The Last Escape

Dedication

This book is dedicated to all the Allied Second World War prisoners who gave their freedom so we could keep ours.

Contents

List of Illustrations

31. George Guderley, Bob Otto and Roger Allen at the Stalag Luft IV memorial in Poland.

Photographic acknowledgements

1, 2: Cal Younger; 3, 4, 5, 15, 17, 18, 19, 20, 21, 22, 23, 29: Courtesy of the Friends of the United States Air Force Academy Library; 6, 7, 8: Vic Gammon; 9: Corbis; 12: Joe O'Donnell; 11: Bob Coles; 13, 24, 25, 26, 27, 28: Imperial War Museum; 14, 15, 16: Courtesy of the United States Air Force Academy; 30: George Guderley; 31: John Nichol.

List of Maps

Acknowledgements

To acknowledge every individual who helped us produce this book would be impossible, but we would like to send special thanks to Dr Patricia Wadley, the national historian at the American Ex-POW Organization, for the use of her thesis *Even One is Too Many* and her encyclopedic knowledge of POW affairs; Duane Reed at the United States Air Force Academy, Colorado, for answering hundreds of questions and seeking out stories, oral histories and photographs; the staff at the Imperial War Museum in London, especially Stephen Walton, for guiding us through the archives; the staff at the Public Record Office, the British Library and the London Library; Jo Cox, for research at the Public Record Office, London; Dr Mikhail Myagkov, for research in the Soviet Military Archive, Moscow; Major Dr Peter Andreas Popp of the German Military Archive, Freiburg; Louise King of the Churchill Archive Centre, Cambridge; Ellis Gibson at Travel Designs, who organized our trips to meet many of the American POWs during the tours of their former camps; Allan Percell, who arranged our tour of Fallingbostel; Dominique Kirkman, for translating German sources.

All who read the manuscript and offered advice and corrections – George Guderley, Batch Batchelder, Stephen Walton, Phil Chinnery, Cal Younger, Duane Reed, Dr Barry Turner, Dr Kent Fedorowich and Sebag Montefiore; the International Committee of the Red Cross in Geneva, for checking its archives and providing information; the staff at the Air Force and Army Historical branches of the Ministry of Defence.

Everyone at Viking/Penguin, especially Juliet Annan, Wendy Wolf and Kate Barker; our agent and friend Mark Lucas; and Suzannah Nichol and Sarah Foot, who read the drafts, acted as unpaid researchers and secretaries, offered help and advice, and generally put up with us – we would be nothing without them.

But most of all we would like to thank the POWs themselves

who, along with their nearest and dearest, wrote to us with information and allowed us to interview them, to read their private diaries, and to force them to remember – sometimes painfully – events long forgotten. We have tried to list them all in the bibliography, but we apologize for any omissions. Without them, this book would never have happened.

Preface

It was a bleak place. Ahead, the road stretched out through the pine forest as far as the eye could see. Above, the sky was grey, and drizzle was falling. But here, in this remote corner of eastern Europe, Roger Allen felt himself on familiar territory. 'It reminded me of home then,' he said, 'and it still does now.'[1]

'Then' was 1944. He was the tail gunner in a bomber flying on his thirteenth mission over Germany when three Messerschmitt fighters came roaring out of the sky, cannons blazing directly at him. Bullets ripped through the fuselage, an engine was hit, flames licked around him. The instinct to survive took over, and at 20,000 feet he bailed out. Three of the crew were not so lucky and died. As his parachute opened he looked up and saw the plane he had left just a split-second before explode. On the ground he was captured by a patrol of soldiers, boys in uniform – fifteen or sixteen years old, he thought. He was all of twenty-one, and for him, in that time-honoured phrase, the war was over.

Instead, a different sort of war was now beginning for him, and one in which his life would be in just as much danger as it had been when he was airborne. What lay ahead was an ordeal he was lucky to survive. Weeks later, on a train nearing his designated prisoner-of-war camp, he looked out and saw the streams, hills and forests of eastern Germany that made him think of home 5,000 miles away in the very heart of the United States. He was a prisoner in a land which, for all its familiar-looking contours, was not his own and where he was not just a stranger but an enemy. 'Yes, I was scared as we marched up to the gates along a path between the pine trees and I saw the barbed wire in front of me. I was in someone else's power. They had me, and I had no idea for how long. As I looked around, I realized that escape was pretty well an impossibility. I would just have to make the best I could out of this situation.'

More than half a century later, Roger Allen returned to eastern Europe on a different mission. A whole lifetime had gone by –

a blissfully happy marriage, a fulfilling job, beautiful children, grandchildren already grown up. Now retired, he felt something pulling him back. There was a gap in his life he wanted to fill, a hole in his personal history that even those he loved knew little about.

When I got home at the end of the war in 1945, I didn't say much about what had happened. Yes, it had been bad – very bad – but I didn't want to burden anyone. Anyway, all I wanted to do was go out and have fun again. I met Flo, and we hit it off really well; we were married three months later. I didn't want to tell her about it, because it was all behind me. We had a new life of our own to lead.

Roger Allen's war experiences were forgotten, a part of himself that he did not visit, until ten years ago, when he retired from his job on a newspaper and started to unbutton the past. He joined an organization for former prisoners of war, and began to recollect and to talk. For the first time, his daughters heard snippets about their father's life in Nazi Germany. Pieces of the jigsaw were put together, but the whole picture was still hazy. Then, in 2001, Allen decided to go back and face his demons. In the autumn of that year, with his family, he joined a party of veterans who crossed the Atlantic to Germany and took a coach to that remote pine forest and the site of the camp which had once housed them and 10,000 other Allied prisoners of war. There was little left to see: the miles of barbed-wire fencing had gone, and so had the watchtowers that stood at every corner. Only a few brick and stone foundations remained.

The authors accompanied Allen on this trip into what had once been Germany but was now part of Poland.[2] He set off into the undergrowth to try to find where his own hut had been, but his legs – bowed and damaged in his experiences back in 1944 and 1945 – stumbled on the rough, uneven ground and he had to stop. He turned away from us, but we knew there were tears in his eyes. We found a hollow in the ground, a cave with a bricked-up entrance that he recognized as a store for potatoes – the one staple in prisoners' diet. Then we came across a water-filled concrete pool, its stagnant contents choked with weed and insects. Things were falling into place. Here was flesh beginning to appear on old bones. The forgotten past was coming back to life.

Except it had not been forgotten. There was a monument there on the site of what had once been Stalag Luft IV, erected as a tribute to brave British and American prisoners of war by the Polish people who had come to occupy the towns and villages nearby when the war was over. Nor was it a neglected monument. The next day, having been told that veterans from America were coming to visit, the locals turned out in their hundreds. Young soldiers of the Polish Army formed an honour guard. Old men with drooping moustaches and wrinkled faces wore the uniforms of the partisan units in which they had fought the Germans half a century before. Wreaths were laid and, as 'The Star Spangled Banner' rang out over a loudspeaker in the still of the forest, Roger Allen, snapping to attention with his fellow veterans, made no attempt at all to conceal the tears running down his face.

To his family, what was happening was astonishing. An easy-going husband, father and grandfather was being hailed as a hero of the Second World War. In the winter of 1945, one of the coldest in modern times, he and all the other Allied inmates of that camp had been marched out into the unknown. The war was coming to an end, the Soviet Army was advancing into Hitler's Germany from the east, and Stalag Luft IV was one of many camps that lay in the invaders' path. Rather than let their captives go, the Germans forced them out of their barracks into the snow and away towards the west. It was the start of a 500-mile journey across Germany. Hundreds died. They froze, they starved, they were broken down by sickness and exhaustion. In their minds was the constant fear that they were marching to their deaths, that they would end up victims of a desperate dictator seeking revenge. Allen's family were shocked by the story of appalling misery and unbelievable human endurance they were hearing. This was the secret he had kept to himself for fifty years.

*

In his comfortable retirement bungalow in a small town 30 miles north of London, 'Batch' Batchelder, a former British airman of the same vintage as Roger Allen, shared the secret. He too had been shot down over Germany, though in his case it had been much earlier, in 1942, and he had been a prisoner in a different camp. As he told us about POW life, he spoke about 'the death march', and we looked at him in astonishment. Neither of us had ever heard of such an atrocity happening to British servicemen in the war in Europe. It was the starting point for the research that has resulted in this book. Batchelder told us that starvation and dysentery had reduced him to a little over 7 stone in weight. At the end of the war, many POWs were skeletons whose appearance would have been hard to distinguish from that of a concentration-camp survivor. The world had shuddered with horror as those sad and debilitated souls emerged from the Nazi death camps. But why did no one seem to know about Allen and Batchelder and the thousands like them?

One of the answers is that, when they returned, their ordeal was indeed overshadowed by the horrors of Auschwitz, Belsen, Dachau. And rightly so, as they would be the first to admit. They suffered, but they were not systematically tortured and destroyed. There was no pile of corpses, no inventory of 6 million slaughtered, no obscene paraphernalia of gas chambers and ovens. Compared with what had been done to the Jews and the other victims of Nazi hate, their experience seemed slight.[3] Then the facts emerged about Japanese ill-treatment of Allied prisoners in the Far East, and the brutality and inhumanity there also seemed to make the ordeal of these men in German hands seem insignificant. Somehow their story disappeared. Their place in history was a footnote: the war had ended, and they had simply come home. In the words of one eminent military historian, 'When finally the Third and Last Reich foundered in a cloud of putrid dust, some 250,000 British, Commonwealth and American prisoners marched briskly out of the ruins.'[4]

March they certainly did, and briskly too, but the impression given of a swift and easy liberation is wrong. However, the former POWs did little to correct it. Many wrote down their stories and showed them to each other, had them privately published, sent them to military archives. But the secret stayed within the group. Time and again they would explain how they could not discuss their experiences with anyone other than another prisoner of war. One of them wrote to a friend:

There isn't a day that goes by that I don't have some thoughts about those difficult days, but I seldom talk about them. The few times that I did, I got the distinct impression that the ordeal I was describing was not fully understood. Only when sharing your experiences with another former POW can you be sure that he knows what you are feeling. You can see it in his eyes.[5]

Why did they keep their stories to themselves? Partly it was because some felt that POWs were looked down on, that being captured had put them in a category that was halfway towards cowardice. Having to surrender was rarely anything other than a humiliating experience, and the trauma of it could last a long time. It would not be eased by the letters that were said to have arrived in prison camps from unsympathetic girlfriends with messages such as 'I would sooner marry a hero than a coward.' Feeling they had let the side down by being captured in the first place, most POWs were reluctant to talk when they got home.

In the years immediately after the war a few memoirs appeared. Among the first books about prisoner-of-war life was writer and broadcaster Robert Kee's *A Crowd is not Company*, published in 1947. Its thrust was in the title: being a prisoner of war was a drab and demoralizing experience. You lost your privacy and your dignity. But this was not a message that the post-war reading public wanted to hear, and in 1952 the hero books began to appear – stories of comradeship and fellowship centred round the activities of the escapers. From then on the accepted image of the prisoner of war was an airman in a rollneck sweater who spent his days tunnelling and his nights plotting new ways of taunting the guards.

In the face of this, who was going to admit to a camp life that was humdrum and fear-filled? RAF pilot Ron Walker, a man whose courage will become obvious in the pages ahead, wrote at the end of his diary:

Any reader will have noticed a difference between this narrative and the scripts of popular POW epics such as The Wooden Horse, The Great Escape and Colditz. A distinct lack of the expected British stiff upper lip! Well, although there were many prisoners of war who did have heroic qualities, I was not one of them. I was, as now, more a canary than an eagle! Naturally I would have liked to present myself in a more favourable light but then it would not have been my war-time diary, and I know that all deficiencies and weaknesses in my character will be accepted by those who love me.[6]

The testimonies in this book fill a gap in our knowledge about the end of the Second World War. This is the heroic story of the Rogers and the Rons and hundreds of thousands like them who made it home in appalling circumstances and against terrible odds. Theirs was the ultimate prisoner-of-war epic – the last escape from Germany.

*

A word of caution. This is not a definitive history of prisoner-of-war camps in Germany in the Second World War. We have not covered every camp and every march or each moment of liberation. To do so would be next to impossible. As a result, there will be those who will read this account and wonder why they have been missed out, or complain that their experiences – those of a father or a grandfather – were different. No man's story was typical. Some sailed blithely through prison-camp life and returned home unaffected. Others were tormented for the rest of their lives. Such was the nature of camp life that one man's experiences could be totally at odds with those of a man in the next hut, let alone the next compound or another camp hundreds of miles away. To be a prisoner of war was to be deprived of certain knowledge beyond your immediate surroundings. For example, there were prisoners at Stalag Luft III, the famous *Great Escape* camp, who had no idea that the camp stretched to five compounds let alone that men in just one of those compounds were digging their way to freedom through tunnels named Tom, Dick and Harry.

The lack of precise information is still a problem. For all our research, we confess at the outset to being unable to answer with certainty some basic questions. How many prisoner-of-war camps were there in Germany in the Second World War? It depends on which month of which year, and whether you count separately the many hundreds of satellite work camps. Official sources in Washington list 238 principal camps spread all over Germany, though some of these may have been civilian camps or transit camps, and their designations – and even their locations – do not always correspond to those in German sources. How many prisoners of war were there in Germany? The same problem applies, and official documents are inconsistent in their estimates of numbers, but it can be said with some (but not total) confidence that in the middle of 1944 Germany had *9 million* prisoners of various nationalities. It is a staggering figure, hard to take in: imagine the entire population of Greater London being held behind barbed wire. But it is also a misleading figure, because it does not take into account the millions of captured Russian soldiers who had already perished, unfed and neglected in the east. Germany in the dying days of the Third Reich was in many ways an armed prison camp – which makes the survival of the estimated 250,000 to 300,000 British and American prisoners even more remarkable. They were spread over the whole of Germany in many different camps, but the bulk of them had been placed in the Stalags* furthest to the east – as far away from home as could be, in order to deter them from escaping.

And it is there, in the summer of 1944, that we begin.

---

* The nomenclature of the camps was:
Oflag – *Offizierlager*, a camp for officers only. Stalag – *Stammlager*, a camp for all other ranks. Stalag Luft – a camp for air-force prisoners. Marlag – *Marinelager*, a camp for navy prisoners. Dulag – *Durchgangslager*, a transit camp or reception camp. Germany was divided into military administrative districts designated by Roman numerals – I, II, etc. Each camp generally (but not always) took its number from the district it was in.

1 The Russians are Coming

Sergeant Jimmy 'Dixie' Deans heard the long-expected good news transmitted from a thousand miles away and, for all his excitement, realized he now had a serious problem on his hands. Problems, though, were his strength. He was just thirty years old, but everyone – prisoner of war and German guard alike – acknowledged his as the wisest of heads on young shoulders. Though there were older and more senior men to choose from, the 3,000 British airmen imprisoned in this wasteland on the north-eastern border of Hitler's Germany had not hesitated to elect him their camp leader – the person who would represent their interests to the Germans.

Minutes before, John Bristow, one of Deans's most trusted men, had hummed along to the last strains of Vera Lynn singing 'I Don't Want to Set the World on Fire', then taken the record off the wind-up gramophone to get at the secret radio hidden inside – known in camp slang as 'the canary'. Outside, from beyond Stalag Luft VI's barbed-wire perimeter fence, a chilly wind, surprising for early summer, was blowing in, kicking up swirls of dust and sand on the parade ground, so that the men posted at the door to keep an eye out for patrolling German guards had to wrap themselves up to stay warm. The radio, built by Bristow from spare parts that had been stolen or smuggled in, was the prisoners' most precious secret. Twice in eight months it had come within a whisker of being discovered when the 'ferrets' – security officers whose job it was to foil escapes – searched Deans's hut. But it had survived – for this moment in history.

That morning Bristow had been carrying out a routine test of the radio, connecting up the clothes line that doubled as a makeshift aerial and twiddling the two knobs fashioned from toothbrushes until he could tune in to London. What he heard through the crackle and hiss of the static made him realize that something big was happening. There would be more on the regular news bulletin. And so, at noon, he crouched over the radio, earphones on, to hear

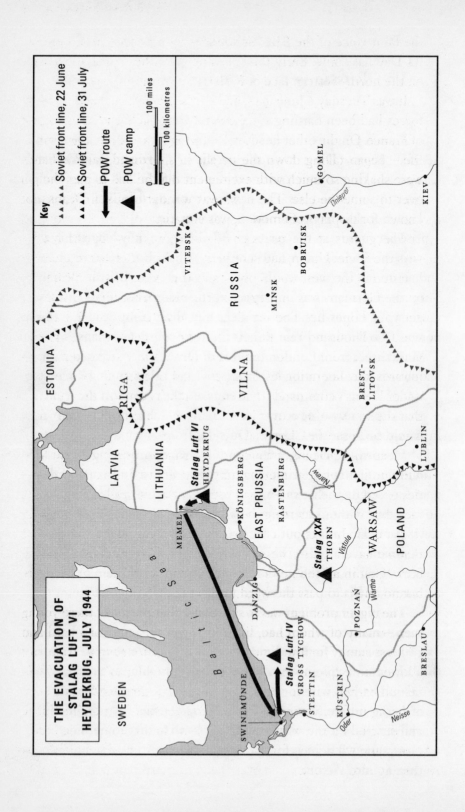

Key

△△△△ Soviet front line, 22 June

▲▲▲▲ Soviet front line, 31 July

POW route

▲ POW camp

0   100 miles

0   100 kilometres

THE EVACUATION OF
STALAG LUFT VI
HEYDEKRUG, JULY 1944

SWEDEN

Baltic Sea

Stalag Luft VI
HEYDEKRUG

MEMEL

DANZIG

SWINEMÜNDE

Stalag Luft IV
GROSS TYCHOW

STETTIN

KÜSTRIN

Stalag XXA
THORN

KÖNIGSBERG

RASTENBURG

EAST PRUSSIA

Vistula

Warthe

POZNAŇ

Oder

Neisse

BRESLAU

WARSAW

POLAND

LUBLIN

Narew

BREST-
LITOVSK

VILNA

RUSSIA

MINSK

BOBRUISK

VITEBSK

GOMEL

Dnieper

KIEV

RIGA

ESTONIA

LATVIA

LITHUANIA

the faint voice of the BBC announcer John Snagge from London: 'D-Day has come. Early this morning the Allies began the assault on the north-western face of Hitler's European fortress.'

It was Tuesday 6 June 1944, and British, American and Canadian forces had been battling since dawn for a beachhead on the coast of France. On the other headset, Ron Mogg – a journalist in civilian life – began taking down the details in shorthand, but his hands were shaking so much with excitement that he had to pass the job over to someone else. The news was wonderful. Even Deans, not known for displays of emotion, was ecstatic.

The guards at the prisoner-of-war camp, close to the border with the Soviet Union, had been bragging for weeks that the coming invasion in the west would never succeed. The Atlantic Wall built by the Germans was impregnable, they told their prisoners. Don't get your hopes up. The invaders would be thrown back into the sea. The Thousand Year Reich still had many centuries to run. The news direct from London told a different story. The first giant step towards the liberation of Europe – and, ultimately, of the men under Deans's command – had been taken. There was a real chance that the war would be over by Christmas – that, God willing, they would be home *for* Christmas.

Meanwhile, Deans, a thoughtful man who never did anything without first considering the consequences, addressed the difficulties posed by the news. He had to find a way of passing it on to the men, but without alerting the Germans to how they had heard it. 'If the camp breaks out cheering, the Germans will know for sure that we have a radio,' he had warned Mogg in his gentle Scottish burr. 'Call in all the news messengers and warn them to be ready but no one is to pass the word until *I* say so.'[1]

The bigger problem was to make sure that the joy of these young men – many of whom had, like him, been prisoners of a hard and ruthless enemy for four long years – was kept under control and not allowed to explode into a premature uprising. They had been behind barbed wire for ever, or so it felt – in that debilitating state of being unfree, eternally hungry, deprived of love and comfort, and scarred by the wasted years and the humiliation of captivity. Now they would see for the first time a real possibility of defeat turning into victory.

But what if demonstrations of joy led to open defiance of their captors? 'Jerry-baiting' – making fun of the German guards, irritating them, pushing back at them without pushing too far – would have a new and dangerous edge as the guards became nervous or volatile or vindictive and certainly more trigger-happy than before. There had been deaths in the camp even at settled times – a prisoner shot while trying to escape; another, in a notorious instance that had enraged them all and nearly led to mutiny, gunned down for having left his hut three minutes early in the morning, before the night curfew was over. Who could tell what tragedies were possible in the unsettled months ahead? Deans knew it would be up to him to guide his men home, to get them through the war's *Götterdämmerung* finale.

His first problem quickly solved itself. As the messengers were doing their job, slipping from overcrowded hut to overcrowded hut, their whispered bulletins greeted in silence, a loud cheer suddenly burst out from A compound and spread round the entire camp. Discipline had not broken down, however – it never would under the rule of 'King' Dixie. Apparently the invasion had been announced on German radio, and one of the guards was spreading the news himself. 'You have invaded Europe but soon we will push you back into the sea, and England and the Americans will want peace, the war will end and you can all help us fight the Russians,' he declared, putting his own chauvinist spin on events happening 900 miles away.

Over in the neighbouring compound for American prisoners, the word was also spreading fast among the 1,500 airmen there, first carried surreptitiously by another eager former newspaperman, Tom McHale, and then broadcast over the camp loudspeaker by the Germans themselves – their bombastic version of what was happening repeating their confident claim that the Allies would be thrown back into the sea.

This was the signal for the *Daily Recco*, the newspaper hammered out by the prisoners on an old typewriter under hand-lettered headlines, to go into production. Soon a front page was posted on the wall of a hut. It ran the text of the official German version: 'During last night, the enemy began his long-prepared offensive against Western Europe, which has been awaited by us ... Bitter fighting is in progress.' The POWs who crowded round to read passed quickly over the propaganda, their eyes returning to fix on the banner headline in bright red across the top – 'INVASION'. That said all they wanted to know.

D-Day had been discussed and awaited for the past eighteen months, ever since Hitler's overreaching adventure of invading the Soviet Union had died in the ruins of Stalingrad and then turned into retreat. At Prokhorovka, on the Russian steppes, 2 million soldiers, 6,000 tanks and 4,000 planes had fought for supremacy in the summer of 1943. The Red Army had won, expelling the German Army from Soviet soil and then pressing relentlessly west into Poland until the front line was barely 200 miles from the camp here at Heydekrug, close to the Baltic Sea. New prisoners brought to the camp had been pumped for information – 'When do you think the war will be over?' was the first thing the old lags crowding around them always asked – and they had told of huge convoys at home, prohibited areas around the southern ports of England, and immense troop concentrations. Now, with the British and American landings in Normandy, the Second Front was under way and the squeeze on Germany and the choking of its military machine could begin.

Flight Sergeant Richard Passmore, a prisoner since 1940, could not contain his elation that an end was in sight – 'an end to hunger, separation, confinement, lack of fulfilment'.[2] For the rest of his life he was never able to forget the harsh facts of life as a prisoner of war. 'We went to bed hungry, we got up hungry, we rose from each mockery of a meal hungry and we sat, stood, lay or walked in a state of constant gnawing hunger. At night we dreamed we were free and at home, and awoke anew to the dreadful reality. Each new morning, despair clawed at the guts again.'

Not this jubilant morning. As the word spread, some men dashed to see the written proof of what they had been promised for so long. Others took their time. Sergeant Cal Younger, a twenty-two-year-old Australian, sauntered over from his hut with his closest friends in the camp, hands in pockets, 'affecting dignity, indifference, nonchalance perhaps', as he recalled many years later.[3] He had been in a state of melancholy for months now, brought on by the arrival of a letter from home – the one that all POWs dreaded:

Nancy had broken off our engagement. An older man would have expected it, would probably have released the girl long before, but I had never allowed myself to believe that it could happen, though her letters had been troubled and less frequent. Yet here it was, in words of kindly finality not so different from those which countless other men here had read.

For some, a shattered romance could be the last straw, bringing an end to that hope of home that got them through each day. A few would sink into themselves, losing interest in life – some to the point where they wandered towards the wire and invited the sentries to open fire on them. Younger had avoided that route, helped by his friends. That was generally the way of camp life. Prisoners had their buddies – two or three, rarely more – and they looked after each other, sharing food and space and pastimes. They were hard-won friendships, ones that 'grew slowly but with great certainty, as coral is built', as Younger himself put it. These 'combines' were the building blocks of camp life, the substitute for the family at home you could no longer turn to.

Not that there was anything soft or sentimental about prison friendship:

It has an intensity possible only where men are thrown together in such a way that they cannot avoid each other, cannot choose when they will meet, or when separate. Even the husband–wife relationship is less absorbing, less demanding, less taut. You sulked or lost your temper or gave way to almost any emotion quite unashamedly. You had friends in other barracks who you saw on an everyday basis, but it was almost essential to have someone to whom you could come with your ego naked, someone who shared with you your hours of melancholy, nursed you in illness, and accepted, without complaint, the spite you felt in your heart for the other fellows, but which, to preserve the peace, you vented upon him.

Time had stood still in the camp. Life there had its own rhythms, its own ups and downs, its fears and its rewards. By and large, if a man kept his head down and his nose clean, didn't get too involved in the antics of the escapers – the 'tally-ho boys', as they were known – and concentrated his mind on getting enough to eat, it was a safe life, defined by military rituals and generally conducted within the rule of law. You were at war all right, but conscious of being away from the sternest realities of violence and death.

It was just over two years since Younger's Wellington bomber had exploded in mid-air and he had escaped from the flames by parachuting into northern France. For more than a week he had been on the run, hiding out with the help of the locals, until he was caught after curfew by the police and handed over to the Germans. He had flown many missions – steering through the flak, seeing friends shot down, grateful to make it home in one piece – but now for the first time he looked the enemy in the eye, saw their jackboots and steel helmets, felt the clutch of terror at being alone and in the hands of men who would not hesitate to kill him. On his way by train to his first camp, sharing a compartment with civilians, boys of the Hitler Youth had hissed at him and menacingly fingered their sheathed knives. Only the armed *Luftwaffe* guards escorting him had kept him from being skinned alive. While the war continued, that hostility was still out there, on the other side of the barbed wire – except now it would be even more intense as a result of the Allied carpet-bombing of German cities, and more deadly as the fight for the survival of the fatherland itself began.

Behind the wire, life was by no means easy, but it had its sense of security. The horizon was a line of trees, the edge of a seemingly impenetrable forest beyond the perimeter of the camp. In one direction a man could see further, to mile upon mile of flat and featureless countryside across which a train occasionally puffed. It was a small world, made bearable by comradeship and routine. 'We were far from the battle fronts,' Younger remembered,

and though we heard about the war's changing patterns, it was all too far away to have any sense of reality. We were in continuous suspense, waiting for the one great event that would affect us, so that suspense became the inspiration of our existence, the drive without which we would have sunk into lethargy and decay.

There was hope in that suspense – and there was security in the arrival of food, mail, cigarettes and books, above all, books. They were our link with humanity, with established and familiar things, with sanity. They were our escape. Men acquired knowledge and learned to appreciate the arts. There was a daily outpouring of verse and story, of painting, of musical composition, of practical invention, the constant taking and giving of ordinary life. *We forgot the crafts of war.*

Was all this about to end? With mixed feelings of elation and unease, the prisoners realized that the 'one great event' their hopes had been pinned on was now upon them. Younger, like every other POW it seems, had been taken into captivity with the immortal words 'For you, the war is over.' Now that war – with its terrors, its uncertainty and its potential for instant death – was coming back into his life.

In the weeks that followed D-Day the prisoners and their captors battled with propaganda. In their huts the airmen drew up maps of Europe, and with coloured pins and strands of blue and red wool they plotted the movement of the Allied front. 'What's the latest gen?' was the first whispered question when friends met in the compound or sat down to eat. The guards retaliated with newsreels of the new, pilotless buzz-bombs, the V1s, that were being launched on London and which they claimed would turn the course of the war back in their favour. Richard Passmore realized that he and other long-term prisoners had witnessed trials of the V1s way back in 1942. They had seen strange objects flying at low level along the Baltic coast and out to sea. The mystery was now explained, and the implications were worrying. The guards never lost an opportunity to boast of these and other unknown new weapons of mass destruction that their beloved Führer had assured them he had in reserve.

Nevertheless, the Germans were becoming noticeably more jumpy as the weeks went by. The camp, being exclusively for aircrew, was run by the *Luftwaffe*, the German equivalent of the RAF. There had always been some mutual understanding and respect between enemies of the same service. The prisoners had even felt sympathy for guards who returned from leave with descriptions of the devastation of German cities by Allied bombing – homes burnt out in firestorms, the people living in cellars, deaths in every family. 'The sadness rubbed off,' Sergeant Vic Gammon remembered. But now there was a new iciness in relations. Tempers frayed more easily, and politeness and respect turned to anger and bitterness. Food supplies were also beginning to run low. The powder-keg conditions that Dixie Deans had feared were becoming a reality.

*

Deans was an ideal man to be in charge of the prisoners at Stalag Luft VI at this time. This was his third camp, and his reputation was growing. There were men here senior in rank to him, but his right to command as the camp's elected Man of Confidence was never challenged.[4] It took a special type of individual to maintain control over prisoners of war, who, as a group, could be undisciplined to the point of anarchy. An officer who was good at leading fighting men into battle was often not suited to leadership here. The legendary Douglas Bader – brave and inspirational fighter pilot though he may have been – was too impetuous and too antagonistic for such a job, and in his four years in various prisoner-of-war camps there were more than a few fellow officers who saw him as a liability, as likely to get his men shot as to get them safely home.

In the words of one military historian, a successful camp leader had to

inspire confidence by showing that he was completely unselfish about food and personal comfort. He had to ensure that everyone in the camp always received a fair share of everything, taking a firm line with those, of no matter what rank, who tried to get more than their share. He had to be indefatigable in negotiating with the enemy to improve conditions and to protect inmates from ill-treatment. He had to bear hunger, cold and other discomforts cheerfully, and by his example help maintain the morale of his fellow prisoners.[5]

Deans could do all this, and more. There was a presence about him that demanded obedience. Some thought him overbearing, and there were those who referred to him as 'the Führer' – though only behind his back. But to most of the men who came into contact with him, his powerful personality combined with an instinctive understanding of human problems made him like a revered head-master. Younger felt that 'any man could take to him a personal trouble and know that when he came away at least some of the burden was transferred to the sturdy shoulders of the camp leader'.

Deans himself was modest about his ability, putting it down to 'a
fair degree of confidence', 'pretty fluent German' for dealing with
the enemy and having 'my finger on the pulse of the camp'.[6]

Deans's authority was evident on the parade ground. The daily
roll-calls were always a shambles – deliberately so. Men would
stroll from their huts late and in any clothing they cared to put
on. Then they would move around to confuse the guards' counts.
There would be catcalls and rude songs – anything to annoy the
Germans. With one barked order Deans could – if he wished –
bring the rabble smartly to attention. He rarely did so, because he
considered roll-calls a matter for the Germans. But, if in the attempt
to gain order, the guards' threats escalated and there was a danger
of events getting out of hand, he would act. Younger recalled how
'one crackling command brought immediate silence, horse-
play ceased and we were instantly transformed into a military
assembly'.

One particular parade stood out in Deans's memory as an
indication of the dangers. On an April evening earlier that year the
men had been called from their huts for a special assembly. The
camp was jittery because an escape had just been foiled, and as
they paraded at dusk the first thing the prisoners saw was the show
of strength. Steel-helmeted reinforcements had been brought in to
bolster the regular guards. They formed a circle around the prisoners and dropped to their knees, machine-guns pointing menacingly from every direction. Richard Passmore could not believe
what he was seeing. 'Were we about to be mown down?' he asked
himself. There was a marked absence of tomfoolery as the count
was taken, and an eerie silence as the guards tallied the figures.

Younger too waited apprehensively in the ranks as

the Adjutant, Major Heinrich, stalked solemnly to the centre of the
parade ground. Behind him the camp interpreter marched, with knees
thrust high, and halted and turned with clashing heels. Then came
Dixie, marching formally, but out of step with the Germans, deliberately
dissociating himself from them. From his attitude we knew that the
Germans had done something unpleasant and were trying to cover it
with this ceremony of self-justification and the reinforcement of guards
in case we were not deceived.

Heinrich read from a document in slow, sombre German. Then the interpreter read the English translation.[7] There were sharp intakes of breath as the news sank in of a mass escape at Stalag Luft III, a prisoner-of-war camp for British and American air-force officers at Sagan, 100 miles south-east of Berlin. Seventy-six prisoners had escaped. Fifty had been shot dead 'while resisting arrest, or attempting a further escape after being recaptured'. In the stunned silence, a voice from the ranks asked, 'And how many were wounded?' Heinrich shrugged his shoulders.

Every man there knew what this meant. They had been murdered. Fifty of them. A few boos broke out, and then there was an instinctive surge forward by the ranks, followed by a roar of almost uncontrollable anger. The ring of guards levelled their machine-guns . . . and Deans's voice rang out. 'Stand fast!' he roared. For just one second, according to Passmore, 'the situation teetered on the edge of a bloody massacre. Then discipline asserted itself. The ranks stiffened. The danger was over.'

Deans dismissed the parade, ordering every man to go straight to his hut 'and wait there for a time. You are to take no action of any kind.' Passmore, streaming away with the others, 'stared with hate-filled eyes at the guards, who refused to meet our gaze'.

Two months on, Deans feared a similar sort of confrontation – but with fatal consequences this time. He could rest assured that there would be no more escape attempts to provoke the Germans – or at least not ones authorized by him. After D-Day the order had been received from London, encoded in letters and in 'personal' radio messages on the BBC, that escape attempts were to stop. The end of the war was in sight, and escaping could only jeopardize lives unnecessarily. But Deans remained deeply worried by the mindset revealed by the massacre of the fifty escapers. The incident had confirmed what he had always suspected: that the Germans were capable of almost anything. Others got the message too. Sergeant Cecil Room remembered how the anger that greeted the news of the killings was followed by fear. 'It put the wind up us when you thought, my God, the Germans could do this to *us*.'[8] Sagan was a warning. It was a sign that the prisoners could expect no quarter in the days ahead before this bloody war was over once and for all.

Deans made what preparations he could. In the early hours of 13 June the camp theatre – which over the years had provided relief, fun and precious forgetfulness for actors and audience alike – went up in flames. Hundreds of prisoners in pyjamas ran with buckets of water to try to save it, but the wooden hut with its tarred-paper roof was soon an inferno and then a ruin. The word was put round that the fire was the result of faulty electrics, but in fact the theatre had been sacrificed. The fire had been started deliberately, to conceal from the Germans the illicit removal that night of some parts of an amplifier. These were cannibalized to turn the POWs' radio receiver into a transmitter which, in an emergency, could be used to send out an SOS. Deans, as he anxiously contemplated the future, at least had a flimsy line of communication established.

But, for all the prisoners' concerns, there was jollity in the air at Luft VI for a few brief weeks that summer. The optimists prevailed over the pessimists, the active over the inactive. Passmore indulged himself in the hope that 'one day we really should be free again, complete people, no longer truncated. An evening walk around the camp became a must as men, scenting real life again, began to slough off the deadly inertia of prison life.' Then again, a man had to be cautious if he were to retain his sanity, and there would be a nodding of wise heads that it might be 1945 before they were liberated. Not one of them, however, could have guessed the full extent of the horrors they would endure before they made it home.

For now, however, a hot sun was shining, the days were long and languid, and, despite an epidemic of fleas that had everyone scratching even more than usual, there were things to celebrate. The Americans put out the flags on the Fourth of July, and there were baseball and boxing bouts – and booze. Using the raisins, prunes and sugar in their Red Cross parcels, the industrious and the desperate found a way of brewing a crude alcohol – 'kickapoo joy juice' as some called it. No one took much notice of their camp leader's Independence Day address. They were too drunk. The British were not so fortunate. Illicitly brewed liquor had been stored under floorboards to be brought out to celebrate news of the invasion, but the Germans had found it and, after sampling, confiscated the lot.

Not long after Independence Day, with the last echoes of 'Yankee

Doodle Dandy' and 'The Battle Hymn of the Republic' gone, a
new sound filled the air. No one could miss it. It was the distant
rumble of heavy artillery. The Red Army's summer offensive was
sweeping the front line through Poland and closer and closer to
the border with Germany. Heydekrug and its thousands of prisoners
of war were in the way. Deans and his close coterie of commanders
had no way of knowing how to react to this. It could be good news
– perhaps they were on the point of being released by the Russians.
On the other hand, there was every chance that the camp itself was
about to become a battleground, with the POWs trapped in the
crossfire. Or that the Germans would withdraw but massacre their
prisoners before they did so, if for no other reason than to stop
them taking up arms and joining the ranks of the invaders. In which
case, what could Deans and his men do to defend themselves? What
last-ditch stand could they make, unarmed and unprepared, against
guards with machine-guns and the defence of their homeland and
their Führer at stake?

*

Adolf Hitler took pleasure from the time he spent with his head in
the clouds at the Berghof, his southern residence in the town of
Berchtesgaden, high in the mountains above Salzburg. There, sitting
in a deep, chintz-covered armchair or wandering the terrace, he
could gaze out at the panorama of peaks, matching the endless
Alpine vista with endless talk. His military commanders often
fought to stay awake during the hour-long monologues in which he
refought old battles and plotted imaginary new ones, increasingly
succumbing to what an attaché described as a tendency 'to wishful
thinking ... [as] his contact with reality was slipping away'.[9]

He was there in the summer of 1944 to hear the news that the
Allies had stormed the beaches of northern France, and he was
back again a month later as it sank in that his personal instruction
to prevent 'the Anglo-Saxons' (as he called the invaders) from
breaking out of the Normandy peninsula could not be obeyed.
Contemptuously, he shuffled his pack of generals and field marshals,
damning their defeatism, questioning their courage and their
loyalty. Then he railed as his army in the east counter-attacked
against the Russians, only to be encircled, outnumbered and
outgunned, unable to dent the Soviet advance. The borders of

Germany were about to be breached. It was time he flew his Eagle's Nest.

On 14 July he left the Berghof for what would be the last time. Despite persistent rumours and romantic fancies that this would be his chosen last redoubt, a defiant mountain hideaway should the war go badly, his fate always lay elsewhere, and he seemed to know it. Nicolaus von Below, a staff officer from the *Luftwaffe* who had been attached to the Führer's headquarters for seven years, watched as, on his way to bed, Hitler strolled the length of the Berghof's great hall, stopping at each portrait on the wall and nodding at it as if in farewell. He stooped a little as he walked, his shoulders slumped as never before.

The next morning Hitler boarded his plane, and his personal pilot, Hans Baur, headed the four-engined Focke-Wulf Condor north away from Salzburg and over a landscape that was still German, but only just. These were no longer the safest of skies for them. For a while Hitler had been the master of a colossal military empire stretching out from Berlin nearly 1,000 miles in any direction – to Athens in the south and Oslo in the north, to Calais in the west and the gates of Moscow in the east. But that overblown bubble had shrunk alarmingly.

Von Below, seated in the plane that day, knew that it was in the air that the war had already been lost and won. British and American bombers had played the decisive part, knocking out the factories the *Luftwaffe* depended on to build new aircraft, and then, in huge, unstoppable waves, pulverizing the citizens of German cities from Munich to the Rhine. The blame for all this destruction was directed at the Allied airmen. They were dubbed *Terrorflieger* – terror flyers – and many of those who were shot down and fell into the hands of German civilians were strung up from lamp-posts or beaten to death by an angry mob, as many men lucky to be saved from a lynching while in transit and now safely imprisoned at Stalag Luft VI knew only too well. Such actions were illegal – the Geneva Convention specifically outlawed reprisals against prisoners of war. But Hitler and his henchmen connived in this summary injustice. When, a year earlier, Heinrich Himmler, head of the SS, had heard that police on the ground were moving in to rescue downed airmen from the mob, he issued an instruction that it was not their job 'to interfere in clashes between Germans and English and American flyers who have bailed out'.[10] The calls for revenge could only get louder.

Later that day, after four hours in the air, Hitler's plane touched down at Rastenburg in East Prussia, the gloomy complex of concrete bunkers covered with camouflage netting, known as the Wolf's Lair, from which the Führer had directed the invasion of the Soviet Union nearly three years earlier. The prisoners of war of Luft VI were just 100 miles away to the north. The advance patrols of the Red Army were even closer.

In the days that followed, as Hitler and his generals stood around the maps in the operations room and planned the defence of the fatherland, bad news poured in from every direction. On 17 July, Field Marshal Erwin Rommel, Hitler's most talented tactician, was injured, strafed in his open car by Allied fighter planes while driving to the front in France. The only good news was that the line was being held in Italy. German troops had dug in halfway between Rome and Florence, and the American and British advance up the peninsula, which had begun eleven months earlier, seemed to be slowing. The army commander there, Field Marshal Albert Kesselring, was summoned from the battlefield for a bauble – to be decorated by Hitler personally with the Knight's Cross with Diamonds, Oak Leaves and Swords. He arrived on 19 July.

On that same day a significant order was issued from the Wolf's Lair, 'concerning preparations for the defence of the Reich'.[11] It put the German civilian population on a total war footing – as if they had not been in that situation for months already. It restructured the military and civilian administration for fighting the enemy on German soil, and it ordered preparations to be made for evacuations from the east, away from the advancing Russians. Among the instructions to move 'foreign labour' – i.e. slave workers – westward, and the civilian population too (as long as they did not panic), item 6(a) called for 'preparations for moving prisoners of war to the rear'. It was a crucial instruction that was to prolong the war for hundreds of thousands of Allied soldiers and airmen, forcing them into misery, starvation and, in many cases, death.

The next day, 20 July, was hot. The officers due to attend the midday conference with the Führer stood around in the open air enjoying the warmth of the sun; then Hitler arrived, shook each man by the hand, and led them into the situation room. They seated themselves round a long oak table, and the conference had just begun when a latecomer arrived, having flown in from Berlin only that morning. The man was a war hero, who had lost an eye and several fingers in fighting in North Africa. Hitler shook his hand and ushered him to a seat close by.

Ten minutes later there was an explosion. The wooden hut shattered. Amid the smoke, the dust and the debris, the dying and the badly wounded lay moaning on the floor. But the target of the bomb had escaped. Hitler, his jacket and trousers torn, was hurried away to his private bunker. Though the bomb, hidden in a briefcase, had gone off under the table he was leaning on, he was unmarked. Later it would emerge that his hearing was affected and the nerves of his left arm damaged.

It was quickly established that the bomber was that late arrival. Colonel Claus von Stauffenberg was an aristocratic Prussian who had at first welcomed Hitler's rise to power but had then turned against him, blaming him for the military disaster the country was facing. His conspiracy to overthrow the autocrat and replace him with an administration that could cut a deal with the Allies had been two years in the making. His chance – his invitation to the Wolf's Lair – had come that day for a simple reason: he was Chief of Staff to General Friedrich Fromm, commander of the Reserve Army, the military forces at home which now needed to be drawn into planning because the Russians were about to break on to German soil.

Stauffenberg had made an excuse and left the situation room before the bomb exploded, racing to a plane and back to Berlin. Convinced that no one could have survived the blast, he ordered the takeover of the government by officers friendly to his cause. The word that Hitler was alive brought his coup to a close. He was arrested and shot on the spot, but the strands of the conspiracy would take months to unravel. Hundreds of senior officers died in the resulting witch hunt. For Hitler it was the final proof that the officer class was disloyal and could not be trusted. Von Below thought the Führer was never the same physically after the attack. He was often in pain, his language coarsened, and he was quicker than ever to anger and to threaten. His incipient paranoia and his desire for revenge were sealed in the explosion at Rastenburg. His view of what lay ahead was apocalyptic. After 20 July he told Von Below, 'We may go down, but we will take the world down with us.'

Stauffenberg's assassination attempt had another significant result. His superior officer, General Fromm, was one of the first to be implicated in the plot and executed. Hitler handed over control of the Reserve Army to one of the few men he felt he could still trust – the SS commander, Himmler. His dedicated Nazis ran the concentration camps and administered the 'final solution' of the Jews. His secret policemen were the feared Gestapo, his private army the legions of the Waffen SS, who wore a death's-head emblem into battle. He was perhaps the most feared individual in Germany – some said even Hitler was wary of the power he wielded. His new responsibilities would shortly give him nominal control over a group who had, until now, largely been protected from him and his thugs – the Allied prisoners of war.

*

At Stalag Luft VI, Hitler's 19 July order to prepare to evacuate the camps came too late. The war was moving fast, and the prisoners had already gone. As the first two weeks of July slipped away, the camp had been overrun by rumour. It was said that the townspeople in Heydekrug had already been evacuated, moving as fast as they could, desperate to escape the advancing Soviet soldiers, whose reputation for plunder, rape and murder ran before them. No woman, man or child was safe. On the road to Moscow, Hitler had categorized the Russians as *Untermenschen* and had ordered them to be treated accordingly. On the road to Berlin, what was to stop them living up to their subhuman designation?

The word was that the POWs would be moved out too, though there was furious debate among them about this. Why would the Germans want to hang on to them? They would just be a burden, needing to be fed and guarded. Surely it would make more sense to abandon them to the Soviets. Others thought the Germans would keep them as hostages – that or shoot them all outright, a possibility that every man was aware of, even if few voiced it.

Throughout Luft VI, men put their minds to work on practical matters – scrounging any sort of material they could find to fashion a rucksack, sewing up a blanket or a shirt so that it could be slung over the shoulder as a bag. On 13 July, with just a few hours' warning, the German commandant gave the order that the camp was to be evacuated. The urgency was such that a needle cricket match between an England XI and an Australian XI on the hard-baked earth of A compound had to be abandoned with just a few overs to go. No details were given of where they were going or how long they would be on the road. Each man would be allowed to take only what he could carry. The camp stores were raided for their stocks – even the toilet paper, and what could not be stuffed away in bags was flung over the barbed wire and the hut roofs like streamers, as if it was suddenly carnival time.

The Americans went first, tramping out into the darkness that night. Earlier, they had thrown any possessions they could not carry over the wire into the British compound. Cal Younger recalled that 'unfortunately they did not warn us, and their first fusillade of tinned foods struck down several unsuspecting British airmen'. Next had come books, clothing, sports equipment and thousands of cigarettes. The Americans left, and then, two hours later, they were back for some unknown reason. For a while the rumour mill ground away with stories that the Russians were closer than had been thought and that the camp was on the point of being liberated. But at 3 a.m. the Americans were rounded up and marched out again. They went noisily, chattering and shouting and singing, and those left behind listened wistfully as the sound swung away through the night air, growing fainter and fainter in the distance until suddenly it was gone.

In the British compounds there was little sleep for anyone that night as each man kitted himself out as best he could, able only to guess at what lay ahead. Inside each hut was like a bazaar. Younger described it as 'the time of levelling up. The rich were no longer rich for they could keep only what they could carry, and the poor were no longer poor for they could choose whatever they wanted from the goods abandoned by others.' One man who had won 7,000 cigarettes betting on the date of D-Day sobbed as he abandoned them. They went up in flames, burned in bonfires that raged through the night rather than give any German guard the satisfaction of a smoke. It was a warm July, but the men took their greatcoats. Who knew how long they would have to travel?

The camp emptied section by section during the next few days, until Younger found himself almost the last remaining. He had eaten as much food as he could without making himself sick, then wandered from empty hut to empty hut. Most prisoners had destroyed what they couldn't carry and the ground was littered with ripped clothing, squashed cigarettes, trails of powdered milk. The gardens once lovingly tended by inmates as a source of vegetables had been trampled. In one hut he found a small library of books above a bunk. It was intact: its owner had not had the heart to tear to pieces a source of solace that had seen him through years of captivity.

As the days passed, Younger's hopes were raised that Red Army soldiers would appear at the gate 'to free us'. Instead the time came for him and his combine to leave too.

Outside the hut, we lay back upon our kit, slid our arms into the straps, and got unsteadily to our feet. There was a pile of Red Cross food parcels, and German guards watched hungrily as we ripped open the boxes and stuffed meat, tea and chocolate into our pockets. We offered tins to some of the guards, who thanked us warmly, until a German in the sentry-box began to shout at them angrily. They should be ashamed, he cried, to accept charity from the murderers of their wives and children. Some threw down the things they had picked up, but others just carried on shoving tins into their knapsacks.

Toby had a brainwave and went to fetch the laundry cart. We piled our kit into it, and within seconds a dozen men had done the same thing. 'March! March!' came the order, and we put our shoulders to the wheel. In his sentry-box the guard wept with anger. With the exception of three men who remained in the camp, hidden in an unfinished tunnel, we were the last prisoners to leave. Ahead of us was a long column of men. At our backs, marched six guards, each with a snarling dog on the leash.

Further down the line, a horse-drawn cart carried the contents of Dixie Deans's camp office – all his meticulously kept paperwork, his typewriter, and his wind-up gramophone with its hidden radio inside.

For some, just being outside the camp was a thrill, and their eyes were overwhelmed by unfamiliar sights – fields where the harvest was being worked, ox carts on the road, children playing. The pleasure was short-lived. The rumour that Heydekrug itself had already been evacuated was clearly not true, because, as the prisoners entered the town, people were lining the road, and they were very hostile. Some threw stones. The prisoners were going, while they were being left to their fate. Meanwhile the road was now littered with greatcoats, blankets and tins of food, 'discarded by men who had set out with more hope in their hearts than strength in their backs'.[12] The column of marching men passed a funeral with elderly mourners in top hats and frock coats. At a church, a burly *Luftwaffe* corporal was marrying his sweetheart, a slip of a girl who glanced up at the passing prisoners with a sad and bewildered look on her face. In the months ahead, more than one of the POWs would remember her and wonder about her fate.

At the railway station, the POWs waited, still watched by resentful townspeople. A train pulled in, and the prisoners were herded sixty at a time into closed cattle trucks. There was no room to sit, so they leaned against each other for hour after hour, the sun blazing down outside and the trucks getting hotter and hotter. Eventually the train began to move, and a nightmare journey began. Men had to urinate and defecate where they stood, and not until they persuaded the guards to slide back the doors a little was there any relief from the stench. They passed a slave-labour camp, and those who could peer out of the ventilation hole saw skeletal figures being whipped by a jackbooted guard. They roared their anger and their disapproval before the train picked up speed and the image of those worse off than themselves was gone.

'Thirty-six hours we spent in the train,' Younger recalled. 'Frequently we were shunted into sidings to make way for German troop trains travelling to the east, and to allow hospital trains westward.' They passed through the whole of East Prussia and deep into Poland, with no idea where they were being taken and aware that the guards did not know either. Eventually the train halted at a remote station and, limbs stiff and aching, they were ordered out. A column formed and, flanked by the guards, they marched 4 miles in the gathering dusk, through a town called Thorn, where pretty

Polish girls called out to them until the guards shooed them away with their rifles.

Ahead they caught sight of their new camp. Richard Passmore's spirits sagged as he took in its familiar 'sandy ground, drab ever-greens, monotonous barrack blocks, goon boxes and barbed wire. I could only imagine that Europe must be covered with these bloody things, and all disgustingly alike.' Stalag 357 – Thorn – was already inhabited by 3,500 British Army prisoners of war, who grumbled at the arrival of the airmen and the overcrowding and half-rations it would mean.[13] But huts had been cleared for the newcomers, and they settled in, able to relax a little for the first time in days. They were safely back behind barbed wire and, despite the grudging welcome, with their own people again. Only later would they learn how lucky they had been.

*

The earlier groups marching out of Heydekrug had suffered unbelievable horrors before they arrived at their destination, a different camp altogether. Their journey to Stalag Luft IV at Gross Tychow in the German province of Pomerania was a story that would spread like poison to every prisoner of war in German hands. It was a warning of the danger they all faced, confirmation of what the commandant at Heydekrug had solemnly told Deans – 'There is a cold wind blowing outside.'[14]

For them the train journey in cattle trucks had been a short ride to the coast. It was night-time when they arrived at the dockside of a Baltic sea town called Memel and were hustled out of the wagons and along a dark quay to a small coal ship. Many men would recall the fear that crept over them. Prodded up the gangplank of the *Insterburg,* they were made to leave their packs on the deck and were then forced down a long vertical steel ladder into a dimly lit, foul-smelling hold. Those who objected looked up to see cocked machine-guns pointing at them.

Nine hundred men were crammed into each of the ship's two holds, huddled below the waterline, sitting or crouching between each other's legs or back to back, knees drawn up. Those on the edge had to try to keep their feet somehow on the sloping metal hull. Others clung to girders and stanchions. Cries that 'There's no room' were ignored as still more were forced down. With the last man in, the hatch was battened and the only light came from a single electric bulb. A rumour went round that the ship was so old and rusty that the Germans must be planning to scuttle it and all of them with it. It was all too believable in that claustrophobic black hole, which one frightened prisoner, looking about him and seeing the tears and the terror in other men's eyes, likened to Dante's vision of Purgatory.[15]

The ship set out into the Baltic Sea in the early hours of 16 July, heading west at a steady 8 knots. Down below, Sergeant Vic Clarke took charge. He had to keep his men calm, to stop the panic that could so easily engulf them. He spoke excellent German, and negotiated with the guards for the hatch to be opened and for a dozen men at a time to go up on deck. As they breathed in the fresh air and relieved themselves over the side, the guards covered them with machine-guns and steam hoses. Behind, in the wake of the *Insterburg*, the prisoners on deck could see a German torpedo boat which, they worked out, had two purposes. It was their escort, but in the event of a mutiny on board it would be their executioner.

Meanwhile, as the sun rose, temperatures soared and the hold became an oven. For those who could not make it to the deck, the only means of sanitation was a bucket lowered on a rope – the same bucket, or so the prisoners believed, as was used to send down drinking water. It was plainly not adequate; dysentery was already spreading, and a corner of the hold quickly became an unofficial latrine. In the heat and the stench, spirits sank and bodies collapsed. Clarke took it upon himself to tell the *Insterburg*'s captain that his name was known and that if anything happened to the prisoners the British secret service would hunt him down after the war and hang him.

This was not enough to calm the fears in the hold. Some of the airmen had been on missions dropping mines on this very waterway; Soviet submarines were also known to operate in the Baltic. Now, every movement of water was a torpedo, every brush of driftwood against the side a mine. It was simple enough to work out that, if the ship was hit, those in the hold had no means of escape. In the heat and the gloom, morale among the frightened prisoners was at its lowest. Then an American – no one ever knew his name, but they never forgot what he did – gave a cry of 'Don't let the bastards get us down' and began singing a romantic Irish lament in a rich baritone voice. 'My Wild Irish Rose,' he sang, and in the hushed silence the notes soared and echoed around the metal hull along with a thousand thoughts of home.

American airman John Parsons went into a dream world – a time and a place somewhere in the future where he would be with his wife, Mai, back in Indiana. It was because of her that he had resolved never to get involved in escape activities, not to make waves. 'I didn't want to take the risk. We had so many plans and I didn't want to jeopardize our future.'[16] But whether or not he had a future was now out of his hands.

After sixty hellish hours at sea the *Insterburg* came into the port of Swinemünde at the mouth of the River Oder to land its dirty, exhausted and frightened human cargo. The prisoners emerged from the hold blinking in the strong sunlight and picked up their packs from the pile on the deck. As they filed down the gangplank, two of them – 'obviously quite crazed', according to one witness – tried to break away, heading in the direction of some trucks parked on the quay.[17] 'A machine-gun rasped out without warning and mowed one of them down. He died where he fell. The other kept on running until he dropped into the water, riddled with bullets.'

On the quayside, more humiliation awaited the prisoners. They were made to remove their boots and were then handcuffed together in pairs. Being shackled was unusual, and it did not bode well. The rumour ran that they were about to be handed over to the SS and paraded naked through the streets of nearby Stettin as *Terrorflieger.*

Thirsty and afraid, they were prodded at bayonet point into railway trucks that had stood all morning in the sun and were now oven-hot. The only distraction from their misery was when the air-raid sirens suddenly began to wail and an immaculately dressed *Luftwaffe* officer threw himself to the ground, covering his white summer uniform in oil and coal dust. The prisoners cheered this small victory. At anchor out in the bay, German battlecruisers fired at an American bomber high in the sky, while down on the quay panic-stricken guards slammed shut the doors of the railway wagons. The prisoners could do nothing to save themselves as bombs exploded all around them – Allied bombs, made in the United States, dispatched from England, marked on the side with messages like 'To Adolf, with love', intended to kill Germans, but now terrifying their own countrymen. It would not be the last time the prisoners faced death from their own side.

This time they were lucky. This was not a proper raid, just a stray bomber which had missed its target and was ditching its payload before heading home. The all-clear sounded and the train set off, and, as it gathered speed, fresh air, salty from the sea, blew into the trucks to give the prisoners some relief. Most were in a bad way, and some slumped to the floor, tongues parched and gasping for breath; but the wagons were so crowded that no one could bend down to help. Percy Carruthers had fought in the desert in North Africa and thought he knew what thirst was. 'But this was different, born of days of lack of sleep and of rough handling with neither food nor water. Everyone suffered the agonies.' Around him he saw nothing but gaunt faces and hollow eyes.

Several hours later the train came to a halt in a siding on a long, lonely stretch of track beside a pine forest. A sign announced the name of the tiny station – Kiefheide. The doors were opened and the *Luftwaffe* guards who had accompanied the prisoners from Heydekrug got out. Then the doors were slammed tight again. They would not be reopened until the next day. Peering out into the gathering dusk, the prisoners saw to their horror that their familiar guards had disappeared. Instead, alongside the track were lines of vicious-looking young men in white uniforms, brandishing unsheathed bayonets. They were marine cadets, a naval version of the fanatical Hitler Youth, teenage Nazis reared on adulation for the Führer. Those inside the trucks saw hate in the eyes staring in at them, and feared for their lives. That night they slept little, kept awake by the sound of steel blades being sharpened on grinding wheels outside and the laughter of the youths as they boasted about how they would teach the *Terrorflieger* a lesson tomorrow.

A tense morning came and went, and it was afternoon before the doors were flung open and the prisoners, still manacled, were hounded out to stand in lines beside the track. A big pile of boots had been kicked off the train, and each man now scrambled to find his own, or ones that vaguely fitted. Then the prisoners were marched past a station building and on to a road. Ahead lay a terrifying sight: a double line of shouting and cursing marine cadets.

Among them stood guards with machine-guns at the ready. Vic Clarke realized that he and his men were being set up. Here was an incitement to panic, to run – and to be shot down 'while trying to escape'. There was even a film cameraman on hand to capture the evidence of them fleeing. He passed the word urgently down the column – 'We're in for trouble but you must restrain your impulse to run. Don't give them an excuse to open fire.'[18]

Sweat poured from every man as they set off down the road in columns of 200. At the very front, an astonishingly tall German officer set a fast pace, which the prisoners – exhausted, hungry, thirsty and with packs on their backs – could not match without breaking into a run. A German major in gleaming white breeches and knee-length boots stood on the running board of a Mercedes staff car as it drove up and down the column, frantically urging the prisoners on at the top of his voice, waving his pistol menacingly at them. To Percy Carruthers he looked 'demented' as he screamed and gyrated, the veins standing out on his neck and 'hate spewing from every expression'.

After half a mile they veered off to the left and on to a sandy track sloping up through the pine trees. As the prisoners slowed, their feet sinking in the soft sand, the major fired a shot in the air. 'Make them run,' he yelled at his own men. '*Alles laufen.* Make them run until they drop!' It was a signal for mayhem. The marine cadets began lashing out at the prisoners, hitting them with their rifle butts, stabbing them with their bayonets. 'That's for Hamburg,' they shouted, or Cologne or Berlin or any of the dozens of German cities the Allied bombers had blitzed. As the blades sliced him, one defiant prisoner yelled back, 'London, Coventry, Liverpool, you kraut bastards!'

Blood oozed from cut flesh, and the smell of it enraged the snapping guard dogs, straining at their leashes. By now the rear ranks were being driven so fast that they cannoned into those ahead of them. Those at the front ran faster, many of them throwing off the packs they had desperately hung on to since leaving Heydekrug, sacrificing their only possessions in the scramble to stay alive. Men fell to the ground, tripping over bags in front of them or simply too exhausted to carry on. The enemy closed in around them.

John Parsons staggered as the man he was shackled to fell

and pulled me down with him. It was difficult to get back on our feet without being overrun by dogs, men and guards. He kept saying that he couldn't make it, so I dragged and carried him along the way. He kept saying, 'Johnny, we're going to die, we're both going to die.' One of the guards took a jab at me and I threw up my hand to protect myself. He cut me badly and I was bleeding profusely.

Cec Room saw in horror that a friend running in front of him had been slashed so often that his trousers were hanging in shreds. To this day he is ashamed at feeling relieved that he himself was not the target. 'The German wasn't stabbing me because he was too busy stabbing old Bob in front. It's a terrible thing to say but you're just glad that it's happening to someone else rather than to you.'

But there were some instances that afternoon of regular German military personnel protecting the prisoners. An elderly sergeant rescued Ron Akerman, on the point of collapse. 'For God's sake, stay by me,' he told the POW. 'I was a prisoner in the last war and I don't agree with this. I'm not going to have it.' But other guards were as vicious as the youngsters, and now they began slashing with their bayonets at any prisoner still with a bag on his back, hacking at the straps until it fell to the ground. A rifle smashed so hard against the head of a burly Canadian airman that the wooden butt snapped off. A giant of a man, he shook his head and staggered on, blood streaming down his neck and splashing over those around him.

Percy Carruthers took a blow that knocked him off balance and into the ditch at the side of the road. There he lay face down, feigning unconsciousness, while the column passed. He was planning to escape.

I kept deathly still, almost too tense to breathe. Then I heard German voices in the ditch. 'There's another one here, Heinz. Get him out.' A boot in my ribs and a prod in my buttocks almost made me squawk but I lay still. 'I think he's out for the count,' said one of the Germans. 'Then put a bullet through him just to make sure,' came the reply. I leapt up in a flash and shot past them. Before they had time to realize what had happened I was back in the column and lost from their sight.

Vic Clarke tried to reason with the German major, to calm him down, but he was ignored. Running ahead to the front of the column, he then tried to slow the pace down. He was helped by a fellow prisoner, a paratrooper, who ignored the German harassment and called out for everyone to 'keep it steady, don't break ranks, keep in close and don't panic'. Sergeant James Taylor of the US Army Air Force remembered 'many acts of courage in the midst of the confusion. All along the route men shouted encouragement to each other. The stronger prisoners moved to the outside of the column in order to protect the injured and weaker ones in the centre.'[19] All the time, shots were being fired, and Taylor was convinced they were being run to their death. In the forest on either side of the track the prisoners could see machine-gun nests. More cameras on tripods were also in position to film any attempt to flee from the beatings they were getting, to make it look like a mass escape. Later, few were in doubt that if they had panicked there would have been carnage.

Ahead, the track through the forest began to turn, and as they rounded the bend the prisoners saw the barbed-wire gate and sentry towers of a camp, and another gauntlet of guards to greet them. They staggered through more blows before collapsing to the ground inside the compound. Hundreds of men nursed wounds as a German doctor walked among them chuckling 'Gut, gut' and refusing them treatment.[20] Percy Carruthers examined himself and counted six stab marks on his body, but others had as many as fifty (and later one man died from his wounds).[21] Vic Clarke's official report on the incident after the war put the number of his men with bayonet wounds at 106.[22] He could not count those bruised by the clubbing they had received or with rips in their flesh from dog bites. There was no water to wash off the drying blood, nor to drink. Nearby, guards sat in the afternoon sun tucking into food they had looted from the prisoners' packs.

As they sat panting on the grass, the prisoners heard more chilling news. This camp, they were told, was a Gestapo punishment camp for *Terrorflieger*. It was kept secret from the Red Cross, and here the Geneva Convention did not apply. Prisoners would have no rights – they would not even be allowed to talk to each other. And, as if to ram the point home, the guards forced them at gunpoint to lie flat on the ground, face down. 'No talking, or we shoot!'[23] They were then strip-searched before at last being allowed what they most craved – water and sleep.

That first night they would sleep where they lay, on the ground, under the stars, cold and shivering. The next day Vic Clarke, though he was in no better condition than his men, went to work, cajoling soup, medical supplies and tents from the Germans. His threats to complain about their treatment to the Swiss – who were the Protecting Power charged with looking after the interests of Allied prisoners of war – were taken seriously, proof that the German claim that it was a special, secret, camp was just bluff.[24]

For a few nights the POWs slept in tents, but eventually they were all allowed into the barracks huts in the main compounds of Stalag Luft IV, near the German town of Gross Tychow, and they settled down to a semblance of normal camp life. However, it would always be a much tougher regime than they had known at Heydekrug. The 'run up the road' – as the violent reception became known – would be repeated to a smaller extent for later arrivals at the camp, and Luft IV would become a byword for brutality. It represented the threat hanging over each and every Allied POW – that they would be slaughtered in the awful endgame of the war against Hitler.

2 Abandoned to their Fate

July 1944 was a good time to take stock in Washington. The United States had been in the war for two and a half years, and, at the War Department, Military Intelligence compiled a special report on American prisoners of war in Europe.[1] The total in captivity in Germany was 28,867, of whom just over 12,000 were Army. The remaining three-fifths were flyers. The men of the Eighth US Army Air Force had joined the RAF's Bomber Command in its campaign to devastate Germany as the first step to victory. Casualties had been high. There were 16,593 pilots, navigators and gunners who had dropped out of the sky and were now behind barbed wire.

The very first was a high-flyer in every sense. Lieutenant-Colonel Albert Clark, a West Pointer, had been second in command of the first American fighter group sent to Britain in the summer of 1942. In a dogfight over northern France, the Spitfire he was piloting was hit. The plane limped towards the Channel coast, losing height and power, before Clark was forced to crash-land it on the German earthworks built on the cliffs at Cap Gris Nez outside Calais, just 20 miles short of Dover and safety. When he went into captivity, the only Americans to precede him had been members of Eagle Squadron, volunteers from the United States who had joined the RAF to fight in the fifteen months before their own country officially went to war.

American prisoners were scattered over fifty-seven different camps and hospitals, though the vast majority were held in just eight main camps, five of which were for aircrew and therefore run by the *Luftwaffe* and the other three for ground troops and run by the *Wehrmacht*. All were in eastern Germany – 'apparently as a deterrent to escapes through France', according to the report.

Generally the prisoners were treated reasonably well, the report said. Its words, chosen carefully, were 'fair' and 'correct'. Certainly, considering what the Japanese were dishing out, the men in German hands could consider themselves lucky. On the other

ALLIED FRONT LINES, AUGUST 1944

NORWAY

SWEDEN

FINLAND

OSLO

HELSINKI

BALTIC SEA

ESTONIA

NORTH SEA

DENMARK

RIGA LATVIA

COPENHAGEN

LITHUANIA

EAST PRUSSIA

MINSK

HAMBURG

BERLIN

AMSTERDAM

NETH.

WARSAW

RUSSIA

BRUSSELS

BELG.

POLAND

KIEV

CAEN

PARIS

GERMANY

PRAGUE

CZECHOSLOVAKIA

FRANCE

SWITZ.

MUNICH

VIENNA

HUNGARY

BUDAPEST

ITALY

BULGARIA

ROME

Key

▲ POW camps

▲▲▲▲▲ Front lines at 25 August 1944

0   200 miles

0   200 kilometres

hand, if you contrasted their lot with the way that German prisoners of war were being looked after in the United States, there was no doubt where it was preferable to be. In the Stalags and the Stalag Lufts, there was a severe shortage of food and clothing. A dietitian in the Quartermaster's office had analysed the quantity and content of the official rations for prisoners in German hands and had concluded they were not enough to keep body and soul together. The camps had come to depend on Red Cross parcels as basic rations. In some places transport problems meant that parcels were now not getting through as often as they should – either that or the Germans were stealing them. There was every expectation that this situation would worsen. For the moment, however, the health of the prisoners was generally good. Serious sickness was comparatively rare, and the worst problem was skin infections as a result of not being able to take regular baths or showers.

Morale among the men was generally high, but two main things could cause it to slump. The first was when mail failed to turn up from home, often delayed by the slowness of the censors at both ends. The second was when POWs read in German newspapers or heard on the radio about workers going on strike back in the United States. 'Prisoners were enraged by such news and many were doubtful that the spirit of the American people was high enough to win the war.' Another gripe, brought on by letters from home, was that the Red Cross had put out literature to their families and friends depicting prison-camp life 'as one of ease and indolence instead of monotony and hardship'. Many felt misunderstood. They were not cowards because they had surrendered or been caught, but they were made to feel guilty. Stories went round of men in the camps receiving white feathers from people at home, and these were bitterly resented. Equally harmful were reports of being jilted in their absence by wives and girlfriends. But, the report maintained, 'while prisoners of war have suffered from occasional depression they have never approached despair. In all camps, American discipline and organization have been excellent. News of the [D-Day] invasion will keep morale on a high level for many months to come.'

Senior men like Colonel Clark had done their best to keep spirits high. He had been in charge at Stalag Luft III at Sagan as more and more of his countrymen arrived, many of them young and very frightened. 'Some of them were just eighteen years old when they got here. They had to do their growing up behind barbed wire,' he recalled later.[2] Barely out of his twenties himself, he kept them busy:

If you had left them alone, they would have gone to seed, grown beards, got slovenly. They would have just unravelled. But we had hut inspections on Saturday mornings; we marched them. From the Red Cross, we got summer and winter uniforms. We took every opportunity to keep them from forgetting that they were military men and their country would need them when they got home. We focused their minds on escape activities, determined to keep fighting the Germans even here behind barbed wire. I was very proud of those kids.

If the young POWs were initially bewildered by where they were and what was happening to them, so too were their folks at home. For most Americans whose loved ones were prisoners of the Germans, Europe must have seemed like another world, almost another time. In Oklahoma City or Wyoming, and even in Chicago and New York, it took an immense leap of imagination to picture the lives that sons and husbands were having to live as captives. The War Department was of little help. The report was the sum of its knowledge of what was going on in the camps. Those nursing their bruises in Stalag Luft IV would have been astonished by the declaration that they were being treated well. As for the huge task that lay ahead – of getting them home in one piece – the real action on that front was taking place 3,000 miles across the ocean from Washington, in England.

*

London was a frightened city in the summer of 1944. For more than a month the pilotless, jet-propelled V1 bombs had been dropping; thousands of Londoners had already died. For the second time since 1939, schoolchildren were evacuated into the countryside away from danger. A million were on the move to safety. The rest of the capital's population waited in dread for the now familiar drone of the engine overhead and the awesome silence as the motor cut out – and those in homes and shelters below counted out the fifteen seconds that would elapse before the doodlebug hit the ground and exploded. There was just enough time to pray that it would fall on someone else.

The attacks were relentless. The Prime Minister, Winston Churchill, told an anxious House of Commons that flying bombs were coming in at the rate of 100 to 150 a day. He was typically ebullient in public, but he could not fail to have been concerned. His armies were just beginning to win the war on the European mainland, but victory might still be snatched from him if the devastation continued on the home front. More than 2,750 bombs had already rained down on London and on 'bomb alley', the track of Kent, Sussex and Surrey countryside over which the VIs flew from *Luftwaffe* bases in northern France. In six weeks they had killed nearly 3,000 civilians and badly injured 8,000 more. The military men in the War Office who were considering how to get the POWs home from the camps could be forgiven if they thought that, in the circumstances, Germany was a far safer place to be.

On 19 July the first document was placed in an empty file at the War Office in London. The buff folder was numbered 0103/5860, and in the space for 'Subject' a clerk had scrawled in longhand, 'Possible treatment of Prisoners of War by Germany in final stages.' From the offices of the War Cabinet had come a paper giving the experts' opinion on the likely fate of the POWs before their arrival home.[3] It was rather optimistic in its assessment.

The report began by considering the possibility that Germany's generals would have taken over the running of the country – presumably after having ousted Hitler, though there is no specific mention of this. If this had happened, it was thought

most unlikely that any action would be taken against Allied prisoners of war. One of the main objects of the military leaders in assuming control would have been to establish an administration which the Allies would view with less disfavour than the Nazi regime. This object would be entirely defeated if they themselves allowed action to be taken against Allied prisoners of war. Moreover, such action would destroy any hope that Great Britain and America would act as restraining influence on Russia, whose vengeance the Germans greatly fear. We therefore consider that if the military leaders are in control at the time of Germany's defeat, wholesale atrocities against prisoners of war in their camps are most unlikely.

The analysis was accurate, but its timing was unfortunate. We do not know if the planners had had wind of a rebellion against Hitler in Germany and this had informed their report. If so, they had miscalculated. The very next day Stauffenberg failed to assassinate the Führer, and the possibility of a military coup was gone. Germany would fight to the bitterest of ends.

The report then went on to examine what would happen if Germany collapsed in defeat under its Nazi leaders. The result would certainly be chaos, though the planners remained hopeful. They were reassured by the fact that most of the camps were run by the military, and that their commandants were old-style 'army' types. 'In the hour of defeat the inclination of these authorities would be to curry favour by considerate treatment of prisoners of war.' Camp guards would also realize they had 'everything to lose and nothing to gain by ill-treating prisoners of war'.

The only faction in Germany that might ill treat prisoners of war would be the SS and Gestapo. The less fanatical and less deeply compromised members of these organizations would be likely to try to win favour by a last-minute show of moderation. The danger would come from a relatively small section of genuine Nazi fanatics [who] will resist to the bitter end. Fully armed, completely ruthless and indifferent to the consequences, either to their country or to themselves, they may try to revenge the defeat of their Führer and their cause, even at 'five minutes past twelve', on both prisoners of war and on the foreign enslaved workers in Germany. To men of this desperate sort, the killing of any member of the victorious nations will appear as an act of heroic resistance or will be resorted to as a means of eliminating dangerous witnesses.

Hitler and Himmler might conceivably order such action in order to cause the maximum trouble and sorrow at the hour of their own ruin. They might also possibly take hostages from among the prisoners in an attempt to save their own lives.

It was a chilling assessment – and one with which the prisoners tending to their injuries at Stalag Luft IV after their 'run up the road' would have agreed. It encapsulated their fears, and their personal experience, precisely. But what the military planners went on to conclude would not have eased their anxieties. The report's assessment was that revenge attacks by the SS and Gestapo 'would *probably* be local rather than general'. Later, some thought that 'probably' was a thin word on which to gamble hundreds of thousands of lives.

No one in London was prepared to recommend immediate, urgent and direct action. There was a suggestion that 'consideration should be given to the possibility of action to protect prisoner-of-war camps that appear to be in danger', but it was made half-heartedly. Instead, the onus was to be put on German camp commandants and guards to resist the SS and the Gestapo, and to that end it was proposed to issue a 'solemn general warning' that they 'would be held individually responsible for the safety of prisoners of war in their charge and that excuses or attempts to shift responsibility on to the SS or Gestapo would not be entertained'. There was no suggestion as to when such a warning should be issued, though the assumption seems to have been the sooner the better. In the event it would be nine months before the precise wording could even be agreed, by which time the war was virtually over. Meanwhile, many prisoners of war had been through hell.

The report had two further recommendations to make. One was for 'speedy communications' to be established with the camps by providing them with radio transmitters. This never happened, and the recommendation seemed to miss the point that most camps had secret radios anyway, thanks to the ingenuity of the prisoners rather than any initiative from Whitehall. The other was that the prisoners should not make a nuisance of themselves – 'instructions should be issued to refrain from any action that might be interpreted as provocative'. They were to be told – not for the first time – to stay put: 'to remain in their camp until they received further instructions on what to do and where to go'.

But the forced evacuation of the camp at Heydekrug showed that this was an issue already out of the prisoners' hands. The military authorities in London were planning for a situation that had been overtaken by events on the ground. There was a crucial gap in their understanding, and it would only widen in the months ahead.

*

The hell of being a prisoner of war would be a mystery to most people. Men locked up in huts a thousand miles from home would receive letters from ignorant friends asking what the local beer was like and what they thought of German women, as if they were on an excursion to the seaside. But at least they could take comfort that the most powerful man in the country knew the facts and sympathized with them. Churchill had been a prisoner himself during the Boer War, and, though his captivity lasted just twenty-four days, the experience marked him for ever. He wrote:

It is a melancholy state. You are in the power of your enemy. You owe your life to his humanity and your daily bread to his compassion. You must obey his orders, go where he tells you, stay where you are bid, await his pleasure, possess your soul in patience. The days are long, hours crawl like paralytic centipedes. Nothing amuses you. Reading is difficult; writing impossible. Life is one long boredom from dawn till slumber. Moreover, the whole atmosphere of prison is odious. Companions quarrel over trifles and get the least possible pleasure from each other's society. You feel a constant humiliation in being confined to a narrow space, fenced in by railings and wire, watched by armed men and webbed about with a tangle of regulations and restrictions.[4]

Churchill wrote with insight and compassion. But, for all his protestations of sympathy, how high prisoners of war ever came on his agenda for winning the war is questionable.

The general problem of what to do with prisoners was one that developed very slowly in the Second World War. The first British servicemen to fall into enemy hands were Sergeant George Booth and Aircraftsman Larry Slattery, who were flying a 107 Squadron Blenheim shot down over the North Sea port of Wilhelmshaven on 4 September, the day after war was declared. Four days later, the first officers, Squadron Leader S. S. Murray and Pilot Officer A. B. Thompson, were attacking German warships in the same area when they too were shot down. The Germans fished them out of the sea and were then flummoxed by what to do with them. At first they treated them like civilian internees, but eventually locked them up in an old fortress at Spangenberg, in the middle of Germany. The Red Cross was asked by the British government to keep an eye on their welfare.

For the next eight months there was the lull of the 'phoney war' – and no fighting meant no prisoners were taken. Then came *Blitzkrieg*, the furious Nazi onslaught on Belgium and France in the spring of 1940. As the remains of the British Expeditionary Force dragged themselves off the beaches at Dunkirk and limped home across the Channel, a heroic rearguard protected the backs of the evacuating troops as best it could. With all the little boats gone, its position was hopeless. There was no choice but to surrender.

In their thousands, British soldiers – bedraggled, defeated, exhausted, bewildered – were marched away from the sea that should have been their route home. There was no food or water along the way. As they were herded east on foot towards the borders of Germany and beyond, they were barracked and bullied, and were liable to be shot with little or no warning. Some were to tramp for six weeks, and the fear and humiliation they felt along the way would never be forgotten. The truth was that their captors had barely made any plans to deal them. With every expectation of the British suing for peace and the war being over by Christmas 1940, the guards would brag that holding the 40,000 prisoners they claimed to have taken was a temporary problem. It was only after Hitler turned his back on an invasion of England five months later that a permanent solution had to be found. A chain of proper camps was built. Prisoners were settled to as normal a life as possible behind barbed wire.

In Britain, too, preparations were made for the long haul. At the War Office, a Directorate of Prisoners of War, known as the DPW, was set up at the end of May 1940. Eighteen months later it had grown into a vast bureaucracy split into three official branches and with many other subdivisions besides. It appears never to have been a happy ship. Its tasks overlapped with those of other Whitehall departments and there were frequent turf wars. Its operations were slow and cumbersome. 'There was much scope for muddle and some vicious internecine departmental warfare,' according to historian David Rolf.[5] Its initial responsibility was to ease the anxiety of those whose husbands and sons had gone missing but had not been reported as dead. It was a snail's-pace process, dependent on information coming out of Germany. The layers of bureaucracy made it even slower. The Foreign Office – which had its own prisoner-of-war department – was involved, and so too was the Red Cross in Geneva and London. Lists of prisoners went through them first before arriving at the War Office. There it was considered unfortunate – though incompetent would be a better word – that for a while no one in the Directorate could read French or German, so that any correspondence with foreign words in it had to be sent back to the Foreign Office for translation.

Problems like this meant that the news that loved ones were prisoners often came through unofficial channels – a note smuggled home, a message via a friend. In such cases the DPW's policy was to tell the relatives to ignore these messages, to reject them as forgeries or propaganda. This set the tone for the War Office's future dealings with the relatives of prisoners of war. Right until the end of the war, it preferred to tell them as little as possible. Their questions were unwelcome; they should be grateful for what little information they had. More than once in the years ahead an MP would rise in the House of Commons to question the War Office on behalf of a distraught constituent. To be fair to the staff of the Directorate, they had a monumental task on their hands. In wartime, information is the most precious of commodities and hard to come by. Nevertheless, too often blind bureaucracy got in the way of humanity.

As for ensuring that food and medicine sent from home got through to prisoners in the German camps, the DPW's reaction was to shrug off responsibility for that entirely. International convention decreed that it was up to the military authorities in the country holding prisoners to feed and clothe them adequately. Prisoners' rations were to be equal to those available to a private soldier in that country. The Germans, as signatories of the Geneva Convention, were expected to honour this commitment. Therefore, the mind of officialdom decreed, any supplies sent from home were extras, and a matter for the Red Cross. There was an almighty row about this which was never satisfactorily resolved. Relatives were posting parcels of food and clothing to addresses in Germany;

nothing was getting through. The *Sunday Express* took up the issue, aided by the formidable Mrs Coombe Tennant, whose son – a captain in the Welsh Guards – was in Oflag VIB. She wrote to Mrs Churchill, mother to mother, telling her that prisoners like her son had been left to 'rot in starvation and rags'. The government had given the job of looking after them to the Red Cross, she said, but it had failed to check if the Red Cross – a voluntary body, after all – was up to the job, which it was not. Mrs Churchill (who also had a son in the Army) may have been moved, but her husband was not, and he refused an inquiry. However, the senior civil servant in the War Office had taken note. Sir James Grigg had heard reports about the shortcomings of the Red Cross, 'and if half what is said is true it looks as if there might be a very considerable scandal brewing', he confided to his colleagues.

Still the parcels were not getting through. The Post Office denied it was to blame; the Red Cross brought in an expert from travel agents Thomas Cook to try to improve matters; an official inquiry was held after all, but its findings were suppressed. More effort went into containing the row than into resolving it. Throughout, the instinct of the civil servants was to let the public go on thinking that the Red Cross was responsible for the welfare of prisoners of war. Then all the flak – and in a sensitive area like this, there would be plenty – could be sent in that direction, as far away from the desks of the War Office mandarins as possible. They won this particular skirmish hands down. The Red Cross unfairly bore the brunt of press criticism that 'our boys' were getting a raw deal, while Churchill and his government got on with fighting the enemy.

As the war progressed and the Americans became involved with the setting-up of a Prisoner of War Information Bureau in Washington, lines of responsibility and communication did improve (though never to the point of being crystal clear – deliberately so, it would seem). The Directorate found itself with new problems to deal with – not least the care of enemy prisoners falling into Allied hands. It also took on the job of organizing swaps of prisoners, particularly the sick and wounded. These were enormously complex operations involving negotiations with third-party countries. Huge amounts of manpower and endless documentation were spent on bringing home a tiny number of men. Finally, as the end of the war seemed a distinct possibility, the DPW took on the responsibility of working out how to get the prisoners home.

It was at one of its very first discussions of this subject, in January 1944, that a meeting chaired by the head of the Directorate, Major-General E . C. Gepp, approved the instruction to be sent out to all camps for the men to 'stand fast': to stay where they were under all circumstances and wait to be liberated. It was an order that would be constantly restated and constantly reissued, as if there was some deep fear that it would not be obeyed. There was reason for such a fear. Because the last time British prisoners of war had been given such a command the result had been disastrous.

Minds had only to be cast back a few months to the summer of 1943 and the collapse of Mussolini's Italian Army after the Allied invasion of Sicily. Seventy thousand British and Commonwealth prisoners – most of them soldiers captured during the desert fighting in North Africa – were held in camps in Italy, mainly in the north of the peninsula. With the Italians on the verge of surrendering, the British military authorities drew up detailed plans for transit camps, for reception centres, for 6,000 staff to be flown in to process the former inmates and see them home. But for now the men had to stay where they were. On 25 July Mussolini was dismissed, the Fascist Party was disbanded, and in each of the camps the Senior British Officer – as instructed – formulated plans to take over from their guards when the armistice with Italy was finally announced.

For some, the unseating of the Duce came too late. A few days earlier, 2,400 prisoners had been shipped off to Germany. Could this still happen to the rest of them? The official line was definitely not. They would soon be free and on their way home. Moreover, a lid had to be kept on any speculation to the contrary by rumour-mongers and cynics who pointed out that the Germans were waiting ominously in the wings. In some camps, news, whether from papers or over the radio, was suppressed to avoid encouraging those prisoners eager to make a run for it while the going was good.

For week after week the majority waited patiently for the Italian surrender to be officially declared. According to the historian W. Wynne Mason, the prisoners, some of whom were into their third year in captivity, were acutely aware of the possibility of transfer to Germany and further imprisonment there under unknown conditions, but there was so little reliable information about what was happening outside that it was well nigh impossible to decide on a definite plan of action. As time went on the atmosphere at some camps became tense; early hopes of release gave place to suspense and anxiety.[6]

On 3 September, British and American forces landed on the Italian mainland and a formal surrender was secretly signed. The news broke five days later, in the early evening of 8 September. In some places, excited Italian guards threw away their rifles and their uniforms, put on civilian clothes, and headed off home. The prisoners remained more phlegmatic, according to Mason. 'There were some scenes of rejoicing and a good toasting where wine was obtainable. But most men went back to their games of bridge or to unfinished snacks of supper. The emphasis was on keeping cool.'

Camp leaders and senior officers had a sleepless night as they worried about what to do.

The whole deadening routine of prison-camp existence had suddenly broken and men had to use their initiative again. They were faced with the responsibility of deciding whether to disobey the War Office order in a very confused situation. In the event, large numbers of officers and troops, well-disciplined despite years as prisoners of war, decided to carry out the last British order they had received. The outcome was the transfer to Germany of tens of thousands of able-bodied British soldiers who might otherwise have rejoined the Allied forces.

Thankfully, some of the prisoners had seen the orders for the nonsense they were and had escaped when they had the chance. Some headed south, some north, some were quickly rounded up and returned. In the end 12,000 made it to the Allied lines and a further 5,000 to neutral Switzerland. But the vast majority agonized about orders, and lost their nerve and their freedom as German soldiers arrived to take over. At one camp the leader held a conference with his senior officers, then assembled all the POWs and told them that, if they so wished, they should consider themselves released from the order to stay put. The meeting was at

2 p.m. At 2.30 p.m. German troops rolled into the camp, slamming shut the gates behind them. Just a handful of prisoners had managed to flee in those thirty desperate minutes. For the rest, there would be a quick transfer by train up through northern Italy and through the Brenner Pass into Germany and what would be another eighteen months of miserable captivity. One sergeant summed matters up ruefully: 'Everything comes to him who waits. We waited and the blasted Germans came.'[7]

It was heart-breaking, and made worse by the realization that the outcome was the result of bad planning. Upwards of 50,000 prisoners fell into German hands because, as Mason insists, of an order 'formulated several months previously which was totally unrelated to the existing military situation'. Moreover, the order had been given despite a warning from MI9, the Military Intelligence department whose job it was to help escapers to get home. MI9 had recommended the opposite course of action: that prisoners in all camps should be encouraged to leave in small groups and make their way to the coast, where, under fighter-plane cover, boats would be waiting to take them off. Such an operation was too much for the War Office. The best that can be said is that the plan had not been totally rejected but was still being discussed in London just as heavily armed German soldiers were climbing up into the Italian sentry boxes and sealing the holes in the barbed wire.

There was no inquiry into this debacle – nor even, one suspects, any sense that there was a debacle to be investigated. If an explanation for the 'stay put' order was requested, the line was that it had been given to prevent prisoners from being massacred if they attempted a mass break-out. This ignored the fact that in most camps (though, it should be said, not all) the Italians were more than happy to shoulder their arms, point their machine-guns in the other direction, and let their prisoners go. The truth was that 'staying put' made sense to the pen-pushers and the desk jockeys. The only way they could make their neat evacuation plans was by assuming that everyone was where they were told to be rather than where they ought to be.[8]

And yet a winter had gone by and here were the same instructions being prepared for the same reasons of convenience, apparently without discussion. Moreover, the instructions were now to be backed up with punishment for those who ignored them. Prisoners of all ranks who did not stay put would be reclassified as 'Displaced Persons' – given the same uncertain status as the millions of refugees and deportees thrown up by the war, unwanted, unrecognized, unprotected. Not one of the documents we have seen – the minutes of meetings, the reports and recommendations – makes any mention of what had happened in Italy as the result of the 'stay-put' order. It was as if noses had been turned up and away from a rather bad smell.

This would prove to be an apt metaphor for almost anything to do with prisoners of war. They seemed to be at best an encumbrance. There was never any way in which they were considered part of the war effort, as was made clear by a general at the War Office. In March 1944 intelligence had been received that the underground resistance in Poland was planning an uprising against the Germans, and he had been asked for an opinion on whether the Allied prisoners of war should be encouraged to join it.

At the time, there were many work camps in Poland, filled with soldiers and airmen below the rank of sergeant, who, under the Geneva Convention, were required to work. For officers and senior NCOs the privilege of rank was to while away their time in separate camps without such distractions or opportunities. But the ordinary ranks, who made up the vast majority of the prisoners, laboured for a living on the land, in mines, in factories – anywhere that did not involve directly aiding the enemy's war effort. Most were quite willing to do so, happy to be relieved of the boredom of camp life and aware of the chances they would get outside the barbed wire for scrounging extra food and even escaping. Large camps like Stalag XXA at Thorn or XXB at Marienburg had a main compound and as many as 500 satellite work camps, usually in the surrounding area but sometimes up to 200 miles away, some just a bunkhouse at a farm or a quarry holding a dozen prisoners and a handful of guards.[9] Could those POWs be used to help fight the Germans?

The general thought not – and, given the dangers of such a course of action, he was probably right. But his reasons reveal an unease about prisoners of war that was not uncommon in military circles: 'They are not trained, equipped or in many cases physically fit for guerrilla warfare. I doubt whether it would be possible to ensure they would be in uniform and properly organized under British officers.'[10] In other words, they were not up to being proper soldiers and not up for a fight. Another memorandum tucked away in War Office files contained a reminder that prisoners of war might well be soft on the Germans because of the shared experience of camp life. They would have learned to distinguish between a good German and a bad German, and as a result 'it may be more difficult to make them hate the enemy than is the case of other British soldiers'.[11]

In all matters to do with prisoners, it seems, it was always easier for the War Office to say no. After D-Day the Red Cross put the case for agreed 'zones of immunity' in Europe – basically no-fly areas where civilians and prisoners of war would be safe. The German high command readily agreed, but the Allied military authorities refused. They would get little or no benefit from such areas, because the *Luftwaffe* was a spent force, offering hardly any aerial threat. The Germans, on the other hand, had much to gain – particularly if, as the Allies suspected, they were to use such areas as a cover for military activities. Where better to place a unit repairing tanks or a factory turning out bullets than next to a prisoner-of-war camp that had been given protected status? No, it was not possible. At their conference in Casablanca in 1943, Roosevelt and Churchill had resolved on all-out war to achieve unconditional surrender. The drive for victory could not be hampered in this way.

It was an understandable decision, though no one was actually prepared to spell out the consequence. Allied prisoners of war would have to take their chances. If necessary, they were expendable. In the event, accidental bombings or strafings by Allied planes caused scores, maybe hundreds, of deaths in the camps. Nor, as we will see much later, would 'friendly fire' – a euphemism which disguises that extra-terrible tragedy of being killed by your own side – stop there.

*

Behind the blacked and sandbagged windows in his office in Mayfair, Lieutenant-Colonel Harry Phillimore pored over the memorandum from the Office of the War Cabinet with its muted analysis of the dangers facing prisoners as Germany sank into chaos at the end of the war. It irritated him. As number two at the Directorate of Prisoners of War, he had the job of trying to protect the POWs' interests. The suggestion that men in the camps should be instructed to be discreet, not to cheer at good news when they got it for fear of provoking the Germans, struck him as nonsensical and unrealistic. It would also be bad for morale if the prisoners were ordered to silence by their own commanders back in London. He preferred to put his faith in 'common sense, on which the prisoners themselves are the best judges'.[12] He did not question that they should be told to 'stay put', though he made it clear that he thought that this message had already got through.

What concerned him most was how to protect the prisoners from those who would harm them. He noted that the Chiefs of Staff had already ruled that dropping weapons into the camps was 'unnecessary', so he came at the problem from a different perspective. What if there was a severe shortage of food in the area of a camp and the local population tried to rob the prisoners of war? For that eventuality, he had been in direct touch with General Dwight D. Eisenhower's staff at SHAEF – Supreme Headquarters, Allied Expeditionary Force – and had requested that plans be drawn up for 'the dropping of arms or armed paratroopers at the camps'. SHAEF, he reported, was also arranging for a huge airlift of food to the camps when necessary – 17 million 'man rations' were being allocated.

Phillimore's report was dated 27 July. Five days later, Eisenhower's Chief of Staff, Lieutenant-General Walter Bedell Smith, confirmed Phillimore's conclusions in writing: 'Should conditions in specific instances demand that steps be taken to protect prisoners of war, it can be done by the dropping of either parachutists or arms, as appears to be expedient at the time.' He added in summary, 'Present planning at this headquarters is on the basis of providing emergency feeding, by air, should that be necessary.' Meanwhile, 105 radio transmitters had been earmarked for delivery to the camps 'within seven days after cessation of hostilities'. Each one would be taken in by an officer, accompanied by a qualified wireless operator.

The military side apparently now taken care of, planning shifted to the huge logistical problem of how to ferry the men home when the war ended and what to do with them once they were there.

Here was an area in which the planners felt more comfortable. They could assume an empty canvas, they could pinpoint reception centres on maps, they could appoint commanders of those centres, and devise the forms that each returning prisoner would have to complete. They could spend day after day sorting out back pay and leave entitlement. They could prepare carrots and sticks for the minority of prisoners who, after years of near-anarchy, might be slow to fall back into the strictures of military discipline. Then there were psychological problems to consider. The small band of psychologists attached to the War Office was giving considerable thought to the rehabilitation of men who had been deprived of freedom of action for so long. They might even become unduly anxious 'over such small adventures in initiative as crossing a crowded road or finding their own way to a railway station half a mile away'.[13] They would have to be eased back into normal society. Their families and friends would need educating on how to deal with withdrawn and possibly difficult husbands, fathers and sons.

There was much humanity in the paper that Sir James Grigg (now promoted to Secretary of State for War) presented to the War Cabinet on 22 August 1944, though his underlying intention was revealed by his early mention of the need for ex-POWs to be available 'after a due interval of leave, re-training etc, to take a further part in the war against Japan'.[14] From the perspective of more than half a century, it is important to remember that, for people in 1944, the prospect of war rolled out into the future almost endlessly. Mussolini had gone, Hitler was next, but still there would be more to do, more sacrifices to make. In Asia, the Japanese were fully expected to die in ditches rather than surrender. One military analyst calculated that conquering them could lead to a million and a half casualties.[15] Grigg had the manpower needs of the Allied armies in the Far East to consider too. Nevertheless, he was filled with compassion for returning prisoners. He thought as many as 35,000 of them might need 'mental rehabilitation', treatment 'to restore their mental balance and outlook'. What he was planning for them was lectures, films and discussions, plus lots of PE and games.

All this would be done within the existing military set-up of

Army, Navy and Air Force, though, in the true fashion of the centrally planned state – for this war and the immediate post-war period would be its finest hour – there would be coordinated action with the ministries of Labour, Health and Pensions.

*

Nearly 2,000 miles away to the east, a regime that had taken central planning to new extremes was about to embroil the War Office, the Foreign Office, the Prime Minister, the President of the United States and the entire Allied command in a problem that would grow and expand until it overshadowed not just the next twelve months but the next two generations. Long before the Second World War was over, the seeds of a new world conflict had been sown, and the first shoots had just appeared in the strangest of guises.

The 1944 invasion of Normandy had thrown up a problem. As the British and American armies advanced into France they took prisoners, and to their surprise they found that vast numbers of those surrendering in the grey uniform of the *Wehrmacht* were not Germans or Austrians, or even Croats and Romanians – other allies of Hitler. They were Russian. They had been recruited from the millions of Soviet foot soldiers who had been overrun on the eastern front as Hitler knifed his way towards Moscow in 1941 and 1942.

Some were dissidents, opposed to Stalin's Communist regime – particularly those who came from areas such as Estonia or the Ukraine, which had only recently been forced into the Union of Soviet Socialist Republics. They had often surrendered to the Germans without firing a shot. Seeing the invaders as liberators rather than conquerors, they needed little persuading to take up arms against the Red Army. But there was evidence that others had been subjected to an especially brutal form of recruitment. A unit of prisoners would be lined up and the first man asked if he would put on a German uniform. If he refused he was shot in the head. The rest of the line were then usually quick to enlist. The precise number who joined up in this way is impossible to say – though, after capture by the Allies, many, many more claimed to have been recruited in this way than is likely to have been the case.

These forces recruited in the east had, sensibly, been posted away from Germany's eastern front, where they would have been fighting against their own people, and been sent in battalion numbers to the western front – which is why they were now turning up as prisoners in such huge quantities in France. But what was to be done with them? Technically they were traitors and turncoats, having defected from the USSR, the Allies' ally. But many of them claimed that their surrender to the Allies was in fact their liberation from forced servitude in the German Army. Instead of being put behind barbed wire, they should be allowed to fight alongside the Allies against the Germans.

Adding to the complexity of the problem was the attitude of Stalin. As far as he was concerned – and despite his own son having been captured by the Germans – there were no Soviet prisoners of war, and never had been. Every true Soviet soldier died for the motherland rather than surrender. Those who had put their hands up and marched into captivity were therefore not Soviet citizens. Despite there being 5.5 million Soviet prisoners of war in Germany – appallingly treated by their guards, starved, beaten and casually murdered – Stalin maintained the fiction that they did not exist.[16] But now that their existence was self-evident – because so many of them had fallen into the hands of his own allies – he would rewrite his own rewriting of history. He wanted them back, and they would pay for their desertion with their lives. He also insisted on getting back all those Russian prisoners of war held in German camps liberated by the British and American advance in the west. They too would suffer for having surrendered to the Germans.

And if they did not wish to return? Here he had an ace to play. The prisoner-of-war camps in Poland and eastern Germany were about to be liberated by the Red Army. Thousands of British and American soldiers and airmen would then fall into Russian hands . . .

At the War Office in London, a top-secret memorandum showed the size of the problem. As of August 1944 there were 160,000 British and Commonwealth prisoners of war in Germany – of whom just over 100,000 were thought to be in the zone that would be liberated by the Russians – and 22,000 Americans.[17] The number of Soviet prisoners of war in the western part of Germany – the British and American zone – was put at 365,000. The report refrained from any political analysis except to say that 'repatriation should be dealt with by a common plan' and that 'the manner in which those released by the Russians are dealt with will be closely studied'.[18] The British and US Military Missions in Moscow were then given the tough task of negotiating the 'necessary arrangements' with the Russian military authorities.

A little education was needed for those unused to the ways of the Russians. From SHAEF headquarters, General Walter Bedell Smith wrote to the US Military Mission in Moscow:

It is possible that the Russian Armies in their advance into Germany may over-run camps in which US POW are located. Under these conditions, it is apparent that the evacuation and repatriation of US POW will have to be effected by a military thrust eastward into Russia and thence outward via a northern or southern route, as may later be deemed expedient. Can you approach the appropriate military authorities in Moscow with a view to making advance arrangements for processing such US POWs.[19]

Did a three-star general really think the Soviets would allow an American military operation deep into their agreed zone of influence? He was soon acquainted with reality.

Even at this early stage it had to be assumed the Soviets would be difficult, and it was made clear to British and American diplomatic staff in Moscow that they should put all their efforts into ensuring that prisoners of war liberated by the Red Army were sent *directly* home. The Russians must not be allowed to transport them back to the Soviet Union first.[20] Unstated but crystal clear was the fear that POWs would be held as bargaining chips. Marshal Stalin gave plenty of smiling assurances that British and American prisoners who fell into Soviet hands would be well treated, but, as the months went by, getting any firm arrangements from the Soviet Foreign Office or the General Staff of the Red Army proved well-nigh impossible.[21]

Meanwhile, Soviet negotiators concentrated their attentions on those Russians who had been caught fighting for the Germans in France. By the autumn of 1944 there were 16,500 of them held in camps in Britain,[22] and the Soviets wanted them sent back immediately. What stirred the Soviets into action was a rumour that some of the 16,500 were about to be shipped out of Britain –

which was now bursting at the seams with prisoners taken in France – to camps in Canada and the USA. This brought Washington into the argument. There the Soviet ambassador claimed that each and every one of the men in question had been 'taken by force' by the Germans and therefore ought to be returned home without delay.[23] Back in London, the matter had reached the War Cabinet. It seems that the issue there was not whether it was right to send these men back to a certain death – their status as traitors was not really disputed – but that Churchill was anxious to retain a bargaining chip of his own. However, when one of his ministers protested at 'the Cabinet's decision to send these men back to Russia; it will mean certain death for them',[24] he relented a little. He ordered the Soviets to be stalled – 'all the apparatus of delay may be used'[25] – and Moscow was told that unfortunately no ships were available to carry their prisoners home straight away. Behind this was a sense that Moscow might well prove difficult when it came to Allied POWs who fell into Soviet hands. According to a memorandum to the Chiefs of Staff, 'It may be necessary to go slow until it is definitely clear that the Russians intend to co-operate on the question of our own prisoners of war.'[26] A complex cat-and-mouse game was beginning.

The Foreign Secretary, Anthony Eden, went to Moscow to thrash out a deal, and over dinner with Stalin he secured a verbal agreement – 'the Marshal's personal word', as he explained[27] – on the mutual return of prisoners of war. The deal having been done, Churchill was soon tetchy about the whole subject when anyone tried to raise it again. He ticked off the Foreign Office for 'making unnecessary difficulties. It seems to me we work up fights about matters already conceded in principle. I thought we had arranged to send all the Russians back to Russia.'[28] A few days later he scribbled a note to Eden: 'We ought to get rid of them *all* as soon as possible. This was your promise to Molotov [the Soviet Minister of Foreign Affairs] as I understand it.' 'All' was underlined.

Shortly after, a War Office memorandum put matters more diplomatically, recording that the Prime Minister and the Foreign Secretary 'consider it most important to send these Russians home. A promise was made to Molotov in Moscow that this should be done as soon as possible.'[29] Molotov had yielded on the general principles of exchanging prisoners of war. He had also yielded on that most precious of commodities to the Soviets – secrecy. There would be 'prompt and continual' sharing of intelligence on the camps that were liberated or about to be liberated, and officers from each side would be allowed to visit those in each other's zones of influence and even take over command during the evacuation period. The harsh side of this agreement was revealed by Major-General Gepp. He told a meeting attended by top brass from the War Office, SHAEF and all of the services that 'His Majesty's Government had agreed to return all Soviet nationals to Russia *regardless of their wishes*'.[30]

There can be no doubt that this far-reaching decision – with its implication that men would be forced back to Stalin's Russia, at gunpoint if necessary and in the face of overwhelming evidence that they would be slaughtered when they got there – was taken to protect the interests of Allied prisoners of war who were about to fall into Soviet hands. In Washington, staff at the British embassy prepared a memorandum which admitted as much, and gave it to their American counterparts. It stated that the British government had been

influenced by the fact that when the Soviet Union overruns Germany, they are almost certain to come across a number of our prisoners of war, whom, naturally, we want properly treated. It is felt very strongly in London that the treatment of our men in Germany will depend very largely upon the way in which the Russians are treated in the United Kingdom.[31]

It was a position some Americans were most uncomfortable with. Forcing men to return to the tyranny of a Communist regime, even if that regime was an ally in this particular war, went against the grain. Secretary of War Henry L. Stimson was among those who objected to forced repatriation, and Washington's original stance also reflected this principle. But then, in the autumn of 1944, it quietly swung around 180 degrees. The Americans would follow the British lead and return Soviet prisoners of war by force if necessary. Only the President could have made such a momentous decision.[32] Roosevelt, like Churchill, had seen the bigger political picture, and this was the policy the two Western leaders would formally adopt five months later at the Yalta summit meeting with Stalin, where the shape of the post-war world was settled. Underlying it was a simple matter of reciprocity. If they wanted to be certain of their prisoners coming home from territory under Soviet control, they would have to guarantee the return of all those Russians in Allied hands – even if it meant turning a blind eye to what the Russians were planning to do with theirs when they got them back to the motherland.[33]

*

The planners had done their bit. But, as autumn turned to winter in 1944, their scheme for getting the POWs home had to be put on hold. It was now clear that the war would not be over by Christmas. There were setbacks such as the disastrous Arnhem campaign in late September. Paratroopers dropped behind enemy lines to seize a bridge across the Rhine were cut off and routed. The door into Germany was slammed shut (and would not be forced open for another six months). Several thousand more Allied troops joined the already overcrowded ranks of prisoners of war.

At the same time there were more and more warnings about the dangers facing the POWs. A note with top-level distribution suggested that 'Hitler may use as a last card a threat to murder all POWs in his hands unless the Allies come to terms. His object would be to avoid unconditional surrender and to cause dissension in the final stage of the war between the United States, Britain and the Soviet Union.'[34] This came up for consideration at the War Cabinet, along with a view from the DPW that little could be done to offer the prisoners direct protection. Because the camps were too widely dispersed to make a military operation feasible, 'there will be no certain method of protecting them'. The only course it could recommend was by now familiar: the issuing of a warning to the Germans of the retribution they faced if they acted in a criminal manner.[35]

None of this was likely to still the anxiety among those at risk. Intelligence gleaned from coded messages and letters, and reports by escapers who made it home, showed fears about the intentions of the Germans in the camps. At Oflag 79 near Brunswick the prisoners were said to be 'nervous about possibility of shootings on cessation of hostilities'.[36] At Nuremberg the men of Stalag XIIID had extra concerns because the SS were very active nearby. Stalag 344 at Lamsdorf was being secretly organized into fighting units which would be the hard core of any resistance to the Germans, if that proved necessary, but there, as elsewhere, there was concern about how they would fare if they became involved in 'guerrilla warfare'. The Senior British Officer in the old castle at Spangenberg (Oflag IXB) was unsure that, when it came to it, he would be able to enforce the 'stay put' order for longer than seventy-two hours – especially, he pointed out, among those under his command who had been in Italy and had paid for their caution (and their obedience) with so many more months of captivity. The reports added up to a plea for help. Those in the camps asked for 'representations [to] be made to the General Staff for protection to be arranged, especially where there are officers, as they seem to be in most danger from the SS'.

A practical way of providing such protection was suggested by a naval lieutenant who had managed to make his way home from the special prisoner-of-war camp for sailors, Marlag Nord, near Bremen. His direct experience suggested that the 800 guards would present little danger. Most of them were 'men of the 50–55 age group. Their fighting spirit was negligible and their loyalty nil. The NCOs were of poor quality while none of the officers had seen active service.'[37] Nor was he concerned about reprisals from the local population. What worried him was 'deliberate Gestapo or SS murder, as part of a policy of "burning boats" to induce the German civilian population to continue the war'.

The lieutenant had a plan. He said there was open country to the south of the camp 'well suited for gliders and paratroopers', but he warned against any premature action to free the prisoners, because this might result in the very outbreak of killing they were trying to avoid. Instead, activities should be monitored by regular reconnaissance flights over the camp. 'From such indications as football matches in progress, washing hanging on the line etc, it should be possible to judge if all is well.' Some signal should be arranged 'in the event of distress or difficulty', at which point a relief force could be flown in. Bravely, he volunteered to lead such a mission.

That the Germans were capable of the worst sort of atrocity was no longer doubted. Grigg put a memorandum before the War Cabinet listing a dozen instances where Allied prisoners who had surrendered during the latest fighting in France had been murdered in cold blood.[38] He also reported that prisoners of war who had recently returned from Germany under one of the swap schemes feared that the mood in the camps was worsening. Normally relations between guards and inmates were civil, but now

fraternization with prisoners by civilians and guards had ceased through fear of the SS and Gestapo. In some camps members of the German staffs have hinted to the prisoners that they will be used as hostages or killed. It was generally felt there was a serious danger of the SS shooting prisoners on a large scale during the period immediately preceding the cessation of hostilities.

The same memorandum noted that the SS were taking over 'some responsibility for security measures' to do with prisoners of war.

For all the concerns coming from the camps, the truth was that the prisoners were on their own. They would have to learn to live with their fears. That autumn, a series of proposals had been made for daring rescue plans. Each had been considered at the highest level – and turned down. One suggestion came from Combined Operations, based at the USAAF Eighth Air Force, acting entirely on its own initiative. It envisaged an untidy ending to the war, with the German armed forces defeated but with resistance continuing among the SS and fanatical Nazis. Amid this chaos, the prisoners of war would experience 'untold suffering and hardship'.[39] They must be brought home as quickly as possible – to leave them to take their chances would be 'an unforgivable indictment'. So all resources would be diverted in their direction for an air evacuation. Airborne forces would seize airfields next to camps, then the camps themselves. Heavy bombers and transport aircraft would then fly in to fly the prisoners out. With all resources thrown in from RAF Bomber Command and the American Eighth and Fifteenth Air Forces, the whole operation could be completed in twenty-four hours, though it might take up to a week. There would be casualties, especially 'if it is necessary to fight for the security of the airfields', but these would be worth risking if the suffering of the prisoners was alleviated.

Two weeks later, on a Thursday morning in Room 342 at the DPW offices in Curzon Street House, the idea was buried with faint enthusiasm.[40] The senior SHAEF representative preferred his organization's own plan – already at its final stages, he assured the meeting – for food drops to the camps, which he thought would use up most of the available aircraft in Europe. He supposed they could ask for planes to be diverted from the war in the Far East, but he thought permission for that was unlikely. The man from the Air Ministry said no one had told him that Bomber Command was expected to take part. Two wing commanders took it in turns to warn that the approval of the Combined Chiefs of Staff would be necessary. Eight of the thirteen at the meeting made no contribution worthy of including in the minutes. If the Combined Operations plan was ever going to fly, there was little here to encourage it.

A fortnight went by and there was another initiative. Brigadier Norman Crockatt, the Military Intelligence officer with special responsibility for prisoners of war,[41] was one of the old school, a First World War veteran and holder of a DSO[42] and a Military Cross. Still a man of action, though just turned fifty, his problem with the SHAEF plan to drop supplies to the prisoner-of-war camps was that he thought it impractical.[43] Take the issue of two-way radio transmitters. When to drop them was a delicate decision. The plan envisaged doing so a week after hostilities ended, but Crockatt thought this would be far too late, leaving the camps without direct communication for a dangerously long period. However, if the wirelesses were dropped too soon, when the German guards were still exercising control, this 'might give the enemy an excuse for shooting our P/W'. He then revealed his lack of trust in the headquarters planners by stating what some might have thought to be obvious – that Germany would be without electricity supplies, 'owing to bombing', and that therefore only *battery* (heavily underlined) sets were likely to be of value. He also had doubts about a suggestion that low-flying aircraft should fly continuous patrols over the camps. Certainly this would do wonders for the morale of the men below. But it might also 'act as a warning to enemy guards'.

The importance of Crockatt's intervention was this: the SHAEF plan had been drawn up on the assumption that conditions in Germany at the time of an armistice would be reasonably orderly; he assumed the opposite. Dropping foodstuffs without dropping armed troops to secure and protect them was ridiculous. He had no doubt that deployment of parachutists and airborne troops was 'essential'. He also wanted secret agents sent into the camps with instructions, and officers parachuted in to take charge of camps of largely private soldiers where there was no proper command structure. In the event of things going wrong – 'any atrocities, such as mass shootings' – he recommended that retaliation would have to be *immediate* (again underlined), another reason for having a proper attack force on standby. What he envisaged was no less than a massive airborne operation into the heart of Germany at a time when there was still likely to be stiff resistance to the Allies. The fact that his plan came up for consideration in the days immediately after the debacle of the airborne operation at Arnhem may explain why it was to be so comprehensively shot down in flames.

Crockatt took his plan in person to SHAEF on 1 October. There, two brigadiers gave him the courtesy of an audience and said they would pass on his suggestions to those heading the assault on Germany – Field Marshal Bernard Montgomery's 21st Army Group and General Omar Bradley's 12th US Army Group – for their observations. Crockatt left the meeting with little hope that he was getting anywhere. 'Advance provision for prisoners of war bristles with difficulties,'[44] he concluded.

This feeling was confirmed three weeks later, when he received a considered reply, on one side of paper.[45] Most of his eleven specific operational suggestions were dismissed with one line – 'not considered practical', 'not considered advisable'. No explanation, no discussion. The use of parachutists and airborne troops as outlined by him was dismissed with a curt 'This is not agreed'. The writer could not even be bothered to get Crockatt's name right – it was spelt incorrectly, and the initial was wrong.[46] The message was clear: get off our territory. At the end, the letter from SHAEF acknowledged the likelihood that paratroopers would have to be used to safeguard prisoners of war, but stated that that would be a matter for the army groups to decide and would only even be considered 'if and when ... consistent with operations'. In other words – and perhaps not unreasonably in the circumstances – the priority of the Allied commanders was to win the war. The plight of hundreds of thousands of prisoners held in enemy hands was not at the top of their list; defeating Hitler was.

World-weariness – weariness of the war itself and of the warring between departments – permeated a DPW memorandum that listed the proposals for direct action and the responses – 'rejected', 'rejected', 'discussed and rejected'.[47] The memorandum concluded that 'there is little which can be done in the way of actual protection by force of arms'. The only general agreement was, yet again, that a warning should be issued to the German military and the German people about their conduct. The precise wording and when it should be released were still under discussion.

On one other matter there was agreement. Crockatt's memorandum to his opposite numbers had mentioned 'the likelihood that camps will be moved back by the enemy as he withdraws'. SHAEF agreed that 'this is highly probable'. In fact confirmation – albeit belated – of the very first such evacuation was on its way. From Stalag Luft IV in eastern Germany, news had been received of Sergeant Vic Clarke's official protest about the ordeal he and his men had gone through in being moved from Heydekrug to Gross Tychow. He had submitted his account to the Germans on 5 August for passing on to the Swiss Protecting Power. It had taken three and a half months to reach Geneva, and was not seen in London much before the end of November.

Shortly after, more alarm bells began to ring in Whitehall. A DPW report at last noted that Himmler had been given overall control of prisoners of war in Germany and that officers of the SS 'are gradually displacing officers of the Wehrmacht in control of the German military machine. It is possible that no decision of importance on the subject of POW can be taken without reference to the highest authorities.'[48] It added that the SS had not actually taken over the day-to-day running of the camps – 'there has as yet been no change in the type of officer selected to take charge of the actual camps' – though Gestapo interference was on the increase, especially over escapes. The German military continued to realize that any mistreatment of Allied prisoners of war would lead to similar action being taken against their men in captivity, whose numbers were swelling considerably as swathes of France fell to the Allied advance. But 'those to whom power is now passing' might work to different rules. For them, reciprocity would not be allowed 'to interfere with whatever steps they may consider necessary to preserve German security'.

The fact that Red Cross supplies were not getting through also made a nonsense of the SHAEF airlift supply plan, which was based on the assumption that the prisoners of war would continue to get half of their food from their usual sources. It had occurred to no one that, as Europe descended into chaos, they might be facing a situation of near-famine.

Over in Washington, the need for direct action to protect prisoners of war was now surfacing as an issue. The number of Americans held by the Germans was thought to have risen to some 50,000 or more. The realization that 35,000 of them were in areas that would soon be controlled by the Russians caused consternation. The Chiefs of Staff made a direct approach to Eisenhower, asking him to prepare an airborne operation to protect 'our nationals'.[49] It went the way of the Crockatt plan. Ten days before Christmas, the Chiefs of Staff had watered down their demand for a full-blown operation to a request for 'a broad outline plan'.[50] Priorities were now clearly and unambiguously stated: 'Protective troops are only to be employed where their use does not conflict with gaining victory in battle.' It turned out to be a sensible precaution. Two days later, on 16 December, the Allies would be rocked back on their heels as eight German Panzer divisions backed by fourteen divisions of crack infantry thrust through the wooded and mountainous Ardennes area in eastern Belgium, forcing a gaping hole in the US First Army's front line and threatening to reverse the whole outcome of the war. The Battle of the Bulge was a savage warning that Hitler was not dead yet, and that there was much to do before any prisoners would be coming home.

3   Out into the Cold

There was something Dickensian about Christmas 1944, and not just because of the 6 inches of snow that fell in the night, covering the pine trees beyond the barbed wire, dusting the roofs of the barracks and the watchtowers, and managing to turn the vast acres of Stalag Luft III, near the east-German town of Sagan, into a charmed place, if only for a few hours. Nor was it because of the shiny decorations that the men had hacked out of old tins and strung in rows across their rooms. What was so special was the spirit of Christmases past and Christmases to come that shone in the camp. A choir of eighty gave voice to Handel's *Messiah*, accompanied by a full orchestra. Then, in their hundreds, the prisoners trooped to 'church', filling the theatre in the centre compound to overflowing. Standing there in long, ragged coats with blankets wrapped tightly round their heads to keep out the bitter cold, they resembled a flock of unkempt nativity-play shepherds, come to hear the good news.

This was despite a Scrooge-like beginning to the festivities. In previous years, the months before Christmas had been used to squirrel away the odd tin of meat or paste, any treats from home that could be kept and brought out for the feast. Not this year. Supplies of Red Cross parcels had dwindled. Luft III was 100 miles south-east of Berlin, 60 miles from the border with Poland, and too close for comfort to the advancing Soviet army. On the choked railways and roads, supplies for prisoners took second place to soldiers and arms heading for the battlefront. For weeks the 10,000 inmates of the camp's five separate compounds had been forced to depend on local German rations: sour bread, sausages of congealed blood (and, so it was said, the occasional human fingernail), mouldy potatoes, thin barley or pea soup, cheese with a taste to make a man vomit. Nor were there the caches of home-brewed alcohol to juice up the merriment that there had been at previous Christmases. Precious few ingredients could be found, and in any case the guards

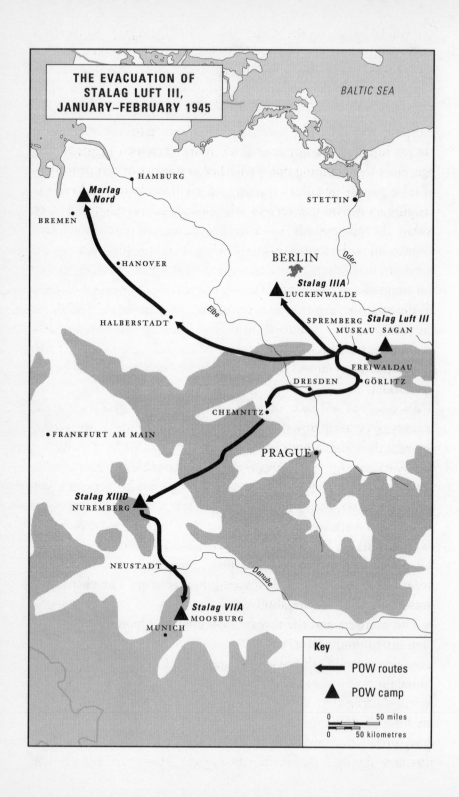

THE EVACUATION OF
STALAG LUFT III,
JANUARY–FEBRUARY 1945

BALTIC SEA

HAMBURG

Marlag Nord

BREMEN

STETTIN

HANOVER

BERLIN

Oder

HALBERSTADT

Elbe

Stalag IIIA
LUCKENWALDE

SPREMBERG *Stalag Luft III*
MUSKAU SAGAN

FREIWALDAU

DRESDEN GÖRLITZ

CHEMNITZ

FRANKFURT AM MAIN

PRAGUE

Stalag XIIID
NUREMBERG

NEUSTADT

Danube

Stalag VIIA
MOOSBURG

MUNICH

Key

POW routes

POW camp

0   50 miles

0   50 kilometres

had cracked down on the illegal stills.[1] The Germans had promised there would be beer, but no one really expected it to arrive. A terrible year was about to end badly.

Sagan was famous for the escaping activities of the air-force officers held in captivity there. Unlike at other camps, where escaping was a minority activity, here the 'tally-ho boys' were always top dog. At any one time, more than two-thirds of the prisoners were helping out – whether as diggers of dirt or forgers of false papers or tailors running up civilian clothes or lookouts keeping an eye on the 'ferrets' who poked and prodded their way round the compounds looking for tunnels. In the twenty-two months after the camp opened, the Germans logged 262 escape attempts, 100 of them involving tunnels.[2] Most had failed, of course, but some had been spectacularly successful. Two men had made it all the way home in 1943 after digging a tunnel from the middle of the compound – disguised from the Germans by the wooden vaulting horse which covered its entrance and was in constant use by a squad of gymnasts while the escapers burrowed away below the surface.

Success had led to overambition and disaster. In March 1944, seventy-six mainly British officers exited from the north compound through the most famous tunnel of the Second World War. Theirs was The Great Escape; Hitler's response was The Great Retaliation. He personally ordered fifty of those recaptured to be shot. An ominous poster went up in all camps, addressed 'To all prisoners of war' and warning that 'Escaping from prison camps has ceased to be a sport ... Breaking out is now a damned dangerous act ... All police and military guards have been given the most strict orders to shoot on sight all suspected persons ... The chances of preserving your life are almost nil.'

The murders and the threats cast a pall of gloom over Luft III that, nine months later, had still not lifted. Some of the prisoners were cheerful enough, busying themselves with plans for the future, confident that the war really was coming to an end and that they would soon be civilians again. One would-be tycoon was spending his time on drawings for a caravan which he planned to put into mass production after the war.[3] But for others the approaching Russians signified not liberty but death. Flight Lieutenant Ron

Walker, an old stager who had been shot down in 1941 after a bombing raid over Düsseldorf, had given up hope of ever getting home. He had not known any of the fifty who had been massacred – they were in a different compound – but he felt sure he would share their fate.

'I could never understand how we were going to survive,' he recalled.[4] 'I thought the Germans wouldn't be bothered about us and they would simply shoot us down. There was a real danger we would be murdered. Germany was in turmoil – how would we survive it? I really didn't believe we would. Not everyone thought that way, but I'd been a prisoner a long, long time.' He was not party to the desperate plans drawn up by senior officers on the escape committee in case a massacre looked imminent. They would go on the offensive: attack the guards with bare hands, storm the German compound, seize some guns, die but take some of the bastards with them.[5]

Then came a small miracle to lift the gloom. A few days before Christmas a batch of Red Cross parcels arrived, and out of them tumbled canned turkey and plum pudding, cigarettes and cigars, candles – a Christmas cornucopia. The Americans in the west compound even had an unexpected seasonal visitor. They were shivering in the cold night air as the roll-call was taken on the parade ground on Christmas Eve, longing to be dismissed to the comparative warmth of their rooms, when they heard the impossible sound of sleigh bells. From behind one of the wooden huts came

a small wagon carrying Santa Claus, resplendent in a red and white suit, pulled by two men dressed as reindeer. As we watched hopefully, Santa made the rounds tossing out bundles of mail to each group as he passed. Faces were a little brighter as we returned to the barracks. Santa had brought the Spirit of Christmas to this lonely camp in the wilderness where the ever-burning light of hope at times grew dim. Mail had been allowed to accumulate over a period to permit Santa's Visit. It was one of the 'not to be forgotten' days at Sagan.[6]

Over in the north compound, RAF pilot John Hartnell-Beavis and his room-mates tucked in. They had managed to save enough biscuit crumbs, sugar and dried fruit to bake a cake, and they took a slice each at teatime on Christmas Day, along with bread and butter and jam from the Red Cross parcels. But the best was yet to come. That evening they sat down to thick soup, tinned turkey, sausages and vegetables, cooked in a makeshift oven. For most of them that was enough. Their stomachs had shrunk, the unexpected feast was too much, and they gave up, groaning with pain and pleasure, before they reached the pudding and half a pound of whipped cream each. Not Hartnell-Beavis. As a matter of principle, he pushed on until every scrap due to him was gone and he felt – for the only time in his eighteen months of captivity – full.

In another hut in the same compound a stray American was enjoying British hospitality. Lieutenant Joe Lovoi was a new boy, shot down in his B-17 bomber scarcely a month earlier. With no room for him in the American compounds when he arrived at Sagan, he had been assigned a place in a hut of sixteen English, Australian and Canadian airmen, all of them camp veterans. They took the twenty-three-year-old under their wings. Things would be done correctly here. They played bridge not poker, chess not checkers. On Christmas Day they all bathed and shaved, even though the water was close to freezing, and then put on their cleanest clothes. 'There were smiles, handshakes, happy greetings and warm embraces,' Lovoi recalled, and a special menu whose mock-sophistication he would never forget – 'sardine au toast' for breakfast, 'sausage au pain frite' for lunch and 'pâté cockerel' (chicken paste on a cracker) for supper.[7]

That evening, Lieutenant Onafrio Brancato blew on his fingers to warm them up, took up his guitar, and, as usual, began to pick out a tune. Another young US flyer, he had arrived at the same time as Lovoi, and his music had helped break the ice. He sat in the middle of the hut, and the others collected round him or just lay on their bunks and joined in at a distance. They began with carols, then 'Jingle Bells', and finally 'White Christmas'. Outside, the wind howled against the window, driving the sleet against the door as they sang and dreamed of home, each one of them 'staring straight ahead, for fear that the wetness under his eyes would be noticeable'. As for what lay ahead, 'only God knew when and where our next Christmas Day would be spent'.

In his bunk that night, Lovoi lay sleepless and restless, unable to get the thoughts of home out of his head. In his mind's eye he was back in the kitchen of his parents' home in Cambridge, Massachusetts. 'The atmosphere was unusually quiet for a normally vocal Italian immigrant family. My three unmarried sisters were going about their activities almost in robotic fashion. My father, Ottavio, sat slumped in a kitchen chair, staring into empty space.'

Lovoi's imagination was uncannily close to reality – as he would later discover. He was one of four brothers away fighting in the war, but he was the one his parents were worried to death about. The others were safe enough, but Joe was 'MIA' – missing in action. Not a word had been heard about him since 16 November, when his plane failed to return to base in Italy. There had been no message from the War Department. His father, who had fought in the First World War, had slumped into a depression and spent hours leaning on the front gate, staring at the street and remembering the children playing there or just hanging out, in better times. Stirred to do something, he tried to join up at the Military Recruiting Office in Boston, begging to be sent to Europe so he could search for Joe.

He pleaded his case in his broken English. He said he would peel potatoes and cook for the American forces. He was an expert tailor and could sew torn uniforms. Through his tears, he proudly showed the recruiting officer his U.S. Citizenship Certificate. He certainly did not lack the courage, but his depression deepened when he was rejected because of his age. He was 56 years old.

The one person who never lost hope was Nancy, Joe's mother, a devout Catholic. That Christmas, even though her boys would be absent from the family home, she set up the Nativity grotto as usual in an alcove on a landing halfway up the stairs – a manger scene surrounded by bright, coloured lights. Now she would pause each time she passed it, cross herself, and murmur a prayer for her missing son. Her eyes flickered over the Virgin Mary with the Christ Child in her arms, then moved on to the figure of Joseph. Falling to her knees, she looked into the face of the saint and hesitantly whispered, 'Is my son alive?' Her tear-stained eyes saw the statue nod its head. Her scream brought her husband and her daughters rushing to her side. 'Joe's alive!' she told them. 'He's alive!'

Three thousand miles away, in England, another mother wept with joy at her home in an outer-London suburb as – through a more conventional method – she learned that her missing son was also alive. Flying Officer Eric Hookings was another newcomer to Sagan, shot down over Holland just weeks before and lucky to survive after falling straight into the arms of the Waffen SS. A major with a death's-head emblem on his cap had held a pistol to his head and threatened to pull the trigger. Later, the two guards taking him to Sagan had had to fix bayonets to hold off a mob of German women who noticed his distinctive blue RAF uniform at Dortmund railway station and tried to attack him. He was now housed in Belaria, an overflow compound at Sagan some distance away from the main camp. There the prisoners had managed to hide their illicit still from the guards, and in Hookings's hut there was hooch to drink, along with carols and good wishes all round. 'We created our own internal happiness and made the most of it because there was no point in doing any other. But most of our thoughts were with families and loved ones at home.'[8] And that was where, on Christmas Day itself, a telegram arrived from the Swiss Red Cross saying that he was no longer 'missing presumed dead' – a prisoner, but alive!

The rest of December 1944 was, in the words of Joe Lovoi, like a lost weekend. Not for him the diversion of hockey matches on the frozen fire pool, using skates which had recently arrived from the YMCA. Though new to captivity, he had quickly fallen into the ennui of camp life, summed up by one army major as 'an endless Saturday and Sunday that never succeeds in getting round to Monday'.[9] Another old stager sank into depression and recorded, 'I look behind me and see an endless arch of wasted years and, looking ahead, just a tunnel of time. The monotony and futility of it all is maddening. When will I break out of the darkness into the light?'[10]

At least the news was brighter. The German offensive through the Ardennes had stalled, falling well short of its objective, the fuel dumps at Antwerp. Without diesel, the Panzers stopped in their tracks, and the Allied counter-attack began to iron out the temporary bulge the Germans had made in the front line. But good news like this, received on secret radios and broadcast by word of mouth around the camp, could not still rumour. Hitler, it was said, had ordered the execution of all prisoners of war unless the Allies diluted their demand for 'unconditional surrender'. It did not matter that, as we will see later,[11] no such order seems actually to have been given. Nor that, with hindsight, such an order was highly improbable. Hitler's generals and even some of his henchmen may have been ready to talk terms, but the Führer was not a negotiator. But the rumour had a life of its own and was highly believable at the time, given what everyone knew about the Nazi mentality and Hitler's fanaticism. Allied governments would come to believe it and make their plans accordingly. To every prisoner gazing into an uncertain future it had the cold steel edge of reality. Joe Lovoi for one believed it. 'I thought we prisoners-of-war might have to pay the price of "unconditional surrender", that there was a real danger we could be shot. We didn't discuss it much, though. It was scary enough just to think about it yourself.'

*

On New Year's Eve, Stalag Luft III was strangely quiet. Men took to their bunks and buried their heads, lost in gloomy thoughts. The new year offered little comfort. In Lovoi's room Brancato broke the silence with a casual strumming of his guitar which then turned into 'Waltzing Matilda'. The Australians perked up, then the rest joined in, tenor matching bass until they sounded like a full male-voice choir. 'We sang ourselves out of breath,' Lovoi recalled, 'and then there was a lull.' Brancato's guitar filled the silence again, this time with 'Auld Lang Syne'. 'Then the room became very serious as we hummed along with him, and as we did so, we were forming a human ring, clasping each other's hands until the human bond was complete. "We'll take a cup of kindness yet . . ." we sang out at the top of our voices.'

All around the camp the word was that they were going to be marched out – despite the weather, despite the obvious lack of transport, despite every argument that it would be easier for the Germans to let the Russians overrun the camp and take over responsibility for another 10,000 hungry mouths to feed. The prisoners looked for some sign from the increasingly nervous guards, but they too were in the dark. Two and a half weeks into the new year, a fresh batch of Red Cross parcels arrived and, after conferring with each other, the senior American and British officers decided to release them there and then rather than store them for later. The men needed fattening up for what might lie ahead. Apart from the Christmas blow-out, they had been on restricted rations since September. Now they were encouraged to eat three hot meals a day.

The men were also encouraged to get fit, and the numbers fast-walking or running the $^3/_4$-mile perimeter track of each compound went up dramatically. On 23 January an order was posted on the noticeboard telling all American prisoners that they should get in ten laps a day while they still could. As they padded round, circuit after circuit, bodies steaming in the sub-zero cold, the breathless talk was of where they might be going, and when.

For all the expectation, when the moment came it was a surprise. The temperature had dipped even further and the snow was falling heavily on the night of 27 January 1945 as guards rushed from hut to hut. '*Raus! Raus!*' The Russian advance had been quicker than anyone could have anticipated.

Stalin's winter offensive had begun just a fortnight earlier. On a 300-mile front stretching from the Baltic to Warsaw, 163 Soviet divisions swept forward against a defensive line of just 30 German divisions. Riding in new American-built trucks and troop-carriers instead of advancing on foot, the soldiers of the Red Army were able to keep up with their tanks as they knifed through 100 miles of Polish countryside in little more than a week. They bypassed city strongholds whose garrisons Hitler had ordered to slow their progress – they could be mopped up later – and now the forward divisions were just 95 miles from Berlin itself. The Third Reich was tottering as if hit by a sledgehammer.

Ron Walker stood at the door of his room and looked out in dismay. They were to leave for an unknown destination. They had thirty minutes to get ready. 'We could take with us only what we could carry. A feeling of terrible desperation broke over me.' His room, like the hundreds of others in Luft III that night, was in chaos as men scrabbled together what they could. Discarded cigarettes littered the floor. Food was top of the list of priorities. What they couldn't carry they tried to eat there and then. Layer on layer of clothing was put on, with little regard to rank or service. One prisoner recollected wearing his blue airman's tunic and a new pair of khaki trousers, two thick woollen jerseys, a greatcoat on top, a naval cap on his head, a scarf round his neck, and two pairs of gloves on his hands. Finally he slipped an extra pair of socks over his boots, to give his soles some grip in the snow. The effect was 'wild-looking and ill-kempt'.[12]

Out in the corridor there were optimistic shouts that 'The Russians are only 15 miles away.' If the prisoners could delay leaving as long as possible, their liberators would be here. Some began practising how to say *'Ja Engliski offizier'* – 'I am an English officer' in Russian – just in case. In the north compound people stood around listening to what they hoped were guns, and there was a general feeling that they would be overrun that night or the following morning. In fact the Soviet Army was still 60 miles away, pushing across the frozen River Oder which marked the Polish border and then turning back to encircle and lay siege to the German city of Breslau.

Over in the west compound, a bugle call summoned the American contingent from their huts. Men stood, heads bowed in prayer, before shuffling out of the warmth to line up in the snow, their makeshift packs on their backs. The thought of the Russians being so close brought no cheer to Joe Cittadini, a navigator from New York. He wasn't sure he wanted to be set free by the 'eastern horde', as he called them.[13] Yes, they were allies; yet, as he recalled, 'all through the last decade our government had told us we must destroy this communistic combine'. He wasn't averse to heading westward out of their way. Nor was Lieutenant Bill Ethridge, who had come to the conclusion that the Soviets had little time for prisoners of war, whichever side they were on, and were just as likely to put Americans to work in forced-labour battalions as any captured Germans.[14] Among those more sympathetic to the Russians there had for some time been a rumour that the guards would turn a blind eye to anyone who wanted to stay behind and await the arrival of the Red Army. The German sergeant who had supposedly said this was approached and asked if it was true. A snarl and a menacing wave of his machine-gun quickly set the record straight.[15]

Bob Neary pulled on his pack (made from a buttoned-up shirt with the sleeves as shoulder straps) and a blanket roll, making sure that the logbook and drawings he had meticulously kept throughout his stay were safe. He was wearing every stitch of clothing he possessed. Round his head he wrapped a hood fashioned from a scarf, to protect his ears. Thirty minutes after midnight, he was among the Americans from the south compound who headed the column out into the night. Some dragged sledges, hastily made from Red Cross crates or an upended wooden bench. Guards with regulation packs on their backs marched alongside, some with dogs on leashes. Each prisoner had a gift in his arms – an unopened Red Cross food parcel that was tossed to him as he left. He also took on board a last-minute warning from the Germans: anyone who lagged behind would be shot.[16]

The same uncompromising threat had been conveyed to the senior-ranking US officer, General Arthur Vanaman. He was playing bridge with three of his colonels in his room when a German major interrupted them to say the camp was to be evacuated in half an hour and that anyone trying to escape or anyone falling out along the way would be shot. Vanaman stood up, looked the German in the eye, and told him they would have to be prepared to shoot him first. He had spinal injuries – the result of bailing out of a plane – and these meant he was sure to be the first to fall by the wayside. Nevertheless, he went out at the head of his men. One of his senior officers thought it a miracle that the middle-aged Vanaman was able to make the journey at all.[17]

They began in formation, four abreast, but soon deteriorated into a single file stretching miles into the distance. The flimsiest of the sledges began to break up after the first few hundred yards. At first there was a lot of shouting from the guards and even some banter. Some of the prisoners found it exhilarating to be out on the road – enjoying 'the freedom of walking through the countryside after so many years of confinement', as one of them put it.[18] But a blizzard was driving hard into their faces, and ice quickly formed on their eyelids and any exposed flesh. The temperature, according to estimates later, sank to 17 below zero.[19] They had only just started, but within the first few miles many were already exhausted. Every two hours the guards called them to a halt for a ten-minute rest, and they flung themselves on the snow and gasped for breath as the storm raged around them. Those who sat on the road itself found their trousers frozen to the surface.[20] Each time it became harder and harder to get up and plough on – so much so that Joe Cittadini preferred to keep going rather than risk seizing up. As he marched he glanced to either side of the road, and in the eerie half-light cast by the moon on the snow he saw German civilians 'slinking along in the small trees and bushes, gathering what we discarded as we were forced to lighten our loads'. Cans of margarine were the first to go, then other weighty and bulky items. In the snow by the roadside, a straw-stuffed mattress lay next to a type-writer.

The prisoners were not the only people on the move that night. Refugees fleeing ahead of the Russians jostled for room on the road. To Bill Ethridge they seemed to be carrying their entire lives with them –

bundles, small pieces of furniture, long-handled scythes, hoes and crosscut saws. They were mostly men and women too old to be useful in the German army, plus small children under 10 or 12. Many were bandaged or walked with a stick. A few rode in two-wheeled carts. An old man explained to me that the small wooden trunk and two chairs he was carrying had been made by his grandfather and he would die before giving them up. I gave him one of my two chocolate bars and thought how lucky we were in America.

His own parents, back in Illinois, had been born in Germany. He was just one generation away from being on the other side. Other prisoners, however, were less generous in their thoughts about these German civilians now running for their lives. This was their reward for the misery their country had brought to the rest of Europe and the world. It could hardly be called unjust.[21]

The POWs were still marching as the night faded and day broke; and now, in the morning light, they could take in the whole mournful picture around them. Not just prisoners and refugees crowded the road, but German troops too: some heading in the opposite direction, towards the Russians; others coming up behind, haggard and wounded, returning from the front. They begged cigarettes from the prisoners and called them '*Kamaraden*', as if somehow they were suddenly all on the same side, united in misery.

By mid-morning the prisoners had reached a small town named Freiwaldau. Already they had come 18 miles, hurried along by their guards with dire warnings that the Russians were only two days behind them. Those at the head of the line found shelter from the driving sleet inside the buildings of a labour camp. They were the lucky ones. Those who arrived later had to warm themselves as best they could out in the open. Some lit fires, ripping planks of wood from buildings while the guards weren't looking, knowing they might be shot if they were caught stealing. The cold was a more immediate killer, and any risk was worth taking if it increased the chance of survival.

Here many men dumped the loads they had been carrying. Bob Neary abandoned virtually everything and ripped up his only towel and wrapped the rags round his feet to protect them from the cold. His treasured logbook and sketches stayed – for now – stuffed into the front of his jacket. Bill Ethridge lightened his load too, giving away a can of powdered milk and trading his cigarettes with a German guard for a piece of smoked sausage. His feet were numb with cold 'and seemed no longer part of my body'. The soles of his shoes were nearly worn through. Fearing frostbite, he took off his shoes and socks and massaged his toes furiously for twenty minutes, until a little bit of feeling returned, all the time vowing to himself 'that if I ever survived this, I would never be cold again if I could help it'. He was lucky to be able to get his boots back on. Others who took theirs off and left them while they slept awoke to find the leather frozen solid. If they could not find some heat to thaw them out, it meant marching through the snow in bare feet.

After a day's rest, taken in the cold and wet, the marchers set off again into another sub-zero night. Six inches of snow fell before the morning. Men were dropping with frostbite and twisted ankles. Order was disappearing. The word came down the line that one prisoner was already dead from cold and exhaustion. Bill Ethridge knew of six men who had decided that enough was enough and were going to find somewhere to hide and wait for the Russians.

He never discovered what happened to them. In fact escape could never have been easier – all a man had to do was walk off into the dark and lose himself. But most, like John Hartnell-Beavis, an enthusiastic would-be escaper when he was back at Sagan, could see no point. 'It would have been akin to suicide,' he decided.

The column was soon swept by panic. They were marching through a thickly forested area over snow that had compacted to ice when there was a terrifying commotion and shouts that a plane was approaching and about to strafe the column. Prisoners scrambled off the road, plunged into the forest, and threw themselves into the undergrowth. Joe Cittadini's heart was beating wildly as he lay in deep snow and waited. Towards the rear of the line, some of the guards interpreted this dash for cover as an escape attempt, dropped to their knees, and fired volleys into the darkness. Several prisoners were hit, and the word was that two were badly injured.

A ridiculous story travelled quickly along the line, passed on by prisoners and German guards alike, that Russian tanks had attempted an ambush. The Germans, in a constant state of anxiety that Stalin's invaders were about to overtake them, believed it. The prisoners were ready to believe it too, and some began to shout out that they were '*camarada*', '*Americanisha*' and 'prisoners of war'. But there were no Russians to heed them. The cause of the commotion turned out to be a cart with a small boy at the reins who had lost control on the icy road. Amid the darkness and the fear, a bolting horse had been mistaken for the Red Army.[22]

The march resumed, and as the column strung out it became easier for exhausted groups to drop out and take shelter if they passed a barn. Bob Neary gave up after falling asleep several times while actually marching. He joined a group who stumbled into a roadside inn and slept on the bar-room floor. Four hours later he pulled himself up and set off again, but more than thirty of his companions could go no further. They could only wait for the horse-drawn wagons that were accompanying the column to pick them up, and in the meantime pray that the rumours that stragglers were being shot was not true.

Bill Ethridge was also close to giving up. He looked at the state of his companions around him and asked himself, 'How much more can we do?' They coated their faces and lips with margarine, to try to ward off the cold, and staggered on.

It would have been easy just to drop in the snow and pass out, even though we knew that would mean we would freeze to death. We found more than one prisoner huddled asleep in a snow bank, apparently unnoticed or avoided by the Germans. We pulled them to their feet, slapped them hard in the face, then pushed them back on to the road.

But some could not be roused. A British chaplain, Murdo Mac-Donald, who was marching with the Americans, remembered how

on the second night out, Lieutenant Jenkins, an All-American football player, decided to die. I heard the summons passed along the straggling line: 'Padre Mac, you're wanted.' I found Jenkins on his back in the snow. He insisted on giving me what remained of his scanty rations. I stayed with him till he died, closed his eyes and ran to catch up with the main column, three miles away. The summons came again and again.[23]

It was not just the prisoners who were suffering. Guards were dropping out too, and some of the prisoners took comfort in a rumour that one of them had died of the cold.[24] Another, known as Shorty, was a favourite among the prisoners and got more sympathetic treatment. He was an older man, suffering from an injured leg, and when he eventually collapsed his rifle fell to the ground and Ethridge picked it up and threw it away into a bank of snow.

We took turns carrying him, two at a time, with his arms around our necks. Then a German officer in a car saw us and ordered us to lift Shorty, who was unconscious, into his vehicle. But when he realized the guard's rifle was missing, he drew his gun and threatened us. He radioed for help and four armed soldiers arrived. We were all searched, but then Shorty came round and told the officer he must have dropped his rifle in the snow when he fell. Soldiers went off and searched until they found it.

RAF bombardier Geoff Willatt was astonished to see a guard he knew – once the most vigorous of 'ferrets' – out cold and being dragged along on a sledge by two children from a village. But what was really worrying about the guards was that they seemed to have no idea where the column was heading. Willatt saw from their behaviour that they – like the prisoners – had not been told the destination. He began to doubt 'whether we are going anywhere. Perhaps we are just marching endlessly west, in which case, how many of us will freeze to death if we have to sleep in the snow?'[25]

For the next rest, as many prisoners as possible crowded into an abandoned inn by the side of the road to sleep. They had come more than 25 miles in less than 24 hours, and Ethridge's feet were more painful than ever. But others were in much greater distress. 'Ten had passed completely out and a few others were delirious. I did what I could to comfort one who had really lost it. I kept reminding him that he had to pull himself together because he had a wife back home who needed him. This seemed to help.'

Another 12-mile march through the night brought them to the town of Muskau, where they were allowed to sleep. Here there was unexpected hospitality. Some German women had set up tables in the street and were serving coffee, soup, bread, sausage and sympathy. They offered their enemies God's blessing. In a quiet voice, the headmistress of the local school hoped 'you boys will be going home soon'.[26]

That night there was no marching, but there was consternation. Ethridge and his companions were directed to new accommodation in a factory with a huge smokestack. Stories about extermination camps had reached the prisoners, retold by some sergeants who had arrived at Sagan via Buchenwald. They panicked momentarily at the sight of the chimney, until a guard told them it was a brick factory with warm kilns and room on the floor for almost everyone to stretch out. Here, despite the dust and the dirt, they could rest and recover their strength. For them the worst was over. It was just 15 miles to what they now learned was their immediate destination. A senior officer had finally wrung some information out of one of his German counterparts. They were going to the railway junction at the town of Spremberg. With the weather easing a little, they would make it there easily the day after next.

It was a time to take stock of injuries. Walter Steck saw hundreds of men around him who needed medical attention because of frostbite and exhaustion. 'I never knew human beings could stand so much suffering,' he declared. But at least there were willing hands to help them. Slave workers who laboured in the factory brought hot water. A Polish boy repaired the sled that one combine had dragged all the way from Sagan. And not for the first time they were reminded that there were people around them in this central-European nightmare whose chances of survival were even lower than theirs.

The stragglers had time to catch up – among them Joe Cittadini, who had dropped out at the last village. His blistered feet would go no further, and he had reluctantly let his room-mates go ahead as he rested. A guard stayed with him and thirty other casualties, and the next day they piled into a hay wagon to be hauled into the Muskau brick factory, 'a wonderland of dust and toasty warmth', as he recalled it.

The factory was very large with prisoners camping in all the nooks and crannies. As I wandered through looking for my friends I spotted one of them on his blanket. I came up behind him. 'Hey, Bob where are all the guys?' He didn't turn to greet me. Then I realized he was kneeling in deep silent prayer, thanking the Good Lord for bringing us through this hardship safely.

Those at the head of the column could now take time to repair the damage done to their bodies, their minds, their souls. But, behind them, thousands were still toiling through the snow.

*

Ten thousand men marched the bitter road from Sagan to Spremberg over five days and nights. Their stories were similar, but each man's struggle was his own, a unique battle to survive, assisted by a collective determination not to give in. You helped the man next to you as you plodded on through the snow, head down, each foot forward a triumph of will-power, getting through the ordeal as best you could.

It had taken nearly eight hours for the whole camp to be evacuated, and as the last man left Sagan the front of the column was already nearing its first major stopping point at Freiwaldau. By then the line was stretched out for 15 miles or more. Somewhere in the middle were Joe Lovoi and his buddy, Onafrio Brancato, who had set off from the north compound of Luft III at just before 4 a.m. 'The only way to march without getting your head frozen was to bend at the waist, twist your shoulders and bow your head into the teeth of the freezing gale,' Lovoi recalled. Nobody spoke, saving all their energy for their legs. The moaning of the wind and the crunch of boots were the only sounds. Thousands of pairs of feet had already passed this way and hammered the snow into a hard surface, and 'we tried to walk in the footsteps of those ahead of us'. For some prisoners, however, the road had already reached its end. As he sat taking a rest, Lovoi saw a horse-drawn wagon go by. Several bodies lay on its floor, as still as death.

He and Brancato began chatting to each other – just small talk, anything to keep up their spirits. Every now and then they would gasp as the wind found an opening in their clothes. Then the chatter stopped as their faces froze and they put their heads down again and marched on in silence. Lovoi remembered getting 'to a point where you are so tired it doesn't matter, so you just keep plugging along'. Eventually, they too reached Muskau. Arriving in daylight, unlike those who had gone ahead, they could see the abandoned factories and office buildings of what had once been a pottery town. They too could now shelter and rest. The best places near the warm brick ovens were all taken, but just being under cover was a bonus in itself. Lovoi and Brancato found a dry spot, sat down, and dug into their dwindling provisions. They split a small can of devilled ham, looked in vain for something to wash it down with, and then lay on the floor and slept.

Ron Walker was among the last to leave Sagan, which meant that he and his companions at least had a night's sleep, however broken, before they began walking. A German guard warned him that the road outside was dangerous because Russian fighter planes were patrolling overhead. Another summed up their chances glumly: 'You will walk with refugees, sleep with them and probably die with them.' It was 8 a.m. when they set out, and there were casualties almost immediately. This group included the longest-serving prisoners, and they tended to be the least fit. The years of semi-starvation had taken their toll. As men fell behind, 'our wing commander constantly walked up and down the column shouting encouragement or threats to anyone he thought was about to give up. He was a tremendous example of the best type of regular officer.'

Walker 'did not think I could be so cold and live'. He tried to take a drink from his water bottle, but it was frozen solid. His fingers were too numb to untie his parcel of food. But help was at hand. Unlike those in front, the prisoners at the end of the line were marching in daylight, and in villages they passed through German girls came out with bread and coffee in exchange for soap and chocolate. His memories were all of how friendly the Germans were, and how sick they were of the war. 'I think they genuinely felt sorry for us.' One morning, after an overnight stay in a school, prisoners let some local children take turns having rides on their sledges. In their Hitler Youth uniforms, they giggled and screamed just like youngsters at play the world over, and Walker was left contemplating the absurdities of war.

For the 2,000 British prisoners in Belaria, Luft III's overflow compound, the march was, if possible, even worse than for the others. Being at a distance from the main camp, they missed the rumours. Eric Hookings had absolutely no idea they were about to be evacuated until the moment yelling guards turfed him out of his hut at three in the morning. 'What the bloody hell's happening? What's going on?' he thought as he grabbed newspapers to stuff inside his greatcoat as insulation.

We were marched straight out with no delay, pushed on the road more or less straight away by Germans prodding us with their guns. We had no idea where we were going. It was terrifying. Even those in the sick bay had to go, and there were lots of them. Jaundice, dysentery and scurvy were rife and we were all lousy with vermin and covered in sores and suppurating wounds.

They slept in barns and cowsheds at night, nestling up to the cattle for warmth, 'woken intermittently by the cries, coughs and wanderings of colleagues, some of whom were mentally scarred for life'. There were thoughts of escape – 'but where could we run to? Better to stick with the misery of the march. There was safety in numbers and comfort in numbers, and warmth at night in being close to each other.' But their guards were particularly inhumane.

In one village an old woman came to the gate of her cottage with acorn coffee. 'She probably had sons or grandsons of her own and took pity on this bedraggled string of exhausted men passing her door.' A guard stepped forward and smashed the cups with his rifle. 'To this day, I'll never know why.'

On the fourth day Hookings went down with dysentery. Racked with pain and filthy with his own vomit and excrement, he felt at the lowest ebb of his life. 'God only knows how I got through as we staggered from one barn, cowshed or pigsty to another.' There was no sign of the sun, and grey days fused into endless winter nights. He remembered coming to a railway siding where men and boys in tattered German uniforms were getting down from a line of railway trucks.

They were emaciated, badly wounded and as filthy as we were, but they had this cadaverous, haunted look of terror, as if they had been to hell and back. They were the remnants of a crack German army unit that had been fighting on the Russian front. To see the enemy, our captors, in far worse condition than some of us, lifted what little hopes we had and put a little aspiration into our souls. We exchanged our few remaining cigarettes for some of the food they still had. We were both beaten people. They were disillusioned with the war as much as we were. They had had their share of physical wounds. We were wounded mentally and by the experience we had just gone through.

We were camped in this siding for some time, guarded by Germans who in turn were watched over by their own SS troops. One of the SS generals had two geese, obviously intended for his dinner. They were too much of a temptation for starving men and one of the geese disappeared. The SS general's fury knew no bounds, and it was only the tact of the Senior British Officer that saved those involved from being shot. The German demanded compensation for his loss and we were compelled to give him our cigarette rations.

Hookings and his fellow prisoners were eventually loaded into cattle trucks for a journey of seven days and nights.

We never left that truck in all that time. Occasionally the train stopped and the doors were opened and we emptied the bucket, which, since many of us had dysentery, was disgusting beyond imagination. But no one was allowed outside. We had no idea where we were. We heard planes but we did not know whose they were. We slept where we stood, leaning against the next man, day after night after day.

When they arrived at their destination, they were driven out at bayonet point and into lorries which took them to their new camp – Stalag IIIA at Luckenwalde, to the south of Berlin. It would be their home for the rest of the war.

We had travelled hundreds of miles on foot, lorry, cattle truck through the utmost depravity, sickness, hunger and despair. We had experienced despondency of such depths we thought we would never recover. But there was always that little spark of hope, the thoughts of seeing our loved ones and, for me, the idea that one day I might be clean again.

*

The rest of the prisoners of war who had started out from Sagan were also arriving at new camps, but in different parts of Germany, many hundreds of miles apart. Muskau had become a makeshift transit camp, with prisoners constantly arriving and dossing down wherever they could find shelter. It was pot luck. Far too many were crowded into the town's cinema; another small group spread themselves out on soft straw in the centrally heated coach house of a country mansion just outside the town – the home of a wealthy German count. There they had the ultimate luxury: a flushing lavatory. Some stayed in and around Muskau for three days before being moved on. Those we left warming themselves at the brick-works had time to recover their strength before being marched on to the railway yards at Spremberg. Different groups were being ordered out at different times, depending on which camp and which train they were marked down for.

By now the sub-zero temperatures had eased, the thaw had set in, the biting chill of the wind had abated. Only those pulling sledges – hard work in the absence of snow – cursed the better weather as they toiled over wet cobbles and tarmac to Spremberg. Soon, abandoned sledges and the piles of clothes and equipment they had once carried lined the road. So too did lines of men squatting. Dysentery was running rife through the column – started, some said, through corned beef and Spam that had frozen in the cold and then been eaten before it defrosted. John Hartnell-Beavis had to make so many stops he fell far behind his place in the column. 'I don't care if they shoot me, I'm not going any further,' he yelled as he sat in agony by the side of the road. The guards waved machine-guns at him as they went by. Eventually he pressed on, and reaching Spremberg was an enormous relief for him.

Here, for the first time since leaving Sagan, there was a semblance of order. A German field kitchen doled out stew, the best Bill Ethridge had ever tasted – or so he thought, until he was told that the 'beef' was horse meat. A raid by British bombers had just beaten up the track and the marshalling yards, but workers were hard at it getting them back in service. Meanwhile, small groups of Home Guard soldiers – none of them young men – were digging in, their guns pointed eastward as they waited for the Russians. 'Some hopes of stopping the advance,' thought Geoff Willatt.

For most of the Sagan prisoners of war the marching was over, but there was still no sign of an end to their journey. In a siding outside of town one group of prisoners was packed into a cattle train, seventy to a truck. There were no windows, and the only light came through cracks in the wooden sides, which also provided some welcome ventilation. Many of these men also had dysentery, and the filth and the stench were overpowering. When the overflowing bucket was passed from man to man – sometimes, by necessity, over their heads – it felt to Joe Cittadini as though 'we had truly been baptized in hell'. Stops were frequent, but the doors were never opened.

During one of these stops a new hazard emerged. A fierce hailstorm suddenly lashed the train, or so it seemed. In fact it was machine-gun bullets from a squadron of American fighter planes. A prisoner looking through a crack saw them as they zoomed over at tree-top level. Ethridge and those around him were unscathed, but the word was that in other trucks prisoners had died.

Finally, on Sunday 4 February, eight days after leaving Sagan, they pulled into the southern German city of Nuremberg, piled out of the trucks – grateful to be in fresh air again – and set off on a mile march to their new home. On the way they stumbled round huge bomb craters. The city was clearly under regular attack from Allied bombers. As he marched through the gates of Stalag XIIID, Ethridge worried. He remembered his own flying missions, and how easy it was to be off target – 'just a slight tip of a wing or a sudden shift in the wind and the bomb would be deflected way off side, like from the rail yards into our new camp!' One nightmare was over; another was about to begin.

Joe Lovoi found himself heading even further south than Nuremberg. He and the column he was in had stayed for many days at Muskau before being marched to Spremberg and loaded on to a train. In his wagon they organized a rota so that everyone changed position once an hour, moving from the cold walls on the outside to the heat generated by all those bodies in the middle and then back again. He choked on the stench of faeces; he would have to close his eyes, grit his teeth, and take his mind somewhere else – anywhere else – to stop the claustrophobia overwhelming him. 'In some ways it was worse than the march. On the march we had some liberty. We could turn our heads, we could walk a little to the right, a little to the left. We could slow down, we could speed up. Now we were jam-packed in like pieces of cargo. If the guy next to you moved, he moved you.'

They made the best of it and managed to joke with the guard who rode with them in the truck – 'we were kidding him and we took his rifle away from him. You should have seen the terror in his eyes. He thought we were going to shoot him. We laughed and gave it back. It was just a joke but it could have been very dangerous.' On this last stage of the journey a number of prisoners did indeed try to escape. Thirty took advantage of a stop to get away. It was foolishness, just as it had been earlier. They were physically exhausted, they had no idea where they were, and they were all rounded up within a few days.

Thirty-six hours and 400 miles after leaving Spremberg, the train pulled into Moosburg, 30 miles north-east of Munich. Stalag VIIA looked for all the world just like the camp at Sagan they had left twelve long days ago. It had the same double-barbed-wire fencing, high wooden watchtowers with machine-gun emplacement, and low, grey wooden barracks, from whose windows the prisoners already in residence were staring at the new arrivals.

Here there would be even less space and even less privacy than before. Here a man could quickly go mad.

Meanwhile the German war machine and transport system continued to disperse the many thousands of POWs across Germany. The train that Hartnell-Beavis was put on took him on a three-day journey in conditions he described as 'a hell hole' until they reached Bremen in the north of Germany. On an achingly hard floor, he and his fellow travellers lay side by side like sardines, overlapping each other so that some inevitably ended up on top of others. Half of them were ill. For one whole night they cowered as the train sat in Hanover station during an air raid. Finally they reached Marlag Nord, a camp normally reserved for naval prisoners of war, which was to be their new home. The Red Cross had already condemned it as unfit and insanitary. As he walked through the gates, Hartnell-Beavis thought it 'the most derelict collection of huts I had ever set eyes on'.

For Ron Walker, like Eric Hookings, the destination was Luckenwalde. On the way he talked to a friendly guard, who gave him an apple and his considered opinion that 'the best thing would be for the Americans and British to occupy the whole of Germany and quickly too'. It was a stop–go journey that took 22 hours to cover just 60 miles, but at the end spirits were high enough for singing to break out as the prisoners marched in pouring rain from the station up to the camp. Voices rang out with 'It's a Long Way to Tipperary', 'Keep the Home Fires Burning' and 'Take Me Back to Dear Old Blighty'. They were soldiers again, in step and in tune.

The community singing was brief. At the gates they were made to wait. First the camp was in total darkness because of an air-raid warning. Then the Germans insisted that every man had to be deloused, showered and searched thoroughly before being allowed to enter. It was eleven hours later before Walker got to his quarters, close to tears with fatigue. He hunted for a spare bunk and collapsed on to the bare boards of the one he found. 'Twenty-four hours later I was still lying there and my friends called one of the British doctors to have a look at me. He said I was suffering from dysentery and exhaustion. When I asked him whether I would live he replied, "Probably . . . if you want to."'

The Sagan evacuation was over, and at the end of it there were thousands like Walker who didn't know whether they wanted to live or die. They had nearly frozen to death in Germany's worst winter for fifty years. They were racked with disease, hungry and exhausted.[27] Some had not made it at all – a small number, impossible to be precise about in the circumstances. All bureaucracy had gone by the board. After the first few hours in the blinding snow on the way out of Sagan, no one, not even the guards, was counting. Geoff Willatt reckoned that, of the 2,000 prisoners from his compound at Sagan, 300 collapsed with cold and exhaustion during the march, along with 40 guards. Most were helped to the end of the road, but not all. Another estimate was that, from the entire column, fifty had gone missing – though whether escaped or dead no one could tell. Exhausted, frightened, sick, most prisoners did not ask what had happened to their comrades. For now it was enough just to have survived.

4   Fears of a Massacre

As the men from Sagan settled into their new camps, they could reflect on a bruising experience in which their most dangerous enemies had been a fearful epidemic of dysentery and the bitter cold that had sapped their strength and morale. And killed them too. After five days on that hard road, then agonizing hours crammed into cattle trucks, surely they were now out of danger. But the question constantly whispered among the huddled groups was 'What do the Germans have in store for us now?'

While the tens of thousands of POWs spread across Germany pondered an uncertain future, word about the marches was beginning to reach home, sketchy though it was. In Britain, those who knew their husbands or sons were held in camps in Poland and the far east of Germany had seen the news of the dramatic Russian military advances and had drawn the obvious conclusion: their men were about to be released. They pressed for information, and, in response to their requests, on 22 January 1945 the War Office issued a press release approved by the Prime Minister himself.[1] It was not very informative. 'So far the War Office has received no information of the release of any British and Commonwealth prisoners-of-war by the advancing Red Army,' it said. 'An announcement will be made as soon as reliable information is available.'

But then it hinted at bad news, with the first indication that the prisoners might not, after all, have been left behind in their camps to be freed by the Soviets. 'It is known that the German authorities have been moving to the west prisoners of war and civilians from camps which are likely to be overrun. It should be appreciated that in the present conditions in Germany it must be some time before details of these transfers reach London.' The hopes of relatives were dashed.

A few days later, in a top-secret coded telegram from the British ambassador in Switzerland, the Foreign Office in London received confirmation that prisoners were indeed to be moved.[2] The Swiss were the Protecting Power for Allied prisoners of war, and one of their inspectors had just returned from a visit to Upper Silesia in the far south-east of Germany. He had been to two of the big camps there,[3] and learned that the Germans were making urgent plans to move the prisoners westward away from the Russians. They would be on foot and expected to march at least 20 kilometres (12.5 miles) a day, which was the maximum laid down in Geneva Convention regulations. The Swiss thought – wrongly – that it was already too late for such an evacuation, 'owing to rapid advance of the Soviet troops'. They were – rightly – concerned about 'the difficulties caused by prisoner health and equipment as well as weather conditions'. A copy of the telegram was circulated as a matter of top priority to all the appropriate ministries in Whitehall, marked 'Immediate'.

Then came confirmation from a different source, as the Germans – always expert propagandists – tried to make sure that their version of events was heard. On 31 January, at 6.15 in the evening, those tuned to the European Service in English from Berlin heard an announcement that Allied prisoners from Stalag Luft III at Sagan were marching westward – *at their own request!*[4] It had originally been intended to leave them to be overrun by the Russians, the German announcer said, but the prisoners of war had refused to stay. 'They did not want to be left on any account and preferred to remain in captivity in Germany than be liberated by the Soviets. They begged the camp commandant to arrange for their withdrawal from the danger zone and gave their word of honour not to try to escape during the evacuation process.' The programme made a further claim, echoing the growing feeling among the military in Germany that it was time for the Allies to recognize that their true enemy was the Soviet Union. 'Thirty officers and a large number of men volunteered to fight against the Bolsheviks in the ranks of the German armed forces.' To press home the point, it gave what it said was evidence that British prisoners liberated by the Russians were being pressed into joining the Soviet forces, and when they refused they were being shot or arrested and 'taken off to an unknown destination'. A few weeks later a similar story appeared in a Norwegian newspaper under the heading 'British flyers preferred German imprisonment to Bolshevist liberation.' Ron Walker, who had been in Sagan and had marched out of it at gunpoint, was amazed when he read the report at his new camp, Stalag IIIA at Luckenwalde. 'Who are the Germans trying to fool?' he wrote in his diary. 'Themselves perhaps.'[5]

The German propagandists' attempt to sow dissension among the Allies made no headway in Whitehall either. A War Office memo of 15 February made it clear that the Russians were 'our allies' and that the Germans were 'forcing' the prisoners to march west.[6] It predicted a calamity. 'It is obvious that under the present weather conditions and with the disorganization which must exist in that part of Germany, our men will be exposed during the long marches to very great hardship and danger.' Members of the Imperial Prisoner-of-War Committee[7] met 'as a matter of urgency' to see what could be done 'to assist and protect them'.

One thing that puzzled the Committee was what motives the Germans had in hanging on to their prisoners. The Germans had provided only a legalistic explanation – that in evacuating the camps they were merely removing the prisoners from the danger of a potential battle zone, as they were obliged to do under Article 9 of the Geneva Convention. If this really was their reason, then the situation could quickly be resolved. General Eisenhower had put forward a proposal whereby Berlin would be formally relieved of that obligation. 'Compelling these men to travel subjects them to much greater danger and hardship than would be involved in leaving them behind. Instead of moving our prisoners, the Germans should leave them in their camps or at agreed safe locations to be overrun by our Allies. This would also relieve the Germans of the burden of maintaining them.'[8]

Another possible reason for the Germans to hold on to the prisoners was that, if released, they might be armed and thrown back into the fighting. To counteract this, the Committee recommended that the government should try to strike a deal in which the Germans would be given an undertaking that men liberated in this way 'would not be used in the British or American forces against Germany for the duration of hostilities'.[9] However, it is clear that there was still a great deal of uncertainty about what the Germans were really up to. On his copy of the agenda, one member of the Committee scrawled his own comment about the evacuations.

'We still don't know why,' he wrote, adding a number of question marks for emphasis.

In London, reports began to accumulate. On 17 February a message from the International Red Cross warned that 'evacuation towards the west is being carried out in most difficult conditions, on foot, without food, in severe cold. Prisoners of war are being assembled in transit camps with no reserves. Further evacuations westward and north westward are projected in similar conditions.'[10] The next day a War Office memo noted that 'some 12 camps involving 60,000 men' were now on the move, and said that the Swiss inspector in Upper Silesia had actually witnessed the departure of the men from one particular camp.[11] They had gone out with a Red Cross parcel and a loaf of bread each, and the memo added – optimistically – that 'a Red Cross parcel is regarded as an adequate supplement for one week'. (Those actually marching might have been tempted to ask, Supplement to what exactly?) But the dangers were recognized. 'The distances involved are in some cases as much as 350 to 400 miles. Stalag VIIIB is reported to be destined for Nuremberg. There is little doubt that in winter conditions great hardship must be involved.'

The Combined Chiefs of Staff in Washington were also coming to the same conclusion. They had received 'reliable information' of prisoners being moved 'under conditions imposing great hardship and likely to result in considerable loss of life'.[12] Three days later, the Directorate of Prisoners of War in London drew up a list of twenty-two camps in the way of the Russian advance. Information about them was sparse and at least two or three weeks out of date. Many were simply described as 'transferred westwards' or 'marching westwards' and 'destination unknown'.[13]

On the same day, 21 February, prisoners' relatives at home in the United States and in Britain got the first inkling that a disaster could be in the offing. The American Red Cross reported that 'prisoners of war in Germany are being marched deeper into the Reich through temperatures as low as 30 degrees below zero without proper clothing'.[14] The news was given by Richard Allen, the organization's vice-chairman, at a meeting of the Red Cross branch in Brooklyn, and was picked up and passed on by newspapers and radio newscasters. 'I am sorry to tell you that, with the structure of Germany breaking up, there is real cause for concern for our prisoners of war. Those of you who have someone in German prison camps must be ready for bad news.'

*

News was the commodity that relatives of prisoners of war were constantly starved of. Good or bad, it was always in short supply. This lack of information began when a man first went missing, and the first indication that a husband or a son might not be coming home was in a telegram. With a war on, everyone came to dread the arrival of the delivery boy on his bicycle, the knock on the door, the ominous brown envelope thrust into your hand. Doug Fry's mother opened the door of her home in Islington, north London, on Saturday 31 July 1943 and feared the worst. The note the uniformed messenger handed her was marked 'On His Majesty's Service – Priority'. It read, 'Regret to inform you that your son 1812146 Sgt Douglas Robert Fry is missing as a result of air operations on the night of 30/31st July 1943. Letter follows. Any further information will be immediately communicated to you.' It was signed 'OC, 15 Squadron'.[15]

Her first instinct must have been that her youngest son was dead. The post on Monday brought a glimmer of hope. Having dispatched the telegram, Wing Commander J. D. Stephens had then written straight away from the airbase at Mildenhall in Suffolk

to express my deepest sympathy with you in your anxiety but also to encourage you to hope that he is safe. He was the mid-upper gunner of an aircraft engaged on an important bombing mission over enemy territory, and after take-off nothing further was heard. It appears likely that the aircraft was forced down, and if this is the case, there is some chance that he may be safe and a prisoner of war.

There could be a long wait ahead before she knew for sure, he warned. 'It may be two to three months before any certain information is obtained through the International Red Cross. May I on behalf of the whole squadron express to you our most sincere sympathy, and hope that you will soon receive good news.' His praise for her son must have helped her to cope – 'he had done excellent work and successfully completed nine operational flights

. . . he will be very much missed by his many friends in the squadron'.

How many similar letters the Wing Commander had written that day was unknown. There would have been at least six for the other members of Fry's crew, and as many again for all the other planes from his squadron that had not returned the previous night. Three weeks later another officer would have to write in similar vein to Wing Commander Stephens's own family – he was killed in action over Germany. But Mrs Fry had hope – as the chaplain from Mildenhall reminded her in a letter of sympathy. He wrote:

Those of us who wait for the crews to return, whether in the control room or on the flare path or the ground staff mechanics, always feel a deep sense of personal loss when an aircraft fails to return. Of all war news, 'missing' is the hardest one to hear. Although we are always hopeful, we must not be too optimistic nor too sad. Yet I would like to stress that what is unknown to man is known to God. Wherever our loved ones may be, we may confidently commend them to Him, and in so doing find comfort and strength for ourselves. You may be sure that your son would not wish you to be overcome with sorrow, as you may be sure that his prayer for himself and crew was less for safety than for loyalty and devotion to duty.

Whether Mrs Fry was cheered by this wise mixture of pride, patriotism and faith we do not know, but it must have been more comforting than the curt letter she received from the Casualty Branch of the Air Ministry a fortnight later, which set out the facts, albeit with 'great regret'. There was, however, a short leaflet headed, 'Advice to the relative of a man who is missing', which listed the procedures the authorities went through to trace missing men. Again, it would all take time:

Continuous efforts are made to speed up the machinery whereby the names and camp addresses of prisoners of war can reach this country. The official means is by lists of names prepared by the enemy government. These lists take some time to compile, especially if there is a long journey from the place of capture to a prisoner of war camp.

But there was a chance of earlier news:

'Capture cards' filled in by the prisoners themselves soon after capture and sent home to their relatives are often the first news received in this country that a man is a prisoner of war. That is why you are asked to forward at once any card or letter you may receive, if it is the first news you have had.

And there was a warning about false hopes –

which may well be raised if you listen to one other possible channel of news, namely, the enemy's broadcasts. These are listened to by official listeners, working continuously night and day. The few names of prisoners given by enemy announcers are carefully checked. They are often misleading, and this is not surprising, for the object of the inclusion of prisoners' names in these broadcasts is not to help the relatives of prisoners, but to induce British listeners to hear some tale which otherwise they could not be made to hear. The only advantage of listening to these broadcasts is an advantage to the enemy.

With only this somewhat stark information for comfort, the waiting went on for Mrs Fry. But there were more official letters. She had been dependent on her son for an allowance of 17s. 6d. a week, deducted from his pay, and that would still be paid for the time being (but not indefinitely); his personal effects would be kept in an RAF depository and would be returned to her only if he was confirmed dead; if she wanted to put a notice in the press about her missing son, she was told not to disclose anything other than his name, rank and number – and certainly not any 'information of value to the enemy'. The RAF Benevolent Fund wrote to ask if she was in need of temporary financial assistance. As August turned to September there was no news – which was good news – but as September turned to October there was news that was bad. The Red Cross wrote with details it had received about the plane in which her son had been flying. From German sources it was known that five of the crew of seven had been killed, though they were as yet unidentified. One named man was a prisoner, but it was not Doug Fry. There was no information about the fate of the seventh crewman. The prospects did not look good, and the tone of the letter reflected this. The report from Germany was 'grievous' and 'can but add most deeply to your already great anxiety'. 'We wish you to know that every effort is being made in order to clarify this distressing situation . . . We ask you to accept our sympathy in your suspense.' A fortnight later an Air Ministry letter confirmed the facts from the Red Cross and was deeply sorry for 'your prolonged anxiety'.

And then, when all seemed lost, Doug Fry was found. His mother was the first to know. She received the 'Capture card' she had pinned all her hopes on. He was alive and in Stalag Luft III at Sagan.

Now she could be busy. There was much to do. The Air Ministry and the Red Cross had to be given the glad news. Then there was his first parcel to prepare – the next-of-kin parcel as it was officially known. Instructions arrived from the Red Cross on how she could get extra coupons in order to buy clothes to send to him, how to pack the parcel, and where to send it. There was no postage charged as long as it carried a next-of-kin label. She was told not to embroider any messages on the clothes – not even his name, though she could mark this in ink. Under no circumstances was she to mention his squadron. Chocolate – a pound and a half maximum – and soap – no more than 11 oz. – were allowed and, for convenience, would be supplied by the Red Cross at a fixed price. Under no circumstances could she send 'photographic apparatus, field glasses, sextants, compasses, electric torches and other instruments that could be used for naval and military purposes'. A cheery note from the Red Cross hoped that 'he gave good news of himself in his letter and that you will soon hear from him again'.

At his squadron in Mildenhall a parcel was also being prepared, with 500 cigarettes and some books and records. He got *The Saint Goes West* by Leslie Charteris, Artie Shaw's 'Begin the Beguine' and the Benny Goodman Orchestra's version of 'Bugle Call Rag'. His former colleagues at the insurance company in the City of London where he had worked before the war had a whip-round and sent Mrs Fry a postal order for £2 5s. 0d. to buy presents for his next parcel.

Just before Christmas she had a letter from the Red Cross saying that Doug had been moved from Stalag Luft III to Stalag Luft VI. 'It may interest you to know that this camp is situated at Heydekrug, about halfway between Memel and Königsberg.' At last she could relax. It was four and a half months since he had failed to return from his mission. Now she knew he was alive and, if she took out an atlas, she could even put her finger on the place where he was. Mrs Fry could sleep at night.

*

It was a relief to establish that a loved one was not missing or dead but a prisoner. But, after that, it was never easy for those at home taking their ease in comfortable chairs, and with reasonably full stomachs, to imagine or understand the life their husbands and sons were now leading on the other side of Europe. It all seemed so unreal. Communication was censored. In the two letters (three for officers) and four postcards they were allowed to send each month, prisoners did not bother trying to describe where they were and under what conditions they were living, because this would simply not get through. RAF airman Norman Leonard, shot down in February 1943, remembered trying to indicate to his father back home in Essex that at one stage he had been put in handcuffs – a retaliatory act ordered by Hitler after he claimed that the same had been done to German prisoners in Allied hands.

Back at my squadron I had an old bike and when I was shot down, it was sent to my father. He wrote he had got my bike but that the chain was missing, and I replied in my next letter: 'Don't worry about the bike, I've got plenty of chains here.' But the German censor didn't like that and cut it out. You had to be really careful what you said. You had to ensure your loved ones knew you were OK, not bleat about the bad things but emphasize the good.[16]

Propaganda could be made out of the smallest thing. The Germans told Red Cross inspectors at Leonard's camp that the water-storage tank was a swimming pool, and, according to Leonard, 'the Red Cross duly reported this and produced a pamphlet that was sent to all of our families saying how well we were being looked after!'

Not surprisingly, those at home were ignorant of the real facts – which accounted for those incongruous letters prisoners would get from home asking what the beer was like in Germany, or the girls. The fiancée who implored her sweetheart in a letter, 'Darling,

I hope you are being true to me' clearly did not quite grasp the realities; nor did the mother who wrote, 'In your May letter you asked for some slippers. What colour would you like?'[17] Right at the very end of the war, one prisoner had a note from his father's boss demanding to know if he was using this time of idleness profitably, so that he could improve himself and make his father proud of him.

Official publications about POWs were few. The War Office was glad to let the Red Cross shoulder the burden of relatives. The Red Cross obliged by issuing a pamphlet, on sale for sixpence, that appeared to steer a careful route between alarming those worried about their loved ones in captivity and over-reassuring them. It listed the camps in Germany – twenty-six at the time the pamphlet was published in 1942 – and their rough location. It explained the prisoners' rights and the organizations looking after their interests. It gave a veiled warning: 'the treatment of prisoners of war in food, clothing, housing, entertainment, discipline, varies greatly between camps and at different times in the same camp. Whether a camp is comparatively "cushy", as the soldiers say, whether it is administered with severe discipline, or with bare or hostile justice depends on the temperament of the camp commander.'[18] And then it reassured: 'there are certain minimum standards set up by the international convention which was signed by Great Britain and Germany among other signatories ... and in general the terms of [this] agreement are fairly observed in Germany, except as regards food and clothing. There have been grievances but after negotiations these are usually corrected as they arise.' Those who had run the gauntlet on the road to Gross Tychow or seen friends lying dead on the barbed wire may have disagreed with this assurance.

The pamphlet made life out to be dull but endurable, cheerless and uncomfortable but not filled with danger. It described how in one camp in the mountains prisoners could go for walks in the country and even have meals at country inns. 'At one camp, after a lecture on bird life, permission to study the birds of the countryside was given.' But then, just in case this seemed too easy-going, it cautioned, 'Do not let these examples give you the idea that prisoner camps are an improvement on holiday camps.' Photographs generally showed men smiling. Those – the majority – with work duties seemed happy enough – 'hard routine work is preferable to the monotony of prison life', according to the caption under a picture of two dozen soldiers, spades and pickaxes in hand, on a work detail. And yet 'it would be a grave mistake to gather ... that they have a highly agreeable life and there is no need to worry about them'.

The overall message was a stoical one: worry about your men, by all means, but not too much. It was an attitude the government undoubtedly approved of. Be concerned for prisoners of war, knit gloves for them, send them all the parcels and help you can (via the Red Cross, please), but don't make waves. Make contributions instead. There was much about activities in the camps – theatre, music, education courses, reading, sport – and their importance in stopping the men from getting 'browned off'. Every encouragement was made to send books, sporting equipment – cricket bats, balls and stumps were particularly needed, since the Germans had none – clothing and lots of letters. 'The highlights in a prisoner's life are letters from home and food parcels,' the pamphlet stated. The job of providing the extras in prisoners' lives that would make all the difference to their welfare had fallen to the Red Cross and the Order of St John, and the best thing relatives could do was to support these charities wholeheartedly.

Doug Fry's mother made full use of the Red Cross. She went to a club that met once a week in the West End of London, and there she talked to other mothers in a similar situation. They kept in touch with each other constantly, pooled information, helped each other out. She knew when her son was moved from Stalag Luft VI at Heydekrug down to Stalag Luft IV at Gross Tychow, but she lost track of him after the POWs were marched west out of Luft IV in January 1945. Nobody knew where they were then – not even the Red Cross.

Betty Batchelder had nothing but praise for the Red Cross when Harold, her husband – a pilot always known by his nickname of 'Batch' – disappeared in June 1942.

The Red Cross was very, very helpful. One of Batch's uncles was quite high up in the organization and he was able to wheedle all sorts of people to get more information. It was the Red Cross who actually confirmed that he was alive [and in Stalag Luft III at Sagan]. But I didn't get any information from the War Office. They didn't keep you updated with regular letters or anything like that. I presume there were just far too many prisoners for them to do that. Or perhaps they didn't want us to know, because they knew we would be horrified. But I did make contact with one or two of the other wives in his squadron whose husbands had been shot down, and if one of them got a letter we would immediately phone each other to say that we'd heard and the boys seemed to be all right.[19]

She and Batch had been sweethearts all their lives. 'We met as small children,' she explained:

I was five and he was seven. We both had older brothers who went to the same school and were friends. They played together, and Batch and I did the same. I think even then I knew I was going to marry him. We hated the days when we weren't together. The link between us was very, very strong right through our schooling, when we went from the infant school to the junior school, and the junior school to the senior school. We would meet in a group of other youngsters and somehow or other we always used to pair off. As the years went by we realized we were very happy with each other's company. We told our parents we wanted to get married, and at first they said no, that we were too young. But then, when the bomb raids started, my father decided he ought to let me have my happiness while I could. We got married on 31 January 1942. I was twenty years old and Batch was twenty-one.

Batch had joined up as soon as he could, anxious to fulfil a boyhood yearning to fly. He was posted to 102 Squadron at Topcliffe in Yorkshire. Betty, a trained telephonist, joined in the war effort too, and went to work as a civilian for the War Office at a large country house it had commandeered in Essex.

In the middle of June 1942, just five months after their wedding, he had some leave, she wangled some time off, and they spent a weekend in Yorkshire.

We had dinner in a lovely old inn, and then went back to the hotel and nattered in the lounge with the other service people and girlfriends and wives staying there. I am so glad I went. It would have been awful if I had said no. But when I left him on the Monday morning I had a strange feeling. Back at work, I was on duty when a sentry came up and said he had a telegram for me. He hoped it wasn't bad news, but I think he knew. I took it and opened it. It just said, 'Your husband has been reported missing on duty last night.' I was so shocked. All I could do was just get on with my job.

I had to tell his mum, and that was the worst thing of all, because he was her eldest and she adored him. She was quite convinced she would never see her little boy again. I was equally convinced that if he had got out of that aircraft alive he would get home. But it was weeks before I heard anything. Then word came via the Red Cross, and then I got confirmation from his commanding officer that he was alive and in a POW camp. It was a fantastic relief. I also knew him well enough to know that if there was any chance of escaping and getting home he would.

For weeks she lived on the illusion that he would somehow cut his way through the barbed wire and get back to her. It did not happen, for all her longing, and after three months or so she accepted that he would be gone for a long time. 'And then I got his first letter. It was very brief and he indicated that things were not particularly good in the camp. But at least he was alive and well. I knew I had to play a game of patience then until he came home.'

But rigid wartime bureaucracy meant that the patience of waiting relatives could be sorely tested. The Red Cross had a rule that it would pass on prisoner details only to the designated next of kin. That meant that if a man was married they would deal with his wife and no one else. Sometimes, if there was a rift in the family or the wife had gone away (some were evacuated), mothers were left with no way of finding out what was happening to their sons or even how to contact them. Another matter of deep concern was whether the time spent as prisoners would count as active service when it came to totting up entitlement to be demobbed after the war. Parents and wives worried that their men would be pushed to the back of the queue, when in their opinion the experience they had been through should entitle them to jump it.

Many relatives of prisoners were far from happy at how they were treated by government. It worried some of them that the War

Office was the ministry responsible for POWs. They felt – probably rightly – that the military arm might not always have the best interests of men in captivity as its priority. All this unease burst out in a House of Commons debate in November 1944.[20] One hundred and fifty MPs signed a motion calling for a senior minister to be given specific responsibility for all prisoner-of-war matters. In putting the case to the House, Lieutenant-Colonel Louis Gluckstein, MP for Nottingham East, spoke of the 'disquiet felt by relatives that the present system of divided ministerial responsibility is unsatisfactory'. Almost every government department, he said, had a say of some sort in POW matters, and 'there is plenty of room for overlapping and even conflict'. At present, coordination was through an interdepartmental committee presided over by the Secretary of State for War – a function that could only be 'a rather vexatious additional task in an already rather over-burdened life'. A specially designated minister to take on this job would make life better for everyone.

Gluckstein had cross-party support for his suggestion, and a Labour MP spoke of prisoners of war having 'a special claim on this country' – a sentiment with which his party boss agreed. Clement Attlee, Labour leader and Deputy Prime Minister in Churchill's coalition government, did not agree, however, that the present arrangements were not working, and rose to defend the status quo. POWs and their relatives had his 'most profound sympathy', and he felt for their suffering and their anxiety, 'which is one of the great human problems of the war'. But he did not accept that there was 'grave disquiet' among relatives, and he was insistent that the majority of families 'have confidence in the way matters are being handled by the Government, by the Protecting Power and the International Red Cross'. There were discussions between government departments, but not 'conflict'. There was absolutely no need for 'one super-minister'.

Attlee was challenged by Irene Ward, MP for Wallsend, who accused him of 'complacency' on an issue that really was causing great anxiety. She said that many senior officers she had talked to were very critical of the War Office's handling of POW affairs. But there the matter rested. The government would not be budged. Relatives – as they faced the most distressing time of all, uncertain about whether their men would ever get home in the chaotic last months of the war – would have to make do with the system as it was.

*

Over in the United States, Mai Parsons's only comfort was her memories. Her mind went back over the long years that she and her husband, John, had been apart – and those distant times when they had been together. They had married in the spring of 1942, less than a year after meeting. He was then twenty, and she was eighteen.

They had their own apartment in a Victorian house in Lafayette, Indiana, and spent 'the carefree days of two young people in love, bicycling, swimming, playing tennis and visiting family and friends. These were the days of the 5-cent Coke and the 10-cent hamburger. Even the "blue-plate special" was never more than 50 cents, so we ate out a lot.'[21] It was a dreamy time, overshadowed by the reality of war and the certainty that John's call-up papers could arrive at any moment.

We dreaded mail arrival each day. His two brothers had enlisted the day after Pearl Harbor. My brother followed them shortly after, as did many of our friends. Then John's turn came, and in October 1943 he left for England. As his plane took off, he had warned me he was going to drop something for me, and as I watched I saw a cardboard box floating down – but, though I looked for it, I couldn't find it. It did make me wonder what would happen if he were to drop out of a plane, just like that box, somewhere over Germany. It was strange waving him off, seeing his plane fly away – really bad. But everybody was in the military then and you just accepted it. I never entertained any thoughts that he might not come home or something horrible might happen. I just knew he was going to come home.

Mai had thought about going to university, but she now changed her mind. The war effort came first, and she took a job in a Lafayette factory making fuel cells for bombers. Letters came regularly from John in England, telling her about his crew and the things they got up to in their spare time – trips to London, for example – but there was nothing about the missions they went on.

Then, on 21 February 1944, he was shot down. It was a week before I heard from the government that he was missing in action. This was a very difficult time for me, particularly the nights. I went to stay with my parents, and they helped me to get through it. Then, after three weeks, I found out he was a prisoner. The information was unofficial. There were people here in the United States who had short-wave radios and they picked up John's name on a propaganda broadcast by the Germans. I got over fifty telegrams from total strangers telling me. It was a relief and a joy to know he was alive. I felt sure he would be taken care of, protected by the Geneva Convention. It also meant he didn't have to fly any more. I felt he was safer there as a prisoner of war than flying on missions.

Mai's workmates did not share her optimism: they thought her cock-eyed. 'They kept telling me he wasn't coming home, and I was foolish to think he would. I should prepare myself for the worst, they said. But there was no way I was going to let myself believe that. I went to church every day and I said lots of prayers for him.' She was inspired by a calendar on the wall at work which had a picture of a soldier in uniform stepping off a Greyhound bus and his wife meeting him. 'I kept thinking about my husband. What if he came on a Greyhound bus? There were all these people around me saying it'll never happen, and I just stared at that ridiculous photograph and believed it would happen to me one day.'

She eventually received a telegram from the government with official confirmation of John's captivity and an address at which to contact him. She started to write every day, and occasionally she received a reply. The first, after two months, mentioned his grandmother's dog – a strange thing to include, she thought, until she remembered that the animal was a Pomeranian and deduced that he was trying to tell her where he was. (He was at Gross Tychow, in East Pomerania.) Then, at the beginning of 1945, the letters from him dried up, and she would not discover until after the war that this was when he was out on the road marching west. At the time, she and the other wives and mothers knew next to nothing – 'only that the war was coming to an end and some prison camps were being liberated. I worried a lot about him then, because information had stopped. We were living on rumours and wondering what was happening. I went to mass every day. People in my office were still saying that I shouldn't have so much hope.'

But hope was all that Mai and the thousands of other relatives waiting at home had. Perhaps it was fortunate that they could have no inkling of the tragedies about to overtake their loved ones.

*

Those very first evacuations of the camps in eastern Germany and Poland were frantic. But was there more to them than just a panic reaction to the rapid advance of the Red Army? The Russian offensive had begun on 12 January, but had quickly gobbled up more miles than anyone could have expected.[22] Not that the German authorities were unprepared. The order from on high to prepare for evacuating the camps had been issued months before in Field Marshal Keitel's instructions for the defence of Germany, issued from the Führer's headquarters on 19 July 1944 and with Hitler's full authority. Presumably – and one has to presume, because there is no document trail to show precisely what happened[23] – it was left to the Army and Air Force, who ran the camps, to work out the details and implement them when necessary. When the orders to move came, they were very late and left no time for delay.

And the orders applied to each and every prisoner in German hands – as if surrendering anyone the German armed forces had conquered was tantamount to accepting the end of the Reich itself. But all this is speculation: precise German intentions towards the prisoners of war in those last months of the war remain obscure.

Accounts of what happened from the German side are rare indeed, but two camp commandants at least were questioned by Allied interrogators after the war, and their testimony provides some insight into events. Von Hovel – the commandant of a camp in the north of Poland – reported that 'months before' he had been ordered by his immediate superior to draw up plans for an evacuation.[24] The order to proceed came during the night of 19/20 January, and the guards were to begin marching the men out that very morning.

The plan was instantly out of date: quarters had been arranged at a village to the west, but this turned out to have already been overrun by an advance party of Russians. The prisoners and their guards had to head in a different direction altogether – north – to avoid falling straight into the hands of the Red Army. 'Confusion ensued,' von Hovel told his British Army interrogator more than a year later. von Hovel received one more order confirming their new line of march and where they should spend the next night, 'But that was the last order we received . . . From that moment on, the Stalag had to act on its own resources' as the column headed west and north through ice and snow. They occasionally made contact with military headquarters and with prisoner-of-war authorities in other areas they passed through, but in essence they were on their own.

They were also in a race – against time. Von Hovel recorded that 'the enemy was following close behind – about one day's march behind us', and so the days up to the end of January were 'very strenuous' for prisoners and German guards alike. His account was one of chaos – lack of proper accommodation, no field kitchens or even kettles to boil water, lorries that constantly broke down, and packs that had to be abandoned by the side of the road. 'We lost many prisoners through flight and illness; hundreds lagged behind and were picked up further back by other units or by police patrols.' Russian tanks caught up with part of the column and a thousand prisoners were liberated – or, as he described it, 'fell into Russian captivity'. His choice of words was revealing of that underlying attitude of the Germans, their conviction that the British and Americans were as scared of the Soviets as they were. Hence the false claim by the propagandist on the radio from Berlin that Allied prisoners at Sagan had pleaded not to be left behind to be liberated by the Russians. The Germans believed the Allies would soon be joining them in a war against the Bolshevik hordes, and that was another reason why they were not prepared to leave their prisoners of war behind in their camps.

An even more confusing story was told by Theodor Lorentzen, commandant of another POW camp based in the north.[25] In the summer of 1944 – presumably as a result of Keitel's directive of 19 July – he too received orders to make preparations to evacuate his camp, and an elaborate plan was worked out. There was even a codeword for the operation – 'Walrus'. On 23 January 1945, Lorentzen picked up the phone and ordered Walrus to begin. He did not say who told him to do this. One of his senior officers left the very next day with a party of 2,000 British prisoners plus guards.

Lorentzen himself stayed behind with the bulk of his men (and possibly some of his prisoners, though he did not make this clear), because he had also received an order that the power plant at the camp was to be kept fully operational. Interestingly, he said that this order had come from a general of the Waffen SS.

A month later Lorentzen himself was on the move – apparently in response to orders from the highest in the land. 'On February 14 1945 I received an order purporting to have come from the Führer through General-major Ihssen ["Commandant of Prisoners of War" for the Danzig area] that all British and American prisoners-of-war would be evacuated to the west at once and that it must be understood by us all that no British or American prisoners-of-war should fall into the hands of the Russians.'

The commandant's account is interesting because of its ambiguities. It is unclear about whose orders he acted on. Reading between the lines, it seems that he ordered the evacuation of his prisoners on the very day that he received an instruction from the SS that everyone should remain where they were. We can only speculate that Lorentzen – an army veteran of the First World War – may have been trying to protect the prisoners, and perhaps even himself, from any deadly intervention by the SS. If true, it would confirm the opinion of some experts that tension between the military authorities – the *Wehrmacht* and the *Luftwaffe* – and the SS was a significant factor in the forced marches. Out on the road, for all its dangers, it was easier to keep one step ahead of the organization that ran the most terrifying killing machine the world had ever seen.

*

It is difficult now to fully grasp the extent of the power that the SS had accrued in Germany by the end of the war. It was a state within a state. Under Heinrich Himmler, the SS ran the concentration camps, the forced-labour factories and the extermination policies that were at the heart of Nazi Germany's ruthless regime of fear. Under his direction, millions were butchered with an efficiency that made their fate even more chilling. He and his SS generals routinely spent hours deliberating on the minutiae of their horrendous acts, creating endless forms, lists and files to impose order on the business of mass murder. To Himmler, getting rid of 30 million

Poles and Russians to make way for a Greater Germany was a problem of paperwork, nothing more. It was this logical reduction of evil into righteous legality – the ability to put a pseudo-civilized veneer on inhuman savagery – that inspired one German general to call Himmler 'a man from another planet'.[26] Though he consistently presented himself as a nice person, the cold-blooded way he went about his work inspired terror in victims and fellow Nazis alike. Only Hitler was said to be entirely without fear of him.

Their comradeship went back a long way. Himmler – at one time a laboratory assistant in a fertilizer firm – had been one of the very first of the *Schutzstaffel*, the 'shock troops' dedicated to the defence of their Führer years before he actually came to power. In their distinctive black uniforms and shiny black boots, with their insignia of double silver flashes, they became an elite force, held together by iron discipline. Himmler manoeuvred the SS into a position where it held all the levers of power in the country. The police – including the secret police, the Gestapo – were under his control, and through them the whole German nation had been distilled into a vast card index. He even had his own army units, the half-a-million-strong Waffen SS. A large part of Germany's economy was also under his control, and Himmler was believed to have transferred large amounts of money into banks overseas for his own use and that of his favourites.

As the Third Reich collapsed, Himmler – amazingly, given the crimes that were stacked up against him – had no doubt that he would survive it. Despite all the atrocities for which he had personally been responsible, he saw no reason why he should not replace Hitler, make terms with the Allies, and prosper in the post-war world. His SS troops were therefore busy trying to hide the evidence of what he and they, in the name of the Führer, had done. Concentration camps were to be razed to the ground; not a single inmate was supposed to survive. The bodies had to be buried. The task proved too great even for Himmler's killing machine, however, and those still alive as the advancing Russians, then the Americans and the British, got closer to the terrible secret of the Final Solution were marched anywhere in their distinctive striped uniforms in the expectation that they would die along the way. Other SS troops were stationed behind the German front line and handed out summary justice to deserters and defeatists. Lamp-posts, trees and bridges were hung with corpses of those who had said too soon that the war was lost.

Meanwhile Himmler was trying to negotiate his own terms of surrender – terms that would still leave him as a major player in Germany and Europe. He had been putting out feelers to the West since as far back as the autumn of 1944. Now his efforts redoubled as the war headed for its obvious conclusion. Secretly he traded a few thousand Jewish lives with the Red Cross and the Swiss.[27] He was in talks with the Swedish authorities and with senior US intelligence agents. And there can be no doubt that having a large number of Allied prisoners of war in his hands would add considerably to his bargaining position.

With Himmler and the SS in control, the future for the POWs looked bleak. And for those waiting in camps in the path of the Russian advance one thing was certain: they would have to be moved west. Whatever the cost.

5   The Retreat from Stalag Luft IV

It was the epic length of the journey, its seeming endlessness, that made the march from Stalag Luft IV at Gross Tychow one of the great – yet unrecognized – acts of heroism of the Second World War. From its start on 6 February 1945 to liberation for the very last man on 2 May, the journey – which, in a serviceman's typical jaunty attempt to turn hardship into humour, the prisoners dubbed The Shoe Leather Express – covered close to 500 miles. It was like setting out from London and tramping north to Edinburgh and then all the way on to Abderdeen. Or starting from Washington along the highway to New York and, having passed Manhattan, keeping on to Boston.

Cecil Room, an RAF observer, lived – and logged – every one of those miles. They are there in blistering, bone-aching, stomach-churning detail in the diary that he, like so many others, managed to keep on scraps of paper, cigarette packets, farmyard rubbish, anything he could lay his hands on during overnight halts.[1] Later on in life, the memory might play tricks, persuade a man in his old age that it had not been that bad after all. Then he could turn to the record he had made at the time and know just how bad it had been.

Stalag Luft IV had never been a good camp to be in. The gauntlet that the men had to run when they arrived in July 1944 – the so-called 'run up the road' – was a foretaste of the hard regime imposed by the guards. In an atmosphere of bullying and intimidation, the prisoners were cowed into being more submissive than at many other camps. A Red Cross report after a delegation from the international agency visited the camp warned in no uncertain terms that 'the relation between the prisoners of war and the Germans is very tense'.[2] The fear went deep. The guards in the watchtowers took delight in practice-firing their machine-guns down into the compound, and RAF Sergeant Percy Carruthers remembered how 'we would throw ourselves on the ground, hoping not to be hit.

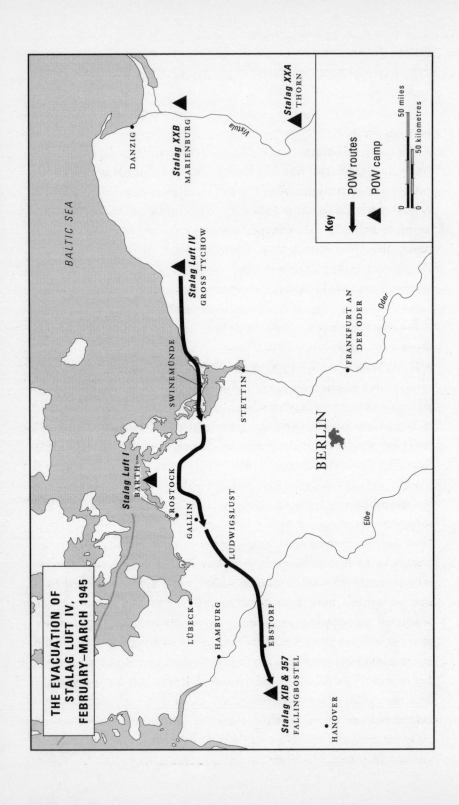

THE EVACUATION OF
STALAG LUFT IV,
FEBRUARY–MARCH 1945

BALTIC SEA

Key

POW routes

POW camp

50 miles

50 kilometres

Stalag Luft I
BARTH

Stalag Luft IV
GROSS TYCHOW

Stalag XXB
MARIENBURG

Stalag XXA
THORN

DANZIG

Vistula

Oder

FRANKFURT AN
DER ODER

STETTIN

BERLIN

SWINEMÜNDE

ROSTOCK

GALLIN

LUDWIGSLUST

LÜBECK

HAMBURG

Elbe

EBSTORF

Stalag XIB & 357
FALLINGBOSTEL

HANOVER

As we lay flat, hearing the metallic chatter and the thuds of the bullets in the ground, many of us thought this was the end. We suspected the exercises were intended to cause panic among us, undermine our morale and put our nerves even more on edge.'[3] Later, Doug Fry wondered if these target practices had been 'rehearsals for getting rid of us'.[4]

One of the guards was particularly unforgettable, not just for his size – he was at least 6 feet 6 inches tall – but for his brutality. He must have felt uneasy about his height, because he had a tendency to walk with his head bent down and his back hunched over, as if trying to disguise his extreme proportions. This had the opposite effect: he looked Neanderthal. But this posture gave him his name. He was universally known as 'Big Stoop', and the prisoners learned to avoid him, saving up their thoughts and their revenge for a better time.

John Parsons was not a man to flinch from horror. By the time he arrived at Luft IV he had survived the unspeakable – seen friends with their intestines hanging out or their faces burnt out of all recognition; cradled a dying man in his arms; watched as a fellow prisoner went stir-crazy and was shot while trying to escape. But in Big Stoop he encountered terror that imprinted itself on his mind for ever. Parsons was being subjected to an intimate body search for contraband.

You stood before a number of guards and they would look in your ears, nose, mouth, rectum – anywhere you might be able to conceal something. I had laid my clothes on the counter and the Germans looked through them, and the first thing they handed back to me was a little woollen military cap. I was standing there naked, and I put it on my head. I suppose it must have looked pretty comical. Suddenly, from out of nowhere, I was struck so hard that I slumped to the floor. I didn't know what the hell was going on. Then Big Stoop stuck the butt of his rifle in my neck and put his huge feet on my back with those old hobnail shoes that he wore. I didn't know what he wanted. What had I done? Then he stuck the muzzle of the gun in my mouth. Amid the noise, the screaming and the pandemonium, I heard a voice – his, I think – say, 'Disrespect'.

He made me get up and stand to attention in front of him. I did as I was told even though I was in so much pain that I could hardly stand.

Finally someone said, 'At ease, soldier,' and I was allowed to get dressed
and he let me go. I went back to my hut and I had dents in my back from
his boots. Big Stoop had a cruel, sadistic streak. He could take against
you just because he felt like it that day, and then he would behave like a
maniac. I never heard him talk much, he usually just made gestures. His
hands were huge, so large that they looked abnormal even for the size of
his body.[5]

The camp's American doctor, Captain Leslie Caplan, knew all
about Big Stoop's hands – 'out of proportion to those of a normal
person' – and the fearful damage they could do.[6] In a witness
statement to a war-crimes-tribunal investigator after the war he
described how the guard 'beat up on many of our men. He would
cuff them on the ears with his open hand and the pressure on the
eardrums sometimes punctured them.'
Sergeant George Guderley had seen those hands in action too.
A B-17 gunner shot down in September 1944, he arrived at Luft IV
with two other newcomers and encountered Big Stoop straight
away.

There was this huge guard standing there with a couple of his goons, and
he said in German, 'Take off your clothes.' I speak German and so I
started to do what he said, but the other two didn't understand and they
didn't get undressed quickly enough. He started yelling at them, and
then he ripped off his belt and swung it at this guy's head and beat the
hell out of him. He put his hands up to protect himself, and Big Stoop
interpreted that as an attack on him and he beat the guy even more. The
wounds that buckle made were so deep I could see the bone in his skull.
He was in really bad shape.[7]

In this atmosphere of fear it was difficult to keep up the morale
of new prisoners, who were arriving in large numbers. Allied
bombers were now pulverizing Germany from every direction, and
inevitably, given the sheer number of planes in the air, there
were more crews forced to bail out over enemy territory. Percy
Carruthers saw the horror on the faces of newcomers, and felt
sorry for them. He had been through the degradation they now
faced as captives, and would not wish it on anyone.

Perhaps only a few days ago they were in the local pub at home, happy and laughing, or having a shindig in the mess. From flying high, on top of their profession, they would be reduced to the humility of incarceration and to the indignity of standing naked and being harangued by a hate-filled enemy. They appeared to be so well fed and healthy as they stared at the emaciated frames of older prisoners like me. I was two stones under my normal weight. They must have been wondering how long it would be before they were just as gaunt and undernourished.

Then, as 1945 began, a new type of prisoner started turning up at Stalag Luft IV – and it became clear that something momentous was happening. These new prisoners were mainly British soldiers who had been captured by the Germans as far back as 1940, and they came in long columns with stories of being force-marched from work camps and Stalags in the east, just ahead of the advancing Red Army. More and more arrived, stayed, and then marched out again, heading west. One, a private named D. A. Harpin, passed through with a group which had already been on the march for ten days from their work camp 150 miles away to the east. He recorded in his diary how they arrived at Gross Tychow at 7.30 p.m. on the evening of 2 February, 'all very tired', and were issued by the Germans with a quarter of a litre of barley soup.[8] But the other prisoners wangled a treat for them, and each man got a quarter-share of a Red Cross parcel and fifteen cigarettes. The newcomers had a whole day's rest before being marched out again on 4 February, unaware that they had a further 520 miles to trudge and would be on the road until the last week of April.[9] Even at this early stage in their trek they were a sorry sight. Carruthers described them as 'footsore and limping, dirty, ill-clad, obviously very hungry and exhausted. They stayed just long enough to allow their blisters to heal before they left. But there were thousands more to come.'

In these matter-of-fact words, Carruthers described the beginnings of that massive exodus which would soon see the arteries of Germany clogged by millions of displaced people heading west in varying degrees of terror and horror. He was just as matter-of-fact about being swept up in it himself:

And soon we ourselves were to be herded out on to the road and to the fields and woods, in snow, frost, rain and sun, to experience frostbite, hunger, thirst, blisters, swollen limbs, spastic muscles, colitis, dysentery, pneumonia, freezing cold and many other afflictions we could never have contemplated.

The Russsians had now reached the River Oder to the south of our camp, had taken Breslau and were moving north.[10] Flap and panic took charge. We were to leave the following day. Kitchen wagons would go with the column, drawn by oxen or horses. We were also told the march would be by easy stages in a south-westerly direction where an empty factory was reported to be suitable for housing us. This information of course was quite untrue, as we were to be marched west as quickly as possible with the object of crossing the Oder before the Russians were able to cut us off. Hurriedly we made makeshift packs from shirts and whatever other suitable articles we could find. The brew pot was never still and we drank tea continuously while we worked late into the night, preparing to leave.

Carruthers, who had been evacuated from Stalag Luft VI at Heydekrug, forced into the hold of a ship for that dreadful Baltic 'cruise', then into a stifling railway wagon, before being chased up a forest track at bayonet point, was one of thousands on the move again. If they had known what lay ahead, they might have tried to stand their ground. If they had known for certain how precarious the German hold was on this area, they might have considered resistance. The Russians were very close indeed. Further south, their drive towards Berlin had already taken them west of Gross Tychow, which was now in real danger of being surrounded. Advance Russian troops held crossings over the Oder at Frankfurt and at Stettin. All they had to do was race north to the coast and the Germans would be trapped and their prisoners free men.

A corridor 50 miles wide along the Baltic coast was all that remained for the Germans if they were to get across the Oder and back into the heartland of their country with their column of 10,000 Allied airmen intact. But, at the time, the prisoners had no means of knowing just how desperate their captors were and just how close they were to being encircled. They gave no thought to resisting the efforts to move them. All those months of intimidation, all those beatings by Big Stoop and other guards, had worked. The fight had been knocked out of them. They would do as they were ordered.

*

George Guderley was dismayed to hear that Luft IV was to be evacuated in just a few hours. He was a member of the camp's escape committee, though there were precious few escape plans for them to consider. Tunnelling was out of the question in the soft sand of the Baltic coastal plain, and anyway the barracks huts were raised 3 feet off the ground. What the escape committee had spent most of its time deliberating was what to do when the Russians arrived.

We didn't worry that the Germans might try to massacre us. Despite the way they had treated us, there was no suggestion that they would turn on us and kill us all, so we didn't draw up any real defensive plans. We thought the guards would just go and then the Russians would turn up. We were sure we would be liberated by them. We could hear their artillery in the distance from around the beginning of the year – huge barrages that got closer and closer. We discussed how we could let them know we were here, how we could help them to liberate us, what we would we do when they came crashing through the gates.

This confidence that they would soon be free changed dramatically at the end of January, when the leader of the American compound was called into the office of the commandant, Oberstleutnant (Lieutenant-Colonel) Aribert Bombach, a short, thin-faced man and a staunch Nazi. He was told, 'Have your people prepared to march out. You will not be left behind for recapture by the Russians.'[11] There would be no option to stay put: everyone was going west. Those who were sick would be sent ahead on special trains, but the only form of transport for the rest would be their own two feet.

As the word went round, just as at Sagan and every other camp where an evacuation was ordered, prisoners frantically tried to loosen their muscles, exercise their lungs, harden the soles of their feet. Some found the whole idea monstrous. Joe O'Donnell, an American B-17 gunner shot down ten months earlier, protested, 'We're aviators; we're not marchers.'[12] But even he saw sense and got some training in – fast! 'I realized we were going to have to survive a severe Baltic winter and that all that inactivity in camp had made me unfit. I had to catch up in one hell of a hurry.'

Guderley made plans for what lay ahead with his closest friend in the camp, a boy barely out of his teens whom he called Buck. Their friendship was astonishing – one of those unbelievable coincidences of war. Five thousand miles away from Chicago, in the middle of a desolate forest in eastern Germany, they discovered they were neighbours at home. When he arrived at Luft IV, Guderley, a sociable fellow, had made the rounds of the huts in C compound, calling out cheerily, 'Anyone here from Chicago?' 'I was just trying to find a friend,' he recalled:

and then in one room this guy called out, 'Yeah, I'm from Chicago', and I said, 'Where do you live?' and he said, 'Up on the north side.' I said, 'Where did you go to high school?' and he went, 'Lane Tech.' I said, 'So did I.' He told me his name was Buchholz, and I said, 'For Christ's sake, you're not Big Buck's brother are you?' Big Buck was a beer-drinking buddy of mine at home. And he said, 'Yes, that's me. I'm Little Buck.'

We had grown up in the same neighbourhood. The coach of the softball team he played for lived just two doors from me. But he was three years younger than me, and when you're a teenager that age difference puts you in another group completely. That's why I'd never met him. But now we became very close. He was someone I could exchange private thoughts with, which is very important. It's very un-private in a prisoner-of-war barrack. There are so many people with their beds crammed together in a small space. You need someone you can relax with, and for me that was Little Buck.

The two of them made plans to stick together on the march, which was not going to be easy because they were in different huts – 'I was in barracks 10 and he was in barracks 4' – and they guessed, correctly, that they would be marched out in hut order. That meant that Little Buck would be somewhere out ahead of Guderley, but

we would try to link up and then travel together, to look out for each other. We had no idea what was going to happen once we got outside the camp. But there was always the possibility that something awful might occur, that some German civilian or the SS might start shooting at us. There were lots of niggling fears in our minds. We had an agreement: if we got separated and didn't see each other at all on the march, then it was a solemn pledge that we would meet up again at Hank's Tavern, a neighbourhood hang-out of mine on the north side of Chicago. And if one of us didn't make it, the other would go and see the other's folks.

The buddies had a target, a fixed point in an uncertain future. A beer at Hank's – a glass of Chicago's best Three Star, sitting on the counter, cool and welcoming – would be a beacon for both of them, a symbol of a time when all this would be over and they could perch at the bar and jaw over what they had been through and how glad they were to be home.

The gates of Luft IV swung open on 6 February 1945. It was cold – below zero – and snow was falling. The Russians, George Guderley reckoned, were just 15 miles away, maybe only 10. That close. 'Behind us, the noise of battle was very, very real.' A rumour travelled through the ranks that, according to a guard, Hitler had ordered that the prisoners should be made to march without their trousers, presumably as an extra hardship and to discourage them from trying to escape. The commandant, it was said, had decided to defy his Führer and had refused to carry out this instruction.[13]

Roger Allen was among the first to set off, and he felt a mixture of fear and jubilation.

The fact that we were being marched out meant that things were looking up for the Allies. But we also discussed the possibility that they were taking us out to shoot us. You'd have been mad not to think there was a chance of that happening, but it didn't scare us to the point where we couldn't function. Let's just say we were apprehensive. But, as we left, we were joking. We were Americans, and we could handle this! I guess there was a little bit of bravado about it. We were trying to keep each other going. But nobody told us how long we would march for, or when it would stop. I don't think the German guards themselves knew.[14]

Guderley was in a good mood too.

I was just happy to be out from behind the barbed wire. I had often stared out from our compound and wondered what was down the road. Now we could see a sawmill, some houses, a railroad. There was lots of joking, smart-ass remarks, laughing at ourselves, at our plight. It's what people do, as a coping mechanism. It's funny how the body reacts. I can't explain this but it must say something about how excited we were because, after our first night outside the camp, sleeping in a barn, lots of the guys woke in the morning and said they had had a wet dream that night. It was so unusual. Sex was not something that ever occurred to us in the camp. We dreamed of food, always of food, but not women. I can only think we must have been too hungry or tired or worn down.[15] But that night, whether it was the exertion of the day's march I just don't know, but there was all this activity, this release. It was a subject of discussion the next day. 'Do you know what happened to me last night?' – 'Oh, really, me too.'

*

In the British compound, the order to evacuate Luft IV had come as a total surprise to Cec Room. 'Camp Leader crashes into the barracks at half past midnight and wakes the whole lot of us, with the news that we're being evacuated on foot at 12 noon today,' he wrote. 'What a bloody panic!' Doug Fry was caught on the hop too:

We guessed that, since we'd been moved out of Heydekrug six months before because the Russians were advancing, the same was likely to happen here. They were going to move us – it was just a question of when. But there was no official communication. We were just turfed out that morning. I remember having a sense of foreboding. No matter how bad a camp you are in, you feel safe and settled. You've got a roof over your head and a bunk to sleep on. Now we had no idea what lay ahead.

Whereas the Americans appear to have had some sort of advance warning of the evacuation, the British contingent, it seems, had been less on the ball. That wouldn't have surprised the Americans one little bit. They always tended to see the Limey prisoners as rather lackadaisical in attitude, badly dressed, ill-kempt – and undisciplined. In return, the British often dismissed the Yanks as loud, bombastic, self-centred – and undisciplined. It was the natural rivalry of military men indulging in chauvinist banter rather than bigotry, and rarely involved any real animosity.

The biggest difference between them, in any case, was due not to nationality but to length of service behind barbed wire. The Americans were generally much newer to prison-camp life. They looked at the behaviour of their transatlantic allies – most of whom had been captives for two or three years, sometimes more – and came to the conclusion that they had gone soft. 'Experienced', 'canny' and even 'laid-back' might have been more appropriate words. The longer a man was a prisoner, the less likely he was to kick against the fact of his incarceration. He had gone through the stages of anger and hurt. He learned to play the system in order to beat it, rather than beat his head against what he could not change. If that meant he became institutionalized, then that was just a way of coping. The British tended to adopt an attitude of 'seen it all before' – which was often true. But it made them slower to react when the decisive moment came.

Then again, Room remembered that, after they were given the news that they were off in twelve hours' time, the British in his hut, true to their national stereotype, brewed tea. They did, however, throw every single tea bag they had into the pot and use up all the tins of condensed milk they would be unable to carry. The result was heaven – 'it was so sweet and strong, you could stand a spoon upright in the cup!' Even then a few men went back to bed, on the grounds that the Germans were always giving orders and nine times out of ten they came to nothing. But this was no false alarm, and at midday, ready or not, the prisoners were on the move.

Room picked up his hastily made pack – 'my pathetic bundle' as he called it – and two rolled-up blankets. He had just gulped down a hasty meal of warm potatoes in their jackets. Now he was astonished to be issued with a third of a loaf of bread, 'the first we had seen for a month'. Then it was out, past a line of sentry boxes standing empty and desolate – 'I never thought we'd ever see them like that.' He was elated.

Fry was not. His hut had set off a few hours earlier, having been assembled in the open air at 6 a.m., when it was still dark. 'Horrible, horrible,' he recalled. 'There was a blizzard blowing and 2 feet of snow already on the ground.' The Red Cross parcels they were issued with were heavy – 7 lb apiece – and unwieldy to men whose arms were already full. Some men ditched them almost straight away, convinced by talk from the guards – whether malicious or out of ignorance Fry never knew – that they were going only a few miles up the road and would not need these extra rations. 'They came to regret this later,' he noted ruefully. Carruthers saw dozens of discarded tins of food lying in the snow and thought abandoning them 'absolute folly'.

That night, covering himself in straw to try to stay warm, Room found a moment to make his first diary entry of the march. It had a jaunty flavour to it:

First eleven kilometres are covered in good time on roads covered in ice, slush, snow. We are all feeling fresh. Then we strike out across muddy fields and cart tracks, to Naffin [a village] where we are bunged into barns for the night. No food issued by the horrible Huns and I have to creep unobserved into the cowshed to get a cup of cold water. Wizard sleep, but during the night a rat bites me on the cheek, gnawing his way through the straw, one blanket, pullover, scarf and cap. Some teeth! – 11 miles that day.

The journey to hell had begun. Nobody but nobody – not even the German guards – had any idea that this was Day 1 of 86.

*

It was after the first few days that Guderley began to wonder

where we were going and when it was all going to end. Before we set out we had been told we would be on the march for two or three days, but we were now well past that. The food was running out. We eked out our supplies – a can of salmon or Spam will last three days, but then you have to eat it all because you know it's going to go bad on you if you don't. But when it was gone we didn't know whether we were going to get fresh supplies. Would there be any Red Cross parcels out here on the march? It didn't look very likely.

At night, if you were lucky, you managed to get into a barn, but the guards would pack us in so tight that no one could lie down. We took it in turns to stand up while the others slept, but you only ever got an hour's sleep at a time before you had to move around and give your space to somebody else. If there was no barn, we slept in a field, in the rain and snow.

Each day began to roll into the next. We just kept going, one foot in front of the other, marching on and trying not to think of the hell we were in. And the weather was getting worse – driving wind and rain and rain and snow mixed, and so cold.

Guderley knew that Buck was somewhere ahead of him in the column, but he could find no chance to sneak ahead to join him. He was marching with three members of his bomber crew who had been in the same hut as him, and one of them was in trouble straight away.

He had broken his leg when we were shot down. He bailed out against the slipstream, and his foot caught between the gunsight and the seat. He was trapped, and it was only because the aircraft exploded in mid-air that he was blown clear. He had multiple fractures and had been in hospital, and he was still limping all those months later. But the Germans refused to let him be evacuated by train as one of the sick. They said he was mobile enough to march. But he was in a bad way from the start. I helped carry his Red Cross parcel for him, shared it with another of our crew. But I lost contact with him after a few days. He teamed up with another prisoner and they decided to stick together, and I did the same with another couple of guys. I didn't see him after that, though I know he made it home in the end. At the time, though, I wouldn't have given much for his chances.

*

It was the mud that stuck in Room's mind in those early days. The lanes were smeared with it, and so were the men after tramping across bare-earth fields. He reckoned he had an extra 5 lb weight on each foot from the cloying black soil that caked them. Later on he would reflect on this and take a strange delight in the mud. He would, he realized, now have no trouble looking veterans of the First World War in the eye. It was commonplace between 1939 and 1945 for those who had fought in the trenches in the previous war to belittle modern soldiering as soft. Room recorded that 'the last war wallahs have nothing on us – they can no longer crow about the mud they used to plough through'.

As he marched through the rain and sleet, he prayed for a warm place to sleep when the night came, only to find himself having to bivouac in the middle of a field. 'Bloody awful night,' he recorded, 'no room in barn, and again no food from Jerry.' Around him on the march were airmen of many nationalities – 'English, Canadian, Czech, Polish, South African, Australians, New Zealand and one from Tahiti'. Ahead and behind was a ragged, suffering army of mainly Americans. As they marched briefly along the side of the fast, straight road that linked Danzig and Stettin before they turned off on to a country track, the size of the column could be taken in at a glance. It was awesome – 'thousands of men, three abreast, stretching into the distance and all strung out; we looked like cattle in a herd, not military in the slightest'.

Not that they had the road to themselves. On the contrary, it was crowded with German evacuees and other lines of prisoners of war, also on their way to God knows where. Some French prisoners came begging for cigarettes and fought among themselves to grab them from outstretched hands before their guards hustled them off. Room was plagued by thirst, and in desperation he broke the ice of a puddle on the ground, persuading himself, against all reason, that the water was 'moderately clean' before drinking it.

Room had the comfort of his chosen buddy by his side – a pilot by the name of Jack Paul, who had been shot down on the first 1,000-bomber raid on Cologne. At the end of a day in which they had marched 20 miles (the last three in the dark along a road knee-deep in snow), they lay exhausted in a shed on a farm. 'Wash our feet in hot water brought to us by a Russian slave worker and I take my boots off for the first time since we set out,' Room recorded. The toll of marching such distances – 'and not on tarmac roads but over potholes and ruts' – was horribly apparent as he stared at his bruises and blisters. In fact the surfaces they marched on could hardly have been worse. 'Rough ground,' remembered Percy Carruthers, 'deeply rutted with snow covering the depressions. Some of the boys seemed unable to "read" the ground and many of them fell heavily.'

Five days into the journey they were issued with a quarter of a loaf of black bread per man. Until then they had had to raid the fields through which they marched to find potatoes, turnips, mangolds, any old root crop that they could gnaw on. Now, amazingly, they passed through a small village and found buckets of cold water, fruit juice and hot ersatz coffee left by the roadside for them. 'What has come over the Germans?' Room asked himself. 'At any other time they would have spat at us without hesitation and called us "Luftgangsters" and "Terrorfleigers".' Percy Carruthers, a little further back in the column, witnessed the same display of kindness and hospitality as he passed through the village, but the guards around him would not let them stop. He remembered a little old lady hobbling along beside the column, 'obviously disturbed by our plight and saying *"Kinder, kinder, warum kampfen wir?"* – Oh children, children, why do we fight?' When he grabbed a cup of soup from a villager, a guard dashed it out of his hands.

As for Room, his kindly impression of the German civilians did not last long. The very next day, marching though a largish town called Greifenburg (though he recorded it in his diary, consciously or unconsciously, as Grief- not Greif-), he was shoved out of the way and into the gutter by 'a particularly nasty-looking civilian' who he reckoned wanted to kill him.

Occasionally there were small unexpected treats. One night the prisoners pooled whatever German coins they had, together with cigarettes and chocolates to make the equivalent of 50 marks, and Carruthers negotiated with a local farmer to buy a small sheep. Room recorded, 'The boys slaughter it, and it is divided among 600 men. My share is as big as a sugar knob. Meanwhile, 100 German officers and men have four sheep between them. This is higher mathematics as taught by the Führer!' There were celebrations too – albeit muted ones. Room recorded, 'Feb 12. Jack's birthday. Today, he's 24. Gets an extra cup of water from me for a present!' A lifetime later he would say, 'I've never seen comradeship like we had on that march. It was vital – vital – to have your good friend along with you. You got each other through it. My friendship with Jack lasted for fifty years, which isn't bad.' In his diary he paid tribute to his friend: 'I never gave up because I knew Jack would always help me, or I would help Jack. You're always chivvying each other along. There was no chance that we were going to leave each other by the side of the road. Good God, no. Never. Together, we would get there, sooner or later.'

Carruthers celebrated Jack Paul's birthday too, but in a black mood verging on despair.

We had now done over 135 kilometres in extremely cold, wet weather on less than a loaf of bread and a few boiled potatoes, along with weak potato soup and a cup of barley. Broken blisters could not be properly cared for and many were becoming infected. This was a situation which was to become extremely serious, claiming the life of one of my men[16] and threatening the lives of many more. How long could we endure?

Meanwhile, despair of a different sort descended on John Anderson, a US Air Corps sergeant. He was convinced he was letting everyone down – and especially himself. It began when, early on in the march, he caught a whiff of freedom and decided it was too heady for him. He stopped by the side of the road to relieve himself, the column walked on and rounded a bend, and suddenly he was on his own. 'There wasn't a soul in sight and I remember thinking, "I'm free." '[17] But the feeling was short-lived. 'I had no way of subsisting by myself in my condition. I had no weapons. I had no food. I didn't even know where I was, except that I was somewhere in Germany. I decided that all I could do was to catch up with the rest.' Back in the safety of the column, he was ashamed of himself for not making the break on that lonely, snow-blown road. In his mind, he beat himself up for what he had done – or, rather, not done – and put it down as a sad case of 'misery loves company'. 'My morale was pretty low most of the time during this period.' He had no need to blame himself. Almost everyone on that march spotted a chance to get away at one time or another – a moment when he was on his own and a quick dash would take him into hiding. All but a very few passed up the opportunity. Their chances of survival alone in a hostile country, or even in a combine of two or three, were slimmer than staying with the main group. To realize that was common sense, not cowardice.

And, anyway, cowardice was not a charge anyone could ever level at Anderson. Waiting for him at home was an Air Medal and three Oak-leaf Clusters for his 'courage, coolness and skill' on bombing missions over Germany. In his absence, the citation was sent to his mother on the very day that he marched out of Stalag

Luft IV. From the outset, however, he found the march tougher going than many of the other men. He was not as prepared for it mentally, largely because, from the time he bailed out during a bombing raid over Berlin in August 1944, his imprisonment had until now been as trouble-free as any man parachuting into enemy territory could expect. He had been swiftly captured, and was not threatened by irate civilians or trigger-happy Gestapo officers. He had arrived at Luft IV without being subjected to the violence of a 'run up the road', and had instantly made himself so busy in the camp that he was never depressed or fearful about being there. He was a classical musician and a churchgoer, and he set to work coaching the camp choir and running Bible classes. When the order to evacuate the camp came, he had given so little thought to what lay ahead that he packed all his music to carry with him, and a book he had borrowed from the camp library. He had started it but not finished, and he wanted to know how it ended.

But very quickly his right foot began to give him problems. His walk became a limp. He lightened his load by ditching the library book – 'there was no time for reading anyway' – and, after much agonizing, his hymn book too, though 'it was heart-breaking to leave it behind'. But still he laboured under his burden, and friends rallied round to carry his pack for him.

If they hadn't done that, I think I would have just quit, just lain down by the road, though that was the last thing I wanted to do. We heard rumours that anybody dropping out would be shot. I worried about that. But then I was also worried that I was letting the others down. I felt weak, and I was ashamed that others had to carry my pack for me.

His feet got better, but his conscience troubled him throughout the march. Anderson was a good man – too sensitive for the cruel realities that went with a struggle to survive. These were not conditions in which a man could always do the right thing. When others suffered, he was tortured by doubts about himself. There was, for example, the night when one of his companions went to fetch water from a well. He brought back half a pint in a cup, to be shared among himself and three others, and asked for his share to be kept for him while he went out again to try to get some more.

Time went on and Nelson did not return, so we split the remaining quarter between us and drank it. Then he returned. He had queued for more water, but the guard had turned him away at the last minute. He came back believing that at least he had his share of the first cup waiting for him, only to discover that we had drunk it. He was very angry. Many times I regretted what we had done. My conscience hurt. We had betrayed him.

Then, when Anderson, under doctor's orders, had to ride on the sick wagon that brought up the rear of the column, because he was doubled up with dysentery and his feet were again giving him problems, he worried about a man with rheumatism who was having to walk behind. 'I almost gave him my place on the wagon, but I didn't. I felt guilty about that. I wish I had, because to this day I worry about him. I didn't know his name, and I have no way of finding out what happened to him. He probably made it, but I would still like to know.'

*

The crippling pace was unrelenting, and no one could get the Germans to slow down. With threats and rifle butts if necessary, they forced the column of frozen, exhausted and sick men to keep going. Carruthers remembered making representations to the Germans,

but they would not listen to our pleas. They insisted that we had to complete 140 more kilometres in the next few days. This was an ominous prospect, and it was clear that there would be many serious casualties ahead. But when we told them this, all they would say was 'Befehl ist Befehl' – 'Orders are orders' – and the Feldwebel [Sergeant] patted his revolver and then pointed his index finger to his temple. That was final.

Stops were now taken hurriedly, if at all. Guderley remembered being forced along

at a pretty fast pace, westward into the sunset, doing between 35 to 50 kilometres a day with no stops allowed for personal comfort. We had to urinate as we walked. Those who had dysentery had to soil themselves. Pretty soon, no one had any shame about this. If we were passing through a village and you had to have a bowel movement, you just dropped your trousers and crapped in the street gutter. Out in the country we were not even allowed to drop out. We just had to do it in our underwear and keep going. We also weren't allowed to stop for a drink of water, so all we could do was reach down and grab a handful of snow and stuff it in our mouths. But the people who had gone before us had soiled in the snow, relieved themselves where they walked because they had no other option. We were just passing the disease from one person to another.

The Germans were frantic in their efforts to push the column on. They firmly believed that the Russians were closing in fast, pressing in from the east behind them, while other Red Army forces were now pushing up the line of the River Oder from the south to close the trap. The last place to escape, to cross the river and get back into the haven of north Germany, was at the wide estuary where the Oder meets the Baltic Sea. Their immediate destination was the ferry at Swinemünde – and they had to reach it before the Russians or, like a man caught by the tide, be overwhelmed.[18]

It was the night of 14 February when Guderley's part of the column swung out over the coastal flatlands and arrived outside Swinemünde. They had been marching for eight days. Those around him were exhausted and sick. That night would stick in many memories as an approximation to hell. They slept in each other's shit. They froze without shelter from the vicious cold. They nearly drowned in flooded foxholes. They cowered beneath bombing raids. Civilized men found it hard to believe that humans could sink so low. To Roger Allen, the cold was like nothing he had ever experienced before in his life, and he and his buddy clung to each other on the ground under their overcoats in an attempt to keep each other warm.

'I wasn't a terribly religious man,' Guderley recalled,

but that night I prayed. The problem was that we were out on open land and there were no barns. We were put in a field which was pitted with bomb craters from a previous attack. The wind and the rain were vicious, and some of us thought we could find some shelter by getting low in a crater, almost digging ourselves into the earth itself. But the snow and rain wouldn't stop and the crater just filled up, so we had to scramble out or drown. All that was left was to break branches from some fir trees and lay them on the ground as some sort of protection, and then, with our blankets, huddle together to share our body heat. Four of us slept together like that. It was the only way we would have got through. But the ground we slept on was disgusting. The snow was the colour of khaki from human excrement from those further up the column who had stayed there before us.

That night bombers came over the area again, trying to knock out some German submarines moored in the river. Not too far from us an anti-aircraft battery was firing, and big chunks of shrapnel were coming down from the flak. It was terrifying. We had no helmets to protect us. But what was happening made me so angry. I was determined to survive – more so than ever before. Come hell or high water, I was going to get home. That was without doubt the worst night of my life. The dawn broke at around six o'clock, maybe later, and I peeked out at the mud and the misery around me, and I knew just one thing – that I had survived.

That night stayed vividly in Cec Room's memory too – and not just because it was his birthday. He was twenty-five, 'but with my aching back, I feel as though I'm 55'. The day had been marked miserably with what turned out to be a long haul, 23 miles – 'a record run, so my feet tell me' – and then he had not expected to live through the night as they waited for the ferry across the Oder estuary. 'No accommodation in barns, so we rough it out in the open, or cleared woodland. Make a tent from bracken but it falls down. Jack and I curl up together and we kip down on the grass with my overcoat beneath us. Heavy frost at night and we wake up absolutely frozen. Can hardly feel my feet.'

As darkness had fallen that night, Percy Carruthers remembered being entranced as he stood in a large open field and looked up at the beauty of the stars. 'It was one of those lovely clear crystal-domed winter skies,' he said, and its very magnificence indicated acute danger. A cloudless sky meant a heavy frost and body-numbing temperatures.

We longed to have the shelter of some barns, but there were none to be seen. The Germans told us we would have to spend the night just where we stood. Many of the boys were in such an advanced state of physical fatigue that they just folded up on the wet ground. In the whole of my life I cannot remember seeing such a totally dejected and alarming sight. There were well over a thousand Kriegies[19] of varying nationalities gathered together on this site. What hope was there for any of us in a snow-covered field?

He determined to stay awake, fearing that to sleep would be fatal. He wandered around the encampment, queued for hour after hour for a tiny cup of thin barley soup, then tried to warm himself at the handful of faltering fires that had been lit on the frozen ground. But eventually exhaustion was too much for him. He had picked up a large multi-layered brown-paper sack along the way, and now he rolled himself up in it, with another man to share their warmth. Then he drifted helplessly into a sleep from which there was no certainty he would ever wake.

Cec Room had done the same.

Most of us thought that we would freeze to death because it was very, very cold – minus 19 was one estimate. Before going to sleep, Jack and I looked at each other with an air of resignation and thought, 'Here's hoping for the best.' We didn't really expect to survive. But, miraculously, we woke up in the morning, every one of us.

Bodies everywhere were white with frost – but they were alive. It was more than they had thought possible.

*

That morning, the column was pushed across the river as soon as possible. 'There was no hanging about,' Guderley recalled.

We were up and out on the road down to the river. We crossed on a barge pulled by a tugboat. As we reached the other side, the German guards lightened up a little. They had been edgy before then – worried that the Russians were going to catch up. They knew that if they were caught as guards with a group of prisoners their life expectancy would be measured in minutes. On the far side of the river they could relax, for a while at least.

But, if crossing the river felt like an end, in truth, it was just the beginning. The column reassembled on the other side – a crucial 150 yards of deep, dirty grey water now between it and the advancing Russians – and plodded off again. They were heading west, that was all anyone seemed to know. But where they were going and what was at the end of this apparently never-ending road was a question so immense – so beyond answering – that the prisoners stopped even asking. All that mattered was the next step, the next rest, the next brew of tea, the next opportunity to eat. 'I put one foot in front of the other,' said Guderley, 'and just kept doing it. We were heading to an unknown destination at a careless pace. We didn't know where the hell we were. We were dispirited, hungry, sick, tired, confused.'

6 The Deadly Road to the West

Now they had reached the west bank of the River Oder,* the German officers in charge of the column had time to take stock. But it was soon clear to George Guderley that they had little idea what to do next. When the column came to a halt, packs dropped from the prisoners' weary shoulders and the POWs milled around in the freezing rain trying to stay warm, or took advantage of what little shelter they could find. The exhausted simply slumped to the ground, too tired even to spread out a blanket. The guards huddled too, a distance away, as weary as their prisoners and looking just as bedraggled and defeated. The haven they had at last arrived at would not be safe for long. The bridges and the ferries destroyed behind them would be repaired or bypassed soon enough, and then the Russians would again be advancing on their inexorable drive to Berlin.

Guderley saw an officer approach the guards and give instructions. 'They didn't have radios, and it was a mystery to us who they were getting their orders from. Apparently the officer used a telephone if and when he could find one. He would ring in to headquarters, wherever that was, tell them where he was with the column, and be told where to go to next.'[1] There is no record of what the German authorities were planning for the prisoners from Gross Tychow, or even of who was giving the orders that would determine whether they lived or died. According to the commandant in charge of another column of prisoners who followed this same route, it was only after he got over the Oder that he managed to make contact with his superiors for the first time since leaving his camp.[2] But he was vague about what orders he then received. It seemed that the column would just head west, stopping on the way to seek instructions on what to do and where to go and then, in the absence of instructions, just surviving off the land. The

* See map 4 on page 106.

only orders that did seem to arrive were those picking out any guards capable of fighting and sending them to join the forces digging in at the front line.

The prisoners were left in ignorance. Later it would appear that their ultimate destination was a prison camp in the west of Germany, some 300 miles away on the other side of the next natural north–south defensive line, the River Elbe. But if the guards knew this they were not saying. 'They didn't tell us very much at all,' Guderley recalled.

Those of us who spoke German would get what we could out of the guards. There were one or two of them who were willing to talk. You would sidle up to them and judge by their body language whether they wanted to chat. Then you would try and glean little bits and pieces: where we were going next, how many miles we were going to have to march tomorrow.

That was if the POWs could be bothered to try and find out. Cold, sick and starving, for day after day they would now trudge west in conditions that seemed to worsen with every weary step. Where they were going was less of an issue than their chances of surviving at all.

The everyday life of Germany was collapsing around them as millions of refugees clogged the roads west. In the chaos, the prisoners had to seize what food they could wherever they could. Guderley was so hungry he remembered looking at his own forearm

and seeing it as a piece of meat. My own arm, for Christ's sake. I would wonder if I could bite into it and not hurt myself. That's how hungry I was – so starving I would have tried to take a bite out of the south end of a bull going north! Once in a while the guards would actually requisition some food and cook it up in big slop pails for 800 or so of us. But usually we had to scavenge for what we could find. On farms we passed through there might be a store of potatoes we could raid and then cook them in a tin can over a fire. Or there would be grain stored in bins for animal feed, and we would grab a pocketful if we could, chew the hulls off and spit them out, and eat what was inside. Best of all, if there were chickens around, we would use the grain to lure one of them closer and closer until you could throw a jacket or whatever over it and grab it by the head and snap its neck. We would skin it, feathers and all, and boil it.

There were a lot of dead animals along the road – mostly emaciated horses that had died pulling a wagon of refugees. They would just leave a horse lying in the ditch. If it looked recent, if it was still warm, we thought nothing of cutting it up for meat.

The days were just a blur of walking anywhere from 10 to 20 kilometres. Most nights we stayed in a barn. There would be two or three hundred of us, drenched to the skin, no food, stinking of shit. We just had to make the most of it. Three of us would sleep huddled together in the straw under a blanket. The lucky guy in the middle was the warmest, but in the middle of the night we would switch positions so each of us got a chance to warm up. We also kept our shoes under the blanket to try and get them semi-dry for the next day.

Now that we were beyond the river we were able to persuade the Germans to allow us to start little fires and boil our own water. This was an old prisoner-of-war trick. An empty powdered-milk can could be converted into a mini-stove. You could get a very fierce heat out of burning just a few twigs – enough to boil some water. A tea bag was used many, many times, until it was absolutely drained.

Guderley was wiser than most, and careful about the water he chose to boil up – 'I avoided the khaki snow!' He lasted more than a fortnight before falling foul of dysentery.

I was trying to be careful, but in the filth it was impossible. There was nothing to wash in, barely enough water to drink, and we were all absolutely filthy. There was so much dirt in my hands I didn't think I'd ever get them clean. You'd rub your face with your filthy hands and then lick your lips and you'd had it. With dysentery, a man loses all his self-respect. Nothing embarrasses him any more. If you need a bowel movement, you just drop your trousers and let fly. I felt just like an animal. We were being herded along like cattle, and we were acting like cattle.

This is not a description that would have sat easily with American airman Bob Otto, who was trudging a mile or so ahead of Guderley. He had grown up on a farm, and he had never treated animals as badly as he and the other prisoners were being treated now.

Fifty-five years on, he would return to that north-eastern edge of Germany and shudder at the memories. A private, dignified man, his ability to be anonymous helped him to survive. 'I was just one of the people in the bunch,' he said.[3] He did his best to 'keep my head down and get through this'. He remembered vividly – and still with shame – the worst time of all for him:

We were in a huge barn and I was sleeping in the middle with fifty guys on each end and I got dysentery. I had to get outside, step over all those other bodies, asking them to move out of the way. By the time I got to the door it was too late. I had filled my trousers, and all I could do was strip down out in the cold and take my long johns off and throw them away. It was so very degrading. All my pride had gone.

Dysentery would catch a man in his guts with cramps for which the only relief was to chew on charcoal. In Otto's case this worked, and he was better a few days later. But then the pain in his bowels was replaced by the pain of hunger. His insides, utterly emptied, called out for sustenance, but there was little or nothing at hand.

I was so hungry I felt as if my stomach was rubbing against my backbone. We were close to starvation. I lost about 25 lb, and when I got home my mother looked at me and all she could say was 'You're awful skinny, son.' It was thoughts of her that kept me going. I used to dream about her cooking: about pies – pies of every sort; even pies filled with chocolate bars. I kept promising myself I was going to eat as much as I could when I got home – and that I would never ever be without toilet paper again in my life. Never. I didn't think about dying. I suppose that was always a possibility, a fear that lingered at the back of your mind, but I just kept thinking with every step I took that I was going home, and I wasn't going to give up. I was going to keep going as long as I could.

In the end, it was the cold he found hardest to fight.

I grew up in Idaho, where the winters are hard, so I knew what cold was. But this was worse than I had ever experienced. And there was nothing you could do about it. It would penetrate right into your bone marrow and drain you of all your strength. When we were walking we were all right, but it was worse when we stopped. You had to stomp your feet and flap your arms – anything to try to circulate your blood a little. But it was hopeless. We shivered all the time. The cold was there continually, day after day after day. In all of those terrible weeks I don't remember ever being able to stand around a fire and feel warmth on me. Others may have done, but I don't recall that I ever did. Cold, filthy, exhausted. At one point I thought I would never be clean again. We were lousy too – covered in lice and itching all the time. It wasn't really living: it was just existing.

Apart from the thought of his mother's home-made pies, there were two things that kept Bob Otto from giving in. The first was his God. 'There is no question that He helped me through. Back in the camp one of the sergeants was a former pastor, and he organized Bible studies and I attended regularly.' He took his inspiration to survive from the psalms.

The 91st was encouraging: it gave me strength – 'The Lord is my refuge and my fortress . . . in Him will I trust. Surely he shall deliver thee from the snare of the fowler and from the noisome pestilence . . . Thou shalt not be afraid for the terror by night, nor for the arrow that flieth by day . . . For he shall give his angels charge over thee, to keep thee in all thy ways.' My faith was being put to the test on that march, but I never once lost it. In fact I think it was strengthened. Some people might question why God allowed such terrible things to happen, but I didn't blame Him. The dirt and degradation were down to human beings.

The second thing that kept him going was the thought of the young wife he had left behind at home.

I dreamed about her all the time. She was so very important to me. She had been my high-school sweetheart and the only girl I ever wanted for my wife. We had only just got married when I was called up, and she stayed behind working on the local radio station in our home town. I had been back a few times on leave while I'd been stationed in the States, and we'd had such good times together. I remembered those as I marched along, and made plans in my head for our home and our future. In my mind I wasn't here in the middle of the rain and the cold, my feet aching,

ill and hungry, I was in another land where I was safe and with her. You
had to live in kind of a dream world or else you would go crazy.

She was his beacon in those dark days and nights – just like the
beer with Buck in that bar in Chicago that was hovering in front of
George Guderley and luring him on.

*

Events were conspiring against Cec Room and his mate Jack Paul.
Room lost the heel of a boot, and from then on walked with a
perpetual limp. Five miles of a cobblestone road flayed their feet –
'I might as well walk on a bed of nails, it couldn't hurt any more.'[4]
One night they found a cellar to shelter in, only to be rudely
awakened by fellow prisoners using it as a latrine.

But little things lifted their spirits. A generous farmer meant a
pleasant change one night. 'Hot water in a tub and I have a shave,
wash and even clean my teeth! Three hot brews and a cup of pea
soup. Morale up by leaps and bounds.' But food – the lack of
it – was becoming a constant worry. Room confided his thoughts
to his diary: 'If we have to rely on our minute quantities of Red
Cross food we'll never see England again, I'm sure of it.' But
to his companions he said nothing. 'We didn't really talk about
it. We tried to be optimistic. Our one consolation was that we
were going westwards, in the direction of home. Next stop the
Thames!'

How many would get there, however, was an increasing worry.
'Several blokes have disappeared from the column; we get smaller
every day. Where the hell they are we don't know. Bit risky buzzing
off at the moment, with the food situation as it is, and the Germans
are rather panicky with the trigger finger.' But it was sickness that
was taking the biggest toll on the marching men, as Room knew
only too well because his friend Jack Paul was now too ill to walk
on his own two feet. It looked as if he would have to be found a
place on the wagon at the rear. But fortunately the column halted,
and as February ended and March began they stayed in the same
farmyard for a week. It was a chance to rest and recover. The really
sick were taken off the march – though Room did not rate the
chances of those who were sent away to a German hospital. 'You've
got to be half dead to be among them. I'm not sure which is best –

going into dock [hospital] or carrying on with the hike. Anything could happen. Two men taken out during the night with internal trouble and we heard later that they passed on. The total number of deaths is now nine that we know of.' The bitterly cold weather – 'I've almost forgotten what it is to be warm' – left Room in little doubt that many more would die. 'We worried about it inwardly, but we didn't talk about it, because morale had to be kept up.'

On the last day of February he struggled to scribble down his thoughts, even though 'hands too damn cold to write'. He shivered throughout the day, stamping his feet in a vain attempt to get some warmth into his frozen toes as he assessed the situation three weeks after leaving Gross Tychow. Things looked very bleak. The weather was appalling. More men were sickening. He recorded the death of a prisoner from an infection, and declared the 'lack of medical supplies now serious'.

But then the mood changed. Out of the blue on that grey day, a truck arrived with American Red Cross parcels, driven 100 miles across country from the Baltic port of Lübeck. There was one parcel each, and the joy of getting one, sifting through and then savouring its contents, was dampened only by the thought that it would 'have to last till the end of the march, and heaven knows when that will be'. The arrival of the parcels was more of a miracle than Room realized. The Red Cross was trying to track this column – and the many others wending their way across Germany – but its drivers had no real idea of where precisely it was.

It was Vic Clarke – 'dear old Vic' – who found *them*, according to Doug Fry.[5] The sergeant gave the German guards his word of honour that he would not escape, found himself a bicycle from somewhere, and would ride out ahead of the column or off along the roads and lanes in the surrounding countryside searching for the Red Cross convoy or places where it had dumped supplies. Fry remembered catching sight of Clarke 'pottering about and going off and coming back'. His foraging trips would become even more vital – even more life-saving – as the weeks went by. But Clarke paid dearly for his efforts. When others were sheltering and resting, he was always out and about, working and worrying, accepting the burden of responsibility. In helping to keep others alive he exhausted himself, and it was not long before he went down with pneumonia, dysentery and frostbite.

When the march resumed after a seven-day halt, it brought an unexpected relief: on the move, prisoners at least had the chance to warm up. But Cec Room, pressing on through driving snow, soon felt 'as weak as a drowned rat', though the pace was so slow 'even a snail would pass us'. In the skies above there was evidence that they were getting closer to the war. They had been force-marched to escape being caught up on the eastern front. Now the western front was the problem. 'Plenty of fighters and vapour trails at 20,000 feet! The USAAF are very much in evidence. Hear the bombs dropping. Lovely sound, but too near for my liking.'

Not surprisingly, air raids changed the attitude of the German civilians they passed. In one town 'an old codger gives me a kick in the pants as I go past, apparently he hates us. I can't do a thing, just swear like fury under my breath.' Encounters like this would happen more and more. In another town an 'old lady and gent of some 80 summers start knocking the boys about with their walking sticks. Can't hit back otherwise the guards will clobber us. Just have to take these swipes. Eventually, the guards call them off. We pitied them more than anything.'

But kindness had not disappeared altogether, though it now tended to come less from charity than from fear of the future. Percy Carruthers did cloak-and-dagger business with a German farmer who helped the prisoners, on a promise that he himself would be protected when the British Army arrived – which, he was assured by the prisoners, was an inevitability.[6] Sacks of peas, beans, carrots, potatoes, swedes and onions were quietly made available, behind the backs of the guards.

Room continued to note every place they passed through with a name, and in his account, as no doubt on the march, they merged into each other – 'Mecklow ... Jungershof ... Alt Schwerin ... Karow ... Walnshof ...' Most would have no meaning – they were just a village name on a signpost – but a few were significant. It was at Walnshof, for example, that he slept with pigs in a sty – much, it seems, to the discomfort of the pigs.

We had bedded down for the night, lying in this lovely soft straw in a barn, just the two of us for about half an hour, and it seemed like such luxury. Then we heard a grunt and we saw three or four pigs in the sty with us. They took a poor view of us at first, but when they realized we weren't going to harm them they stayed at their end and we all fell fast asleep. The next morning we feasted on some of the rotten potatoes the farmer had put out for the pigs. We were desperate. We skinned them until just the good bits were left, and then cooked them. A good night's sleep and some food – that made it a good day. And the fact that we were among pigs didn't make a damn bit of difference.

The town of Gallin – another name, another place – stood out because an incident there brought a deep longing for home and loved ones. The march was winding past the railway station of this town, a train had just arrived, and all eyes turned to a German officer in his *Luftwaffe* uniform who had clearly just come home on leave and was being greeted by his wife. As they threw themselves into each other's arms, Room was consumed with jealousy. 'It made us think of home.' His thoughts raced ahead to his own homecoming – to tears and smiles and hugs and happiness – and he could only hope and pray that 'in about three weeks' time, we'll be doing that'.

Fifty years on, he could still feel the desperate childlike emotions and thoughts that overwhelmed him then. 'You think about home a lot: just to be back home, safe in a bed, in a real bed. I had a blanket wrapped round me which my mother had sent in a clothing parcel, and that blanket was my link with home. It was pretty special, I was determined to bring it back, and I did. I've still got it upstairs.' His mother was often there in his mind on the journey. On more than one occasion, forced to do something against his correct upbringing, he thought of her. 'Picked up a dirty old piece of bread this morning, weeks old, but I scraped it and chewed it. Better than nothing. If my poor mother could see me now.' But he should have heeded her words, because he then went down with dysentery.

*

Guderley had still not found Buck, nor heard any word of him since they had made their plans back in the camp. He too was now ill – another case of dysentery – and he sought out the 'hospital', an area in a barn which Dr Caplan had commandeered. Caplan was a towering figure for the American marchers, just as Dr Robert Pollack was for the British contingent. He was a source of strength and survival, though he took it hard as he watched his comrades, his patients, suffer, grow weak and die for no good reason. After the war he gave a medical man's account of the march to war-crimes investigators:

Hundreds of men suffered from malnutrition, exposure, trench foot, exhaustion, dysentery, tuberculosis, and other diseases. So little water was issued to us that men drank water or snow from the ground or from ditches that others had used as latrines. Men collapsed from hunger, fear, malnutrition, exhaustion, or disease. Many marched along with large abscesses on their feet. Mud and cold brought frostbite and even gangrene and amputation. I personally slept beside men suffering from Erysipelas, Diphtheria, Pneumonia, Malaria and other diseases. Dysentery was so common and so severe that wherever our column went, there was a trail of bloody movements and discarded underwear (which was sorely needed for warmth).[7]

He and other volunteers marched at the rear with the stragglers, and when they saw a prisoner in trouble – slowing down, his breathing laboured, his legs giving way – they would walk with him, giving encouragement. If he fell totally behind, then a medic would stay with him, in the hope that his Red Cross armband would offer some protection against whatever the Germans had in mind for those who could not keep up. 'In that way the straggler was much less likely to be bullied by the guards,' Caplan recalled, 'but sometimes it didn't work, and both medics and stragglers were gun-butted.'

A substantial 'slow party' established itself at the back of the column, proceeding at its own pace. A few farm wagons were commandeered to carry the sick, and, 'uncomfortable and cold as those wagons were, there was a long line of men waiting to get on them every morning. There was room for only the sickest.' With no other means of power – no cars, lorries or even horses – the volunteers themselves pushed and pulled the carts along the rutted roads and snowy tracks in Dürer-like scenes of human misery that could have come from barbaric European wars of 500 years ago.

Caplan had so little equipment and so few medicines that he was reduced to the level of a medieval surgeon in dealing with his patients. Before listening to a man's chest for signs of pneumonia he would first have to scrape off the lice from his patient's body before putting his bare ear – he had no stethoscope – to the skin. All he had to lance the hundreds of abscesses he treated was a razor blade.

For medicines, we had some Red Cross parcels which gave us a small supply of bandage, tape, aspirin, lice powder, and salves. For hot water-bottles, we heated bricks. For dysentery cases, we made charcoal and let the patients chew it and swallow the powder. I had a small supply of sulphur pills which were doled out only to the most serious cases of pneumonia.

And not even then, it would seem. One prisoner who went down with an infection in his lungs and was so delirious with fever that he thought the snow was purple said all the doctor could give him was a small piece of cheese.[8]

Often all Caplan had to offer the sick was what he called 'a pep talk'. He would tell these suffering men:

The human body is the toughest device ever built, for it is fearfully and wonderfully made. You fellows are young. You are far stronger than you realize. You can take an unbelievable amount of punishment and make a snappy comeback and be as good as ever. Hundreds of men in this column have already done it, and you will do it too.

Caplan was right: each man on that march had to find his own medicine within himself or die.

The lucky ones had friends to pull them through, as Guderley was about to discover. In the makeshift hospital, he stumbled on a slumped figure he barely recognized at first. To his horror, he realized it was Little Buck.

He was terribly weak and in distress; he had given up. It was a condition that a lot of guys succumbed to. They would just stop bothering, and even refuse to be helped. 'Don't do anything for me,' they would say – 'I'm OK.' But they weren't. They were wasting away, dying. I yelled at him, 'What the hell are you doing lying there, you son of a bitch?' It was no time to be nice. He needed a kick in the ass – something to get him pissed off, to make him fight back. But he just looked at me and said, 'I'm in bad shape. I'm not going to make it.'

I was utterly distressed. He was as good as saying, 'I'm never going to get home, so I'm just going to lie here until I die. Being dead is better than this.' I told myself I had to do something for him. His older brother, Big Buck, was my best friend back at home, and since he wasn't around to look after him it was up to me. Then, looking round, I saw some big cans of fresh cow's milk sitting on the ground in the courtyard. There were two 5-gallon cans of cream and one 10-gallon can of milk, waiting for one of the Polish slave labourers to load them on to a wagon and take them into the creamery in town. Here was a potential life-saver. 'If only I could get some of that for Buck', I thought.

Guderley formed a plan. He spruced himself up as best he could to make himself look like someone important –

someone who was fully entitled to walk up to those cans of milk and just take one. Then I swaggered back to where the milk was just as if I was acting under orders, or maybe even giving the orders. Then I reached out and grabbed the handle of a can of cream, and when nobody shouted at me to stop I walked out with it. The guards stared at me, but they did nothing. They must have thought I had permission.

Guderley hurried over to the sickbay and handed the can to Dr Caplan. 'See what you can do with this,' he said, 'just as long as the first swig goes to him' – and he pointed at Buck.

Buck put the can to his lips and gulped, and the cream dribbled down his face and his chin, but he managed to get a couple of pints inside him – maybe more. Then it was my turn. It tasted pretty good – best thing I'd had for a long time. After that it was passed round the other patients. I was concerned that as I hadn't had anything as rich and as fatty as that for such a long time I might be pretty sick. But I couldn't care less. If I died, I would die happy.

The cream had barely been consumed and the can hidden under straw when the guards came looking for it. Guderley was immediately suspected and accused.

They were shouting and yelling, and I was scared. They told me they were going to shoot me. I denied it – told them it wasn't me: that they must be mistaking me for another prisoner, that we all looked alike. But they weren't having any of it. I was standing there, and they were all around me, hollering that I had stolen the property of the Third Reich and that this was a crime for which I would be shot.

I stood in that barnyard in the cold, waiting to die. They would leave me for a while standing to attention there, and then come back and shout at me and wave their guns and threaten to put me up against the wall. Was I scared? I just thought that I'd finally gone and done it. I was resigned. They were going to kill me, and there was nothing I could do about it. I suppose we had lived with the possibility of dying for so long – it was always something that might happen to you as a prisoner. I wasn't being brave or noble, but I do remember telling myself that I was glad I had stolen the cream if it helped Buck. The one thing I wasn't going to do was try and run, because then they would feel justified in shooting me. They could put me down as 'shot while escaping', which was one of their favourite expressions – one they liked to taunt us with. So I just stood there and waited them out. I'd seen scenes like this before, back in the camp, and there was always a lot of fuss and shouting before everyone calmed down. And that's precisely what happened. I out-waited them, and eventually they had all gone away for so long that I just sneaked back to my barn and went to sleep. And that was that.

The next morning I went to see Buck, and he seemed better. He said I'd saved his life, that if he hadn't had that cream he would never have made it, he would have died. I'm not sure about that. There wasn't that much sustenance in the cream. But what I think it did was give him his will back. Feeling that cream in his stomach gave him hope. On that march, in those terrible conditions, a little thing could make a huge difference. And, anyway, I had accepted responsibility for Buck. It was up to me to be like his older brother. He was so sick he could hardly stand, but it was my job to make sure he was going to make it home for that beer we had promised each other at Hank's.

At that point we were near a town called Neubrandenburg, and there was a prisoner-of-war camp there. Our medics got permission to take our sick there, but only a few of them. The camp was already overcrowded, and they would only take those who were so ill they would die if they were moved any more. We left Buck there. I watched as he was taken off to the camp, and I didn't know if I would ever see him again.

Cec Room also had to leave his buddy behind. Despite his rest, Jack Paul had not fully recovered and once more was too ill to march. He was left with the stragglers. Room was devastated. 'I felt lost without him. We were mates, and it was your mate who was going to get you through.' Room also became sick, and in his illness he soiled his trousers so badly he had to throw them away. As the journey continued, a place was found for him in a wagon and he lay on the floor wrapped only in a blanket, 'cold and miserable, in a heavy rainstorm, blankets soaked as usual'. In three days he had eaten one spoonful of tinned salmon and evacuated his bowels seventy times.

After all his exertions, Vic Clarke was also too ill to continue, and Percy Carruthers, whose responsibilities had been growing throughout the march, assumed leadership of half the British contingent – largely because he spoke German and had shown himself to have a knack for nosing out the best places to sleep and the best supplies of food. He had 'a serious talk' with the German officer in charge of his part of the column, explaining that they would all waste a lot less time if he was allowed to go out ahead of the column on what had been Vic Clarke's bicycle and make advance arrangements with farmers on where they could be billeted. The German saw the sense in this and, 'from then on it was not an uncommon sight to see me pedalling along, sitting on the crossbar, with a German guard seated on the saddle with his rifle over his shoulder. Christ, it was hard work sometimes. Those three stones in weight I had lost would have helped tremendously.'

Carruthers would pick somewhere to stay for the night, and then discuss food and hot-water supplies with the farmers. He could, by all accounts, be very persuasive. He would ask them to start boiling up water then and there, so that it would be ready 'when the boys arrived'. He would then cycle back to the column and complete the walk along with everyone else.

Meanwhile, winter was turning to spring, and a burst of sunshine gave Cec Room a lift. He began to shake off the effects of dysentery. He ate a little – 'a few small spuds and a handful of old carrots' – but preferred to live with his hunger rather than have the illness return.

Main trouble is weakness, now. Can count the old ribs quite easily and I don't suppose I'm more than $6^{1}/_{2}$ stones. [He had lost 2 stone in just over a month.] The boys here are in a grim state. No Red Cross food, hardly any bread, and our food for a day consists of a few spuds and a cup of watery soup. They cannot continue to march much longer without a high rate of sickness. We are told we are to proceed to Ludwigslust, 20 miles away, and then transport will be provided. Camp Leaders have been in touch with the Red Cross Distribution Centre at Lübeck. Need for parcels is vital, the Germans can't or won't feed us. Up to date, we have been on the road for 37 days, covered 288 miles and our food supplies have been 2 loaves, $4/5$ lb margarine, $2/11$ lb meat (from the Germans) and $2^{1}/_{2}$ food parcels from the Red Cross. Speaks for itself I think.[9]

At night he dreamed of fish and chips – 'never-ending plates of fish and chips. I'd pay 20 quid for some right now, if I only had 20 quid.' But it was another wish that came true: he met up with Jack Paul again. Paul had recovered, and rejoined all his old hut-mates. 'It was wonderful to be together again, but we weren't over-demonstrative about it. "Hello, Jack." "Hello, Fred." "Nice to see you again" – that sort of thing.' Room disguised his true feelings. Behind the polite, hand-shaking reserve, what he was really thinking – as he admitted years later – was 'There's no way that I'm letting him get away from me again. No bloody fear.'

*

It is safe to say that every man who made the horrific journey from Gross Tychow had a moment when he stared into the face of utter despair. For Joe O'Donnell it came on 12 March – Day 35 –

when I saw my reflection in a dirty, ice-encrusted pool of water. I had not seen my face since we set out. I was a harried, starved, unshaven and unbathed skeleton, that once walked with pride and dignity and now

walked with animals, like myself, as companions. I urinate and defecate
in the woods and the streets of towns like a dog. As I stared into that icy
pool, I questioned why I was here. 'Why me?' I asked.[10]

In his own reflection he saw all the horrors of war and 'the
indignities that only man can force upon another man'. For weeks
he had noticed his companions deteriorate to the 'thin, pale, wild-
eyed creatures' they now were, but his mind had fooled him into
thinking that this was not happening to him too. It was a shock to
see himself as he really was, and to realize he was the same as
them.

Around me were 2,000 mirrors. They were my own reflection. I no longer
needed that icy pool to see my degradation.

This was my day of reckoning. It was raining. I was sick with dysentery,
and I sat down beside the road. We'd heard rumours that the Gestapo
were behind the columns and any stragglers would simply be shot. I'd
gone from 160 lb to something like 120. I was ready to give in. But two
guys got me to the barn, got me out of my wet clothes, made a bunk out
of straw and they made some hot coffee. One of them was a gunner from
my plane and we'd been shot down together, but I was so far gone that I
didn't recognize him. I just collapsed. Next morning I wouldn't have
known anything had happened – I was back on my feet. But if it wasn't
for those two guys . . . I still think about that day 55 years later.

O'Donnell meticulously recorded the indignities he and the
thousands of others endured on the march. The lice, for example,
were 'little bastards. Once on our bodies, they always sought greener
pastures, travelling from our necks to our waist or vice versa, and
we would continually pinch and squeeze to interrupt their travels.
We always lost the battle and conceded that if you kill one, a
thousand will come to its funeral. At night their crawling would
stop you sleeping.' They were much more than just a nuisance, a
constant itch to be scratched: they were also a time bomb of disease.
Back in the camp Dr Caplan had given regular lectures on what
he described as 'that close, but treacherous companion of mankind,
which has devastated armies, which carries a wallop like an atomic
bomb, and which has killed millions'.[11] Lice, he reminded his

patients, carried typhus fever. But the hygiene he had pressed on the prisoners was not possible out on the march. O'Donnell remembered trying – and failing – to clean himself up. 'I went out to a pump, put some water on my face and was shaving away with the razor but nothing came off. The water had frozen on my beard and I was just scraping away at ice.'

Then there were the routines for coping with the most basic of human needs, normally so elementary and easy, but in the conditions of the march turned into torments of indignity. O'Donnell recalled weather so bitter that it was impossible to urinate without help. 'We could unbutton and get the old fella out, but you couldn't button the flies because your fingers were like ice. Another guy, hopefully a good friend, had to get down on his knees and put you back together. At first it was pretty humiliating but in the end it didn't matter if it meant we were surviving.' Defecation involved even more indignities. At an overnight stay on a farm a slit trench would be dug by an advance party, or they would use the trench abandoned by a group of prisoners ahead of them in the column who had been there the night before.

On one occasion the previous occupants of the barnyard toilet covered the trench with straw instead of refilling the trench with earth. One of our guys stepped into the trench, hip deep. There he was, dripping with crap. It was like a comedy show for us but it wasn't funny for him. He stripped off every stitch of clothing and, after breaking the ice on the water trough, we rinsed his clothes while he bathed in freezing water. He recovered, but I doubt if he ever forgot.

If a man wanted to go outside during the night to relieve himself, the procedure was complex. It would be pitch black, and lighting a match was strictly forbidden because of the fire risk. A signalling system was used, and the person concerned would be passed from man to man, following the calls of his friends in the darkness, 'Hey, Red', 'Over here, Joe', and so on. Outside, the biggest difficulty was to avoid stepping in another man's mess and then trailing it back into the barn.

O'Donnell admitted that he was 'not above eating anything. I wonder how many German farmers realized what happened to their pets after we left their farms. I would have eaten a dog or a cat.' Others did – among them T. D. Cooke, who shared a dog with two Russian prisoners of war.

I told them that if they killed it, I would skin and butcher it. They went off and came back five minutes later with the dog. I hacked it up and we partially cooked it in an old boiler, though we barely got it warm because we only had a little fire. But we threw in some carrots and it was a real treat. Another time we ate uncooked rats – raw – and you'd be surprised how good they were.[12]

And, when there was nothing else, Cooke ate grass – 'just as fast and as much as we could'.
  O'Donnell did the same:

We stopped by a rye field and little shoots were coming up. I pulled them out, scraped off the dirt and ate them. They were soft and sweet, like the cat-tails that grew in the swamps near the small town where I was born. But those days of starving on the march still affect me. I got used to making do with less and less in my stomach. I can't eat like other people even now. My wife gives me hell every night because she'll cook two potatoes and I'm full after just a half.

  For O'Donnell, Day 35 had been his worst. With the help of his friends he had survived.

But, after that, my emotions and my feelings would still go from one extreme to another. One minute you wanted to give up, the next you told yourself that we were going in the right direction, the Allies were advancing towards us and we could not contemplate such a thing as defeat. We knew it had to end at some point – and we had the arrogance of young Americans that no one could beat us.

But other days had touches of that earlier depression about them – 'the day we heard a report that some guys had both legs amputated because of gangrene, related to frostbite. It was a bitter blow to our morale.'[13]
  John Anderson narrowly escaped a similar fate. His feet had

given him trouble from the very start of the march, and they were now beyond help. The problem was frostbite. Strangely, while his feet remained frozen they didn't hurt. But, as the weather improved and the spring thaw began, so his flesh began to burn. Any hint of heat on his feet and he was in agony. Now his toes were turning black, and 'Dr Caplan told me that he was considering amputation, but he only had a razor blade. I don't know how he would have done it. I suppose they would have had to put me out somehow. It was a terrifying thought.'[14]

Eventually Anderson was left with a dozen others in a barn with a medic to look after them while the column moved on. The Germans came, picked them up, and put them on a train. Anderson pressed his feet against the cold glass of the window to refreeze them and ease the pain enough for him to fall asleep. But finally he just had to grit his teeth and let his feet warm up again, despite the agony this caused him. And, in the end, he was lucky. 'I didn't lose my feet like the doctor suggested. The weather warmed up enough for them to thaw out and I just could not stop the process. But ever since then, and even today, I never cover my feet at night. I prefer them to be cold.'

His conscience still troubled him, however. On the march, men acted with supreme decency to him and he felt spiritually uplifted by those times when he had been helped to survive. He described them as nothing short of 'miracles'. But he found this hard to reconcile with the selfishness he also witnessed as men fought for scraps of food or a place in the warmth. 'Some days we were just a bunch of animals, complaining and fighting each other.' He was bewildered by the cruelty of men who had lost all their humanity, and he tried to block those memories out of his mind, 'because they were the low point in my entire life'.

*

By now, with March nearing its end, streams of men pouring across this northern edge of Europe were beginning to flow together. Cec Room spotted another group of prisoners taking it easy by the side of the road. Familiar faces smiled in recognition. They were a contingent of army boys who months before had stopped off at Luft IV for a while en route from a camp near Danzig. The excitement of instant camaraderie – Englishmen abroad – filled the air. 'We yell at one another and they call out the good old Army cry "Are we downhearted?" and we roar back emphatically, "No!" You'd think we were meeting each other in Piccadilly on a night out!' And that again brought thoughts of home. That night Room 'couldn't sleep at all, dreaming wild dreams of freedom. My God, what I won't do when that day dawns.'

There was a new air about the marchers now, a sense that an end was in sight. A sense of discipline returned too, and they began to march in step again, just as they had in the first few days out of Gross Tychow. A new lightness crept back into Room's diary. The sun was out; snowdrops were blooming; suddenly things were 'wizard' again. The guards were being generous with bread and margarine. Another Red Cross parcel was issued, and Room and Jack Paul dined on bread and jam, prunes and powdered milk. 'We cross the River Elbe. Rhine next stop, boys, then dear old Father Thames. Sun really hot by now and I'm perspiring like mad. Seven weeks ago we were marching in deep snow and ice and now we're being bitten by mosquitoes.' Even so, the effects of long-term exhaustion and lack of food were not shrugged off so easily. The spring in their steps was a triumph of mind over flesh. Every man was a shell of what he had been on 6 February, the day they had set out.

A train was waiting for them at a town called Ebstorf. They cheered. Never had men been so anxious to be locked inside. They raced to the cattle trucks – once symbols of degradation – eager for any form of transport that was not their own battered feet. They didn't mind where they were going, as long as it wasn't under their own steam. Memories of earlier train journeys seemed miraculously wiped from their minds. Crammed into the trucks, they decided to blow all their remaining food rather than have it snatched from them at the camp they were being taken to. Spam, cheese and jam were hauled out of packs and Red Cross parcels, and everyone dived in – except Room. 'This is the most tragic moment of my life. I have been longing for a blow-out for weeks and now I am sick.' With the dysentery back, he spent a horrible night – as did everyone else on board. All too soon they were back in the claustrophobic horror of a German prison train they knew so well from the journey to Gross Tychow. 'Everyone swears he prefers marching to this hell on earth,' Room declared.

To make matters worse, the train stood in a siding all night, with them locked inside, packed eighty to a truck. The smell and the distress rose in equal measures.

Next morning, when the train set off, the journey was mercifully short – just over two hours. They arrived at Fallingbostel in north-west Germany, halfway between the cities of Hamburg and Hanover, and the gates of Stalag XIB were waiting for them to walk through. Joe O'Donnell was glad to get to Fallingbostel, and 'as we approached the camp I remember the familiar smell of burning wood and coal. It was a strange situation – the ones inside want to get out and the ones on the outside wanting to get in.' But hell was about to take on a new form:

We didn't know what the conditions were really like until we got inside. Then we realized we were in a huge international prisoner of war camp housing tens of thousands of people. And there were more to come. We were put in a big circus tent with straw on the ground, animals again. Relief turned to despair. We had marched all those miles just to end up in this place and be no better off than when we were out on the road. In fact, we were in a worse condition – little food and only the ground to sleep on. Two months of marching had been for nothing. And we felt as if we were nothing too. We were back where we started. I was desperate. For me it was Day 35 all over again, but worse.

As Percy Carruthers and his companions entered the camp, they had an inkling of what was ahead. A funeral party was lining up. The coffins were laid out, and they counted no fewer than fifteen of them.

A few days later it was Easter Sunday, and John Anderson celebrated the resurrection of Christ with special prayers. 'I was lucky to be alive. I was thankful to be alive. Wish I were home. Soon, I hope.' His wish would not be granted. The bedraggled lines of exhausted and diseased prisoners of war still struggling into the camp and trying to make themselves at home in worsening conditions would have been distraught if they had known that freedom was still many hard weeks away and their ordeal was far from over.

To those who made it, that horrendous journey from Gross

Tychow to Fallingbostel would always stand out in their memories as 'the death march'. How many failed to reach the end is unclear. Many men disappeared along the way, but the German guards had given up counting almost from the moment they left Stalag Luft IV. Conditions were simply too chaotic along the way, and by the time they arrived at Fallingbostel nobody cared. Some deaths were logged, however. Cec Room tried to keep a tally of those he knew about, and reached double figures from just those in the British contingent around him. After the war, the British doctor on the march, Captain Robert Pollack – who, like the American Dr Caplan, became a hero among the prisoners for his tireless work to save limbs and lives in those terrible conditions[15] – told Room that as many as 150 men might have died on the march. Though there is no independent verification of this, Room felt the doctor was in a position to know. 'We tended to keep the same place on the march all the way, but he went up and down the line and he knew the whereabouts of people. He would come along and say so-and-so had died last night. I don't remember it happening in the first two weeks, but towards the end of the march it was pretty regular.'

Dr Caplan also recorded the deaths of at least ten Americans, but there must have been many more. While Pollack's policy was to move up and down the column giving aid where he could, Caplan deliberately positioned himself at the rear with the stragglers and did his medical work there. He may simply not have known about casualties further up the meandering line of suffering humanity. Nor could he ever know what happened to all the sick and lame who were taken off supposedly to be treated at German hospitals. We know about the ones who made it – John Anderson, for example – because they were reunited with their comrades later. But what about those who did not return? The simple fact is that no one knows.

Whatever the number of deaths, the vast majority of them were undoubtedly the result of sickness, exhaustion and cold. But there is a persistent belief that some prisoners were also killed by the guards. Clarence Brower, from the American 96th Bomb Group, remembered that after a night in a barn some POWs tried to hide themselves in the hay to escape the march. He then witnessed 'something that I hope never to see again. [The guards] set the barn on fire, and as some of the men ran out they were shot as they came out of the flames. This I will never, never forget.'[16]

It was also a common belief that those who fell behind were butchered. One POW, John Lensburg, wrote that 'During the walk, if you fell behind, the guards prodded you with their rifles to keep up with the main column. If you fell behind consistently, a guard would fall behind with you. About five or ten minutes later, the guard would rejoin the column without the POW.'[17] On the other hand, Sergeant Frank Paules, the leader of the Americans, wrote how the Germans 'allowed me to fall back to the rear. We had to look out for the casualties and protect the guys in the back from getting batted on the head by the guards if they were too slow.'[18] His words certainly suggest harassment by the Germans, but not slaughter. It could be argued that the guards would not want to commit any act of murder in his presence, of all people, but the important fact is where he says he was: at the rear, the very place where others allege the killings were taking place. Dr Caplan, who was also travelling at the rear with the wounded, gave evidence that stragglers were sometimes 'gun-butted', but he gave no examples of men being shot.

Although there are archive accounts of prisoners being killed, none of our interviewees who were on this march from Gross Tychow had actually seen this happen or knew the name of anyone who had died in this way. But it remained – and remains – a powerful belief that POWs were murdered. Joe O'Donnell – who heard the reports that stragglers were shot but could not verify it – made the common-sense point that people only ever saw what was immediately around them. 'It depended on where you were in the column. If you were up at the front you wouldn't hear what was happening at the rear, and vice-versa.'

Whatever the mortality statistics, there can be little doubt that what happened over those 500 miles amounted to an atrocity of war, not least because it was largely avoidable. The prisoners could and should have been left where they were, to be liberated by the Russians. Out on the road, arrangements to feed and shelter them were non-existent, and they were marched much harder and further than allowed by the Geneva Convention. Men froze, starved, suffered terrible sickness and sometimes died, all unnecessarily. As

Dr Caplan summed it up, 'We marched long distances in bitter weather and on starvation rations. No doubt many men are still suffering today as a result of that ordeal.'[19]

And the ordeal was not over once the column had reached Fallingbostel. The 'death march' would resume, and the hardship and the dangers would increase as the prisoners were forced out on the road again. Their battered feet would take them closer and closer to the battle zones where Hitler's army was fighting to a standstill – and where a man caught in the middle could lose his life just as easily to a bullet from a friend as to one from a foe.

But that is to jump ahead of ourselves. We will pick up the story of the men from Gross Tychow later. Meanwhile it is vital to remember that their journey was just one out of hundreds of similar journeys made by British and American prisoners of war at this time, as the east of Germany was evacuated ahead of the Russians. And keeping track of them was proving an impossible task.

7 The Rivers of Humanity

Streams of people were winding through the wreckage of Germany in those final months of the war. German refugees, slave labourers, concentration-camp inmates and prisoners of war of every nationality flowed westward in the cold and the damp, bedding down where they could, living off the land – or what was left of it by now. Life was cheap. One British prisoner remembered getting stuck in a colossal traffic jam of refugees and fleeing soldiers trying to cross the single remaining bridge over the Vistula. They all stood waiting their turn in the freezing cold for two hours before taking the only other option, a perilous one: they walked over the frozen river. 'We heard later that the ice had given way and 70 wagons containing German refugees had gone through with heavy loss of life.'[1] The hard-pressed International Red Cross found it almost impossible to keep track of the millions on the road and then try to feed them. It seemed that half the world was on the move, hurrying away from their homes in fear of their lives, or hurrying towards homes they had not seen for years. Central Europe was a seething mass of the dispossessed.

More than half a century later, it stretches the imagination to the limit to take in the full extent of the evacuations. It was even harder to grasp at the time. Some Allied prisoners of war had been on the road for several weeks before a startled world had even begun to catch on to what was happening. All plans for bringing them home had started with the assumption – then followed by the instruction – that they would stay where they were and wait for their liberators to come to them. But the kaleidoscope of men and camps had now been turned, and a new picture was emerging. However, accurate and up-to-date information to bring that picture into focus was now almost impossible to obtain. Mail to and from the far-flung camps in Poland and eastern Germany, erratic at the best of times, had ceased with the evacuations. That meant no more coded messages between camp leaders and Military Intelligence

THE MAIN POW
EVACUATION ROUTES

BARTH

LÜBECK •

SWINEMÜNDE

• HAMBURG

STETTIN

Stalag XIB & 357
FALLINGBOSTEL

BERLIN

Oder

HANOVER •

Stalag XIA
ALTENGRABOW

WERDER

Stalag IIIA
LUCKENWALDE

Oflag 79
BRUNSWICK

Elbe

HALLE •

Stalag VIII
GÖRLITZ

LEIPZIG

G E R M A N Y

Oflag IVC
COLDITZ

• DRESDEN

Oflag XIIB
HADMAR

• FRANKFURT AM MAIN

• KARLSBAD
MARIENBAD

Oflag XIII
HAMMELBURG

PRAGUE

• HEPPENHEIM

Stalag XIIID
NUREMBERG

• STUTTGART

Danube

Stalag VIIA
MOOSBURG

• MUNICH

KÖNIGSBERG

EAST
PRUSSIA

DANZIG

Stalag XXB
MARIENBURG

Stalag Luft IV
GROSS TYCHOW

Vistula

Stalag XXA
THORN

POZNAŃ

WARSAW

POLAND

Stalag Luft III
SAGAN

Stalag Luft VII
BANKAU

BRESLAU

Stalag 344
LAMSDORF

KRAKÓW

Auschwitz

Stalag VIIIB
TESCHEN

CZECHOSLOVAKIA

VIENNA

Key

POW routes

POW camp

0   50 miles

0   50 kilometres

in London. A secret radio was carried on many of the marches – in the column from Gross Tychow it was smuggled in the pack of a different prisoner every day, for added security – and was listened to clandestinely at night for news of the war and the Allied advance on the Rhine. But this was only one-way communication. The prisoners – if they could see beyond the tunnel of their present woes as they slipped and stumbled through ice and snow and starvation – could keep abreast of events in a wider world, or at least their leaders could. But when it came to making that world aware of their position or their plight, they were out of touch, isolated, all but abandoned.

One of the first to grasp the scale of the problem facing the hundreds of thousands of British and American POWs was a leading light in the Red Cross in Britain, Major-General Sir Richard Howard-Vyse. He told a colleague in a memo, 'We are about to witness a complete breakdown of transportation in Germany', and that left him deeply concerned about how food parcels would get to the prisoners.[2] Their 'vitality has been lowered by half rations since September and by exceptionally cold weather; now they are faced with the prospect of starvation', he wrote. Nor was the problem confined to those on the move from the east. Consideration also had to be given to prisoners 'in camps which are not likely to be moved and whose position is known accurately. To such camps an effort should be made to get supplies by air.' He knew there could be no guarantee that air drops would get through to the right people, but equally 'no one can say that they will *not* reach them'. He suggested parachuting in 1,000 tons of food, in the hope that at least half of it – 100,000 parcels – would get to those who needed it. 'This would keep 100,000 men alive for a month, to say nothing of the effect on morale.'

The retired general strongly urged his colleague to put this plan to the government. 'There is no time to lose. Whatever the decision may be, we shall then have placed ourselves in a position to say that we have left no stone unturned. I might add that this particular stone has already attracted the notice of many relations of prisoners of war.'

Shortly afterwards, on 28 February, Washington and London received details from Switzerland of what the International Red

Cross believed was the present position of Allied prisoners of war in Germany. The information had come from Robert Schirmer, the organization's delegate in northern Germany. It appeared that he had just been in Pomerania and had seen some of the marchers on the road – possibly the column from Gross Tychow, which was then well to the west of Swinemünde, though travelling quite slowly. He had also arrived at an overview of the whole prisoner-of-war situation after talking to other Red Cross representatives in Berlin who had knowledge of other parts of Germany.

According to Schirmer, there were three main groups of prisoners of war on the move: a northern line of march, a central line of march, and a southern line of march.[3] On the northern route – that corridor close to the Baltic coast through which, as we have seen, the marchers from Gross Tychow were travelling – there were said to be up to 100,000 prisoners. Schirmer reckoned that the great mass of them were at present 'resting' somewhere in the area between Swinemünde and Neubrandenburg. It sounded like a precise enough location, giving the impression of a situation well in hand. In fact the area in question was more than 500 square miles, covered in forest and fields, and criss-crossed by a maze of country roads and tracks. Moreover, there was a 'rear guard', which was still strung out along the 'the roads west of Danzig'. The vagueness of these locations was hardly reassuring. Nor were the designated destinations of the columns – said to be 'the region of Hamburg, Bremen and Lübeck'. Bremen and Lübeck were 100 miles apart. For anyone trying to keep track of the prisoners, this was little more than identifying the particular haystack in which the needle might be found.

It was acknowledged that there were problems in the north. That 80 per cent of the marchers had dysentery was recorded, as well as the fact that they were having to scrounge and barter for food, often 'with little success'. However, Schirmer also made the point that 'the prisoners, German officers and German guards are eating the same rations' – which would have come as a surprise to the likes of Cec Room, who had seen a single sheep stretch to a meal for 600 RAF prisoners one night while their 100 guards had four sheep between them.[4] Sixty tons of food had been ferried to the area on passenger trains, Schirmer said, and was being stored in a warehouse at Neubrandenburg (where there was a camp, Oflag 67) and in smaller depots in other towns. The Germans had provided him with two trucks, and 22,000 food parcels had already been delivered to marching prisoners. (Again, Cec Room would have been surprised. Whoever Schirmer had doled his parcels out to, it wasn't him. Room would have to wait until 28 February until he got his first one since leaving Luft IV.) Particular attention was drawn to the plight of a group of 800 officers who 'were in a soft physical condition because they did no work in their camps and, consequently, are in the worst condition yet seen. Some have lost between 15 and 20 kilograms [33–44 lb]. Some are not able to carry the 11 lb food packages which were given them.' Apparently Schirmer had negotiated with the German guards for these men to be allowed to rest for three or four days until they got better.

The central line of march involved some 60,000 prisoners, who were in a triangle formed by the cities of Leipzig, Berlin and Dresden. A supply of 110 tons of food parcels had been established at Luckenwalde, the camp where a large number of the evacuees from Stalag Luft III at Sagan had ended up about three weeks earlier after their nightmare march and train journey. Marchers from other camps were also heading there, and the word from Schirmer was that Red Cross parcels would be sent out to them on the road. There was no mention of the ordeal the marchers from Sagan had been through, only a reference to 300 'severely wounded' officers who had stayed behind in the Luft III hospital when the rest were evacuated and who, it was presumed, had now been overrun by the Russians. Just one specific case of hardship was recorded – that of 350 severely wounded prisoners of war of various nationalities who had endured an eight-day journey on coal barges from a military hospital on the River Oder to Werder, a town just outside Berlin. They had been 'without light, heat or bedding. Two blankets were provided for each man but there was practically no food or medicine. Seven died.' Otherwise, the prisoners were reported as being 'in relatively good condition', particularly those who had reached safe areas in the middle of Germany 'where trains still run and which are relatively tranquil'.

Down in the south of Germany was the biggest collection of POWs on the move. Schirmer put their numbers at an astonishing

800,000, though he did not know how many were British and American. It can only have been a smallish proportion, though still running into tens of thousands. The vast majority were Russians, who had been scattered throughout the myriad labour camps in Poland and the German borders and were now being shepherded south-west in columns of various sizes. The message received in London and Washington was that 'this group has suffered particularly because it has been repeatedly strafed by Allied planes, because of the bad weather and because it crossed the Czech mountains with but little food'. They would all eventually end up in Stuttgart, Nuremberg and Munich.

The Red Cross sit-rep was difficult to evaluate. Schirmer had clearly been out to see some of the marchers in the north, and had been present when some Red Cross parcels were distributed. But the detail he chose to highlight is revealing – the officers in physical trouble because they had not worked and were therefore unfit to march; the reference to Allied strafing; the unknown fate of the men left behind at Sagan for the Russians to overrun; guards and prisoners sharing rations. It all added up to a softening-down of what was really happening on the marches – and pointed away from any blame attaching to the Germans. It is hard to resist the conclusion that Schirmer had seen what he was allowed to see and had reported back in terms that, while not pretending the evacuations westward were a picnic, nevertheless presented a picture of an orderly and compassionate exodus carried out in difficult circumstances. It came nowhere close to reflecting the true awfulness of the situation on the ground.

But at least some urgent supplies of food were now being earmarked for the prisoners on the march, and some had even got through already. Whether any more would arrive became a moot point as bureaucrats and military men in London wrangled about how much help to give the Red Cross in this mercy mission. The International Red Cross had asked for 'hundreds of lorries' and the petrol to run them.[5] But the vehicles would have to be diverted from the war effort, and SHAEF did not think it could spare them. The bureaucrats had objections in principle. Throughout the war the agreement had always been that the Germans would use their own railway trains to transport Red Cross parcels. If lorries took over the job, the German railway system would be relieved of 'this burden'.[6] The Germans might also 'take advantage of the situation by reducing even further the rations which they are now supplying'. Then again, the Germans might 'decide to seize the Red Cross lorries for their own use'. There was just as much anxiety over the request from the International Red Cross that, if lorries could not be provided, then at least the trains carrying relief supplies should be protected from air attacks. This raised the issue of immunity – 'a difficult question of principle'.

A meeting of the Chiefs of Staff, which might have been expected to call for action, called for more discussion instead. There were 'administrative and organizational problems', it was told.[7] 'Further information' was needed, and 'further consideration'. Its best bet, in any case, was that 'relief on the scale envisaged could [not] be supplied before the greater part of the movements [of prisoners] have been completed'. That, in the chaos of a collapsing Germany, vast numbers of Allied prisoners of war faced starvation for many months ahead, not just a few days, did not seem to have occurred to those at the meeting. They decided to stall. The Foreign Office would be invited to obtain further information, and the War Office to 'prepare a report'.

In due course, men from these two ministries consulted the Swiss government and the International Red Cross and came to the conclusion that assembling a convoy of lorries raised 'serious technical difficulties'. Even if Swiss drivers were allowed into Germany to drive the lorries – which the Germans had not yet agreed to – it would be difficult to find food and lodgings for them. And what if the lorries broke down? Where would garages and spares be found? Armed guards would also be necessary on the convoys, but the Germans would have to provide them and they were unlikely to want to spare the soldiers for this. Problems, problems, problems.

The Swiss tried to cut through them, to broker a deal. But the British officials seemed to react with a bureaucratic lethargy, a willingness to be daunted by the hurdles. There was particular concern about guaranteeing that any supplies that went in under the auspices of the Allies got to British and American prisoners only. A War Office mandarin put his foot down with the Red Cross, making it clear that, without naming names, he wasn't in the business of bringing relief to Russians or the French. British Commonwealth and American prisoners would have to get priority treatment, he insisted, though he wanted to be reasonable and flexible:

We would not raise any question if, in a camp containing 10,000 British and American prisoners and 1,000 others, the parcels were spread evenly. On the other hand, we should be gravely perturbed if supplies sent to a camp for 1,000 British Commonwealth and American prisoners were regarded as available for the whole of that camp if it contained, say, 10,000 other Allies.[8]

Nevertheless, a relief convoy began to be assembled in Sweden to cross to Lübeck in northern Germany, from where marchers in the north could be supplied. The British Red Cross came up with the money to buy fifty steam-driven lorries from Sweden, which would run on burning wood instead of petrol. The British government agreed to underwrite the cost of oil and new tyres. From SHAEF headquarters, General Eisenhower, the Allied supreme commander, cut through the red tape. He had been given full authority by Washington to deal with relief matters as he saw fit and without reference to the politicians and bureaucrats at home.[9] The War Office in London also stepped back, agreeing that sending in relief 'should be left to SHAEF to handle since they alone were in a position to do so'.[10]

Eisenhower ordered 100 army lorries to be made available to go to Lübeck. He also gave the go-ahead for two relief trains, each with 500 tons of food, medicines and other supplies, to head out from Switzerland for Moosburg, 30 miles north-east of Munich in southern Germany, one of the points to which columns of prisoners of war were believed to be heading. The first train left on 6 March. The next day a convoy of twenty-five lorries, each with a trailer carrying enough petrol for the return journey, headed out along the roads of Switzerland and across the German border en route to the towns of Karlsbad and Marienbad, where those on the southern line of march were congregating. These were risky journeys for the Swiss drivers, despite the safe-conduct deal brokered by the Swiss with the Germans and despite the presence of a German guard on each truck. The areas they were heading into were diehard Nazi territory. But, if this convoy got through, a further 175 lorries were on stand-by to follow it. For extra security, all rail and motor vehicles were 'conspicuously marked for air identification'.

*

How many Red Cross parcels got through is impossible to say. Many did, and from the accounts of those who received them we know they were life-savers. That is undeniable. At the same time there were men like Private W. Bampton of the East Surrey Regiment who walked from the far side of Danzig all the way to western Germany and had only one parcel the whole way. In his diary he wrote, 'Still no Red Cross parcels, and yet there must be thousands in Germany somewhere. We have heard there were loads at Stettin and that they were deliberately issued to civilian evacuees. Also we know that we have been deliberately marched through towns where Red Cross stores were. Why?'[11] Another prisoner recalled getting three parcels in two months, and having to share each one with four other men. 'They put no fat on our gaunt frames, but they kept us alive,' he recalled.[12] For weeks on end, the closest others got was rumours of Red Cross parcels, but no parcels themselves.[13]

Private Les Allan certainly never saw one in his marathon journey across Germany. His war ended as badly as it had begun. A nineteen-year-old stretcher-bearer with the Oxfordshire and Buckingham-shire Light Infantry, he had been in the perimeter line around Dunkirk in May 1940, desperately trying to hold back the tide of German tanks to give the men on the beaches 30 miles away a chance to get home to England. 'We were the sacrifice,' he said. 'We were told to do as much damage as we could to the enemy and then it was every man for himself.'[14] Stuka dive-bombers and tank fire destroyed the building he was holed up in. Sixty of his comrades died around him. He was pulled from the rubble unconscious, a prisoner. Back in Slough, his mother's hair turned white overnight when the telegram arrived saying that her son was missing. It was a while before she learned he was now 1,000 miles from home at Stalag XXB at Marienburg in East Prussia. 'We ended up in work camps. The first job they put me on was sawing ice blocks from the river. Then I was sent on roadworks, and after that farms and sugar-beet factories. On one work party a guard beat me senseless with his rifle butt and broke my jaw for no reason that I could fathom.' For four and a half years he slaved away from dawn to dusk – just like tens of thousands of other ordinary British soldiers, required under the Geneva Convention to work while imprisoned by the enemy.

Towards the end of December 1944 he was in a work detachment with 200–300 other British soldiers at Königsberg, a long way from the base camp at Marienburg, and freezing.

It was about 25 degrees below and there was 3 feet of snow on the ground. We had a clandestine radio and we knew the Russians were on their way, and that led to terrifying rumours. Would we be shot out of hand by the Germans? We could not imagine them handing us over peacefully. We thought we would have to fight our way out to avoid being massacred.

Then, early one morning, without warning, the guards forced them up and out of the barracks hut to stand in the cold outside. Allan thought it was a snap roll-call and, instead of pulling on his leather army boots, which he had managed to keep with him and in good trim ever since Dunkirk, he stuck his feet into the wooden clogs he used for working.

I went out on parade like that, and the next thing I knew we were being bullied and threatened to march. We went straight out on to the road – with me and half a dozen others still in our clogs – and began what turned out to be a horrendous march of close to 600 miles. It was a couple of days before Christmas, and we would be on the road until well into April.

They marched more than 100 miles back to the main camp at Marienburg, where they merged with other columns arriving from the surrounding countryside. Together, they all headed west. Allan bound his feet tightly with a piece of flannel that served as socks, and, in his clogs, just kept going. He scavenged to stay alive.

I can truthfully say that, if we went through a town or a village, nothing was left behind alive. Dogs, pigeons, chickens – they all went into the pot. We wasted nothing. A dog's skin made excellent gloves or covers for your feet. It was a primeval existence, back to the caveman. We lived on our wits and killed what was necessary for life.

He thought the casualties on his march were high.

Men would fall asleep in the snow. You would see a hump on the ground and know they were dead. I saw about twenty like that. We just left them there. More often than not we were too busy saving our own lives to be able to help others. It was the survival of the fittest. Sometimes I felt as if I just wanted to lie down and go to sleep and never get up again, but I forced myself to carry on. Thoughts of home kept me going. As for escaping, where was there to go? We were in deep snow, it was 25 degrees below, and there were wolves in the forest.

I did see one man shot. It was about five weeks into the march and we were in the middle of a blizzard. I noticed this chap huddled up in the ditch and a German shouting at him and getting no response. Then the guard just shot him, shouldered his rifle, and walked on. My only thought was that if he could do that to one man he could do it to me next. But we had always been under that sort of threat as prisoners. Rifles and machine-guns were always being pointed at us, and all it ever took was an extra squeeze on the trigger and you would be dead. And nobody was ever going to make enquiries about what had happened to you.

Eventually Allan's column stumbled into Fallingbostel after three months on the road, joining the tens of thousands of men from Stalag Luft IV and other camps who had been making their way west along that northern line of march. Allan could at last rest, though he would never totally recover.

I had been in my clogs for the whole of the march. I stuffed them with leaves and rags as insulation, and tied them to my feet. I always kept a dry rag in my coat, and at night I would rub my feet to get the blood circulating. Because of this, by the end, I only had very mild frostbite. In fact I was better off than those men in army boots, because they never got to take them off and they couldn't warm their toes up. But I did have a broken ankle. I hit a hard ridge of ice and twisted it. A doctor on the march bound it up tight.

To this day he still hobbles. Mile after painful mile – from one side of Hitler's Greater Germany to the other – through snow and ice and mud, in wooden clogs, disabled him for good.

For Private Bampton there was a different destination, though he too had begun his march from a Stalag XXB work camp. He was on a farm to the east of Danzig when the order to march came. With the Red Army only a few miles away, he thought about lying low in the woods and waiting for the Russians, 'but the winter was very severe and the retreating SS were ruthless. Later on I regretted this decision.' After a few days, trudging through the dark, he and two other prisoners and a single guard became separated from the main column. It was not an unusual occurrence. They kept going until they found another group of prisoners and teamed up with them. But it was important to be wary about who you joined with. Bampton saw a column of prisoners from a concentration camp[15] – 'poor devils – many are left to die in the ditches; they were dressed in what looked like striped pyjamas'.

There were constant rumours among the men as they marched – a stock of Red Cross parcels was waiting at the next village, or they were about to be provided with transport. 'Rumour lifts you up in the morning only to dash you down at night,' Bampton noted. As he trekked through the flat and featureless country by the estuary of the Oder, he reflected on a war that had been started because of Hitler's demand for more territory, for *Lebensraum* for the German people. 'There is miles and miles of unoccupied land here, yet Germany wanted more. Was this really worth fighting over?' Three weeks into the march, and with more than 200 miles behind them already, he and his group found themselves near Swinemünde and camping out in that same bleak open field as the column from Gross Tychow had slept out in. For him too that was a night to remember: 'How we got through it I will never know.'

He forever puzzled about what he saw of human nature around him. At night there would be a fight for the best place to sleep and the pick of what little food they had. Some stolen milk almost provoked a riot as other prisoners demanded their share, and

Bampton thought he was in danger of being lynched by 'a snarling mob'. When his pack was rifled and three packets of tea were taken he despaired. The column he was in was now entirely British, but, apart from his closest buddies, he thought his fellow countrymen on the whole 'a surly, miserable, rotten crowd. I can see a terrible change in people I know.' He was not the only one who thought his own side were behaving badly. Another British soldier who had started out at Marienburg recalled that 'the scenes at night when pig-potatoes were issued became a disgrace not only to the army but to England'.[16]

One night Bampton's thoughts turned forlornly to home. It was a Saturday, 'always a happy family day for me in the past', and he longed for a taste of his mother's rice pudding. 'But now I think I belong to the Forgotten Legion.' He was not totally forgotten, however, as the first appearance of a Red Cross parcel on 28 February proved. He stuffed chocolate and biscuits into his mouth, and was lost for words that could come anywhere close to describing the taste except that it was 'great'. 'Good old Red X!!' he wrote in his diary, and then moaned as his stomach went into a painful spasm because of the prunes he had eaten.

But there was good news from home – further proof that they not been forgotten after all. The secret radio picked up a broadcast from London: the marchers were to get regular Red Cross food; they were also to be allowed to rest and to have 'a definite destination as soon as possible'. The latter was increasingly important. Where *were* they going? There had been talk of Hamburg and Hanover. Then they passed a signpost pointing to Lübeck 172 kilometres away. The loneliness returned. 'We seem to be forgotten. Nobody seems to know where to take us or what to do with us. Why don't they send us home instead of treating us like animals?'

He scratched out his despair:

It is March 12 and we have been almost seven weeks on the march. I started off this [diary] taking a fiendish delight in recording a true account of our suffering and hardships. Now I'm just tired of it all and am yearning for a bit of peace and a place where we can make ourselves clean. Oh, God! What would I give for a day at home. But I think the Germans will hang on to us until the war is over and ill-treat us as much as they dare.

The sight of an old friend from a camp back in Poland alarmed him. 'He had been a 15 stone lad last time I saw him but I didn't recognize him now and I had to ask him his name to make sure. He was a mere shadow of his former self, unshaven and dirty and all self-respect gone. His helplessness had made him child-like in his speech.' The guards never ceased to be jumpy, and Bampton noted that two of 'our boys' were shot while trying to escape even very late into the march. He reckoned that his column – and all the others that had set out from the depths of Poland – lost two-thirds of the men along the way. 'Hundreds have escaped, some were killed in German-Russian cross-fire, some have died through lack of attention.'

Finally his group came to a halt at the town of Brunswick. It was Easter. They were put to work. They had been labourers on a farm within earshot of the Russian artillery when they started the march. Now, after close to 500 miles, they were labouring on a bomb-damaged railway line and dodging bullets from British and American fighter planes. 'Our one hope is that our boys will get here and release us from this hell . . . but I don't think freedom will come that quickly.'

And for some it would never come at all. Somewhere in the region of Hamburg, another group of prisoners who had set out from Marienburg back in January buried Trooper B. Smith of the 15/19 Hussars. He had gone down with dysentery, and for days his comrades had carried him until finally they found a handcart to push him in. By then he had gone blind and was very sick. His friend Bandsman Charles Houston of the Royal West Kent Regiment helped bury him after he died on 3 March. 'We wrapped him in a blanket and put him in a grave in a small village cemetery. Since the column could not be delayed, we did not have time to erect a cross.'[17]

One of the more extraordinary accounts to emerge from this time is that of Private F. Coster, an Englishman who had fought with the 51st Highland Division in the retreat to Saint-Valéry near Dieppe in 1940. He had spent four long years at Stalag XXA at Thorn in Poland before, with the Russians almost at the gates of the camp, he decided to escape. Overnight, the ranks of German soldiers guarding the prisoners had thinned as reinforcements were called upon to try to stem the Russian advance. Coster and a large group of other prisoners approached the main gate.

The few guards left stood eyeing us apprehensively and nervously fingering the straps of their rifles. Then one of them shrugged his shoulders and walked off, and was followed by the others. We walked out to freedom.

We decided to make our way to the Russian lines, thinking that this would be the quickest way back to England. We set off enthusiastically through the snow, pulling our sledges behind us. We had no idea how far away the Russians were, but after about an hour of marching through the empty snowy, icy and frosty land, a Russian tank nosed its way round a hillock and confronted us. We waved and shouted 'Comrades . . . *tovarich* . . . friends . . . English.' The Russians' reply was to open up on us with machine-guns. Instinctively, we all dived down into the snow, and were fortunate not to suffer any casualties. We realized that the Russians had been brutalized too much by the Germans to be prepared to practise the niceties of war. We decided we would have to march home the other way. We turned our backs on the Russians and headed out of Poland into Germany in order to reach our own lines, where we would be sure to receive a better welcome.[18]

Coster and his group headed west without any guards or escort. They passed unchallenged through lines of German soldiers digging in. An SS officer asked who they were, was told they were English prisoners of war, and waved them on their way. Shells burst behind them, and the sound of machine-gun fire got closer and closer. Russian fighter planes flew overhead, 'so low that in the dull light it was as if they were travelling on skis across the snow, rising only to clear the hedges'. They got caught in a jam of people trying to cross the Vistula, and heard the dynamite explode behind them as the bridge was blown up by the retreating German infantry. Sleeping wherever they could find shelter, and scrounging food, they kept going.

Then, late one afternoon, two SS soldiers stood in their way and herded them to one side of the road at gunpoint.

I was very nervous, particularly as they made us wait for a long time. Then along the road came a column of pitiful women, dressed in concentration-camp garb, all absolutely exhausted and dragging their feet. Black-uniformed guards goaded them onwards, prodding them with their guns. As the women passed us we surreptitiously handed them bits of food, only small amounts because we had to preserve our own rations. But one of our men gave them every bit of food he had and he spoke quietly to them in Yiddish, words of comfort. His name was Freddy Fried, and he was a Hungarian Jew who left before the jackboots trampled that way and joined the British Army to rid the world of as many Nazis as he could. I had tried to restrain him from handing over all his food and from drawing attention to himself in this way, but to no avail. The straggling column of tortured women passed, and then, lagging well behind, came a very old lady, accompanied by a soldier in black. When she came opposite us she stopped and sagged. It was obvious that she could not go one step further. Without any hesitation, he put his revolver to her head and shot her dead. We had great difficulty in holding Freddy Fried back from getting at that young German. Had we not done so we would surely have been massacred ourselves.

*

One hundred and fifty miles due south of Stalag XXA at Thorn was a camp for RAF prisoners. This was Stalag Luft VII at Bankau, close to the Polish border. The march-out from the camp was accompanied by the severest of threats. As the men stamped their feet in the snow in the early hours of the morning of 19 January, the air so cold that breathing in was painful, a German corporal, a tough man in his fifties who had been hardened by years of fighting in the North African desert, told them that for every one of them who went missing five others would be shot. RAF pilot Alan Clarke was among a group who quickly raided the camp's sports store, full of equipment sent by the YMCA and the Red Cross, to grab whatever was adaptable for what lay ahead. 'One of us had half a rugby ball crammed down on his head, and another split a leather football into two and wore it as a hat with ear flaps. One guy put on wicketkeeping gloves and pads – anything that would give you an extra layer of warmth. We must have looked a funny lot – or sad, maybe.'[19]

His group took what the International Red Cross had described as the central line of march. They raced to the Oder to cross the river before the Russians cut them off. But the pace left many men too exhausted to continue. Each morning it took kicks and prods from the guards, and even rifle shots fired at feet or over their heads, to get them back on the road. Unusually, a check of numbers was made at one point, and twenty-three were missing. Whether they had escaped or simply fallen in the snow and died no one ever knew. Fortunately the German corporal's threat turned out to be bluff, and the mass shooting he had promised was not carried out.

But the guards never relented in their harassment of the prisoners until one morning all 1,500 of them mutinied. They refused to leave the barn they had been in overnight, rejecting orders even to stand up. Threats were made with machine-guns, there was a great deal of shouting, and then

the Germans gave in. They backed down, which was surprising. With hindsight it might have got pretty serious. They could have started to open fire, and if the SS had been there they most certainly would have. But it was so near the end of the war, and they were so scared of the Russians. They gave in, and we were promised a train.

They were packed into cattle trucks, and after a horrific journey lasting three to four days they arrived at Luckenwalde, Stalag IIIA, just 25 miles south of Berlin. Clarke collapsed, past caring, in agony and so thin that he was grateful just to have a roof over his head, even if he was sleeping on the floor. They were all 'gaunt and wasted', more dead than alive.[20]

Though filled with horrors, their journey across the centre of Germany had, at three weeks, been mercifully short. It was a sprint compared with the marathon endured by those evacuated in the south. Stalag VIIIB was at Teschen in the far south-east corner of Germany, on the frontier with Poland and Czechoslovakia, and was a focal point for work camps at the many mines in the area. Coming from the seaside resort of Eastbourne on the south coast of England, Private D. Swift of the Royal Sussex Regiment had no experience or knowledge of pit life; but here he came in 1943, and here he worked. He was a captive from the fighting in northern France in 1940, and since then, step by step, Stalag by Stalag, he had been transferred eastward until he reached this furthest-flung part of the Reich. The flight from the Russians just after Christmas

1944 took him completely by surprise. He and the twenty-seven other prisoners he worked with were hustled out of bed by their two guards in the middle of the night and were on the road immediately.

It was pitch dark in the countryside and freezing cold as we trudged along narrow winding roads. Suddenly we heard gunfire from machine-guns and tanks. Then flares went up, illuminating the snow-covered landscape, and we ran into a patrol of German soldiers on skis, dressed all in white with rifles slung on their backs. Our German Kommandant spoke to them and it turned out that we had been marching in the wrong direction and had wandered slap bang into the middle of a battle. We turned round and just kept going as fast as we could in the other direction. In the next 48 hours, we stopped for two hours only, so desperate were the Germans to get away. We were keen to keep on the move too because the Russians were just as likely to mistake us for Germans and shoot us. When they finally decided we were out of the immediate danger area, they allowed us to sleep. But by then we were lost. Apparently we should have rendezvoused with the main body of British prisoners from Teschen but we had missed them and we were on our own.[21]

As they marched along country roads heading for the Oder, Swift watched elderly German Home Guard troops digging in with anti-tank mortars and heavy machine-guns, saw the fear and the hopelessness in their eyes, and was reminded of those days long ago in France when it had been his job to try to halt a seemingly invincible invader. In towns and villages along the way, the people were in out-and-out panic. The SS were shooting Russian prisoners of war and leaving their bodies to line the very roads that the Soviet tanks would soon be sweeping along. With good reason, the locals feared they would pay with their lives for this brutality. No one was safe. In the chaos, a wrong move meant death. A party of Ukrainian slave labourers had heard that their Russian liberators were close and had risen up against their guards, 'but they had jumped the gun and were all being shot'.

Swift's small group headed south-west towards the mountains of the Sudetenland, struggling through deepening snow. He tried to fight off frostbite in his ears. In a small village in the middle of a pine forest that stretched as far as the eye could see he was billeted in the home of an old couple who fed him a feast of potatoes boiled in their jackets and, luxury of luxuries in those hard times, sprinkled with salt. 'We all sat around in the lamplight thinking how marvellous it was.'

Eventually they came down out of the mountains and turned on to bigger roads, where they found the main column of prisoners – 'thousands and thousands of them' – and joined up with them. Many were Russians, and still being appallingly treated by the German guards:

I saw a group of Russian prisoners lying in the snow, their bodies still twitching in death after being shot just behind the ear or in the temple by the SS. One of our own guards was ordered to take a Russian prisoner into a field and shoot him. The Russian had to dig his own grave. The guard let him say his prayers, then he shot him. This guard was an elderly man and he came back shaken and trembling, muttering that all he wanted to do was to get back to Vienna and peace.

But then they caught sight of a column whose pitiful state was beyond all human belief:

A thousand, maybe two thousand people were standing beside the road, having been made to wait for us to overtake because they were slower than us. They were in blue and white striped pyjama-type clothes and wearing big clogs. They had no overcoats. They were from Auschwitz, which was in southern Poland, not too far from where we had come. As we slowly moved by them, I looked at their faces. I looked in vain for a vestige, a flicker of human interest, of recognition, a hint of understanding, anything in their faces showing they were aware of us or anything. There was nothing. The treatment, the weather, had sucked the life out of them. They stood like zombies on the roadside. Their heads like skulls, their eyes large, luminous and staring, all the same, not a flicker of feeling, like dead men but still alive. It still wrings my heart to think of them. I have tried but my words are inadequate to describe what I saw in those faces.[22]

The trail went on along minor roads, missing the towns and winding through the forests of Czechoslovakia.

1. Sergeant 'Dixie' Deans at Stalag Luft III in 1942.

2. Sergeant Cal Younger in 1939.

3. A typical room at Stalag Luft III.

4. Prisoners at Stalag Luft III, cooking their meagre rations.

5. Fourth of July celebrations at Stalag Luft III in 1944.

6. A secret earphone built into Sergeant Vic Gammon's plastic toothpowder box.

To all Prisoners of War!

The escape from prison camps is no longer a sport!

Germany has always kept to the Hague Convention and only punished recaptured prisoners of war with minor disciplinary punishment.

Germany will still maintain these principles of international law.

But England has besides fighting at the front in an honest manner instituted an illegal warfare in non combat zones in the form of gangster commandos, terror bandits and sabotage troops even up to the frontiers of Germany.

They say in a captured secret and confidential English military pamphlet,

THE HANDBOOK OF MODERN IRREGULAR WARFARE:

". . . the days when we could practise the rules of sportsmanship are over. For the time being, every soldier must be a potential gangster and must be prepared to adopt their methods whenever necessary."

"The sphere of operations should always include the enemy's own country, any occupied territory, and in certain circumstances, such neutral countries as he is using as a source of supply."

England has with these instructions opened up a non military form of gangster war!

Germany is determined to safeguard her homeland, and especially her war industry and provisional centres for the fighting fronts. Therefore it has become necessary to create strictly forbidden zones, called death zones, in which all unauthorised trespassers will be immediately shot on sight.

Escaping prisoners of war, entering such death zones, will certainly lose their lives. They are therefore in constant danger of being mistaken for enemy agents or sabotage groups.

Urgent warning is given against making future escapes!

In plain English: Stay in the camp where you will be safe! Breaking out of it is now a damned dangerous act.

The chances of preserving your life are almost nil!

All police and military guards have been given the most strict orders to shoot on sight all suspected persons.

Escaping from prison camps has ceased to be a sport!

7. (*Above*) The German warning . . .

8. (*Right*) 'Dear John' letters were not uncommon in the camps.

*'... I'm sorry, dear, but I love a soldier.
I know you'll understand...'*

9. (*Above*) Reichsführer-SS Heinrich Himmler inspecting Russian POWs.

10. (*Left*) SS Generalleutnant Gottlob Berger.

11. Fallingbostel, 1944. Allied airmen watch an overhead air battle despite German attempts to force them into barracks.

12. 'A' laager at Stalag Luft IV. The warning rail can be clearly seen: to step over it meant being shot.

13. POWs taking exercise at Stalag Luft III before the evacuation.

14. POWs march out of Stalag Luft III (taken with a secret camera).

15. American POWs on the march out of Stalag Luft III.

16. A rest stop on the march out of Stalag Luft III.

What food we received was watery dried vegetable soup and that not very often. We drank from cattle troughs. At night we were packed into big barns but I don't remember taking my clothes off during the whole four months of that march. One afternoon we passed a long funeral procession wending its way out of a village and up to a churchyard. It must have been the local mayor being buried, because the entourage was large and dignified. Fine black hearse pulled by black-plumed, black-draped, black horses. Wreaths and flowers covered the coffin. It was like opening a window on to a world I had forgotten, a sane world after the butchery and the bodies on the roads behind us.

Now their route took them out of Czechoslovakia and into Germany. They first headed north towards Dresden, then the Germans changed their mind and the column turned around and swung south towards Bavaria. By now, they had come so far west to escape the Russians that they were pushing up against the Third American Army as it thrust into Germany:

An SS soldier came by us in a panic, telling our guards that American tanks had annihilated his unit. He was the only survivor and he said he had torn off his insignia because the Americans were shooting SS men. One of our guards sat down and was wrapping his feet with cloth, which was all he had instead of socks. Then he took two wizened potatoes from his pocket, which was all he had to eat, and he quietly sang '*Deutschland, Deutschland über Alles*' in a mocking tone. He knew the grandiose schemes of Hitler, of race and domination, had gone and all they had left were ersatz socks and old potatoes.

The point was reinforced when an RAF fighter plane roared low over the column, shot up a German lorry, and hurtled away doing a victory roll. 'The lads cheered. It was April now and we had been on the march since just after Christmas. We felt sure the end could not be too far away. I was never so glad to see a spring as this one.'[23]

*

In London, relations of prisoners of war were offered honeyed words of comfort by the Secretary of State for War, Sir James Grigg. On 28 February he told the House of Commons that the men were being moved west under conditions he described as 'harsh', but that 'the representatives of the Protecting Power in Germany are doing all they can to secure improvements from the Germans, and their efforts have not been without some results'.[24] These 'improvements' included an agreement that the sick and the weak would be transported by train and lorry – which missed the point that almost all the prisoners were now exhausted and ill with dysentery and yet were destined to be on the road for many weeks to come. Grigg also spoke of British prisoners of war as being 'transferred', and he highlighted the period 'between 19th and 24th [of February]' as when this had taken place. The clear implication was that the movement of prisoners had been short and sharp and was firmly under control. This was becoming a common misconception in Whitehall. Two days before Grigg's statement to the Commons, General Gepp told a meeting of the DPW that 'the latest information from the Protecting Power indicated that the moves of camps in Eastern Germany had been largely completed'.[25] This was not the case. Though the camps had been evacuated, long and arduous marches were continuing, and would do so for a long time yet.

Magisterially, Grigg also claimed foresight on the part of the government in having expected the prisoners to be moved and having acted ahead of events to deal with this situation. With the Red Cross, he said, 'efforts had been made to establish substantial reserves in the camps of Red Cross food parcels, medical supplies and comforts, clothing and boots'. There is no evidence of such efforts whatsoever. Nobody, least of all the government, had foreseen the evacuation of the camps in the east. Not a single prisoner's account mentions extra supplies arriving at camps for use on the marches. The notion that they had been equipped with 'medical supplies and comforts' would have had Dr Pollack and Dr Caplan gasping in disbelief. As for relief to the camps receiving the marchers, and to those tens of thousands of British and American POWs still on the road, we know that a rudimentary operation was only now creaking into action.

Nevertheless, Grigg felt pleased with himself:

I hope I have shown that the Government in this country, the Supreme Allied Command and the British Red Cross Society are doing all in their power to see that any request from the International Red Cross for vehicles, fuel or maintenance stores which can be effectively used to supply our prisoners is met, subject only to the condition that such assistance will not weaken the attack on Germany and so delay the conclusion of hostilities.[26]

There was nobody to contradict him then, but the documentary evidence available now fails to back him up. It would have been more accurate if the Minister had reported that the British government was actually doing as little as it could get away with to aid the prisoners, while trying to pretend to the relatives of those men enduring conditions of indescribable horror that there was nothing for them to be concerned about.

Grigg may well have had good reason to believe the worst was over for the prisoners when he made that Commons statement. He appeared to be taking his optimistic line after receiving reassuring reports from the Swiss Protecting Power. In which case he would have been horrified if he had been party to a conversation that took place ten days later between American diplomats in Berne and Gilbert Naville, a member of the Swiss Legation. Far from being reassuring, Naville pointed to a total breakdown in communication and an absence of reliable information.[27] Pressed by the Americans to have Swiss inspectors on the ground report regularly on the whereabouts of the prisoners, he could say only that 'telephonic messages are virtually impossible'. As for identifying POWs from the air, this was next to impossible, because their routes were usually along secondary roads and it was hard to distinguish them from any other line of marching men.

For a while now it had been dawning on many in senior positions in the Allied chain of command, particularly the military planners at SHAEF, that the orderly finale to the war they had envisaged was not going to happen. From even before D-Day, headquarters staff had been preparing for the end, and, in particular, for what would happen when the Germans surrendered. Committees had pored over the precise terms of an armistice agreement and how the German military would hand in their weapons. An interim administration for the conquered country was drawn up on paper. The overall plan was called Operation Eclipse,[28] and a sizeable part of it was elaborate schemes for getting the liberated Allied prisoners of war home as efficiently as possible. These covered every detail, from delousing treatment to the supply of daily newspapers, even down to the sending of ENSA singers and comics to the camps to keep the men in a jolly mood while they waited to be shipped home.[29] The entertainers were to arrive 'as quickly as possible' but – perhaps as a precaution, given an audience who had been deprived of female company for many years – the 'live entertainment parties' were to be 'of male personnel'. In February, the army groups on the western front – whose task it would be to put the plan into operation – each received a lengthy document marked 'Secret – on no account to be allowed to fall into enemy hands'. Its five chapters, eighteen sections and numerous appendices seemed to cover every eventuality. But one small tucked-away sentence gave the lie to that impression. Information 'does not reflect the considerable movement of prisoners of war which is taking place', it stated. This sent many of the plans into cloud-cuckoo-land. It was assumed, for example, that the Germans, when they surrendered, would agree to feed the released prisoners for the time being. The reality was that they could not feed them even now. And the medical arrangements were predicated on there being only a small proportion of sick prisoners, whereas by now four out of five men were down with dysentery.

The plan had been distributed despite growing reservations that it no longer fitted the bill. In the middle of January, one SHAEF planner had warned another:

I have become a little uneasy that some of the 'Eclipse' memoranda have not taken into account recent trends of thought. Plans are based on the assumption that (a) there will be a formal German surrender; (b) that there will be comparative law and order; (c) that the German channel of command, including the service ministries at Berlin, will be functioning; (d) that the majority of POW will be found concentrated in camps and thus readily accessible to control; (e) that the majority of POW will obey the stay-put order. It is doubtful whether any of these conditions will in fact apply during 'Eclipse'.[30]

Two months later, as news of the evacuations sank in, fears were growing that there might be an outcome that had always been a possibility but which no one had planned for. The fact that the Germans were hanging on to hundreds of thousands of prisoners of war when it would have been easier to let them go was increasingly worrying. Suddenly, official documents were full of fears. Military Intelligence received a particularly chilling piece of information from the military attaché at the British embassy in Sweden.[31] A German-language newspaper in Stockholm, quoting an unnamed but reliable source, disclosed that Himmler had 'a devilish plan' to be put into force on what it called 'N-Day' – *Niederlagstag*, the Day of Defeat.

According to this plan, all preparations have been made for the liquidation of all prisoners in Nazi hands, including political prisoners and the inmates of concentration camps, those under arrest, and, worst of all, all prisoners of war and foreign workers in Germany. The larger prison camps are to be liquidated by bombing and machine-gunning, or, where there are sufficient SS guards, by shooting.

The report said that 'reliable SS personnel' were being infiltrated among the regular camp guards, and that camp commandants were being provided with Nazi Party 'advisers' who had 'carte blanche authority for N-Day'.

The attaché commented that he could not vouchsafe for the reliability of the story, but he had had a sort of confirmation. 'I can confidently report that Count Bernadotte (of the Swedish Red Cross) told a friend of mine that he was most concerned over the possibility of the Germans running amok against Norwegian and Danish prisoners in Germany.' If the extremists in Germany were planning to take revenge on Scandinavians, how much more would they relish reprisals against the British and the Americans?

A similar warning came from the embassy in Switzerland. Rumours were coming from Berlin that 'the Germans intended to liquidate, ie massacre, such prisoner of war camps as were in danger of being overrun by the advancing Allied forces, rather than try to remove prisoners or allow them to fall into Allied hands'.[32] The Swiss government thought that now would be a good time for the

Allies to issue the official warning to the German people that had first been discussed back in July 1944.

Interestingly, the bogey figure in these rumours was not Himmler but Hitler. The Führer, it was said, had been incensed by the carpet-bombing of Dresden in the middle of February and had wanted to take reprisals against prisoners of war then. Himmler, apparently, had restrained him. This indicated two things. First, that, as defeat neared, the jostling among senior Nazis to blacken the reputation of others and whitewash their own was already in full swing – and it would have an important part to play in the fate of the Allied prisoners, as we will see later.[33] Second, that the destruction of Dresden had indeed added considerably to the danger the prisoners of war were in. The bombing of the ancient city in Saxony remains a matter of controversy. Eight hundred Allied planes dropped their payloads on it. The resulting firestorm caused between 40,000 and 140,000 deaths – the uncertainty of the figures reflecting the fact that the local population was swollen by vast numbers of civilian refugees from the east who had crowded into the city's streets in their flight from the Russians. It was, according to historian Ian Kershaw, 'the most ruthless display experienced of Allied air superiority and strength'.[34] Reprisals were very possible.

In Washington the Combined Chiefs of Staff urged Eisenhower to formulate plans to protect the lives of prisoners from what were described as 'subversive German elements'.[35] He should consider sending in troops by land or air, and even bombers to ferry the men out if necessary. The order of priority – which camps were to be relieved first – was to be decided 'on the basis of potential threats of violence', and he was to act 'at the earliest possible moment' – as long, of course, as these operations did not conflict with 'gaining victory in the battle'. The General's response was to issue full instructions to every division under his command to cooperate in planning an operation. A special war room was set up at SHAEF headquarters to monitor information on the prisoners of war.

Intelligence arriving from the camps themselves was increasingly desperate in tone. Through clandestine channels, on 5 March a message arrived from the Senior British Officer at Oflag 79 near Brunswick with a request for 'either sufficient airborne troops to be dropped to guard the camp against SS and hostile Germans, or arms to be dropped to the POW'.[36] But if either troops or arms were sent they had to be in adequate numbers. The last thing the SBO wanted was what he called 'penny packets' – a few troops who would be hopelessly outnumbered by the guards, or a handful of rifles that would be useless for the prisoners to defend themselves with. He said that, in the event of the Germans going on the attack, he and his men would attempt to break out into the wooded country-side. In the hope of being rescued from the air, they would carry white cloth that could be laid out on the ground to make a letter P 15 feet high. In response to his and other requests, SHAEF stores stockpiled 20,000 rifles in containers in readiness for air drops.[37]

Other camps had been asking for help too – notably the inmates of the legendary Oflag IVC near Leipzig. Colditz Castle was a special-category prison camp. It held those hard-case escapers who had caused so much trouble to the Germans that they warranted the highest security, plus a group of VIPs – the '*Prominente*' as they were known. Some of the latter were high-ranking officers – Polish and French generals – but others were chosen for special treatment because of their family connections. One was Lieutenant John Winant, an airman whose father happened to be the American ambassador in London. Among the British *Prominente* were a nephew of Winston Churchill (Giles Romilly), two nephews of King George VI (Lord Lascelles and the Master of Elphinstone), the son of Field Marshal Haig, and a cousin of Field Marshal Alexander. There had always been a handful of these special prisoners housed at Colditz, but now others began to arrive, as if the castle was a collecting point for them.

Early in 1945, news of them was brought back to London by a sick prisoner who had been repatriated in one of the few exchange deals with the Germans. He thought the men in Colditz were in serious danger, and he went to the War Office to urge that 'when the time came, Oflag IVC should be the objective of a special parachute operation designed not to fail'.[38] There were other voices pitching in strongly for action there – among them Pat Reid, one of only a few British officers to escape from the supposedly escape-proof castle. He knew the rambling building's secrets as if he had been its architect. He had one very direct suggestion: 'Blow the garrison courtyard and the guard house to bits by very low accurate bombing and then drop arms in the inner courtyard and give the officers a chance to fight for their lives. Simply warn them to be ready and they will do the rest.'[39] The DPW were convinced, concluding 'it may well be necessary to organize some such drastic measure',[40] but when the suggestion was put to SHAEF it was turned down because Colditz was in an area which the Russians were expected to liberate and to send in a British task force would be considered provocative.[41]

But plans were now going ahead at great speed for military operations to protect those camps that fell within the British and American zones.[42] A SHAEF memo on 17 March spelled out the scale of the problem.[43] There were believed to be 257,000 British and American prisoners of war in the whole of Germany, of whom 97,000 were already in the British and American zones and would be joined there by a further 70,000 who were being marched by the Germans out of the Soviet zone. That left approximately 90,000 in the Soviet zone, to be liberated by the Red Army. It was on how best to protect the 167,000 in the western and southern parts of Germany that Eisenhower's planners concentrated their attention. To boost the POWs' morale, Allied fighter planes would fly over the thirty-five camps in which they were thought to be held, demonstrating Allied air supremacy to the prisoners, their guards and the surrounding civilian population.

It was now accepted that, as Churchill put it in a note to Roosevelt, there was a danger of 'a deliberate threat by Hitler and his associates to murder some or all of the prisoners' or to keep them as hostages.[44] He speculated that 'the object might be either to avoid unconditional surrender or to save the lives of the more important Nazi gangsters and war criminals, using this threat as a bargaining counter, or to cause dissension among the Allies in the final stages of the war'. These thoughts were echoed by Eisenhower in a message to the Combined Chiefs of Staff in Washington. He told them, 'Acts of violence may be perpetrated against prisoners of war and massacres might be instigated by SS troops or the Gestapo under cover of the general disorder.'[45] It would be no mean feat to stop this. The 'penny-packet' approach would not do. 'The camps are well guarded and [enemy] military forces may be in the vicinity, therefore protection of prisoners of war must be in force rather than in small detachments if it is to be effective.' That meant sending land troops into those camps close to the front line, and airborne troops into the camps further back:

Army Group Commander will be prepared to despatch relief columns to POW camps near their axes of advance, provided that such actions are not at the expense of the success of the main operations. First Allied Airborne Army will be prepared to despatch airborne detachments each of the strength of not less than one battalion for the protection of POW camps outside of reach of our advancing Ground Forces.

Once airborne troops had taken a camp, they would hold it until land forces arrived to relieve them. The prisoners would then ideally be sent back to the west by road, but the RAF and the USAAF would also be on standby to evacuate them by air if that proved necessary. 'These plans will cover protection from enemy action of the maximum number of camps possible in Germany and Austria containing United States/British prisoners of war.'

In the first instance, however, because information was unreliable, small reconnaissance teams would be dropped behind enemy lines near to the camps and would go to ground. Their task would be to send back intelligence and to open up two-way radio communication with the prisoners. Volunteers were called for from British, American and Belgian paratroopers to go on this 'dangerous' undercover mission, which was designated Operation Vicarage. One hundred and twenty teams were sought, each of three men. They were to include 102 British and American officers up to the rank of major. The group, according to its appointed leader, Brigadier J. S. Nichols, also needed 'an attractive title and proper status so members are proud to belong'.[46] So SAARF – the Special Allied Airborne Reconnaissance Force – was born, and began to assemble for training in England at the end of March 1945. The British Special Operations Executive (SOE) planned the training course with the help of the American Office of Strategic Services (OSS), and it was intended to have sixty teams ready for action by the beginning of May. 'The utmost speed and energy will be required and I look to all under my command to work flat out till our object is achieved,' the Brigadier said.

It was all remarkably similar to the sort of operation that Brigadier Crockatt, head of MI9, had taken to SHAEF planners back in October 1944, only to be sent away with a flea in his ear, his ideas dismissed as 'not considered practical' and 'not considered advisable'.[47] But now events had moved on, and what had once been impractical or inadvisable was not only possible but essential. The needs of Allied prisoners of war were now at the top of everyone's agenda. When a daring plan was conceived to drop hordes of secret agents into Germany to track down 100 top Gestapo leaders and assassinate them, the impact on prisoners of war was considered. 'Request your estimate as to the danger of reprisals on Allied POW in Germany,' the mission's planners wrote to those responsible for prisoner welfare.[48] The reply was thoughtful:

The enemy might well be tempted to indulge in reprisals but it is doubtful whether these would be serious or widespread since the number of German prisoners in Allied hands is now so much greater than that of US/British POW in Germany. The consciousness of immediately impending defeat would moreover act as a deterrent. It is therefore thought that the risk [to] Allied POW as a result of this plan is a reasonable one to accept.[49]

It was a helpful response, but what was most remarkable was that it had been requested in the first place. It showed just how significant the prisoners had become – and not before time, some might say.

Efforts on their behalf were redoubled after Eisenhower sent a round-robin memorandum to everyone involved in relief plans. The Rhine had been crossed. The drive into Hitler's heartland from the west had begun. Marked 'top secret' and dated 29 March, the memorandum said, 'Present rapid advances necessitate that preparations for relief of Allied prisoners of war should be completed.'[50] Operations to protect prisoners would now take priority over plans being drawn up to drop troops into Berlin and Kiel.[51] This new sense of urgency may well have been prompted by what Allied troops were finding on the other side of the Rhine. Eisenhower was told that American ground forces had liberated a prisoner-of-war hospital at the town of Heppenheim to discover 'shocking conditions, 53 of 309 having died of starvation, infection and lack of medical care'.[52] If that was the state of the hospitals, what must the camps themselves be like?

But there may well have been another reason why the release of the POWs had become a priority. It was dawning on the military planners that the prisoners might be a crucial factor in whether the war was to be won swiftly or whether there would be a long-drawn-out ending. Pat Reid's plea for special help to liberate the inmates of Colditz raised an issue that began to resonate among Allied military planners. Reid was convinced that the prisoners there were going to be taken away as hostages.

The SS will try to move them from Colditz to the centre of the Nazi ring, wherever that may be (their redoubt). Something should be done for them before they are shifted. I am not a brave man but I know that if I was offered a last chance to be free, preferably with a weapon, rather than becoming a Nazi hostage, I would choose the former course every time.[53]

The idea was taking root that the Nazis were planning to dig in for a last stand and to use the prisoners of war as hostages, prolonging the war for many months. The suggestion was not new, but suddenly it took on a new urgency. If this was the master plan, the evacuations, the marches, the refusal of the Germans to give up their prisoners against all odds began to make sense. It was the Allied military's greatest fear that they would become engaged in a lengthy and costly battle to winkle out the last of the enemy from the mountains of Bavaria and Austria. Now this looked increasingly likely. That Churchill believed that this was the plan is shown by a message he sent to Stalin on 21 March saying, 'it looks to me as if Hitler will try to prolong the war . . . by a death struggle in southern Germany and Austria'.[54] A US Army special report listed the evidence:

1. A German officer in Italy states that his troops would withdraw to become part of the Army Group being formed in Austria for the defence of the Redoubt.
2. Himmler has ordered that provisions be provided in the Vorarlberg

[an area in the mountainous region 90 miles south-east of Munich] in February for 100,000 men.

3. 1,800 Signal Corps men trained for mountain warfare have recently arrived in the Vorarlberg.

4. It is reported that with Hitler and Himmler, the Nazis will defend with 80 crack units of from 1000 to 4000 men each.

The Nazi Party's complete domination of German thought and action must be reckoned with. These people cannot surrender, and a determined continuation of the conflict must be expected so long as there remains a semblance of an army and terrain to defend.[55]

Everything pointed to 'a fanatical "last man" defence at the redoubt center'. And the Allied prisoners of war, held as hostages and as a human shield, would inevitably be at the heart of this resistance. A memo from Field Marshal Alexander, leading the Allied troops up from Italy and into the south of Germany, made this absolutely clear: 'May need substantial forces to evacuate/ protect POW.'[56] It was obvious that only a raid behind enemy lines, through either airborne forces or a special task force on the ground, could achieve this.

Then, out of the blue, an event occurred that threw into question the whole argument for sending troops ahead to fight their way into the camps and liberate the prisoners. Not for the first time in his career, the gung-ho American general George Patton went his own sweet way. He was notorious for his impatience, frustrated by what he saw as the overcautious advance of the British Field Marshal Montgomery and even his own fellow countryman General Bradley. There was a reason for the slowness. The Allied front line now stretched 450 miles, from Holland to the borders of Switzerland. With their backs to the Rhine, the Germans had been putting up the fiercest of fights, taking huge casualties but also inflicting them. The British alone had lost 6,000 men in their sector of the line in the latest push towards the river. But Patton, in the centre of the line, refused to take his time. He didn't want his Third Army to be 'sitting on their asses', as he put it, waiting for the war to end.[57] That would be 'foolish or ignoble', he declared. Ordered to wait until he had assembled four divisions before attacking the city of

Trier, he won it with half that number and then cabled SHAEF headquarters, 'Have taken Trier with two divisions. Do you want me to give it back?' Inevitably, his army was the first to cross the Rhine, on 22 March, and he was like a delighted schoolboy to have beaten Montgomery to it. As he marched over the pontoon bridge thrown up by his own men, he stopped in the middle, pulled down the zip on his trousers, and 'took a piss in the Rhine'. He felt invincible.

So invincible, in fact, that he went too far. The day after he crossed on to German soil on the east bank of the Rhine, Patton ordered one of his tank brigades to make a raid more than 40 miles into enemy territory. Its target was the prisoner-of-war camp Oflag XIII at Hammelburg. When his officers questioned such a high-risk mission so far behind the lines, one of the General's aides explained to them quietly that Lieutenant-Colonel John Waters, Patton's son-in-law, was one of the prisoners there. Captain Abraham Baum was put in charge of a task force of 16 Sherman tanks, 27 half-tracks, 3 self-propelled guns, and 300 officers and men. They set out on the night of 26 March, fought their way through the town of Hammelburg itself, and then smashed through the barbed-wire gates of the camp. The German guards fought back, there was a fire fight, and the casualties included Waters – shot in the thigh and the backside. The camp doctor, a Serbian, saved his life, performing an emergency operation with a kitchen knife. But the camp was taken, and 5,000 prisoners, most of them Yugoslavian but nearly 1,300 of them American army officers, were free – for now.

The task force prepared for its return, though it had room on its vehicles to carry only 250 American prisoners. Ironically, the wounded Waters was among the majority who would have to stay behind. It set off back the way it had come, but the path it had pierced through German lines to get to Hammelburg had now been closed behind it by three German divisions. The task force was, in the words of Patton's biographer Carlo D'Este, 'chopped to pieces'. Nine men were dead, sixteen were missing presumed dead, and there were scores of other casualties. The rest were captured and returned to Oflag XIII, which was now back in German hands. The liberators were now themselves behind barbed wire. Patton's raid had succeeded in increasing Germany's prisoner-of-war population by upwards of 250. They included Patton's own personal aide and bodyguard, Major Al Stiller, who had gone along on the mission 'for the thrills'.[58]

The Hammelburg incident showed the dangers of any mission to leap beyond the front line to protect and free prisoners of war. As news of it filtered out, it could not but give the planners at SHAEF headquarters pause for more thought.

There were always plenty of military men who saw ventures such as the raid on Hammelburg as too great a risk. Armed intervention to protect prisoners would always be fraught with danger, always threaten to lead to the loss of the very lives it was intended to save. Thoughts like these had certainly troubled Field Marshal Alexander when he put down on paper his conclusions about the Nazi redoubt and what should be done to save the Allied prisoners of war from being dragged to it. He stated his concern that dropping arms to them 'would provoke attack and the Germans could argue they forfeited their POW status'.[59] As in so many of the discussions about direct action at this time, the dangers seemed to outweigh the benefits, and his argument turned in favour of mounting a 'propaganda campaign to warn enemy that in event of molestation of POW, all personnel involved will be held to account as war criminals'.

Here was another manifestation of the idea that had been kicked around since the middle of 1944. The Germans must be warned not to commit atrocities, and that those who did would be rigorously hunted down and dealt with. The idea had recently been given a new twist by a man who had every reason to know what he was talking about. Brigadier George Clifton was a New Zealander who had been captured in North Africa, at El Alamein, in September 1942 and had been a prisoner at Oflag XIIB near Frankfurt am Main until the camp was evacuated and he had taken his chance to escape. An advance patrol of American soldiers had found him, and now he had a suggestion to make in the hope of saving the lives of the 268 other British officers he had been imprisoned with. He was fully aware of the dangers the prisoners faced, and thought 'the most effective action to prevent the massacre of Allied prisoners of war by SS troops would be to drop pamphlets informing the population that any hostile act would be followed by large scale air raids'.[60] He thought a similar threat would also stop the Germans moving prisoners again, instead of leaving them to be liberated by the advancing Allies.

Looking back, it seems extraordinary that explicit warnings like these had not been made to the German people already. The reason was that the wording and the timing of such a warning had for many months been caught up in the wrangling that was now beginning to bedevil relations between the Western allies – Britain and the United States[61] – and the third member of the alliance against Hitler, the Soviet Union. Disputes were multiplying and intensifying. The fate of thousands of prisoners of war had for a long time been in the hands of one dictator, whose grip on them was being prised open. Now another dictator – Stalin – threatened their liberty and even their lives.

8   Liberated by the Red Army

The German guard knew all about Russians. Though he was only eighteen years old, he could tell these soft Englishmen a thing or two about the real horrors of war. He had fought on the eastern front, the posting every German soldier dreaded. Stan Moss listened. He had just been through the worst experience of his own life, marching west from Stalag 344 at Lamsdorf in eastern Germany in the bitter snow, threatened with execution by the SS for looting – another word for stealing food to stay alive – sick with dysentery, seeing friends slaughtered in a hail of cannonshot from a passing fighter plane. But this, the young German told him at a camp where they had temporarily stopped to rest, was nothing compared with what he had been through, and his eyes widened, the terror visible in them, as he remembered trying to halt the Soviet advance. 'You mow them down,' he kept repeating, staring into space, reliving a memory that haunted him always, 'but they just keep on coming, from ahead, from the flanks, just coming at you, and you have no choice. You have to retreat.'[1] The Russians were devils: they were either superhuman or *Untermenschen*, but, whichever it was, they didn't care about life – theirs or anyone else's.

To prove his point, he told the story of a village near Leningrad that he and his company had recaptured. They had held it once, lost it to a Russian counter-attack, and then won it back. When they marched back in, they found a line of dead Russian women spiked by their genitals on the iron railings of a fence – a warning to other Russian women not to fraternize with the enemy. As the German told his horror story, Moss was not sure if the young soldier had really seen this himself or whether it was one of those incidents that had passed into myth. But it didn't matter, the message was clear: this was what the Russians did. Moreover, this is what they did to their own people. What could they be expected to do to their enemies? This question lay behind the visceral fear that was driving millions of refugees westward, away from the Red

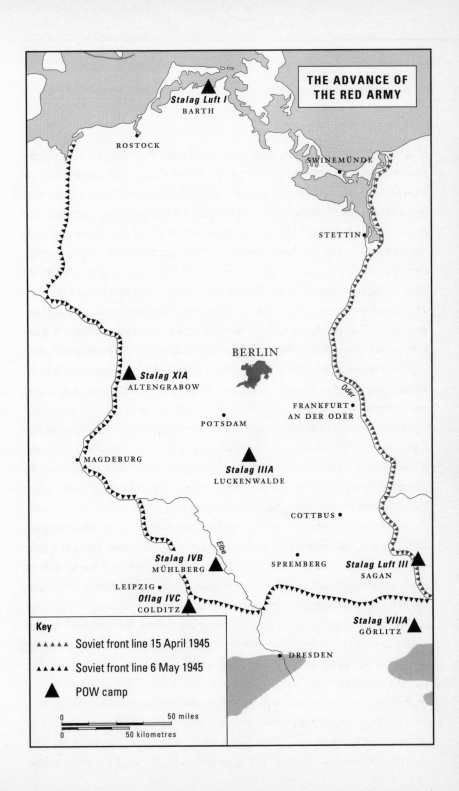

THE ADVANCE OF
THE RED ARMY

Stalag Luft I
BARTH

ROSTOCK

SWINEMÜNDE

STETTIN

BERLIN

▲ *Stalag XIA*
ALTENGRABOW

FRANKFURT
AN DER ODER

Oder

POTSDAM

MAGDEBURG

▲ *Stalag IIIA*
LUCKENWALDE

COTTBUS

Elbe

SPREMBERG

Stalag Luft III
SAGAN

▲ *Stalag IVB*
MÜHLBERG

LEIPZIG

Oflag IVC
COLDITZ

Stalag VIIIA
GÖRLITZ

DRESDEN

Key

▲▲▲▲▲ Soviet front line 15 April 1945

▲▲▲▲▲ Soviet front line 6 May 1945

▲ POW camp

0   50 miles

0   50 kilometres

Army's line of advance. To many a British or American prisoner of war thinking of lying low to be liberated by the allies from the east, the propaganda gave pause for thought.

Ron Walker, however, had a different view of the Russians, having seen the barbaric way the Germans treated them – worse than animals. Having been marched from Stalag Luft III at Sagan, he had ended up at Luckenwalde, designated Stalag IIIA, a huge holding camp south of Berlin, now home to tens of thousands of prisoners of all nationalities. He had arrived there more dead than alive from the march. Only the urging of a doctor had persuaded him to turn and face the world again instead of lying in his bunk and staring at the wall – a common enough condition in the camp to have its own name: 'pit-bashing'. Walker, an expert linguist, spoke German and was fast learning Russian, and interpreters were desperately needed. The job took him to the Russian compound, and he returned in tears, filled with disgust – and admiration. Until then he had tended to believe that the Russians were peasants and barbarians. 'I remember that when I first saw a Russian fighter plane I found it difficult to believe that a Russian would have the intelligence to fly one!'[2]

What he saw now was a revelation.

It was just unbelievable how anyone could survive in such conditions. It was dark in the barracks, because most of the windows were bricked up, and indescribably filthy. There was water and excrement swilling around the floor. No bunks, no straw, no tables or stools – nothing. And yet, unbelievably, the Russians, the Communists, the so called anti-God nation, had built an altar with a cross and decorated it with scraps of silver paper, bottle tops and fragments of broken glass which reflected the little light that penetrated the barracks. Whether my shock at finding it transformed I do not know, but it was one of the most beautiful things I have ever seen. So much love and patience had gone into its building, though they were literally dying of hunger.

He remembered the 400 Russians who had starved to death at a previous camp, and how he and his companions had tried to throw food to them over the wire, only to be stopped by the German guards shooting at them. 'The sad songs they sang in the evening will haunt me for ever.' Faced with a choice between the Germans and the Russians, it was no competition for Walker as he remembered the horrors he had seen – 'the Germans beating Polish women with sticks in a field, and the murder of our own friends as some, driven by desperation, tried to climb the perimeter fencing'.

The suffering of the Russian people is hard to comprehend. It was once said that to be born British in the nineteenth century was to have drawn a winning ticket in the lottery of life.[3] Similarly, to be Russian in the twentieth century was to be an abject loser. Generation after generation had been victims of one war or another. More than in any other nation, Russian women bore their sons for the slaughterhouse. Close to 2 million Russians died in the First World War – twice as many as the British, fifteen times the number of Americans. Then came the Revolution and five years of fighting between the Reds and the Whites. Then Stalin's purges, in which 10 million peasants were either executed or starved to death for resisting collective farming and an unknown number of dissidents were eliminated or sent to labour camps for what were dubbed 'crimes against the state'.

The Russian death toll in the Second World War was in the region of 17 million. Put starkly, Adolf Hitler's war cost the lives of 6 million Germans, and Joseph Stalin's resistance to him nearly three times as many Russian lives. Was it any wonder that the Russians behaved without mercy as they first reclaimed their own country from the aggressor and then proceeded to claim the aggressor's country for themselves? As they marched west, the Soviet troops were encouraged by commissars and political propagandists to 'kill, as you storm onwards, you gallant soldiers of the Red Army. Break the racial pride of these Germanic women. Take them as your lawful booty.'[4] Their ruthlessness was not excusable, but it was understandable. The Germans had had a word for the terror they deliberately inflicted on their eastern neighbours in order to subdue them. They called it *Schrecklichkeit*. Now it was being paid back with interest.

Fear of the Soviets was widespread, but those British prisoners of war who were among the first to get home via the Russian back door had reassuring stories to tell of their time as unexpected guests of the regime in Moscow. Captain N. Maclean of the Royal Artillery was too sick to walk and had been left behind in the hospital when his camp at Stalag XXB at Marienburg was evacuated at the end of January 1945 as the Red Army swept along the Baltic coast and into East Prussia.

As the camp emptied at top speed, he was one of just over 200 prisoners told by the Germans to wait for transport. It never arrived. Little more than twenty-four hours after the last of the column had gone, the spearhead of the Red Army rolled in and for a day and a night the hospital was in the middle of a battlefield. Medical orderlies ran around clamping steel helmets on the heads of bed-ridden patients and ushering those who could be moved to shelters. Finally the German resistance crumbled and the Russians took charge. Maclean had nothing but praise for his liberators. Over the next two weeks they 'produced as much food and medical comforts as they could, pillaged from the countryside. A Russian officer said he had reported our presence to Moscow and appeared to have some idea of the plan for dealing with recovered prisoners of war. He promised us we would receive visits from British representatives as soon as possible.'[5]

Then they were ordered to be moved back from the front line. The seriously ill went under escort, but the remainder were left to make their way east as best they could. It was a haphazard journey, in which they took transport where they could and walked if none could be found. Maclean described it as 'hitch-hiking', and it was apparently the normal method used by any Russian soldier moving to the rear. Some of his men decided to stay behind with Polish families they were billeted with, because it meant food and shelter rather than the uncertainties of the road. They were also slowed down by the lines of German prisoners of war being shepherded along the roads to the east, and by making sure that they were not caught up in the wrong columns. The fact that the British spoke no Russian and had to communicate with their liberators in German led to anxious moments. This was not a good time to be mistaken for a German.

A train took them to Warsaw, which the Red Army had liberated only a month earlier and which was now in ruins. From there they were directed south-east to Lublin, where they made contact with two American officers from the US Military Mission in Moscow.

Then they took a train to the Black Sea port of Odessa, which the Russians had decided should be the sole collection and exit point for POWs being returned to the West.

This journey was highly organized and on it we were excellently fed on American rations. At Odessa, we were received by a Russian general and his staff and then taken to a barracks to be deloused. The food they gave us was soup and fried cabbage – good by Russian standards. They appeared anxious to make a good impression. Our officers were supplied with beds, blankets and a mess complete with two waitresses. Other ranks were given straw mattresses and blankets.

Finally, they were cleared to leave. They received Red Cross 'comforts', were kitted out with new clothes if they needed them, and were then put on board a ship for the Middle East and then home. The War Office major who interrogated Maclean in London on 19 March, seven weeks after Stalag XXB had been overrun, noted, 'Captain Maclean considered that the Russians had done their best.'

Others, however, were discovering that Soviet hospitality was not always so generous.

*

Stalag IIIA was a brutish prisoner-of-war camp. Ron Walker, arriving there exhausted from Sagan, had begged to be let in as he and the rest of his column had been made to wait outside for hours in the rain and cold. Soon he would be desperate to leave. 'Our quarters here are by far the worst that I have encountered,' he wrote in his diary.

There are about 200 in our block and we are terribly crowded. This is an enormous camp, there must be about 10,000 of all nationalities including Polish civilians from the resistance movement. Today [it was 7 February 1945] our numbers were increased by the arrival of 5,000 Yanks who had marched from Frankfurt. They only have tents to live in and the straw that was put on the ground for them to sleep on is soaking. They do not have any water laid on and throw their water bottles over the fence dividing us for us to fill. One of our chaps was nearly lynched today when he was discovered demanding an American's watch before he would fill his water bottle. This place definitely does not bring out the best in people.

The sanitation appalled him beyond the point of disgust – a common complaint of Luckenwalde prisoners.

This camp stinks and I mean that literally! Lavatory arrangements were never very good in any of the camps I have been in, usually a big wooden hut where pits were dug and boards stretched across them. No privacy and no flush. Here however there is an added refinement. The pits are not emptied so that one has to search for a place where the excreta has not covered the boards. Couple that with a lack of paper and very limited washing facilities and it all becomes very depressing. If we're still here in the summer, God forbid, I believe a typhus epidemic is a certainty.

Eric Hookings, another RAF man who had been on the march from Sagan, lived in fear of falling in the latrine. It was no laughing matter. He had suffered so many indignities already, but this was his ultimate nightmare. 'There was a pole that you had to grasp to crouch over the pit. The terror was that you would fall in to what would be a horrendous death.'[6]

Another Sagan man, Leonard Pearman, thought Luckenwalde 'a terrible place', where only the indomitable fighting spirit of the men kept them from going under.[7] He realized too that it could only get worse, and it did as more prisoners flooded in every day, doubling the population. Some were new captives – many of them young American soldiers overrun by the Germans in the early days of the Battle of the Bulge, shaken to the core by their encounter with the battle-hardened Waffen SS and stunned to be behind barbed wire. Others were columns of marchers from the prison camps in the east, arriving exhausted and starved. Bunks were three-high; barracks were crammed; marquees erected on the muddy ground were soon filled to overflowing. With so much unhappy humanity to contend with, the Germans rolled out more barbed wire, making sure the compounds were cut off from each other, minimizing the chances of collusion and cooperative action. There were roll-calls all the time, but many men stayed in bed, too sick to make it on to the parade ground. The only thing that lifted spirits was a delivery of Red Cross parcels on 2 March – the first to reach the camp for two months. It felt like Christmas as peanut butter, meat, jam, sardines, salmon, raisins and chocolates were poured out and shared.

Amid the chaos, Ron Walker had developed a routine. In the morning he lay in bed and worked on his Russian phrase book. In the afternoon he tried to mend his clothes or did some washing – 'if there is any water coming through the taps'. And in the evening, when the electricity invariably cut out and there was no light to read, he would 'lie on my bunk and dream of home'. Hope sprang eternal:

Although today we have not enough to eat, to smoke, to read. Although we dare not wash too often, because we do not know how long our few cakes of soap will have to last and when we go to the lavatory we have to be careful how much paper we use because we may not get any more. Although hunger makes us watch our friends when they divide a loaf into six parts, ready to snarl if there is the slightest sign that one's own ration might be the smaller. Yet underlying all this there is hope, hope that before the summer has passed I shall be home, that I shall be sitting in the drawing room talking to my mother and my adorable little sister, yes, even my awful brother!

He longed to go 'for a quiet evening drive, stopping frequently to look at the view from the hill tops'. And, having been deprived of so much for so long, he longed to have possessions of his own – particularly to buy a house, 'preferably in the country for then it will be peaceful and beautiful', and to have a sense of permanence.

His dreaming contrasted with the discordant voices of the prison camp around him. They were mainly complaints: 'I am so cold, I haven't been able to feel my feet since we came here'; 'I'd just put one of my bed boards on the fire to heat a drink when the lights went out'; 'In her last letter she said she was going on holiday with Brian. So who the hell is Brian?' Food was a constant problem. The bread ration was cut, and seven of them would have to make a loaf last a day. 'In addition we get three-quarters of a mug of soup and the same of potatoes, enough margarine to cover one slice of bread and paste or cheese to cover a quarter of a slice. Twice a day we get a mug of mint tea or acorn coffee.' The arrival of some food parcels – one divided between five men – put the hunger on hold for an hour or two, but it was apparent that communications were now so bad that the chances of any more getting through were remote. Aircraft filled the skies, there were frequent raids, and the roads outside must have been nearly impassable. It would be several weeks before any more parcels arrived.

What was demoralizing was that the end had to be in sight, and yet it seemed as far away as ever.

Today is Saturday, just another Saturday wasted in a prison camp. Is it possible this one could be the last of the war? I keep on saying that the war will be over next week but it doesn't mean anything to me. I can't get excited or particularly happy about it. On the contrary I have been more depressed during the last few days than I was during the march and yet there is a very good chance that the war will end next week or anyway next month. I think I know the reason for this depression. I have had so many disappointments that my mind, or rather subconscious mind, refuses to accept what I keep on telling it is true. But maybe that is a good thing, maybe I'm trying to fool myself again. Oh God, I pray not. Please let this really be the end.

But who would their liberators be? That was the big question. Who would get to them first? The Russians advancing from the east, or the British and the Americans advancing just as rapidly from the west? For all his newly acquired sympathy for the Russians, Walker had no doubt that he would prefer to be set free by his own people. 'I would not mind the Russian front staying where it is for now and the western front moving closer. If that happened, we would feel much more secure.' Instead, the word whistled round the camp that they would not be allowed to stay to find out: the Germans were soon going to force them out on the road again. They would be marched somewhere – though whether east or west, north or south, no one knew. In Walker, the very thought 'produced the same feeling of despair as the last time'.

They had been at Luckenwalde for only three weeks when the first of these rumours of another evacuation began. For more than a month nothing happened, then, on 11 April, Walker noted that 'the second part of this nightmare has begun'. They were told to get ready to move again. But this time it was not to escape the Russian advance. A more sinister reason was suspected:

Evidently we are to be taken north to Berlin as hostages. Hostages for what? Are the Germans going to write a letter saying 'Dear Mr Churchill, please issue a warrant to allow Herr Hitler to go to South America or we will shoot all your RAF prisoners.' It's all going to end as I thought it would, in total chaos and farce.

It was a false alarm: they stayed put after all. But this failed to reassure Walker, who felt sure that he would never see his home again.

If we stay here, this place will probably become a battle zone and if we move our chances of getting to Berlin without casualties are not very high. Yesterday afternoon five Thunderbolts [US fighter planes] were playing around at about 3,000 ft without any opposition. How are we to fare if we have to travel on the railway which is being constantly attacked? Perhaps for once fate might be kind to us and the Russians start their attack or even our own army make a quick advance in the south and cut us off. What the hell anyway, I'm nearly past caring.

Two days later, however, they were marching – down the road to the train station, to be loaded into trucks. For a day and a night the train was shunted from one siding to another. It was noticeable that the guards were intent on currying favour with them: 'All they seemed interested in was telling as many of us as possible that Hitler was a *Schweinhund* and that they were anti-Nazis and always had been. We lay in the sun on the railway embankment, made ourselves hot drinks and discussed all the possibilities.' They painted 'RAF POW' in yellow paint on top of the wagons in preparation for the journey, and were glad they had done so after watching a train pass through the station pursued overhead by a dozen Thunderbolts. 'Next there was a large explosion and a cloud of black smoke coming back down the track. It was all very exciting but it did not fill us with enthusiasm to go on a train journey. Most of the very few trains running were travelling north carrying troops, coal and guns to defend Berlin.'

And then they were ordered off the train to return to the camp. They trudged back up the road – but with a lighter step, because, 'unbelievably', the Germans had provided transport for their packs. 'We had the feeling that we were not really under guard but just allowing ourselves to be taken back to the camp for a short time.' The stroll ended in dismay. While they were away, their barracks had been stripped by other prisoners – mainly the Poles. Walker found all the bed boards gone from his bunk, and had to sleep on a blanket slung across the frame. But the sense that tomorrow would be a day unlike any other day was overpowering, and he fell asleep 'a tired but very happy POW'.

His optimism was misplaced.

Within a few hours I was woken by a dull booming and vivid flashes which lit up our hut. I went outside and it was like looking into hell. The whole sky seemed to be filled with aircraft. They were pounding Potsdam, just outside Berlin. Flares of every colour were falling and below these was the top of an enormous smoke cloud which reached down to merge with the red glow of the fires below. It was so awe-inspiring that I felt physically sick and started to shake. This would undoubtedly finish the war but I had to wonder whether any nation had the right to employ such a diabolical means. And I wondered too what kind of people the Germans were to withstand attacks like that for so long or their leaders to subject their people to such horror.

Fear caused by the raid went deeper when there was yet another change of plan the very next day and the prisoners were told that they were going to Berlin after all.

We are to be moved in two days' time. We were also told that Berlin was to be turned into a fortress and defended to the last man. We are going to be hostages. There is a real possibility of being murdered. It seems this nightmare will never end. As soon as I dared to think that things were going to be okay, there is a new bombshell.

Fear was again the master, only to be again dispatched. They were not to be moved after all, 'and so all is well, once more!'

They could only wait. The Americans had paused at the River

Elbe after taking the city of Magdeburg 60 miles to the west. The
Russians were beginning to throw a ring of armour round Berlin
and were 40 miles away to the east. So near and yet so far. 'Am
terribly excited and nerves completely strung up, even finding it
difficult to write. Want to talk over possibilities and look at maps
all the time. The Germans worried stiff. Too bad for them. Several
sounds and sights of explosion clouds on the horizon today.' Again
they were woken in the dead of night and warned that they were
to move. 'We could only go north and that means either being
trapped in Berlin or getting through to the Lübeck area. Both
prospects are appalling, let alone the almost suicidal journey. Oh
God how I wish it were over.'

Walker put his faith in the Senior British Officer, Wing Commander Dick Collard, who was in constant talks with the Germans.
'I believe he may be able to keep us here long enough to allow us
to be over-run. If we do move and the opportunity arises I think I
shall try to escape. God, how I wish it would end. I never dreamt
it would be as uncertain as this.' Walker got into conversation with
a Russian prisoner, who assured him that life under a Communist
regime was fine. Living conditions in Russia were improving. 'He
thought that if the Russians over-run us we would be allowed to
live in Russia or return to England *if* we wanted to!'

*

And then the end came. Walker recorded the moment with calm
simplicity. 'I am no longer a prisoner of the Germans,' he wrote.
But events had been far from calm, or simple.

On the night of 20 April the German doctor had rushed into one
of the huts and called for the British doctor to help him. 'Come
quickly,' he said. 'Our orders have arrived.' There was a groan.
Most of the prisoners thought this meant they were about to be
forced out on to the road and up to Berlin. In fact the orders that
had come were in expectation of Russian tanks arriving at any
moment. The Germans were to defend the camp to the last man.
The doctor had been told to prepare for heavy casualties, and was
assembling all the medical help he could get. He fully expected
there to be casualties among the prisoners as well as the guards.

'The atmosphere was really tense, and then all the lights went
out. In the darkness we heard the sound of a violin being played.

It was so beautiful, so peaceful, so full of goodness that everyone stopped talking and listened in complete silence for the next hour. Whoever it was will never have a more attentive or appreciative audience.'

At midnight, the Wing Commander brought all his men together in the darkened barracks. He had no real news, but thought the stories of the nearness of the Russians were probably exaggerated. Equally, he doubted that the Germans would obey their orders to fight to the death. He wanted everyone to be on the alert and ready to do whatever was necessary to safeguard their lives. Precise plans were not made and, looking back, Walker could remember only his deep anxiety. 'Would we really have allowed ourselves to be shot? I don't know whether we would have done anything to defend ourselves, I just don't know. I think it came quite near though.' He went to his bunk that night grateful at least not to be en route to Berlin.

The next morning two German fighters flew low over the camp and fired their cannon at a target nearby. The prisoners assembled for the normal roll-call, and then at 10 a.m. the Germans began to leave. They went singly – and furtively – to begin with, then in pairs, and finally streamed away in large numbers, taking off their uniforms and slipping into civilian clothes as soon as they were through the gates. The prisoners crossed over the wire into what until now had been the death zone – put a foot over the warning wire and the guards would shoot to kill – and lined the fence to cheer them off. Walker noted that

by 12.30 p.m. there was just one old soldier at the main gate. As soon as he was alone the poor chap burst into tears but was quickly comforted by our chaps who gave him a cup of tea and a cigarette. There are some very loud explosions coming from just north-east of the camp and I am so excited that it is difficult to think.

Senior officers among the 20,000 Allied prisoners started to take command of the camp. Order had to be established, and looting stopped. Russian prisoners broke into the potato store, though no one begrudged them their booty – they had been starved for far too long – and when they were brought into line they offered no resistance. Meanwhile patrols were sent out to try to find the Russian front line. White flags were hoisted from the watchtowers, and a 'POW' sign was laid out in the compound as a signal to aircraft. 'There is a rumour that we have a transmitter so I hope we may be able to get in touch with someone,' Walker noted. Some German soldiers had surrendered rather than run off, and eighty were being held prisoner. The wheel had turned. The camp had also very quickly become a focus for refugees trying to escape the Russians. They stood at the gates and begged to be let in, among them a German general. He was turned away.

The day dragged on. It rained ceaselessly, and the cloud was low. Expectation turned to anxiety. Where the hell were the Russians? A patrol had returned with news that a German mechanized mortar unit was about half a mile away. What were they going to do? The town of Luckenwalde itself was deserted, and parties of ex-prisoners seized lorries and went looking for food. 'The Wing Commander has moved into the German headquarters. Good for him and I hope he can find a nice bottle of brandy!'

Walker contemplated the next few crucial hours of his life.

The alternatives seem to be either the Germans will return, in which case our German prisoners will be an embarrassment if they claim we captured them and they did not ask for asylum, or we shall be fought over, so I dare not think of home at this time. I had always considered that we might be shot just before the end of the war.

His fears were not groundless.

It is now 7 p.m. and after the ominous quiet some small-arms fire is coming from the woods, some explosions to the north-east and some fires to the south-west and east. At 8 p.m. a detachment of SS troops with a major in charge turned up. He seemed very angry and threatened to open fire unless we all returned to our huts, so we went! Where are those damned Russians?

They came at five in the morning – or rather *he* did. Just one man, a captain in a fur cap, arrived in a reconnaissance car. A little earlier three figures on horseback had been seen at the edge of the woods before they turned away and disappeared back into the trees. Presumably they had reported finding the camp. Now this officer had come. Remembering this half a century later, Leonard Pearman could still feel the emotion, his voice cracking as he recalled that 'marvellous, marvellous' moment. In the headquarters building, the Russian embraced the senior officers among the prisoners, put on an American hat, and then went back outside to find his jeep had gone. It had been taken for a joyride by excited POWs. When it was returned, he headed out of the camp with the two senior officers – and straight into the path of a German armoured vehicle just outside the gates. Shots were exchanged, but the jeep raced on and reached the main Russian forces, and at 9 a.m. on 22 April a lorry full of Russian troops arrived to formally liberate Stalag IIIA.

Walker, in the front row as an official interpreter, took in his first sight of the feared hordes from the east. 'They were an incredible mixture, some with immaculate uniforms covered in decorations and others more ragged than we were but all looking as tough as hell. Then came their spearhead, six T34 tanks and 12 open lorries. The tanks drove at the wire fences and right through them.' Another prisoner recorded how

with a big splintering crash the big double gates were brushed aside as if they were made of paper and to a tornado of cheering the Red Army rolled majestically down the central road of the camp between the compounds while hysterically-happy prisoners shrieked and waved and tossed cigarettes to the smiling crews. They were as tough a looking lot of men as you could possibly imagine, all bristling with weapons. Each man seemed to be equipped not only with a rifle but with a pistol and sub-machine gun as well. The leading armoured lorries were towing anti-tank guns while further back others towed mobile flak guns and mortars. The lorries were crammed with troops and they clustered on the backs and sides of the tanks like leeches.[8]

It did not go unnoticed that there were women in the column – nurses and soldiers – all armed, and just as frightening as the men.

There was still a battle to be won, however. German machine-gunners were firing from the woods. Two Focke-Wulf 190s screamed over the camp and strafed the compound. The Russian spearhead had to mop up the resistance here before moving on west in its drive to complete the encirclement of Berlin. Luckenwalde's 4,000 Russian POWs, starved and sick though they were, were thrown straight back into combat. Within half an hour of their army liberating the camp, they were rounded up, armed, and sent out to fight. 'They made a tragic spectacle as they marched out with their hammer and sickle flag flying but they managed a cheer as they left,' Walker noted. The other prisoners were not sorry to see them go. The Russians had scores to settle for all they had suffered under the Germans, and keeping control of the camp would undoubtedly have been more difficult had they stayed.

But the Red Army was anxious for even more manpower, and suddenly the atmosphere in the camp turned nasty.

A tank stopped in front of me and an enormous Russian officer brandishing a cane shrieked at me and others around to get on board and come and fight too. If the situation had not been so frightening the look of sheer horror on all our faces would have been really funny. Apart from the fact that POWs are supposed to be non-combatants, how do you explain, in the middle of a battle, that RAF officers just do not go to war like that? And anyway, we just wanted to go home! He took out his revolver and for a moment I thought we had had it but instead he just spat at us, which I suppose said it all! As he left, two other tanks followed and they had some German prisoners on board. God they looked wretched, poor bloody humanity!

One Russian officer had a girl with him, presumably a German civilian as she had a dress on rather than a uniform. However she seemed happy enough. She was laughing and hugging him. In the armoured cars that followed there were several girls, all dressed exactly like the men. One of them had an arm band showing she was a nurse but she still had a tommy gun slung around her back. She was about seventeen, blonde and very pretty with a big bunch of wild flowers tucked in her uniform. She gave me a lovely smile, the first time a girl had smiled at me for four years and it was wonderful. She was the one exception to all the other Russian troops who seemed fighting drunk and incredibly tough. They appear to think that being wounded is no reason to stop fighting. Many of them have bloody bandages on their arms, legs and heads but they are still brandishing their guns. I don't think we want to pick too many quarrels with them in the future.

Then, just as quickly as they had come, the rest of the Russian tanks left. They roared out of the camp, smashing through remaining sections of the fence as prisoners scattered to get out of their way, and drove off down the road until nothing could be seen of them except a cloud of dust in the distance. Leonard Pearman was almost sorry he had not gone with them, not taken up the invitation to go in the vanguard to battle for Berlin. 'They were marvellous,' he recalled – 'absolutely great. They were like us.' He felt new life in him – 'that we had hopes of living and getting home, and all because of them'.

It was only now that Walker grasped how lucky they were not to have been caught up between the two armies. Sixty minutes more and the bullets would have been flying everywhere. The Germans had pulled out of the town of Luckenwalde only an hour before the Russians arrived. The mayor had then come to the camp and surrendered to the senior Allied officer, a Norwegian general. 'That is why we were spared a full-scale battle being fought over us.' But skirmishing was still going on in the countryside to the north, and the prisoners were instructed not to go out of the camp. 'Some of our own chaps are ensuring that we don't.' There were also Germans to be rounded up who had tried to hide among the POWs.

The danger was clearly not over, because the next night the camp was strafed by a German fighter plane. Walker heard it approach and circle overhead before its engine note changed as it went into a dive.

Suddenly there was the most appalling noise just above our heads as it opened up with its cannon. It sounded like an enormous firecracker going off. The men in the second and third tier of bunks leapt off and crashed to the floor. I was on the bottom bunk and didn't have anywhere to go! Terror like this had happened to me just once before when I caught sight of the reflection of my burning aircraft just before I bailed out. Both times my mind flashed to home and my mother. Perhaps that is what happens when we think we are going to die – we desperately make one last grasp at the things we love.

But luck was on his side again. There were no casualties. Survival seemed more likely than ever now, even though shells from Russian guns were flying over the camp to targets in the distance.

Despite his confrontation with the Soviet tank commander who wanted the RAF men to join the fighting, Walker remained positive about the Russians, more of whom were now arriving.

This afternoon one of their colonels came to inspect the camp. He looked very smart in his brown uniform. Most of them seem extraordinarily decent and they are doing their best to help us. They bring us most things we want, though their method of obtaining these from the Germans in the town is quite straightforward. They ask quite politely but, if they are refused, they shoot. Some horrors in the camp have come to light. Six bodies were found in a hut in the Russian compound, together with a whip and several truncheons. I hope I shall never forget how cruel the Germans have been to the Russian prisoners, nor the indignities that I have suffered for the last four years. As far as I can gather the Russians have behaved in an exemplary manner. The Germans are very surprised, and well they might be because they don't deserve the slightest bit of mercy.

But others were less comfortable at finding themselves in Russian hands. Alan Clarke felt less safe than he had under the Germans. He remembered Russians stealing watches from Allied prisoners.[9]

Some Russian behaviour surprised Walker too.

Two of our chaps got hold of fishing rods and settled down at a nearby lake to wait for a bite. Along came a couple of Russian soldiers who watched them for a few minutes and then threw a couple of grenades into the lake. The surface was soon covered in dead fish, and the Russians just could not understand why our chaps were so angry with them.

There was a diversion for the Allied prisoners in the number of women in the Red Army ranks – and much raising of eyebrows.

There were 150 men, 50 girls, 11 male officers and 2 women. Some of the girls were quite pretty but all very squat by our standards. We had prepared four barracks for them, one for the male officers, one for the women, one for the male soldiers and another for the women. They nearly died of laughter when they realized we were trying to segregate the sexes, although there was no question that the officers would consider sharing the same billets as the soldiers. There is no segregation whatsoever in where they sleep or what they do. When they line up for inspection, the girls line up with the men in a completely random fashion. How does it all work? Quite simply, the penalty for getting pregnant as a front-line soldier is to be shot.

Other prisoners were forthright in their descriptions of the Russian women soldiers. 'Husky Amazons with large breasts and larger behinds,' said one.[10] This, however, could not be said of the interpreters who now arrived:

Young, smart, attractive and speaking good English, they were dressed in well-fitting, military-style tunics with stand-up close-fitting collars, short pleated skirts, silk stockings and jackboots. Each of the girls wore captain's rank epaulettes. The Norwegians invited one of them to tea. She told them that she had fixed up a nice little apartment for herself in the town and she then openly invited their Roman Catholic padre to come and spend the night with her. The poor man's embarrassment was extreme. He was a giant of a man, and we reckoned it was his size rather than his cloth that attracted her.

The veneer of civilized behaviour was thin. Pearman recalled a girl soldier sitting on a tank with an elderly German guard she had taken prisoner. She was holding a bayonet to the man's throat and asking the British whether she should slit it now or later. They remembered that he had been one of the more humane guards, so they called out, 'No, don't hurt him', and she stopped, though no one knew if she carried out her threat later. This undercurrent of violence and revenge was ever present. Walker, as interpreter, arranged for two of his friends to borrow rifles from the Russians to go out hunting rabbits.

Duly armed, they set out with two Russian soldiers. Not far from our camp the Russians had set up a cage for the German prisoners and on reaching this the Russians ordered out six of the Germans and told them to walk on down the road. 'Shoot, shoot!' yelled the Russians, followed quickly by two guns being dropped by my friends as, very shaken, they ran back to the camp as fast as they could. They blamed me for the misunderstanding, for getting my translation wrong.

But there was no misunderstanding when three Red Army deserters who had fought for the Germans arrived at the camp gate and asked for help. The Allied officers handed them over to the Russians, who marched them down the road and shot them.

The emotional side of the Russians came as a surprise, though it could be unnerving. Walker was introduced to a Russian officer, 'a huge man, well over six feet tall and in an immaculate uniform topped by a magnificent fur hat', who, after seeing how awful conditions had been in the camp under the Germans,

grabbed me in a bear hug which I thought would crack my ribs and said, with tears streaming down his face, 'Oh my eagle, my little eagle, how could they treat you like this?' Then again, you had to be terribly careful not to upset them, otherwise you were soon facing a gun. On seeing a Norwegian for the first time a Russian did not recognize his uniform and lunged at him with his bayonet. When he realized his mistake, he insisted that he came with him to the town, where they both got hopelessly drunk.

They are great drinkers. It seems to be their favourite pastime. At a recent dinner party for senior officers there were numerous toasts proposed by all present. By the time it came to the turn of our Wing Commander most of the heads of state and well-known generals had been toasted. He stood and named those three well-known generals Freeman, Hardy and Willis – in fact the name of a well-known chain of British shoe shops[11] – and the Russians solemnly tried to repeat the names while the British contingent tried to keep straight faces.

The men causing real trouble, however, were the French. 'Rotten eggs,' Walker called them. 'Four have already been killed in a brawl with some Russians and our chaps are constantly arresting them for thieving and other charges, their own officers having given up trying to control them. Oh how I want to get home. I'm tired, so tired, of it all.' His wish seemed close to being realized as news spread that the Russian and American spearheads had now linked up. There had been a historic meeting of troops of the US 69th Infantry and the 58th Guards Division of the Red Army on the River Elbe just 40 miles south of Luckenwalde on 27 April. East had met West with handshakes and smiles for the cameras on both sides. The next day the rumour was that there were Americans in Luckenwalde. 'Surely', Walker wrote in his diary, 'someone is going to get us out of here soon.'

Gradually he realized that the Russians did not share his sense of urgency. A bigger game was being played, and he was getting

very concerned about the political situation. There did not seem any military reason why the link-up between the Russians and the Americans took so long. What on earth is going to happen? I just hope this waiting to be evacuated does not go on for too long. I suppose the real problem is that for the first time I have allowed myself to acknowledge what a terrible existence this has been. Filth and squalor, appallingly crowded conditions, not enough food, hemmed in by barbed wire – and now I'm supposed to have been liberated it is just the same. Of course I'm still terribly grateful for the Russians driving out the Germans but I want to be home: not England necessarily – I'm afraid a lot of my patriotism and nationalism went a long time ago – but in my own home with my loved ones.

He talked to one Russian officer, who told him, 'Tomorrow we go to Berlin and then on to Paris.' The idea that the Red Army was planning to continue westward brought Walker up with a jolt. 'But what about the British and Americans?' he asked. The Russian replied, 'Oh there is no need to worry about them. They are tired of fighting and if not, well we shall have to see.' Appalled at the prospect that had just been unveiled to him, Walker asked himself, 'Is this the reason for the delay? Is another nightmare about to begin?'

Strains were beginning to show.

This afternoon a Russian general arrived at the camp. He had the most evil face I have ever seen and a temper to match. This exploded because although our Senior Officer sprang to attention and saluted him he did not stay at the salute while he addressed him, which apparently is customary in the Russian army. The general's escort cocked their guns and a tragedy was only just averted by some hasty explanations.

Nor, when he had satisfied himself that his dignity was intact, did the general have good news to convey. 'He said the exchange of prisoners was not a military matter but a diplomatic one. In his opinion we would be under their control for some considerable time.' The Russian proposed that the Allied prisoners of war should move to a different camp, with better conditions than Stalag IIIA. It may have been a humanitarian offer, but it had political implications too. The Senior British Officer refused. His orders from London were to stay put. 'He was quite adamant that we would not move from the camp until arrangements for our evacuation were made. After a flaming row the general stormed out but his last action was to order that the watchtowers be manned by Russian guards and patrols reinstated along the barbed-wire perimeter. We really are back to being prisoners.'

April was now turning into May, the Germans had been gone for more than a week, and Walker's trust of the Russians had turned to total suspicion. After witnessing – and interpreting – the exchange with the general, he sat in an office with a young Russian interpreter.

She is blonde, very shy, dressed in a uniform similar to our ATS. She is drinking a cup of coffee – but her free hand is fingering her tommy gun. They never let go of them. Looking at her I wonder what my feelings are for the Russians after today's events. Most of them are very friendly, but they have no idea of time and they are apt to promise the world and do nothing. Do I trust them? No longer, I'm afraid.

More and more prisoners were slipping away from the camp to try to reach the American lines on their own. But they were taking their lives in their hands. The situation was increasingly volatile. Next day fifty Cossacks rode into the camp, and although they had rifles slung around their backs they were all brandishing sabres. Never have I seen POWs disappear more quickly. Through the windows of our barracks we saw a Russian officer shouting at them, presumably telling them that we were allies. At that they galloped off, obviously disappointed that they could not have taken a few chunks out of us!

A few days later came the development that Walker and all the other Allied prisoners had dreaded. Events started well enough, however, with a few Allied prisoners getting away in individual acts of liberation. 'Some American jeeps came, their drivers looking for friends and relatives whom they took with them. In one of the jeeps was an American war correspondent looking for his son. He found him and they drove off. I bet that guy thought he had one great Dad.' But the rest had no choice. They would have to wait. Then came apparently the best news of all. 'We heard that the Americans were nearby with seventy trucks to take us out. I was so excited, so relieved, I wanted to weep.'

A convoy of Red Cross lorries arrived, and there was an altercation with the Russians at the gate before it was allowed in to take away the sick and wounded from the hospital. This did not bode well. The American trucks waited outside. Alan Clarke was in a group who managed to slip past the guard and get on one of them. He was gleefully shouting, 'We're going home, we're going home' when Russian soldiers ordered him off. When he was slow to comply they fired shots in the air, 'and of course we all jumped off and we were back in camp again'. Flight Lieutenant Tony Barber (later to be a prominent British politician and Conservative Chancellor of the Exchequer) was climbing on to a truck when a burst of machine-gun fire went over his head. He quickly got down.

The Russians had refused to accept the credentials presented by the American drivers. Confrontation loomed as the Americans were given five minutes to leave. They were told to get back to the River Elbe, where the US military advance had halted, or else they would all join the prisoners behind the barbed wire. The convoy left. Patrols of Russian soldiers were then sent out to round up those prisoners who had attempted to get away. Armed guards were stationed round the camp at 50-yard intervals, and another cordon was set up 2 miles away. The prisoners – for that is what they were again – were warned they would be punished if they tried to leave.[12]

Walker's anxiety was complete:

So where does that leave us? Will the convoy come back or not? I just don't know whether it is deliberate obstructionism by the Russians or just masses of red tape, because most of them are still very friendly and try and re-assure us that everything will be fine. I just wish they would not keep on saying that we will be really welcome in Russia! I think we must remember what the Russian general said. 'The exchange of prisoners is a diplomatic one, not a military one.' So presumably they will not let us go until Moscow gives the okay.'

Barber had no doubt about what was happening – 'we were being held as hostages'.[13] This was confirmed by the Senior British Officer at a parade the next morning. Hookings recalled, 'He told us, "I'm sorry, chaps but we're not going back with the Americans. The Russians won't let us." That's when the fear started. We thought we were going to be shipped off to Russia, to Siberia, and into their labour camps.'

In his diary (it was now 7 May), Walker recorded his frustration and his fear:

The Russians have at last stopped pretending that they care about us. Five miles away there is a convoy of empty trucks waiting to take us home but we cannot get to it because we are surrounded by Russian guards who shoot at any attempt to cross the wire. It is an absurd and dangerous situation and I have had enough. So within a few days all the goodwill, all the parties where sentiments of undying friendship between the Russians and ourselves were made, have resulted in this. Is this how the future is to be? Is the defeat of the Germans going to end in a war with Russia?

Meanwhile, Pearman was told explicitly by a Russian colonel, 'I'm very sorry. I know how you feel, but I am not allowed to let you go until the Yalta Agreement has been fulfilled.'

'The Yalta Agreement?' the bemused Englishman roared at the Soviet officer. 'What the hell is that?'

9   Hostages of Stalin

The carve-up of Germany had begun even before the chicken had been fully plucked. And the kitchen table where the three most powerful men in the world met to pick over the carcass was Yalta, a town on the Crimean coast of the Black Sea. Inevitably, bones would be broken in the process. In a fifty-room white-walled palace that had once belonged to the Tsar but which had since gone to seed and was riddled with lice, Stalin, the Soviet leader, entertained his Western allies, Churchill and Roosevelt. In a week of talks, beginning on 4 February 1945, they divided Hitler's collapsing Third Reich into zones of occupation[1] and redrew the borders of Poland in a way that would soon make 6 million Germans refugees. Like gods, in seven days they created the post-war world. As a side issue, they also nodded through a deal that all prisoners of war would be returned to their countries of origin, regardless of the wishes of individuals.

It was Churchill who raised the matter, telling Stalin that 10,000 Russian prisoners of war in Britain had already been returned home but that 90,000 remained. What did the Marshal want done with them?[2] Unspoken by the British Prime Minister was the fact that large numbers of them were Russians who had defected to the Germans and had been captured wearing the uniform of the *Wehrmacht*.[3] Stalin asked to have them back 'as quickly as possible'. The Soviet government looked on them all as Soviet citizens, he said. He requested that there should be no attempt to induce any of them to refuse repatriation. As for those who had fought for the Germans, 'they will be dealt with on their return to Russia'. The threat drew no comment from Churchill or Anthony Eden, his Foreign Secretary. Instead, the Prime Minister agreed that the prisoners should be repatriated, and said the only difficulty was finding the ships to take them home. Earlier there had been some dissension within the American ranks. In pre-conference discussions with the Russians, the Secretary of State, Edward Stettinius, unhappy with the idea of forcible repatriation, had tried to argue for a less all-encompassing definition of the phrase 'Soviet citizen'. Knowing this was non-negotiable with Stalin, Roosevelt had simply bypassed his colleague's sensitivities.

Churchill then turned to the issue of British prisoners of war who had been liberated by Stalin's troops, and begged for them to be well treated. 'Every mother in England is anxious about the fate of her prisoner sons,' he told the Soviet leader. Stalin's response was that 'very few' had been liberated by his armies as yet, but there would probably be more soon. He agreed that British officers should be sent to Russia to help get them home. On the following day, 11 February, all this was enshrined in a formal agreement signed by Eden and his Soviet counterpart, Vyacheslav Molotov.[4]

The agreement was a confirmation of what had been happening for some months anyway – at least as far as the British and Americans were concerned. Already a shipload of prisoners of war had been sent back to Russia from Britain, and there had been unfortunate scenes at the dockside. The Americans – after first resisting compulsory repatriation but then falling into line with it because of anxiety for their own prisoners – had had the same experience. In December 1944, Soviet prisoners of war held in a camp on the west coast of the USA were sent home, but not before several of them had committed suicide by jumping into the sea from the ship they had been forced to board.[5] The need to cooperate with the Russians had become more urgent as the Red Army moved closer to the camps in Poland and eastern Germany containing British and American prisoners of war. A War Office memorandum on 22 January 1945 noted unequivocally that 'one of the reasons for us repatriating Russians has of course been the question of the treatment likely to be accorded to our own men, and I think this point is now assuming greater importance'.[6] This was not the time to be stalling, and a troop ship was pulled off other duties to speed up the process. The Chiefs of Staff were anxious that the political quid pro quo should be pressed home. They asked the Foreign Office to make sure that 'the generosity of our action should be impressed upon the Russians with the object of obtaining the maximum chance of reciprocal treatment for any of our men who may fall into Russian hands'.[7] That was the hope. That was the deal. The big question after Yalta was whether the Soviets were playing the British and American game or one of their own choosing.

Sir James Grigg, the Secretary of State for War, was quick to have serious doubts. He was no admirer of the Russians. As allies they were loyal only to themselves – they 'did very little for anyone's beautiful eyes but their own', as he later expressed it.[8] The ink was barely dry on the agreement with them when he took up his pen to voice his anxieties to the very man who had signed it. On 22 February he wrote to Anthony Eden that the Russians were stopping British liaison officers from travelling beyond Odessa into the Soviet-occupied interior, even though this had been a specific requirement agreed at Yalta. 'We shall therefore know nothing about what is happening to our prisoners until some of them arrive at Odessa. If, as I suspect, they bring back stories of hardship and even maltreatment, we shall be responsible for not having done more for them, and public opinion may well be inflamed against the Russians.'[9] He guessed that hundreds of British servicemen were 'wandering' in Poland and southern Russia without anyone looking after their interests, and he was worried for them. He suggested threatening to delay the next batch of Soviet prisoners due to be sent home from Britain. Eden replied with reassurances. Moscow had now given entry visas to British liaison officers, he said, which dealt with the immediate difficulty. He was not minded to issue threats to hold on to Soviet prisoners. He thought it would 'not be wise . . . and in any case we are most anxious to get rid of these people as soon as possible'.

The Russians, however, were still insisting that any Allied prisoners went home the long way round. Instead of sending them west, they sent them east, to Odessa, and many were, as Grigg feared, getting lost on the way. Some would not make it at all. Eight liberated British prisoners died in a train crash at Kraków on their way from Katowice to the Black Sea. Twenty-three were seriously injured, and another fifteen hurt.[10] Then a group of British Army medical staff arrived in Odessa with news that they had had to leave sick and wounded companions behind at numerous hospitals. In Odessa itself, as the British ambassador reported, numbers were building up, but little was being done to get them home. There were problems in finding ships – or so the Russian authorities claimed. The situation was further complicated by Stalin's man-oeuvrings over Poland, where a struggle was going on for control. Moscow backed a pro-Communist interim government; the British and Americans wanted free elections. The American ambassador in Moscow was certain that Molotov, the Soviet Foreign Minister, wanted to link the return of British and American prisoners to recognition by Washington and London of the Moscow-backed puppet government in Warsaw. The British ambassador agreed, describing Molotov's attitude as 'blackmail'.[11] The stage was set for retaliatory action.

Once again the Foreign Office in London urged caution. It was reluctant – frightened, some might say – to send Molotov a formal complaint. 'Our impression is that generally speaking the case that there is ill will has not yet been proved,' an official wrote to the ambassador in Moscow.[12] It was thought that the slowness in getting prisoners home simply reflected the inefficiencies of life in the Soviet Union rather than anything more sinister. 'We should avoid protests which might be interpreted as charges of bad faith and concentrate on inducing Russians to produce more rapid results on the basis of the Crimea Agreement [at Yalta], which, if properly interpreted and applied, should give us all we need.' The ambassador in Moscow concurred. 'There is some evidence of neglect and maltreatment of our men,' he cabled back, 'but I agree it is better not to bring forward such accusations without full chapter and verse.' A week later the Foreign Office woke up to reality and urged the ambassador into action. It was receiving far too many reports of Allied prisoners still stuck in Poland. The British liaison officers must be given full licence to go and check on them. 'You should leave the Soviet authorities in no doubt of the very great importance attached to prompt visits being paid,' the ambassador was instructed.[13]

The kick in the pants for the Foreign Office appears to have come from Churchill. Told by Eden that there were problems brewing over the return of prisoners, he sent a personal note to Stalin regretting that there seemed to have been 'a lot of difficulties since we parted at Yalta'.[14] 'We are very much distressed,' he wrote.

There is no subject on which the British nation is more sensitive than the fate of our prisoners in German hands and their speedy deliverance from captivity and restoration to their own country. I should be much obliged if you would give the matter your personal attention as I am sure you would wish to do your best for our men, as I can promise you we are doing for your men as they come into our control along the Rhine.

The reference to the Rhine was significant. Now that the Western Allies had crossed into German territory, the prisoner-of-war camps in the west were about to be liberated. And by far the largest single national group in these camps was the Russians. There were close on 500,000 of them in the combined British and American sectors. Those terrible marches from the east had in fact changed the balance significantly, leaving just 123,000 British and American prisoners of war in the Soviet sector.[15]

Stalin – the 'Bear', as Churchill called him – replied promptly, full of sweetness. 'You have no grounds for anxiety so far as British prisoners-of-war are concerned,' he wrote.[16] Then he tried a little sharpness. 'They are living in better conditions than was the case with Soviet prisoners-of-war in English camps, when the latter, in a number of cases, suffered persecution and even blows.' Then he dissembled. 'Moreover, there are no longer any English prisoners-of-war in our camps. They are en route for Odessa and the voyage home.' The date was 23 March, and at that time the statement was true. But the Red Army was advancing on more camps – Luckenwalde for example – with clear instructions not to let the British and American prisoners go home until Stalin was certain he had cemented his control of Poland.

The Americans also had difficulties with the Russians.[17] Shortly after the Yalta meeting, the US Military Mission in Moscow had established that there were at least 3,000 American prisoners of war in Soviet hands, whereas the Kremlin had owned up to only 450. Most of them were stuck in Poland, but when a request was made to send in a team of liaison officers to make contact with them it was refused. As with the British, the Russians were willing to allow US representatives to go to Odessa, but no further. The interior was a no-go area. The Military Mission was stunned at this blatant violation of the agreement at Yalta, but, along with the US embassy in Moscow, it reacted cautiously. A confrontation with the Russians would be in nobody's interest. The Americans were mindful that they wanted the Soviet Union to join the war against Japan once Hitler had been dispatched. Moreover, the realities of the situation were that they had no way to force the Soviets to speed up the repatriation of American prisoners of war without a public show of hostility – and an open split among the Allies at this stage would not help win the war. Gentle diplomacy – rather than outrage – was the only way. For public consumption, problems with Stalin were to be downplayed.

On the ground, however, negotiations continued until, after ten days of wrangling, Moscow finally granted permission for a US team to set up in Poland. Led by Colonel James Wilmeth, on 28 February it flew to the city of Lublin, where from the outset the Soviet military authorities put every possible obstruction in its way. The Americans were virtually under house arrest in their hotel, and, though they had flown in on a transporter plane with their own jeep, they were made to use a Soviet driver. Every move was watched. At night Soviet troops slept in rooms next to theirs. Wilmeth had no communication with the outside world. The telephone operator had instructions to cut him off every time he tried to ring the US embassy in Moscow. Meanwhile, the American prisoners they did come across confirmed to Wilmeth that there were thousands of others like them wandering around in Poland without help or transportation, and that some were even locked in 'Soviet concentration camps, where they received practically no food, no news, no nothing'.[18] In Lublin, the Allied prisoners – 91 Americans and 129 Britons[19] – were being kept in a ramshackle building with broken windows, no doors and no heating. They slept on benches or on the floor. They said they had wandered around Poland for a month without getting any help. They told of being beaten, robbed and kicked by Red Army soldiers.

Wilmeth wanted to arrange air transport to fly them out. The Russians refused to allow it, insisting on the overland route to Odessa and then an exit by ship. A phrase slipped into the agreement at Yalta gave them this right. The original document had given each side the choice of transport for taking its prisoners home. At the last minute, Soviet negotiators had inserted six deadly words: 'in agreement with the other party'. As American historian Patricia

Wadley has concluded, 'This change in Article 4 gave the Soviets total control over the movement of American and British prisoners-of-war. In effect the United States and the British had agreed to a hostage situation. Allied prisoners would be held at Odessa and returned only when the US or UK repatriated Soviet prisoners-of-war.' With no alternative, Wilmeth put the prisoners – now numbering 267 – on a train to Odessa.

The Russians expected Wilmeth to leave Lublin too, but he refused to, adamant that he would wait for more strays to turn up, which they did. Picking up a propaganda line that Radio Moscow and the Soviet press had been pursuing ever since Yalta, the Russians told him how abominably the British and Americans were treating Russian prisoners of war in the west. In the ever souring atmosphere, Wilmeth retorted that he was sick of Soviet lies and the failure to cooperate. The whole repatriation exercise, he now realized, was being run not by the Soviet Army but by the secret police, the NKVD. For the Russians, this was a political operation, not a humanitarian one.

They were, however, capable of embarrassment. Wilmeth's suspicions were raised one day when he was invited to visit a hospital in Lublin, where he found seven newly arrived American prisoners of war. They were survivors of what the Russians fell over themselves to explain had been an accident. A camp in Poland – Stalag IIIC – had been liberated, but a Soviet tank had fired on the inmates. Many had been killed, and these seven were among the wounded who had survived. The Soviets offered explanations – a mix-up, a misunderstanding – and said they were very sorry. Wilmeth had no choice but to accept their story.[20]

He finally left Lublin on 28 March – much to the relief of the Russians, who were desperate to get foreign observers out of Poland. Stalin's designs, his intention to turn that country into a satellite of Moscow, were not for the eyes of prying Americans. When the head of the US Military Mission in Moscow, General John Deane, requested permission to fly to Lublin to join his colonel, the answer was no. It came personally from Stalin, breaking the word he had given at Yalta.

Like the British, the Americans protested at the highest levels. Averell Harriman, the US ambassador in Moscow, asked Roosevelt to have a word with the Marshal. Stalin replied in the same way as he would do to Churchill a fortnight later. He could not see what all the fuss was about. His people were dealing swiftly with all American prisoners they encountered, but in reality they had not come across many of them, and those they had were already in Odessa waiting to go home.

Harriman knew this was a lie, and he told his president so. It was proving impossible to get the Russians to stick by the terms agreed at Yalta. Harriman suggested 'retaliatory measures which affect their interests' – some economic sanctions, plus restricting the movement of Soviet liaison officers in the west.[21] But retaliation was more than likely to backfire. By insisting on their right to move any prisoners of war they liberated eastward to Odessa as the first leg of the journey home the Russians had bought themselves valuable time. If the Americans wanted a speedier repatriation, they would have to play the game the Russian way. Roosevelt fired off a bad-tempered letter to Stalin: 'This Government has done everything to meet your requests. I now request you to meet mine' – but there was no sting in the tail. Stalin responded with the absurd claim that there were only seventeen Americans in Poland. He then accused the United States of mistreating Soviet prisoners of war and also of failing to return a number who had been captured in German uniform. The arguments were just going round in circles.

Relations with the Soviets seemed to be touchy on all subjects now. The politicians and diplomats were going through the same experience as Ron Walker in the camp at Luckenwalde. He had started with an open mind about the Russians, prepared to put aside the propaganda – of which there had been a lot since the Communist revolution of 1917 – and, as he might have put it himself, speak as he found. What he first found was a people who had suffered terribly but were misunderstood, and after his initial happy encounters with them he thought the Soviet Union 'deserves an apology for all the lies and slanders our press printed before the war'.[22] But, as we have seen, the reality slowly dawned as he became their prisoner, and a pawn in a ruthless game of international politics. In the Allied corridors of power, the same thing was happening. Of necessity, doubts about the regime in Moscow had been put on hold; the great betrayal of 1939, when Stalin had temporarily sided with Hitler, was forgiven, if not forgotten. London and Washington were prepared to speak as they found. And what they were finding now was deeply perplexing and deeply worrying. Their so-called ally was obstructing their every move.

For example, it was still proving impossible to get an agreement on issuing a warning to the German people not to ill-treat Allied prisoners of war. On 22 March, Churchill complained in a letter to Roosevelt and Stalin that he had proposed this through diplomatic channels as far back as October 1944 and was still waiting for a response. Roosevelt cabled back the very next day with his approval, 'if Marshal Stalin agrees'.[23] But the Marshal was not saying anything. Not yet, anyway. In dealing with his partners, he was prone to make trouble for trouble's sake. In the final weeks of the war, he never lost his suspicion that the British and the Americans were on the brink of making a separate peace deal with some faction or other inside Germany – a deal that would leave him out. He always reacted badly to any hint that Nazi leaders like Himmler or Goering were seeking their own self-serving agreements with the Western Allies – almost as badly as Hitler did when he got to hear about them.[24]

Churchill's correspondence with Roosevelt was now filled with his worries about what he called 'the deterioration of the Russian attitude since Yalta'.[25] He was concerned by the increasingly clear signs that Stalin was not going to back down over Poland. He felt he had been 'defrauded'. Barely six weeks ago he had returned from the summit in the Crimea and told the House of Commons that Britain could trust Stalin. Now, if he was honest, he would have to admit this was no longer true. 'Surely,' he said to the American president, 'we must not be manoeuvred into becoming parties to imposing on Poland – and on much more of Eastern Europe – the Russian version of democracy?' Desperately he wrote to Stalin on 31 March, 'It is as a sincere friend of Russia that I make my personal appeal to you and your colleagues to come to a good understanding about Poland with the western democracies and not to smite down the hands of comradeship in the future guidance of the world which we now extend.' There is nothing to suggest that he got any response. The Soviet Union was going its own way. Just six weeks later, Churchill would make his first reference to an 'iron curtain' coming down over eastern Europe.[26]

As attitudes hardened, direct action was taken. With the Russians now about to arrive at camps full of British and American POWs, such as Luckenwalde in the middle of Germany, Grigg wrote again to Eden with his fears for Allied prisoners of war. 'It is essential that the Russians should hand them over to the Americans at the earliest possible moment' and not 'send them marching back to the rear to turn up some time later at Odessa'.[27] Plans were drawn up to prevent this happening at one particular camp. The newly created Special Allied Airborne Reconnaissance Force, whose hand-picked teams were in urgent training back in England under their commander, Brigadier Nichols, would get their first chance to go into action.

The target was Altengrabow, 45 miles west of Luckenwalde and about 25 miles ahead of the front line of the American Ninth Army at the time the plans were drawn up.[28] One camp, Stalag XIA, was known to be there, but the area could be overflowing with prisoners evacuated from the east. Reports put the numbers there at nearly 150,000, of whom 10,000 were thought to be British and 8,000 American, though the figures were admitted to be guesses. A secret drop would have to establish the facts without provoking the Germans into retaliatory action against the prisoners. Then ground troops could go forward from the American front lines to liberate the camp or camps.

Just after midnight on 25 April, six teams of three men parachuted into the area and discovered that the camp was in a bad way. There was little food, and an epidemic of typhus was beginning. Fortunately the number of prisoners had been grossly exaggerated. There were 20,000 in all, of whom 2,000 were British and American. However, conditions were deteriorating badly. It was also suspected that a detachment of the Soviet 28th Army was very close by and would probably reach the camp before the American front line could overrun it. Contact was made with the German commander in the area and, after delicate negotiations, he was persuaded to agree a truce so that the British and American POWs could make their way to the Allied lines, which were now just 15 miles away. The British and Americans headed west with a thousand of the sick. Hundreds of French and Belgian POWs made it too before further evacuations came to a halt on 4 May, when the Russians arrived and, in the words of the official report on the operation, 'ordered all evacuation suspended'.[29] The SAARF team headed back smartly to their own lines, leaving thousands of Russian and Polish prisoners in Red Army hands. If the Russians had been after more hostages – if they had been under orders from Moscow to seize the British and American prisoners in Stalag XIA just as they had at Luckenwalde – they were too late. Thanks to Brigadier Nichols's raiders and a deal struck with the Germans, these pawns had been taken out of the game.

As April ended, the Russians began to show signs of relenting. Their tight grip on the situation relaxed a little. Now it was just a squeeze. In Moscow, the Ministry for Foreign Affairs suggested that, since the American and Soviet armies had now met at the River Elbe, there was no reason why prisoners of war could not be handed over across the front line. It was what the Allies had wanted all along – no more trips home via Odessa, 2,000 miles away. But George Kennan, the US chargé d'affaires, was suspicious. He thought the Soviets were, as usual, serving their own interests. This was really a way of getting Russian prisoners in the west back as quickly as possible and cutting short any debate about those whose status as Soviet citizens was in doubt.

But, by suggesting repatriation across the lines, the Russians had made it an issue for the military to get involved with, as opposed to just the diplomats. General Eisenhower displayed his impatience. From Supreme Allied Headquarters he told General Deane at the US Military Mission in Moscow that he wanted the 'thousands of US and British prisoners-of-war held in close confinement under unsatisfactory conditions' by the Soviets brought out by plane immediately.[30] If the Russians were being uncooperative, they had better shape up or 'there may well ensue most undesirable consequences'. His view was bolstered by a report from the Norwegian general who had been the senior officer at Luckenwalde. He told American diplomats that conditions in the camp were 'extremely bad', and that the Russian major who had taken charge was usually drunk and his men were 'venting their resentment' on the prisoners.[31] When these points were put to the Russians, they protested their innocence. But they did agree to a formal meeting to resolve all problems, and on 16 May all sides got together in the

German city of Halle. The war with Germany, it should be said, was now officially over, and had been for more than a week. Berlin had fallen to the Red Army, and Hitler had killed himself in his bunker on 30 April. The German forces had surrendered to General Montgomery on 5 May, and the armistice had come into force on 8 May, VE Day. Surely it was time for everyone to go home.

Eisenhower sent his Chief of Staff, Major General Raymond Barker, to Halle. There he found himself facing a Soviet delegation of forty officers – eight of them generals – and a bodyguard of fifty troops. They were all heavily armed with pistols, rifles and machine-guns, and had brought a radio truck for instant consultation with Moscow.

At the first session, Barker proposed the use of aircraft to bring the British and American prisoners home. The Russians flatly refused. They would not allow Allied planes to touch down on what they considered to be their territory. Moreover, the Russian delegation had no powers to negotiate. They had come with their orders, and they would not deviate from them. Barker had no doubt in his mind that the prisoners were now in effect hostages.[32]

The price being demanded for their release was a fresh endorsement of the Yalta Agreement, with an added pledge that it would be complied with 'to the last degree'. Barker stood his ground. There was no need for this. 'Since an agreement had already been signed between the three Governments on this subject, it was superfluous to enact any further ones,' he recorded. They were there to work out practical details on how the Yalta Agreement could be implemented. After spending hours on the radio phone to his superiors, the senior Russian general relented, and they got down to business.

One issue almost wrecked the talks completely. The Soviets insisted that no Russian prisoner of war should have to walk. Transport must be provided for the whole distance. The Americans pointed out that this was simply impractical. While every effort would be made to provide trucks, they could not be guaranteed. It was a point the Russians reluctantly conceded, and an agreement was signed. Prisoners would be 'delivered through army lines to army commands on each side' at specified points.[33] At last the Luckenwalde 'hostages' were coming home.

*

Many at Stalag IIIA had not waited around for the international wrangling to take its course. They had seen which way the wind was blowing, and after years as prisoners of the Germans they were not about to submit to the prospect of new jailers. Ron Walker's despair turned to anger and then to action. He packed his kitbag and, with four friends, made his escape.

We found a part of the wire that been damaged by the Russian tanks, crawled underneath, slipped past the Russian sentry, and ran like hell for the nearby woods. We stuck to the woods until we were about 2 miles from the camp, and then started walking west along the road, diving into ditches when any Russian vehicle appeared.

Towards evening we saw an American convoy heading east in our direction. The last lorry stopped, and we piled in. When the driver realized who we were, he turned round, put his foot down, and we went at a hell of a rate until we reached the Elbe. Crossing it was the greatest moment of my life. The nightmare was over. I really was going to get home.

When we arrived at an American camp, the commanding officer welcomed us. 'You'll find everyone here willing to help you in any way they can,' he told us. 'Good luck, and may you soon be back where you want to be.' These were the first kind words I had heard for four years.

Walker had two thoughts nagging at him. First, he was concerned about what was happening back at Luckenwalde. Second, he realized he had disobeyed the 'stay put' order and 'I will probably be in big trouble when I get home. My only hope is that just before I left there was a strong rumour that the Commanding Officer had, due to the extraordinary circumstances, withdrawn his order for us to remain in the camp. I can only hope it was true.'

It was not true. On the contrary, Wing Commander Collard, worried about the gun-toting Russians and their belligerence after the American trucks were turned away, confined the entire British contingent to the camp. Ironically, it was 8 May, VE Day – the day when all hostilities were to cease. He resigned as Senior British Officer in protest at the prisoners' treatment. Leonard Pearman and Alan Clarke had both attempted to get away in the US convoy and had been hauled back by the Russians. Now all they could do was wait and hope. On 19 May a Russian general brought news of the talks going on at Halle and promised them they would be leaving the next day. He was true to his word. The next morning there were 100 trucks waiting, and the POWs climbed aboard, twenty-five men to a truck. 'You are going home, we are taking you to the Elbe, all is well,' a Russian driver told Pearman.[34] But the Englishman was not totally convinced. Half in jest, he called out to his mates, 'Don't let them fool you, we're going to Siberia.' A Russian officer turned on him and said in perfect English, 'Oh no, no. You're not going to Siberia, you're going home to England. You will see.'

It was a tortuous journey through countryside devastated by war. Road bridges had collapsed, and detours had to be found through fields and woods if necessary. It took eight hours to drive the 60 miles to the Elbe. There a convoy of American trucks was waiting to pick them up. With whoops of joy, they climbed down from the Russian lorries and boarded the American ones. For some it was then a brisk ride across a swaying pontoon bridge – built by US engineers to replace the normal road bridge, which had been blown up – and they were on friendly soil at last. Others walked or went on barges. Alan Clarke remembered crossing the river and seeing a batch of Russian prisoners of war coming in the opposite direction, heading east. He didn't give a thought to what the Russians were going home to. 'We were just pleased to be going home ourselves. We didn't know anything about what would happen to them.'[35]

The fate of those liberated Russian prisoners of war would not be clear for years to come, though senior politicians and military commanders must have had an inkling at the time. Certainly they would have realized there would be no mercy for those who had fought in German uniforms.[36] But it was perhaps too incredible to think that Stalin would really exact revenge on every one of his soldiers who had been taken captive, dubbing them all traitors, murdering them, driving them into labour camps, filling his Gulag with them and their families. Even if such thoughts did cross the minds of Western leaders, they could not be allowed to dictate policy. Hitler was the enemy. Stalin was an ally without whom the war could not be won. If unpalatable decisions were made, deals struck with the devil, then it was because, as the German guards used to tell their prisoners with a knowing shake of the head, *Krieg ist Krieg* – war is war.

Decades later, such decisions have been condemned by some. The forcible repatriation of Russians at the end of the war became a cause célèbre in the mid-1970s and the 1980s, when allegations were made against British politicians and military men about the circumstances in which Cossacks who had fought on the German side had been returned to the Soviet Union to be executed in the last weeks of May 1945. These Cossacks were described as 'victims of Yalta', and their fate led to bitter public controversy. But it is hard to see what else could have been done at the time.

Could Stalin really have been resisted? Almost certainly not. Churchill knew that Britain was exhausted – and bankrupted – by six years of war, and he was not about to prolong hostilities if he could avoid it, and certainly not with a different enemy. Meanwhile the Americans had one eye on Japan and the Pacific, where there was still a ferocious war to be won, and were desperate to switch their focus there.[37] Stalin was the one with the appetite for more bloodshed. Despite the losses the Soviet Union had taken – or perhaps because of them – the Russians were prepared to continue the struggle. It was uncanny how often Red Army soldiers would tell their British and American counterparts that, after taking Berlin, they were ready to march on to Paris and London even. Uncanny and frightening. The truth is that Stalin won the peace in Europe because he alone had the stomach for more war.

Those British prisoners of war held in Luckenwalde and other camps overrun by the Russians were part of a necessary bargain struck at Yalta. RAF airman Leonard Pearman had no doubt that the Cossacks paid the price for him to go home. In an interview conducted at the Imperial War Museum in London in 1989, he was emphatic that, if the Cossacks had not been forced back across the border into the Soviet Union, then he would not have been returned home for many years, if at all. 'Many of us felt it would be a very dismal outlook for us if the terms of the Yalta Agreement were not carried out,' he said. 'We would have been sent to Siberia.'[38] He quoted with approval a statement attributed to Grigg, the Secretary of State for War, in 1945: that 'if the choice is between hardship to our men and death to Russians the choice is plain'.[39] Even after Pearman and his Luckenwalde compatriots had crossed the Elbe and were in safe hands, thousands of British and American prisoners of war were still waiting to be returned in other battlefronts throughout Europe. At the very time that the Cossacks were being dispatched to the Soviet Union, US military sources estimated there were still 15,597 American and 8,462 British prisoners of war in Soviet hands, waiting to be allowed home.[40]

In one instance it is claimed that the release of British and American prisoners of war by the Russians was directly conditional on the handing back of a particular traitor, high on Moscow's wanted list. The camp in question was Stalag Luft I at Barth, a small town on the Baltic coast. It had 6,000 air-force prisoners in late 1944, but numbers had swollen to more than 9,000 by the spring of 1945. Eighty per cent were Americans. It had a reputation as a good camp to be in: the facilities were fair, as was the regime, and morale was generally high – dipping only towards the end, when for six weeks there was a severe shortage of food supplies. Even this privation was short-lived. Red Cross parcels were piling up at Lübeck, and prisoners were allowed to drive lorries the 80 miles along the coast to stock up. Morale was restored to such an extent that Luft I was the one camp where, with the Russians approaching, the prisoners refused German orders to evacuate. The Senior American Officer, Colonel H. Zemke, told the German commandant that he had a trained 'fighting force' who would resist any attempt to move them, and that, though his men could arm themselves only with knives and clubs, there were thousands of them against the hundreds of guards and in the end they would prevail.[41] The commandant decided to avoid any bloodshed, marched his own men out, and surrendered the camp to his prisoners. Zemke sent out scouting parties in two directions – east to locate the Russians and west towards the Allied front line. The ones who went east ran into a Russian patrol just 20 miles away.

On 2 May the Russians arrived. Gordon Hemmings recalled, 'Cossack types on horseback, mostly armed with Tommy-guns and mostly drunk.'[42] The prisoners all put on white armbands with 'American' or 'English' in Russian on them, and were treated with respect. The German population in the town was attacked mercilessly. 'These Russians were nothing more than savages armed to the teeth. I saw one of them with three or four gold pocket watches on chains hanging from his hand, and he was swinging them against the wall and appeared to be highly amused at the way pieces flew off them.' Things settled down when the main force arrived and a Russian colonel took charge. The prisoners turned their efforts to clearing mines from a nearby airfield, in the hope that they would soon be flying home. The suggestion that they would be going via Odessa instead was depressing beyond belief, and VE Day was enlivened only by ceremonially burning down the camp watchtowers.

It was then that the two senior Allied officers decided to push matters along. They contacted the local area commander of the Red Army, who received the all-clear from Moscow for an evacuation by air. Hemmings said:

The next morning [12 May] we were told to be ready to leave at three o'clock. Nobody really believed it. But we marched out of the camp and as we got close to the airfield we heard the sound of approaching Fortresses and we had to believe it. I was in the fourth aircraft. We took off at five o'clock and three and a half hours later we landed in England.

Could it really have been that simple, given the Russians' down-right refusal to allow evacuation by air at any other of the camps they controlled? Historian Patricia Wadley thinks not. Four hundred miles away, on the far side of Germany, a renegade Russian general was being handed over to the army he had deserted three years earlier. The much decorated and highly regarded Andrei Vlasov had been captured by the Germans in 1942 and had joined forces with them against Stalin. Hitler allowed him to recruit a 50,000-strong Russian Liberation Army from Russian prisoners of war. He and his men had ended up in Czechoslovakia as the war came to an end, and it was there that they had surrendered to the Americans. The Soviets were desperate to get their hands on Vlasov, and a deal was struck. Citing confidential government records in

Washington as her evidence,[43] Wadley says he was handed over in return for the agreement to airlift the prisoners of war out of Barth. 'Vlasov was handed over at 2.30 p.m. on May 12,' she says. 'US bombers, which had been circling the Barth airfield, were allowed to land at 3.30 p.m.'[44]

Vlasov was executed in Moscow. Hundreds of thousands, perhaps millions, of his fellow countrymen met a similar fate. The captain of a British ship, the *Empire Pride*, saw what happened for himself after delivering a cargo of Russian prisoners of war to Odessa. Thirty of them had gone under protest, and they spent the entire journey locked in cells. When the ship docked, these men were singled out and

marched or dragged into a warehouse 50 yards from the ship and after a lapse of 15 minutes automatic fire was heard coming from the warehouse. Twenty minutes later a covered lorry drove out of the warehouse and headed towards the town. Later I had a chance to glance into the warehouse when no one was around and I found the cobbled floor stained dark in several places around the sides and the walls badly chipped for about 5 feet up.[45]

For many Russians, home proved to be a terrible death trap. But this was a time when the lives of many prisoners of war hung in the balance all across Europe.

10   Waiting for Patton

From below they would have looked as if they were dropping bombs, but what fell from the Allied planes was not death and destruction. Not this time. Instead, thousands of leaflets fluttered through the air like snowflakes caught in the wind. They dropped to the ground with their message to the German military. Do not think of taking revenge on Allied prisoners of war, the Germans were urged. Their safety is the responsibility of every single one of you, and you will – have no doubt – be called to account.

It was 23 April, and the warning that had been discussed among the Allies for so long had finally been issued. The message – repeated over the radio – fell on a Germany that was collapsing in ruins. The main Allied force had crossed the Rhine just a month earlier, and since then Bradley's and Montgomery's tanks had been rolling east across the flatlands of western Germany almost unopposed. Field Marshal Walter Model's Army Group B, ordered by Hitler to dig in and defend the industrial heartland of the Ruhr, had been surrounded and 325,000 German soldiers had surrendered, among them thirty generals and an admiral. In the south-east, the Russians had taken Vienna. In the north-east, the road to Berlin was wide open.

It was already a time for dying. Model, who just months earlier had wished long life to his Führer and declared that 'none of us gives up a square foot of German soil while still alive',[1] had driven to a forest near Düsseldorf and blown his brains out rather than go into captivity. Others more fanatical than he might wish to take as many of the enemy with them as they could. For those so tempted, there were easy targets in the dozens of overcrowded prisoner-of-war camps in areas soon to be overrun by the invader. For now, the inmates were fish in a barrel.

Winston Churchill had made desperate efforts to have the warning issued a month earlier. In a strongly worded telegram to Roosevelt and Stalin urging them to approve his plan, he told them:

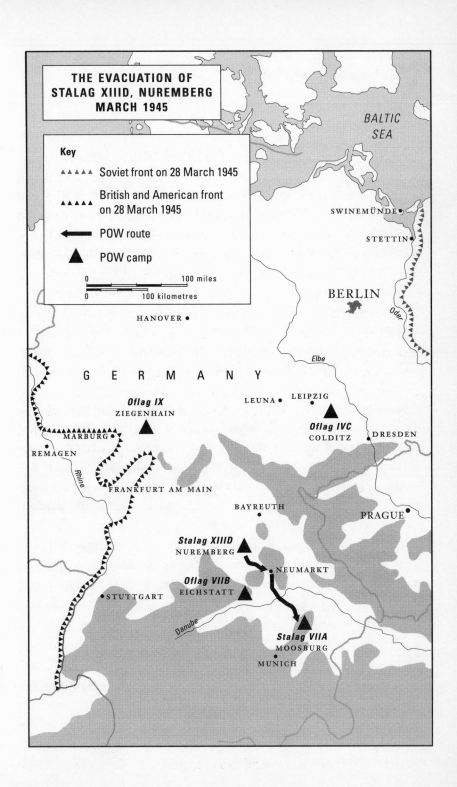

THE EVACUATION OF
STALAG XIIID, NUREMBERG
MARCH 1945

Key

▲▲▲▲▲ Soviet front on 28 March 1945

▲▲▲▲▲ British and American front
on 28 March 1945

← POW route

▲ POW camp

0   100 miles
0   100 kilometres

BALTIC
SEA

SWINEMÜNDE•

STETTIN•

BERLIN

Oder

HANOVER •

G E R M A N Y

Elbe

Oflag IX
ZIEGENHAIN ▲

LEUNA • LEIPZIG
•

MARBURG•

Oflag IVC ▲
COLDITZ

DRESDEN•

REMAGEN•

Rhine

FRANKFURT AM MAIN

BAYREUTH
•

PRAGUE •

Stalag XIIID ▲
NUREMBERG

•NEUMARKT

Oflag VIIB ▲
EICHSTATT

•STUTTGART

Danube

Stalag VIIA ▲
MOOSBURG

MUNICH •

We have long foreseen danger to these prisoners arising either in consequence of chaotic conditions resulting from a German collapse or out of a deliberate attempt by Hitler and his associates to murder some or all of the prisoners. The object of this manoeuvre might be either to avoid unconditional surrender or to save the lives of the more important Nazi gangsters and war criminals, using this threat as a bargaining counter, or to cause dissension among the Allies in the final stages of the war.[2]

He accepted that bombarding Germany with leaflets was not a foolproof method for preventing a massacre:

An SS general is now in charge of prisoner-of-war matters in the German Ministry of Defence[3] and the SS and Gestapo are believed to be taking over control of the camps. On such people a warning will have a limited effect, though at the worst it can do no harm. On the other hand, it is by no means certain that the SS have completed taking over from the regular army officers and on them the letter might have real effect. We should surely miss no opportunity of exploiting any duality of control.

Roosevelt agreed to an immediate release of the warning. Stalin, playing power games, stalled. Urged again by Churchill three weeks later, he insisted that the warning had to be signed personally by all three heads of state (which would now mean Harry S. Truman for the Americans, since Roosevelt had died). That meant another delay. Then the French decided to get involved. De Gaulle wanted his name on the leaflet too.[4] Finally – with the horrors of Buchenwald and Belsen having just emerged[5] – the Russians suggested that the wording be changed at the last minute to include concentration-camp inmates as well as prisoners of war. It was not an unreasonable suggestion, but, given that the Russians had liberated Auschwitz three and a half months ago, it could have been made earlier.[6]

Agreement was finally reached, the planes went out with their leaflets, and the Germans were put on notice. 'The governments of the United Kingdom, the United States of America and the Union of Soviet Socialist Republics,' the message said,

here issue a solemn warning to all commandants and guards in charge of Allied prisoners of war in Germany and German-occupied territory and to members of the Gestapo and all other persons of whatsoever service or rank in whose charge Allied prisoners of war have been placed. They declare that they will hold all such persons, no less than the German High Command and the competent German military, naval and air authorities, *individually* responsible for the safety and welfare of all Allied prisoners of war in their charge.

Any person guilty of maltreating or allowing any Allied prisoner of war to be maltreated – whether in the battle zone, on the lines of communication, in a camp, hospital, prison or elsewhere – will be ruthlessly pursued and brought to punishment.

An excuse of 'acting under orders' was specifically ruled out. 'This responsibility [is] binding in all circumstances and one which cannot be transferred to any other authorities or individuals what-soever.'[7]

Against all expectation, there was no response from Berlin. No threats were issued in return. The month before, Hitler had issued what has become known as his 'Nero Order', which was an instruction to burn and destroy anything useful – whether military or industrial or economic: a bridge or an armoured car or a store of grain – rather than see it fall into the hands of the invaders. Then, on 16 April, from the bunker in Berlin, he tried to rally his troops for one last time with bloodthirsty threats and historical grandiloquence, as if he were still on the podium at Nuremberg and the Nazi faithful were massed before him, hanging on his every hate-filled word.

All his darkest thoughts were about the Russians – 'the Jewish Bolshevik arch-enemy', as he called them – who were 'attempting to smash Germany and to eradicate our nation. You soldiers know what fate is threatening German women, girls and children. This time the Bolshevik will experience Asia's old fate. He will bleed to death in front of the capital of the German Reich.'[8] It was time to fight, not to run, he thundered.

Whosoever does not do his duty at this moment is a traitor to our nation. The regiment or division that leaves its position acts disgracefully. Whosoever gives you a command to retreat is to be arrested and executed immediately, irrespective of his rank. In this hour the entire German nation looks to you, my soldiers. By your fanaticism, by your arms and by your leadership, the Bolshevik onslaught [will be] drowned in a blood bath.

Ironically, however, the greater threat to Allied prisoners of war at this time was coming not from the dictator, besieged and just a fortnight away from taking his own life, but from bombardments by their own side.

*

Bill Ethridge's fears about how easy it was for bombers to miss their target had been totally justified. Back at the beginning of February he had arrived at Stalag XIIID at Nuremberg after the journey from Sagan, picking his way round the bomb craters in the road outside. These were the work of American bombers – B-17 Flying Fortresses – being flown by men just like him. His life depended on them being able to tell the difference between friend and foe from 27,000 feet. During the next months he looked up and was able to pick out the distinctive yellow wing tips and tail sections of planes from his own 447 Bomb Group as they headed for Nuremberg and its vast railway marshalling yards – twenty-five tracks wide in some places – which were no more than 2 miles from the camp. He took what comfort he could from them. 'The raids surely endangered us in the stalag but they also meant the increasing certainty that Germany was losing the war and we would soon be on our way home.'[9]

The bombing went on day and night – American B-17s from dawn until dusk, then British Lancasters and Halifaxes in the dark. The prisoners – those not too weak from lack of food as the daily ration was cut by half – dug foxholes and trenches in between snowstorms, and waited and watched. Joe Cittadini could not take his eyes off this grand spectacle of Germany's defeat. At night, British pathfinder planes would come in and drop parachute flares and incendiaries to light up the target area. Anti-aircraft guns would open up from either side of the camp.

Then for the next half hour the heavy bombers would fly in. The first bomb would get us out of our crude beds to huddle around the windows. Explosions lit the sky over Nuremberg, and we would count the seconds until the sound reached us to work out the distance. They were just a mile away. Our wooden barracks would shake with the tremor. It was exciting and disquieting. Then, during the day, American bombers in rigid formations came over to bomb the same targets.[10]

The sight of Mustang fighters nonchalantly drifting overhead and banking lazily from side to side at about 3,000 feet thrilled the prisoners. There was no opposition. German fighters were conspicuous by their absence. But Allied domination of the air brought terror too. Colonel Walter Arnold of the US Army Air Corps, commanding officer in one of the compounds, would never forget one raid when panic swept through his men. 'They were crying, yelling, wailing and praying. One young airman threw his arms around my waist and fell to his knees hugging my legs, in such distress, lost and frightened. I told him and the others that Jesus Christ would protect us.'[11]

To Bob Neary, the attack on the night of 16 March was 'magnificent, yet horrible'.[12] He threw himself into a slit trench when he first heard the sound of engines in the distance. Then the rumble got nearer and turned to a roar as wave after wave of bombers dumped their loads into the city. 'It soon became a raging inferno and the night was as bright as day from the flares and the fires. Anti-aircraft shells were exploding in the sky like fireflies, and spotlights were desperately probing the heavens. Falling planes were on fire from wing tip to wing tip.' John Parsons wept as he watched an RAF plane brought down. 'It was hit and it made a sharp left turn and came back towards the camp. Then, just outside the fence, sheets of fire were coming out of it. I saw this fellow trying to get out, but the plane exploded and he went up with it. Many of the planes were hit and didn't make it back to England.'[13] And after each raid the stench of cordite and smoke hung in the air for hours.

Private Len Jepps, a prisoner since 1940, who had recently arrived at Nuremberg from Lamsdorf, felt the full force of the Allied bombing when he was sent into the city to bring back a small supply of Red Cross parcels that had unexpectedly turned up in the rail yard. He thought himself strangely invincible as the bombs rained down – 'as though it wasn't possible for us to become the victims of our own forces after we had travelled so long a road and lived to tell the tale'.[14] These were foolish thoughts, as he realized when he surveyed the damage around him afterwards. 'It was chaos. Huge locomotives and wagons were strewn in all directions and fires were burning everywhere. An ammunition train was on fire and hundreds of thousands of rounds were going off like a firework display. Oil tankers were blazing, sending up huge columns of black smoke.'

While Nuremberg burned, the prisoners froze. There was little coal, and fires were kept going only by tearing planks from buildings in the camp. This was a risky thing to do – punishable by death, they were warned. John Parsons took a chance and was stripping wood from a latrine

when I realized there was a guard standing 3 feet away from me. He reached in his holster, took out his weapon and stuck it right in my face. Somehow I managed to distract him and then I just ran like you never saw anyone run before in your life. I got to the window of the barracks, which fortunately was open, and I just threw myself right through it. I got down in the lower bunk and covered myself up with a sack. The guards came through and poked bayonets here and there and walked out. I was lucky as hell.

'Home seems pretty far away right now,' Ethridge thought as he wrote a letter to his wife, Mary, not knowing what were the chances of it getting through. News came over the hidden radio that the Germans were blowing up all the bridges along the Rhine to try to slow the Allied advance. 'We are hoping that the big push is NOW!' The gloomy faces of the guards told him he might well be right. One was overheard saying the war would be over in a few weeks. Why else was the camp loudspeaker blaring out 'In the Mood' and other American dance tunes?

Hunger became a serious problem. Joe Cittadini remembered the Germans providing rancid cheese and soup in which the only protein was the worms floating in it – which was 'kind of discouraging'. The POWs consumed the soup without looking too closely. Moose Moulton recorded that he had been a prisoner of war for exactly a year and 'I have never been so hungry in my life.'[15] His weight was down to 100 lb (just over 7 stone) from 190 lb

(13.5 stone). He wrote in his diary that 'my ribs are sticking out like the black keys on a piano and my legs look like a scarecrow's'. The next day he did not have the energy to get himself out of bed. 'If only parcels would come.'

For others, sleep offered no relief. At night Ethridge would sit up in his bunk because lying down made the stomach cramps unbearable. Supplies could not get through to the camp, and 'I savoured my last piece of Spam, along with one of my two remaining pieces of bread. Along with a bowl of thin barley soup earlier this morning, that's all the food for today. I have enough food on my person to last for about four days, if I am careful. After that, I don't know.' But then, as if by a miracle, food parcels arrived by the lorry load. Six Red Cross trucks arrived from Switzerland. Ethridge gorged himself on toast with real butter, and mashed potatoes with cheese on top – 'PLUS gravy from a can of liver pâté and powdered milk! For dessert, chocolate pudding. A great day!'

The relief and the joy were such that the Senior American Officer, Colonel Darr Alkire, offered to share the food with the guards, whose supplies had also run out. This was seen as 'a smart gesture', particularly since he had earlier been bold enough to make an official complaint to the commandant about violations of the Geneva Convention.[16] He argued that the camp was dangerously close to military targets and that no proper bomb shelters had been provided, that food supplies were 'less than that required for basic metabolism' and of such poor quality that there was a danger of disease, that the barracks were overcrowded with 'only 19 sq. ft of floor space and 119 cu. ft of air space per man', and that there was no heat, a shortage of beds and blankets, poor lighting, and inadequate washing facilities. The prisoners suffered from rats, mice, lice, bedbugs and fleas. Fifty rolls of toilet paper were expected to last 5,000 men more than a month. There was no chapel, library or theatre. He had a suggestion. Let the prisoners march to the Swiss border – which was 150 miles away to the south-west – and stay there until the war was over. Nothing had come of this, but, as Cittadini noted, 'it was heartening to see our thoughts recorded in this manner'.

In the end the prisoners were moved – though in the wrong direction. At the beginning of April, Patton was said to be just 55

miles away with the US Third Army, but the Germans made it
clear that the prisoners were not going to be allowed to stay
around to be liberated. They were to march *south-east*, to Bavaria.
Fortunately the weather had taken a turn for the better – sunny
and warm, the first days of spring after weeks of snow and cold.
The prisoners were in two minds. They would be moving away
from the Allied front, but they would be spared the bombing, which
in the last few weeks had become intensive to the point of shattering
nerves. While some were almost happy to be on the road again,
Moulton was less sure. He had logged every single air raid on
Nuremberg in the past three weeks – there had been 125 in all –
and some had come too close for comfort. But his legs had been
wrecked on the march out of Sagan and had not fully recovered.
'Got my back-pack ready but we are all so thin and weak that I
doubt that I could march again with my knees in such bad shape.'
The next day he wrote:

We are ready to go again. I have put my name on the hospital list due to
my damaged knees. At least our bellies are full right now [they had
stuffed themselves with every bit of food they had left] and the way
Patton is driving eastward right now we might be overtaken. Expect the
war to end very soon but can't tell what the Germans will do. Russians
are driving west too. What is going to happen? We'll see very soon.

They left on 3 April. As they marched out through the gates, they
looked back to see Nuremberg ablaze once more. Ahead lay only
uncertainty. But Ethridge was sure of one thing: 'I will not miss
this place.'

*

While the marchers set out south from Nuremberg, forced out of
the immediate reach of General Patton and his army, there was a
camp 150 miles to the north which was directly in the line of
General Bradley's line of advance. Oflag IX was near the village
of Ziegenhain, and it had been a welcome sight for those English
prisoners of war who had arrived there a month earlier after a 600-
mile march from the east. It had shelter for one thing, even if it was
under canvas, and the *promise* of Red Cross supplies, though none
actually came. Jim Badcock, a navigator in Bomber Command,

arrived there on 12 March 1945.[17] He and his fellow prisoners had been on the road for forty-nine days, tramping across the middle of Germany from Stalag 344 at Lamsdorf, close to the border with Poland. They had experienced the same horrors as others whose journeys we have traced more closely – freezing cold weather, hunger to the point of starvation, sickness and exhaustion. They had seen friends drop out and left to die. Now the survivors from the east had a new home, even if it was perilously close to the battle-front.

The main camp was full of French and Russian prisoners. There were also some American and British troops captured fairly recently, either at Arnhem or in the Battle of the Bulge. The 750 new RAF arrivals were housed in three marquees and slept on blankets on the ground, in rows, packed tightly against each other. Many of them had had dysentery, but their guards refused to give them clean clothes in exchange for the soiled ones they had marched in. 'I hope the whole lot of you shit yourselves to death,' a German officer told them. It was a foolhardy attitude for him to take, given how close the Allied forces were. Just two days earlier, fighter planes had strafed the camp after a guard unwisely drew attention to it by firing his machine-gun at them from one of the watchtowers. The planes had wheeled round and their cannon had taken out the watchtower – and seventeen French prisoners of war with it. Badcock could only reflect on the 'hard luck of being killed by your own people after being a prisoner for five years'. He had been in captivity since 1942, and he felt that much of what lay ahead would depend on being lucky. For now, he could only crouch in a narrow trench as the RAF Typhoons roared over each day at noon, finding it 'curious to be back in the shooting war again after so long cooped up behind the wire'.

Then something happened that made him worry that the war might not be close to its end after all. 'We saw a new squadron of German fighters come into the neighbouring airfield, all the latest type of Messerschmitt fighter.' Could these be part of the secret new weapons the Germans had been boasting about, the trick up the Führer's sleeve?

We thought that when our lot come over tomorrow this lot will murder them. The next morning we saw the Messerschmitts take off and we feared they were going to sit up in the sun and dive on our planes as they came in and massacre them. We needn't have worried. The Nazis formed up over the airfield and then set off eastwards. Then, right on time, over came the RAF and shot up the local railway goods yard, the airfield and a couple of odd factories. Half an hour after they had disappeared, back came the *Luftwaffe* in their smart new planes, though they had difficulty in landing as our boys had made such a mess of their flying field. A few days later this squadron was captured complete – on the ground. How is the mighty *Luftwaffe* fallen.

This was something to celebrate. Clearly, the end really *was* near.

Then we got a terrible shock. We were ordered to get ready to march again. This caused pandemonium. We could just about walk but marching was impossible. Furthermore, we knew (from our temperamental radio) that the Americans were only 20 miles away, so what was the use? Where was there to go? It was pure Nazi bloody-mindedness. We held a meeting of the marquee commanders and the decision was to tell the Kommandant we would not go. We got the reply we expected – if we resisted they would shoot.

When it came to the crunch, half of the British flyers decided to stand their ground, claiming to be sick. The other half left. Badcock was the senior man among those who stayed, and for several days he had to deal with some unpleasantness from the remaining guards. Then, one morning, no Germans came to unlock the compound after the night curfew.

We waited until 08.00 hours and then we lifted the gates off their hinges and sent some men down to the main part of the camp. They came back with the news that practically all the Germans had gone. Just 26 were left, led by a major. It was time for us to take over. There was very little argument from the Germans. We hauled down the Nazi flag and hoisted a Union flag, which we had hidden away. This worried the German major, who warned us that SS troops were still in the district, so we hauled it down and put up a Red Cross flag instead. As a precaution, we left the

German sentries on the gate but we took over the running of the camp, including the cookhouse, so at least we got something to eat. But we weren't home yet. The Americans were still about 11 miles away.

The next couple of days were the weirdest I have ever spent. We were right in the thick of the battle for Germany, still stuck in a prison camp, with Germans still walking about, but yet we were not really prisoners any longer. On the other hand we were not free to go outside. It was like being in a small neutral country. And we were very scared. What would happen if the Nazis counter-attacked? And what if the Americans mistook us for Germans and shelled the camp?

The distant war got closer – louder and louder – in the next 48 hours and on Good Friday, March 30, 1945, most of us were up very early. We posted lookouts on any vantage point to keep scanning the horizon for troops. A German sergeant felt sure we would be caught up in a tank battle and he was right. Suddenly there was tremendous excitement as a lookout spotted a column of German Tigers. I looked in the other direction and saw another column of American Shermans. We were right in the middle. I heard a bang and an unfamiliar whine, and I hit the deck faster than I had ever done in my life. Then came the aircraft, ours fortunately, and we hugged the ground and crawled towards the trenches. Two kilometres away was a village, and as we looked up from the ground we saw a white flag, then another, then another, as the local inhabitants forgot all about their beloved Führer and hung out their nice, clean bed linen as a token of total surrender. The firing stopped. For a moment there was total silence and then the boys let out a cheer. It was all over.

I went to the main gates where a poor, frightened-looking guard was still standing with his rifle and bayonet. He sprang smartly to attention and gave me a salute. In my best stalag German I said to him the words I had longed to say ever since my own capture: '*Ach so mein Freund, fur zu der Krieg ist fertig, nicht wahr?*' 'For you, my friend, the war is over.' With a grin, he dropped his rifle, fumbled in his haversack and produced an enormous bread and cheese sandwich (ersatz cheese of course). He cut it in two with his bayonet and handed half to me. I took it and ate it. It was like manna from heaven.

It was a job now to keep his fellow POWs in check, but this had to be done because no one knew for sure what was happening beyond the wire.

Obviously, we were right in the front line and we must not do anything rash which might place the camp in peril. It was no easy task. Some of my chaps had been taken at Dunkirk – nearly five years ago. However, we just had to be patient for the next three hours, but what a long wait it was! Then I heard a tremendous roar. Hampden Park, Wembley or the Kop at Anfield have never heard anything like this. A seething mass of people was at the main gate. The Yanks were here! A US Army jeep, complete with a crew of six husky GIs, was being lifted from the ground and borne in triumph through the gate. What was amazing was that the men doing the lifting had hardly had the strength to lift a comb to their hair an hour before.

It was pandemonium. Everybody was talking at once. Strangers hugged each other. This was freedom at last! On the road outside, the main columns of the American Army were now speeding by. The GIs in the armoured cars seemed to be as excited as we were. One of them shouted and threw something. I caught a pack of 20 Camels. Real cigarettes at last! I sat by the roadside for a few minutes and really enjoyed a smoke. It truly was Good Friday.

*

A fortnight later the American spearhead had moved 150 miles further into the heart of Germany. Lieutenant Kenny Dodson stood in the turret of his tank and trained his binoculars on the small town half a mile away in the distance. He could see the half-timbered houses, the narrow streets, the people hurrying for shelter. And he could not miss the castle that loomed over them from the top of the hill. Here was the next target. It was midway through April 1945. A few weeks earlier he and his men had crossed the Rhine at Remagen. Now the River Elbe was just 30 miles ahead. But first they had to cross a minor river, the Mulde, on whose banks sat this monstrous late-medieval fortification, guarding the bridge. Dodson peered at his map to see the name of the obstacle in his way. They had just flattened the village of Hohnbach, following orders to stop at nothing and to meet any resistance by pouring in firepower and then driving on over the rubble that remained. Was this town ahead going to give them trouble too, this place called Colditz?

Shells had been lobbed into the village, and a few had dropped into the castle. But there was no sign of surrender. Now it was time to blast a way in. Dodson called out his order for his gun to be zeroed in on 'the schloss', and the muzzle swung round until it was fixed on the front of the hilltop fortress. The line of mobile artillery he also commanded swivelled in the same direction. A high-explosive shell was loaded into the breach to blast through the walls. A shell of phosphorus was lined up to follow, to incinerate the interior and anyone inside. 'Battery, one round, fire,' he called down the phone.[18]

Inside the castle, the 400 Allied prisoners of war were seconds away from being blasted into oblivion. By their own side.

Suddenly, down in the belly of the tank, the driver, 'Mac' Macasland, yelled a warning. 'Hey, lieutenant. Hold it!' He had spotted a Union flag being waved frantically from a window in the castle and, further along, a French tricolour. 'Don't do it! I'm sure some of our boys are in there.' A patrol was sent to find some civilians, who told them that the castle was a prisoner-of-war camp. Dodson should have known this. He was part of General Bradley's 12th Army Group, which had been sent an urgent message from SHAEF headquarters two days earlier alerting it to the existence of Colditz, giving a map reference (K 546935) and explaining that it contained important prisoners of war. '12th Army Group will take appropriate action regarding this camp when uncovered by ground advance and keep this HQ informed,' the message added.[19]

Inside Oflag IVC, the official name for Colditz, a power struggle was reaching its conclusion. For days the Allied prisoners had known the Americans were nearby. They had heard the distinctive crash of artillery shells exploding in the distance, so different from the sound of air raids on the factories and oil installations of Leipzig, 25 miles away, that had kept them awake every night for a month. After dusk, they could see the glow in the sky from fires burning beyond the horizon.

Captain Dick Howe, the British officer in charge of escape attempts, had been among the first in the camp to realize the war was nearly over as he listened on the prisoners' clandestine radio to reports of the Allied charge into Germany. At breakfast on 12 April he announced that the Americans were at Leuna, just 35 miles away. A cheer went up and a thrill of excitement ran through the vast dining room, followed by a silence of foreboding. As Pat Reid, the camp's historian, recorded, 'There were so many imponderables in the atmosphere surrounding them and in the kaleidoscopic nightmare of events taking place in Germany. There were maniacs at the helm in Berlin. Anything might happen.' Chief among the prisoners' worries was that they would be hostages. At midnight, the *Prominente* – the castle's twenty-one VIP prisoners, consisting of generals and others with important family connections – were hustled out of their special individual cells, assembled in the courtyard, and then pushed and pummelled into buses. They were driven off to an unknown destination. When he heard what was happening, the Senior British Officer, Colonel Willie Tod, a tall and imposing man with a coolness that would prove a life-saver in the coming days, went to see the German commandant to protest.

Oberst (Major) Prawitt, white-haired, his face lined and visibly aged by stress, was in a state verging on hysteria. He was too terrified of doing the wrong thing to be able to do what was right. He knew how close the Americans were. He also knew that the Russians were advancing almost as quickly from the east. He did not know who would get to him first, but he hoped it would not be the Russians. And there was a more immediate danger already encamped at his door. The night before, a division of the SS had marched into Colditz village, fresh from performing 'special duties' at a work camp for Jews 3 miles away. The camp's 400 inmates had been slaughtered and their bodies burned. Were the SS now in Colditz to carry out a similar operation? The SS troops were digging in, taking up positions in the buildings below the castle, carving out trenches, mining the bridge over the Mulde, preparing to stop the Americans in their tracks. They seemed determined to put up a fight, to make Colditz their last stand if necessary. If that happened, the lives of the Allied prisoners would mean nothing to them.

In Prawitt's office, Tod took the letter the German was eager to show him – from Heinrich Himmler himself, the head of state security. It ordered Prawitt to evacuate the *Prominente* immediately, on pain of summary execution if he disobeyed or if any escaped. Germany might be shrinking by the day as the Soviet and Allied armies advanced from east and west, but the writ of the SS leader still ran here, particularly with a division of his black-shirted soldiers, still the most feared in the land, camped outside. Prawitt had to obey the order, he told the British officer. If he refused, the SS would march in and carry it out anyway, over his dead body. He feared for the consequences – and not just for himself. 'There will be many deaths throughout the camp, and still the *Prominente* will depart,' he told Tod. 'And what will you have achieved then?'

Tod returned to his quarters, aware that he could do nothing to save the *Prominente*. He didn't even know where they were being taken, though he guessed it would be south, towards Bavaria, the fabled last redoubt in the mountains. Now he had to think about the hundreds of prisoners left. There might come a time when they would have to make a break for it: overpower the few remaining guards and make a dash for the Allied lines. If he got the moment wrong they could be slaughtered by the storm troopers and gangs of Hitler Youth outside. But if they stayed too long they could all be lined up against the walls of the fortress and shot. There was also a third possibility, though the records of those anxious last days in Colditz do not show whether the Colonel realized this straight away: that American shells raining down on the castle would kill them all.

It was that fate rather than any other that they were seconds away from as Lieutenant Dodson levelled his guns at the castle, only to call a halt when friendly flags were spotted. American infantrymen went forward into the town, ready to take it street by street and building by building. As Allied reconnaissance planes flew overhead, Prawitt called Tod to his office and instructed him to get the men ready to leave at once. He had received orders from Dresden. 'You are to move out of the castle towards the east under guard.'

This was Tod's moment. He refused to move, he told the German commandant. He and his men would have to be forced out at bayonet point, and they would resist with violence.

Below the castle and from the woods nearby, the SS troopers in their dugouts were in a fire fight with the American advance patrols. Shells were zeroing in on the town, and some reached the castle, punching holes in the roof, starting fires, and even knocking Douglas Bader, the disabled RAF fighter pilot, off his tin legs. The shelling concentrated Prawitt's mind. He knew he could not use force against the prisoners: shooting just one of them would have him dangling at the end of a rope as a war criminal when the war was over. Tod had made this perfectly clear to him. Now he decided to go one step further. If Tod would give his word of honour that he would keep the German major from being taken by the Russians, Prawitt would quietly hand the castle over to the prisoners. His condition was agreed, and, smiling at Tod – almost fawning over him – he surrendered Colditz to the Senior British Officer.

For the next twelve hours, Tod and the men he now commanded lived on their nerves. They convinced themselves that the American forces in artillery range of the castle must have grasped precisely who was inside. The number of near misses suggested that the castle was being deliberately avoided, but they could not be sure. What if it was just plain bad shooting? What would happen when the US artillery outside found its range? Equally, they could not advertise that they had taken over their prison, for fear of a reprisal attack from the SS troops in the town.

That night, a power cut shut off all the lights of Colditz. A ghostly moon lit the sky, and the men huddled in the cobbled inner courtyard of the castle or tried to snatch some sleep in their dormitories. Explosions outside shook the building, and the machine-gun fire seemed louder and longer as dawn began to break on a beautiful spring morning. Freedom was so close, but one stray shell or a reverse in the fortunes of battle, a counter-attack, could result in the dreams, the longing for home, being shattered.

Down in the town, the SS were withdrawing, rolling their tanks over the bridge and heading away to the south-east. With their last tank over, they blew the bridge. In the castle, John Watton, a painter, retreating into his art to take his mind away from danger, jumped as the boom of the explosives reached him. The chalk in his hand scored across the paper, across the face of a French officer who had chosen this morning to sit for his portrait. The picture was ruined. The bridge was not. In their haste, the SS troops had done a bad job – the piers were shaken but the roadway remained. The American advance would not be stopped.

Now American tanks could be seen in the streets below. A youngster in the khaki uniform of the Hitler Youth – a boy of perhaps fifteen – lay in the gutter, legs spreadeagled behind him, firing a machine-gun. From a window above him, his mother screamed at him to come inside. She was too late. From behind an advancing American tank, a burst of bullets ripped into him. He rolled over, and the GIs marched on over his body.

In the castle's courtyard, officers were standing in groups talking, or walking the cobbles for exercise, as they had done every morning for years, when the wooden gate swung open. An American infantryman stood there and stared around him. The officers stopped and stared back. There was a moment of silence, of incredulity. Those who had been sitting on benches and reading, feigning calm, looked up. A roar of cheering broke the spell, as the officers rushed forward to greet the American. Many of them wept, but the light rain which had begun to fall hid the torrent of tears. Other inmates hung out of the windows cheering as more Americans arrived.

It was only later, after they had shaken Kenny Dodson by the hand and drunk the health of Winston Churchill and Vera Lynn and the Andrews Sisters, all in liberated German wine, that they discovered how close they had come to not going home at all. If Dodson had opened fire ... Stunned men realized they had been just seconds away from being blown to smithereens. On the very brink of liberation, with the worst seemingly behind them and at last able to believe in a future as free men, they had come perhaps closer to dying than at any time in this long war.

*

As more and more camps in western Germany fell to the advancing Americans, the prisoners of war from Nuremberg were still strung out on the road south. 'We know we are headed for Bavaria,' Bill Ethridge noted as the column reluctantly marched further and further away from their would-be liberators, 'but we don't know exactly where.' There was a lightness about them, however – spring fever compared with the icy winter blues of their previous journey from Sagan. 'The guards occasionally showed signs of being relaxed and now and then a hint of a smile would seem to say "this will soon end and we can all go home".' He had brought as much food as he could carry. 'I was not going hungry again!' But this time there was a different danger. They had left the British and American bombers – the Lancasters and Flying Fortresses – behind at Nuremberg, but not the fighter planes. There was a rumour that word had somehow been sent to Allied headquarters alerting them to this column of prisoners of war. If so, the information had not been passed on to the American P-47 pilots now overhead.

The planes were upon us and firing! I was walking on the outside of the column and I hit the ditch as soon as I heard it. Bullets rained down along the road where we had been and some clipped leaves off the trees above our heads. Our guard fell in beside us. Several men were hit and subsequently bandaged with socks, twine and whatever strips of cloth could be made. One man had been killed.[20] We were most fortunate that the pilots had not made a second pass. Apparently they had recognized us after the initial bursts and pulled up early. Throughout the following days whenever P-47s appeared overhead they would come down low and wiggle their wings in recognition. We felt safe again.

The threat of air attacks like this had been much in the mind of Colonel Walter Arnold, in charge of another compound at Nuremberg containing nearly 2,000 American and British prisoners. He had led the POWs out, marching at the head even though he had a gammy leg – wounded when he was shot down, and still plaguing him. They had an escort of eighty-seven guards and two dozen dogs. Some way down the road it became clear that they were heading for the railway station, where a train was waiting to take them to Moosburg and Stalag VIIA. When he learned this, Arnold refused to go any further. Trains were targets, easy pickings for pilots. The Germans fingered their rifles and insisted they would have to take their chance. Arnold would not be intimidated – walking would take longer but would be safer. Eventually the camp commander agreed to abandon the train: they could march the whole 100 miles south.

With the German officer in charge of his group, Arnold plotted a route along back tracks and forests that they hoped would avoid not only American fighter planes but retreating German troops and SS contingents too. The dangers became more apparent when Arnold scouted ahead one day and watched from a distance the goings-on in a town.

A dozen German soldiers were in the middle of the street, surrounded by SS troops. We heard a lot of machine-gun fire, and the soldiers fell to the ground. They were massacred because they were retreating. We stayed in the trees and gave orders to the column to keep quiet. The next day, the SS had all gone and we passed through it but we marched pretty damn fast.

The prisoners went through more villages, slept overnight in barns, and generally found plenty of food along the way. Some parts of the column became a slow meander, and Ethridge's account changed from a catalogue of misery to more of a travelogue of a hike through the rural delights of southern Germany. Only fierce showers of rain spoilt the sightseeing, turning the roads into mini-lakes and forcing the prisoners to tramp through ankle-deep mud.

April 10 – we crossed the Danube at noon. Truly a beautiful river with its gentle sounds bringing to mind memories of Strauss and his famous waltz. We are about 100 kilometers out of Nuremberg but can't get a fix on how much further it is to Moosburg, which we have now been told is our destination. The spirits are ebbing from high to low. Anxious about not knowing when or how this journey will end. Haven't had any word from home since December. Miss that.

Joe Cittadini was not impressed by the Danube, which he thought grey rather than blue. The colour reflected his mood. That this was no holiday jaunt after all was made clear by the cold eyes of some towns' inhabitants who lined up sullenly to watch the bedraggled men march through. The mood deepened further when there was a casualty to bury. One of Ethridge's buddies, Edward Riding, with whom he had travelled ever since they left Stalag Luft III at Sagan, developed a sore throat which turned to a virulent infection. He was dead within three days.

Six of us lined up along side the coffin in a village churchyard and the German soldiers fired three volleys from their rifles. We each saluted as the coffin was lowered. That night we thought about those makeshift graves hacked from the ice and snow during our winter march and were thankful that our friend had at least been given a decent burial.

This was not the only mourning they had to do. The news came through of Roosevelt's death on 12 April. His health had been declining for some time, though this had been concealed from the public. The brain haemorrhage that suddenly killed him was a terrible shock. Cittadini was grief-stricken because he saw the President as 'more than our commander-in-chief, he was a father figure; the sadness was shared by all'. The Germans, though, took it as a sign that perhaps all was not lost after all. In Berlin, Goebbels broke out the champagne and told Hitler, 'Fate has laid low your greatest enemy. God has not abandoned us.'[21]

Some of the guards picked up on this renewed defiance and made it clear that they were still very much in charge. The war was not lost, and they were in no mood for compassion. Each morning they emptied a magazine of bullets into the straw when they left an overnight stop, just to make sure no one was trying to hide and escape. This was no joyride, as John Parsons discovered. 'What the guards told you to do, you had better do – for your own good,' he said. His journey from Nuremberg to Moosburg was dogged by bad experiences. Whereas others in the column found food relatively easy to come by, he struggled. Sickness added to his difficulties. One morning he found it hard to rouse his buddy, Paul Goecke. The two of them had been virtually inseparable for years. They had met back in training in the USA in 1943, had been together on missions, were shot down together, and had been in the same camps. 'What he had was half mine and what I had was half his.' But Goecke was ailing.

He kept telling me that he could not make it. Then, on this particular morning after we had had to sleep out in some woods because there was no other shelter, he would not get up. The guards were shouting, '*Raus, raus*' but he said he was too sick. 'Go on without me, John,' he said. I just jumped on top of him and pounded the hell out of him. The whistle blew. It was time to go. I got him up on his feet and put what clothes I could on him and with another man I started walking him down the road. But others resisted the guards that morning. They stayed in the woods because they were sick and they were not going to move. It wasn't too long before we could hear machine-gun bursts in the woods. There was a lot of screaming. We just kept going, did not even look back. I suppose they were all killed, just like that. The guards meant what they said.

This was reinforced days later, when Parsons saw several of his companions try to cut the corner of a long hairpen bend by slipping through the woods and across a stream instead of sticking to the road. 'I told them that they were nuts. The guards would think they were trying to escape. "If you go down in there, they will kill you," I warned them. About five of them stepped off the road, and they never came out. The guards killed them.'

Meanwhile Goecke's condition had worsened, and in a village Parsons traded some cigarettes for eggs.

I had some crackers from a former Red Cross parcel and I borrowed a Klim [powdered-milk] can from someone and whittled up some wood. I sat there and poached both eggs. By this time Paul was very sick and hallucinating but somehow I got the food down him. But it was clear that he was not going to be able to go on. Someone told me that there was a medical man in the village who might be able to help. I borrowed an ox cart from a farmer and Paul was taken away. He lay in that cart in the straw with my blanket covering him and off he went. It was the last time I saw him until we got back to the States.

Parsons now had the sort of problem that anyone who marched always dreaded: he had lost his partner and was on his own. There was no one to forage for food with, no one to share with, no one to lean on if he got sick. And he did get sick – to the point where

I couldn't walk and all I could do was lie down on my belly and pull myself around with my elbows. I seemed to go where I wanted to go, although it was a crude way of doing it and took any energy that I might have had. I managed to find somewhere to sleep that night and the next day I felt a little bit better so I could walk upright. But that was the day I took potatoes from a pig pen and ate them raw I was so hungry. I got in between the pigs and stole their dinner.

The column meandered on in a strange state of limbo. The prisoners knew that somewhere out there, not far away, Patton's forces were heading towards them. The secret radio told them the

American general was driving towards Munich. They knew their destination was Moosburg, which was close to Munich. At some point, they had to meet. But when? It would be too late for Ed Riding and the ones who had been killed taking that deadly short cut. Would it be too late for the rest of them as well?

By now the column was stretched out over many miles, and they straggled into Stalag VIIA over many days. Parsons's relief at passing through the main gates turned to fear when they were directed to an area of showers.

They told us that we would have to take a decontamination shower. I thought we were going to be gassed. But they turned out to be real showers, and it was a pleasure to have warm water and soap.

There was a tall guy standing in the shower and I tried to speak to him. He gave a sound from his throat like an animal and pointed at his mouth. He had no tongue. Apparently the Germans had cut it out. There were four other guys with him who had been starved near to death. All the flesh on their arms had settled down below the elbows and all the flesh on their legs below their knees. They were the most pathetic group that I had ever seen. How could one human being treat another human being this badly? It made me feel so terrible to think that these men had been treated as they were.

*

The camp at Moosburg was overflowing. It had been built to hold 10,000 men. Now there were 80,000 – predominantly French (38,000) and Russian (14,000). Nearly 14,000 were British and American,[22] and that did not include the constant new arrivals, whose numbers, some said, pushed the total population to 130,000. There were 2,000 guards. Joe Lovoi had been there since early February. He had marched from Stalag Luft III at Sagan to the railhead at Spremberg, and, while others had gone to Luckenwalde and Nuremberg and Marlag Nord, he had been put on a train all the way here. The lucky ones were crammed in twelve to a room in three-tier bunks with no headroom. He and his buddy, the guitar-playing Onafrio Brancato, ended up in an old stable block sleeping on straw. Tents were erected as more and more prisoners arrived, though conditions inside them were terrible after the early spring thaw turned the ground into a sea of mud. Twice a day there were roll-calls, but

Lovoi thought the Germans didn't have a clue what the accurate number of prisoners was. Discipline was poor, there were places in the camp where it was thought unwise to wander, and the whole place had a seedy and desperate air of 'every man for himself'.

A long trench served as a common open-air latrine. Dysentery was rampant, the queues endless, and using it 'just less than torture'. Food was scarce and barely fit for human consumption. With few Red Cross parcels getting through, they had to rely on sauerkraut out of large wooden barrels. It made everyone sick. Time was spent plotting the advance of the Allied front line on maps and counting the days to liberation. But there were also old friends to catch up with. So many people were flooding into Moosburg that inevitably some were former comrades – and some even sounded like voices from beyond the grave.

My heart stopped when I heard a Brooklyn twang yell, 'Hey, Lovoi, do I have to travel halfway around the world to find you and take care of you?' It was Vinnie Niemann, a close classmate from Navigation School. But he had been reported MIA (missing in action) about nine months ago after bailing out of his crippled B-17 after a bomb run over Hamburg. And here he was, with a lip-stretching grin from ear to ear. We hugged each other and cried.

Meeting up like this also brought thoughts of home. Lovoi had imagined that Niemann was dead. Did his family think the same about him? He thought of his brothers fighting in the Pacific against the Japanese, and prayed they were well. With the end clearly so close, he was more nervous than ever before.

Because we had a radio we knew what was going on and we knew we were going to win the war. The question now was, were they going to machine-gun us before then? We weren't sure what they were going to do. But we knew the moment was coming when it would either be 'OK, guys, it's over, you're free,' or 'Here's a bullet in your head.' We knew we had to face it sooner or later.

Private Maurice Newey thought the Americans a particularly despondent lot. He arrived at Moosburg after a marathon trek from eastern Germany. He and his fellow prisoners were on the road for months tramping through Czechoslovakia, and had marched close on 400 miles to Bayreuth before being put on a train to Moosburg. He had been a prisoner since the Battle of Tobruk in North Africa in 1942. He had been imprisoned in the desert, then in Italy, then taken to Germany, where he had been forced to work in a chemical factory. But his spirits were astonishingly high. 'Most of the American GIs had been in captivity for just a few months,' he commented, 'and we were appalled at their lack of morale. They were lying around unwashed and unshaven and seemed to be full of self-pity.'[23] The morale of British soldiers like Newey made a huge impression on one of the senior American officers, Lieutenant-Colonel Al Clark, who had come to Moosburg directly from Sagan. He recalled a group of British privates – they might even have been the column Newey was in – arriving after months marching from Czechoslovakia.

They were from one of the regiments captured at Dunkirk and had been separated from their officers ever since. They had been sent into the mines to work, and here, four years later, they came stumbling into Moosburg. These guys were skeletons. They had been marched all winter, and they were in terrible shape. They put them in an open compound with no shelter for that night, and the next morning those guys had their buttons shined and their shoes shined; they were shaved, and they had really shaped up. It was one of the most remarkable examples of high military morale I have ever seen.[24]

Meanwhile the marchers from Nuremberg were settling in, though they found Moosburg worse than anything they could have imagined. It was, however, thankfully free of the lice that had plagued them back at Stalag XIIID. Bill Ethridge couldn't believe the mud. It was ankle deep after just a day of rain. 'We were told this area had been a swamp at one time and that it was always wet. Further, the mosquitoes breed here by the millions during the summer months. That's something great to look forward to!' He discovered that anything made of wood – from bed boards to door posts – had been whittled down to almost nothing by thousands of men desperate for fuel for their Klim-can blower-cookers. The slats of his bunk should have been 3 inches thick. They were just an inch and a half – and by the time he left Moosburg he had pared them down to an inch. Miraculously they did not snap. Others did not have the comfort of a bunk but slept on the ground in tents with just a layer of wood shavings as a mattress.

For some, arriving at Moosburg was a shock. Lieutenant Frank Stewart of the Lothian and Borders Yeomanry could not get over how 'squalid' the place was.[25] In the compound, clouds of smoke were rising from hundreds of small fires as men brewed tea in the open air, and there was a constant hubbub as anything that could be exchanged was. 'The Americans were terrible lads for trading – they would buy the blouse off your back, the ring off your finger or the food out of your mouth, as one of his friends put it.'[26] Stewart had come just 60 miles, from the Oflag at Eichstatt, which had been a haven compared with most camps in Germany. It was in a pleasant valley with pretty views of forests and a river. While he was there he had read extensively from the library, played cricket and tennis, listened to the orchestra, and discussed theology – and all that just a few days before being turfed out and sent to this hell-hole.

Stewart was a long-term prisoner, captured in France in 1940, and had been through five other camps before getting to Eichstatt. For months there had been rumours that evacuees would be arriving from camps in the east, and they had seen columns of prisoners passing by on the road outside. But none had actually stopped, and in the middle of April they themselves had been forced to move. It had been a disaster. Half a dozen American Thunderbolts flew over and raked the column with machine-gun fire, over and back, five times. Nine men died and thirty-nine were wounded.[27] He realized how close he himself had come to dying only when the man who had been lying next to him on the ground found that a bullet had ricocheted off a tobacco tin in his pack. A friend who was a noted jazz pianist lost his right arm. Stewart wrote:

Most of us had experienced no real personal danger for upwards of five years, and what we had we'd forgotten. We had seen little of battle and fighting and it was one of our consolations for our generally uncomfortable life that for us, at least, the war had passed us by. I think it was this and the complete unexpectedness of it all that accounts for the shattering effect it has had on us. Naturally, we were all extremely frightened at the time, and it has taken time to recover. For days after, we've jumped at the slightest noise, everything has sounded like an aeroplane or a machine-gun, and everyone is restless and nervy. A typical case of shock, I suppose.

The real world disturbed him greatly. Out on the road, 'we met every sort of humanity, all moving aimlessly in every direction, north, south, east and west, having nowhere particular to head for, but just keeping moving, waiting for life, or the Russians, or the Americans to catch up with them'.

With the arrival of warm spring weather, a new problem arose at Moosburg. In the heat, the latrines gave off a terrible stench. They had filled to overflowing and apparently could not be pumped out because there was no petrol to drive the pump. An epidemic seemed inevitable. The senior Allied officer called a strike. No one would go to roll-call. The guards tried to use force, pushing the prisoners out on to the parade ground, but as soon as they left them to get more the ones on the parade ground slipped back inside. Dogs were brought in; pistols were drawn. Lovoi was horrified at what was happening. 'Was the German commandant bluffing? Was it worth even one man's life to find out?' It was the commandant who backed down, calling off his men and his dogs. The senior Allied officer held more talks with the commandant and then came out and ordered everyone to roll-call. 'We lined up quickly, were counted, and dismissed but we couldn't help wondering if he had given in. But that night "honey wagons" rolled into the compound and cleaned out the latrine.'

This successful defiance was a rehearsal for a much more important moment. As Patton's Third Army rolled nearer, the commandant called in the senior Allied officers and told them that the British and American flyers were to be marched out and taken deeper into Bavaria – to the redoubt where the Third Reich would make its last stand. There had been rumours about this for days. Now he was confirming it. But such a move would contravene an understanding that had just been made between Berlin, London and Washington. It was the Germans who – through the Swiss as

Protecting Power – had requested an agreement that Allied prisoners of war would no longer be moved if the Allied governments would agree in return that, when liberated, those prisoners would not be thrown back into the fighting.[28] The US, British and Soviet governments had accepted the proposal, and it came into operation at midnight on 22 April. Fortunately the Allied officers in Moosburg knew this. Al Clark remembered that 'we had been monitoring Radio Luxembourg and the BBC and by sheer coincidence that night there was a broadcast about this agreement. So the next morning, when the Germans told us to line up at the gate, we said, "You had better check. There has been a new deal, and we ain't going." And they checked and we didn't move.'[29]

There were more and more signs of liberation in the air. Nuremberg had fallen to Patton's troops, and Munich became the target for Allied bombing. American fighters flew over Moosburg and waggled their wings in recognition. One came so low and fast that it sent everyone running for cover. As the fighting got closer, 'nerves were raw, stress was high, and anticipation was rampant', according to Lovoi. The men were ordered to stay in their barracks, but as they peeped out through holes in the walls they saw what appeared to be Allied soldiers in fields around the camp and German troops on the retreat. Ethridge lay in his bunk 'mentally helping Patton to come through'. Artillery shells flew over the camp 'like a mid-West thunderstorm'.

The guards gave every indication that they were going to make a fight of it. Instead, they left in the middle of the night. From inside his barracks, Frank Stewart heard a German sergeant run up to a sentry outside and shout something. The sentry left his box and joined the others, and together they all marched out of the main gate. When those prisoners who had managed to sleep through the shelling and the excitement woke on the morning of 29 April the camp was silent. Lovoi

peered out of the windows of our barracks and could not see any guards. The watchtowers were empty. No one knew what to do. Was it a trick to get us to break out so we could be killed? Slowly, we opened the barracks doors and ventured out just a few feet. One prisoner climbed up a watchtower and verified that it had been abandoned.

In fact a deal had been done – not a formal surrender, but an understanding. Al Clark was privy to it.

The Germans called in our senior officer, Col. 'Pop' Goode. I went with him because he had selected me to be his operations and intelligence officer. The Germans said we would probably be free the next day but that the German commander of the area wanted to talk to the colonel. So they put 'Pop' in a jeep and took him to the headquarters of whoever was defending that sector, and there the German general asked him to take a proposal to the local American commander to demilitarize this particular sector because of the POW camp. 'Pop' said he couldn't give him any promise but he would be happy to take the message. He suspected anyway that the Germans had another reason than just the safety of the prisoners of war – there were two crucially important river bridges in this sector and the German general didn't want the Americans to cross them. Anyway, Pop took the message.

He was away all night. He got to the command post of the leading US division and they gave him breakfast of bacon and eggs. The commander, who was an old friend of Pop's, told him he would have to reject the offer 'but we will be through there at, let's see, 8.30 tomorrow morning. There will be a few shots fired, and that's all there will be.' So he took the rejected answer back to the Germans and then came on back into camp. He got back to us just about daylight, and we all gathered around him in his room. He told us about his bacon-and-egg breakfast, and then said very casually, 'They are coming through about 30 minutes from now.' And as he said that, the shooting started.

A fierce battle raged. SS troops were dug in down by the river and along the railway embankment a mile away and ready to defend the town of Moosburg. In the camp, prisoners scrambled for safety, hugging or diving for any scrap of cover they could find as bullets flew through the air. The fighting was confused, and Ethridge thought he saw German troops firing at each other and could not make out what was going on.[30] John Parsons saw a German sniper firing from the top of a church tower in the distance and then watched as he was hit and went spiralling to the ground.

Suddenly the firing stopped and, cautiously, men began to make their way out into the compound. Those brave enough climbed up on the roofs of their barracks, and from there they could see a column of tanks on a hill in the distance. As these got closer, their shape showed they were Shermans. The American star stencilled on the side confirmed it. 'The news spread like wildfire,' according to Lovoi.

Men screamed and yelled. Then a jeep raced ahead of the tank column carrying an American flag. A tall soldier was standing in the passenger side. He was helmeted and stood very straight. As he got within 50 yards of the open front gate, we recognized him. It was General Patton himself, looking like a cowboy with his pearl six-shooters strapped to his sides.[31] His jeep came to a stop just inside the barbed-wire fence and we just knew this was liberation. It was like visiting heaven.

He was immediately surrounded by hundreds of thin, grateful, and home-sick young men. The senior Allied officer made his way to the jeep and stood before the General. He snapped a sharp salute. The General stood tall and returned the salute with the words: 'It is we who salute you and all these brave men.' Then the two men embraced, and we were yelling and shouting, lots of crying and a lot of screaming and hugging your friends.

A prisoner of war took the Stars and Stripes from the jeep, climbed up the camp's flagpole, and replaced the Nazi flag. According to some reports it was Patton himself – 'Old Blood and Guts', as he was known – who demanded this. He pointed to the German flag and yelled, 'I want that son-of-a-bitch cut down, and the man that cuts it down, I want him to wipe his ass with it!'[32] The sight of 'Old Glory' sent the men even wilder. Lovoi remembered that 'a thunderous cheer erupted which could surely be heard as far west as New York City. Thousands of young men looked up at the American flag as tears streamed unashamedly down their grimy youthful faces. I felt com-pletely drained and I sat down and said, "Well thank God it's over."'

Patton toured the camp, speaking to as many of the prisoners as he could. Ethridge was thrilled to shake the General's hand and hear his promise that 'we will whip the bastards all the way to Berlin' – unfulfilled, of course, because the politicians had already agreed that the Russians would take the German capital.[33] Joe Cittadini squeezed into a room and listened to him 'tell us we were great soldiers and would soon be transported to France'. Then some trucks arrived in the camp with food and water – and doughnuts for the Americans, served by two blonde girls from a lorry. For some an even greater pleasure was the taste of white bread – 'like angel food cake'[34] – after years of living on German black bread. There was also chicken, turkey, ham, beef stew, salmon, pasta, and meat loaf. Lovoi managed to get a can of spaghetti and meatballs, but 'we were warned not to stuff ourselves because we might get stomach cramps from the sudden impact of food on our digestive system'. John Parsons took no notice, and was soon throwing up everything he had just crammed inside himself.'

Over in the British compound, the mood was calmer. Ken Searle was thrilled to see the American flag waving

proudly and firmly on top of the town hall in Moosburg, between us and the fast-retreating enemy. We got our own very precious Union Jack hoisted without further delay. But we British prisoners were mostly quiet, only slowly and hesitantly allowing ourselves to smile in a bewildered sort of manner. We were nearly all old kriegies of many years standing and we watched while the Americans and all the younger ones went wild with unrestrained excitement. Later we celebrated quietly on our own by having a peaceful brew of tea out in the sun.

Lieutenant Geoff Wright of the Durham Light Infantry restrained himself too. He celebrated on half a tin of salmon with his buddies, and swore he would stay calm. But then

I get up, I start to walk, I start to run, I nearly fall down a trench and break my bloody neck. And then I am in the middle of a mad throng. My throat tightens and I let out a strangled yell. I am yelling and roaring and waving my arms. So much for my resolve. Free and liberated. It's funny after five years. It's cold but the sun is shining. I am coming and going and I don't know where I am.

On the next page of his diary his writing was a mess of squiggles as he confessed to his wife that he had fallen into bad company: 'Joan, darling, I'm tight, with one pull of best Scotch from these two magnificent American officers. God bless the bastards . . . This diary is all topsy-turvy, darling, but so am I. I am wild, happy and mad. After five years, free at last. May be home next Sunday.'

11   The Hell of Fallingbostel

For all those tens of thousands of prisoners of war who had slogged their way along the northern line of march – from camps in the east such as Stalag Luft IV at Gross Tychow, Stalag XXA at Thorn and Stalag XXB at Marienburg – the destination was usually the same. Some had walked the whole way, in pitiful condition as they were rushed along that corridor of land beside the Baltic Sea, then crossed the first natural barrier they came to, the River Oder, and then plodded west until the next one, the River Elbe. The lucky ones had travelled at least some of the way by train. But they all ended up in the vast prisoner-of-war complex at Fallingbostel on the windswept north-German plain.

Australian Air Force sergeant Cal Younger might have counted himself one of those lucky ones as he sat in the overcrowded compound and listened to the harrowing stories of those still arriving there as numbers increased every day during the spring of 1945. But, as he ruefully pointed out, his was akin to the luck of a one-legged man in the company of those with no legs at all. He had begun his odyssey at Stalag Luft VI, that far-flung camp on the Baltic coast which had been the first to be evacuated way back in July 1944. But, instead of the long march, Younger and his group had travelled south by train to Thorn in Poland, where they had stayed for three weeks before another train journey across the middle of Germany. Both train journeys had been hellish, the prisoners crammed in railway trucks for many days, the conditions insanitary and inhumane. If he was a lucky one, then God help the others. He had now been at Fallingbostel for eight months, and it was far from a picnic.

But Fallingbostel did have one thing going for it: being there brought the thoughts of home closer. The countryside between Hamburg and Hanover was distinctly north-west-European, heathland rather than flatland, lived-in rather than desolate and empty. Younger felt as if he was in '*our* theatre of war' – one that was

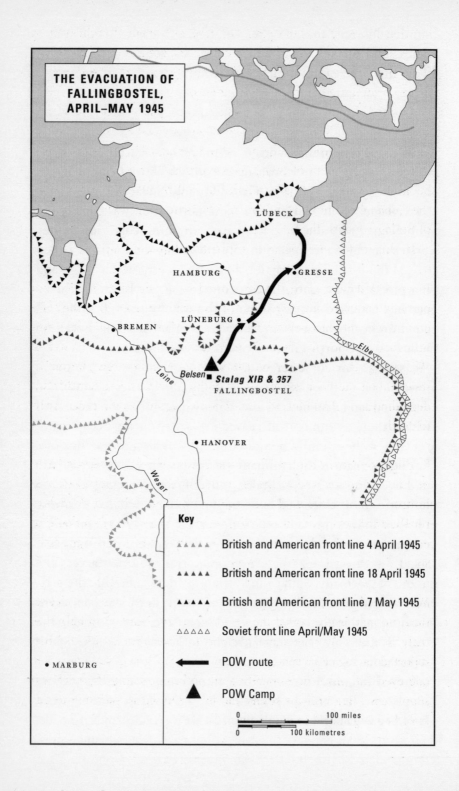

THE EVACUATION OF FALLINGBOSTEL, APRIL–MAY 1945

LÜBECK

HAMBURG

GRESSE

BREMEN

LÜNEBURG

Elbe

Belsen ■ **Stalag XIB & 357**
FALLINGBOSTEL

Leine

• HANOVER

Weser

Key

▲▲▲▲▲ British and American front line 4 April 1945

▲▲▲▲▲ British and American front line 18 April 1945

▲▲▲▲▲ British and American front line 7 May 1945

△△△△△ Soviet front line April/May 1945

← POW route

▲ POW Camp

• MARBURG

0   100 miles

0   100 kilometres

familiar in a way that the plains of central Europe, fought over by Poles and Russians and Slavs for centuries, could never be.[1] At the same time, the camp itself was 'dark and brooding'. There were in fact two separate camps, sprawling across hundreds of acres. They had housed Poles, French, Russians and Italians over the years, and at one stage conditions had been so bad that 6,000 Russian prisoners had died of typhus. The bigger camp – Stalag XIB – now held close to 100,000 prisoners of many nationalities. The second camp had been closed for a year and a half but had then been reopened for the 8,000 newcomers from Thorn, who brought its new designation of Stalag 357 with them.

In this new home, Younger's spirits had quickly sagged.

It was a miserable place. The grey-brick huts were long and low and partially underground so that when you looked out of the window the ground was only just below you. The winter was severe and we had so little food that I lost four stone in weight and four inches off my waistline. We were practically living on swede peel, and even then we had to scramble on the floor and fight one another for it. It was horrible and degrading and I swore I would never do that again. I would rather starve to death.

Flight Sergeant Richard Passmore remembered the degradation of scavenging for scraps like an animal outside the German cookhouse – where huge vats of thin soup were boiled up – though he recalled that everyone was so desperate for anything that could be eaten that there was a properly drawn-up rota for the right to do so.

We removed the suppurating potatoes and slimy swede peelings, cleaned them up marginally, boiled them and ate them. People who have been truly hungry will understand; those who haven't won't. Several men reported having eaten sparrows. Many of us had greedy eyes on a lean, one-eyed cat which occasionally appeared, negotiating the wire with supple ease, but, perhaps suspecting us, it refused to succumb to outstretched fingers and soothing noises.[2]

Cold and hungry, Passmore admitted to despair, being laid lower by the absence of letters from home – 'our spiritual lifeline' – as communications in Germany collapsed.

The present was grim and the future was uncertain. It was tempting to lose hope and relapse into apathy. There were needless deaths of men who could not be bothered to fight back so that comparatively trivial ailments developed into things far worse. The piper, playing 'Flowers of the Forest' as he led a funeral cortège, was no longer a rarity.

He knew the temptation to give up. Sick with pleurisy, Passmore was put in the sickbay and

I just waited to see what would happen to me. I submitted. If I died, I died. I stored the pills they gave me with the vague idea that I might take them all at once and make an end of it. Somehow I didn't. Perhaps the flame of self-preservation was stronger than I knew. Perhaps it was the knowledge of the suffering I would bring to several other people which restrained me, people who were waiting in love and faith for my return. Or perhaps it was seeing a Mosquito fighter fly over the camp on a grey January afternoon without any opposition. Was this the dove returning to the Ark bearing clear signs of life not too far away? At any rate, I stayed in the hospital for a fortnight and one way or another I survived. Which was the aim of that time – to survive each day, and the next and the next.

When a man gave in, death could come frighteningly fast. Private Jim Sims remembered a comrade – a veteran paratrooper, with the physique to match – who came to him one day and said, 'I've come to say goodbye. I can't stand any more of this place. I'm getting out, and you won't see me again.'[3] He was going into the sickbay for a small operation to remove some shrapnel, and Sims told him not to be so dramatic.

Two days later I was asked to be a bearer for his coffin. I just could not see how a seemingly fit and tough young man could go off and die as if he had willed it. But he could never reconcile himself to the prison camp. It appeared to hold some special horror for him, especially when someone told him it might be another eight months before we would be free. But his death haunted me, with the result that his surname is one of the very few I remember from those days.[4]

Sims himself survived, but the scars never completely healed. 'I was a prisoner for just eight months but in that time my weight dropped from 11 stone 7 lb to under 7 stone. I had been a normal healthy young man, but I was never the same again. I suffered physically and mentally ever since.'

Such hardships paled into insignificance in comparison with the treatment meted out to the Russian prisoners in the next compound. What astonished Younger was the routine way in which the German guards would whip the Russians, and the routine way in which the Russians seemed to accept it. They expected no mercy – and could be guaranteed to show none when their turn came to be the masters. And that time would soon come as the news on which the Allied prisoners increasingly relied to boost their morale made clear. The 'canary' on which Dixie Deans had heard the D-Day announcement back at Heydekrug had survived the journey across Germany. It had been hidden in the hand-made model of a racing car – lovingly built to scale and perfect in every detail – belonging to John Bristow, a work so admired that German guards often picked it up and commented on its exquisite design. They never realized the secret inside. Now, with the signal from home closer and stronger, it was more than ever a lifeline of hope.

Ironically, it became harder to receive specific instructions from London. Some bright spark in Whitehall changed the cipher for the radio broadcasts without first making sure that those on the receiving end had been told. RAF sergeant Ron Mogg remembered spending

worried weeks trying to decipher garbled instructions from home. The best brains in the camp – and they included Senior Wranglers [top Cambridge mathematics graduates] and men with high mathematics degrees – covered acres of paper with hopeful deductions, but still the messages came out gobbledygook. The problem was not solved until, eventually, a new prisoner arrived carrying the secret coding information we needed.[5]

The prisoners also retained the equipment that could turn the receiver into a transmitter.[6] This was for the direst of emergencies only – if the prisoners were threatened with massacre and needed urgent help. It could only ever be used once, because its operation would have been immediately detected by the Germans. Fortunately it was never needed.[7]

Deans had taken over the leadership of the British men in the camp. Given the usual inter-service rivalry, it was extraordinary that the large army contingent had voted for an RAF man. But they clearly agreed with Younger's belief that Deans 'would fight for our wellbeing until he collapsed. Rank did not awe him; he was as much at ease with a Nazi general as with a Cockney sergeant. And he knew the Geneva Convention as a priest knows his Bible. He insisted upon its observance by us, and, as far as was possible, by the Germans.'[8] Now he was on constant watch to make sure that men who were bored and depressed did not cause trouble for themselves and others by confronting the Germans – particularly the Gestapo, who arrived for snap inspections. 'One hothead could provoke an incident of much gravity, and Deans wanted to prevent any ugly scenes if it were possible.' He liked to smooth away difficulties, but he stood his ground too, and would protest vigorously about any German behaviour he found unacceptable. One Gestapo officer in his black uniform was so exasperated by Deans that he grasped him by the neck. The British sergeant kept his cool, refusing the dangerous open invitation to strike back. He waited until the man loosened his grip, then turned smartly on his heels and marched to the commandant's office. There he was met with a helpless shrug. What could the commandant do? That was the knife-edge they all lived on now.

But Deans refused to let animal behaviour make animals of him and his men. In the next compound, fifty Polish women[9] – believed to be survivors of the Warsaw uprising against the Germans – had been brought for a shower. Their clothes were being deloused, and they were made to stand naked out in the open. The Germans delighted in the peep show, but not Deans. His men were lined up for the morning roll-call when the women appeared. Angrily, he called out, 'Parade – Attention! About face!' As one man they turned away so as not to add to the women's humiliation.[10]

There was one other unforgettable personality among the POWs at Fallingbostel, who had arrived as a result of the operations at Arnhem. The daring airborne assault behind enemy lines in September 1944 had failed, and the disarmed and weary red-bereted British paratroops had been marched into the camp, evidence that there were going to be no easy roads to victory. They were led in – their wounded hobbling with them – by Regimental Sergeant Major John Lord. His head was held high and his moustache was waxed; he swaggered as if he were parading for the King rather than marching into captivity. Ron Mogg was one of those lining the fence of Stalag 357 to watch the paras enter the neighbouring Stalag XIB.

We did not cheer. We came instinctively to attention and John Lord, noticing our two medical officers standing with us, gave his party 'eyes right' and snapped them a salute which would not have been out of place at Pirbright or Caterham [training camps]. This was the sort of show England could really put on. None of us would have missed seeing it. The impression [it made] on the Germans was incredible.

Lord brought immediate discipline to the compound he took charge of. The soldiers already there had become, in military parlance, a 'shower'. They were scruffy, and morale was nonexistent. Lord sorted them out in a week. The one thing he lacked was an interpreter, and he asked Deans if he could provide one. 'He arranged an official visit to us at 357 to consult with Dixie,' remembered Mogg.

The splendidly upright figure of [Lord] appeared at our gate escorted by two German soldiers who were doing their best to look smart. We presented him with a man who was one of the best German linguists in the camp but whose sartorial standards and hair were hardly regulation. Three weeks later duty brought him back to our camp, and his long hair was short, his side-cap was glued on the side of his head at the correct angle and his cap-badge and buttons blazed. Even his trousers were creased and you could see your face in his boots. To cap it all, he was wearing a belt and gaiters. And they were all scrubbed white. He marched up to the camp with a back like a ramrod and, although not a particularly tall type, managed actually to look down on some of his old comrades.

'You scruffy looking lot of sods,' he shouted, 'it's about time you smartened yourselves up.'

But, for all his force of personality and the fear and respect he commanded, Lord had his work cut out when it came to keeping the bulk of his men clean, tidy and disciplined. It didn't help that they were dressed in an array of ragged clothes. 'We looked like a mob of starving tramps, which is in effect what we were,' according to Jim Sims, one of those captured at Arnhem. But the problem was much more than what they wore. Sims was appalled by the attitudes he encountered. 'There was no mucking-in spirit. It was just dog eat dog and the weakest to the wall.' He remembered the bitter arguments, and even fistfights, over how to slice up a loaf of black bread fairly, or whether a window in the barracks should be opened or shut. Sometimes the bickering would last for hours and then end in blows. There were brawls between men of rival regiments – the paratroopers blamed the Guards for not coming to their rescue at Arnhem – and honour was served only by a bruising. Not that the fights lasted long: after ten minutes the antagonists, weakened by lack of food, were too exhausted to go on.

Lord did his best. He ordered all the men out of the barracks every day, to give them exercise and to get some air into the fetid huts. Some defied him, though if he marched through and caught them they normally leaped through the windows rather than face his wrath. But discipline was a problem, because the usual military punishments for misdemeanours could not be applied. As Sims noted, 'You could not stop a soldier's pay or confine him to camp', and, in the absence of these sanctions, there was always a minority who told the NCOs to their faces that 'We're not in the bloody army now', and 'You're not in charge, the Germans are.' The fist was the only answer to insubordination. Sims recalled a young Canadian soldier nicknamed 'Sunshine' who was lying in his bunk and refused to report to a company sergeant major (CSM) when requested. 'If the CSM wants to see me, I guess he knows where I am,' he said cheekily. The CSM marched from his office and slugged 'Sunshine' on the jaw. It did the trick.

Rain sapped the soul. Cal Younger counted forty-one days out of fifty when the heavens opened, and we lived rain-curtained and mud-carpeted, in clothes that were never quite dry, in boots that were always a little damp. Trails of running green slime coursed down the inside walls, and water, condensing on the ceiling, or leaking through, spattered on our bunks. We slept in beds that were sometimes secretly, shamefully wet because bladders could not be controlled. In everything we did we thought more of our own welfare, and less and less frequently stood aside for anyone else. Hardship, such as it was, brought out the worst in many of us, aggravated our faults, or exaggerated our attributes until they became vices, and sharpened our awareness of faults in others.

Nor was morale helped in mid-January when the Germans removed all tables and benches, straw mattresses and half the bed boards from each barracks in an officially inspired act of retaliation for some apparent injustice done to their own prisoners of war in a British camp in North Africa. Compassion seemed to be a thing of the past, as Younger discovered when he encountered the rule of the mob.

A young soldier – 'more a boy, really, certainly not long a prisoner' – took a beating from other prisoners after being caught stealing food. They stood round him and clubbed him to the ground with their fists.

The youngster was trying not to defend himself, was giving himself, almost gladly, to the flogging, but involuntarily his arms tried to fend off the blows. Then he coiled slowly into the snow and lay still before trying to get to his feet again, as if he knew, and the men flogging him knew, and we who were watching him knew, that his punishment was not quite complete. Two more blows struck him and he fell, a picture of humiliation and misery. The nonchalant pitilessness of it was frightening. He was hauled away to the sick bay on a makeshift sleigh. A man picked up a parachutist's beret, brushed the snow from it, and ran after the sleigh. Gently, almost apologetically he placed the beret on the unconscious but convulsing chest of the man of Arnhem. I went round a corner and was sick.

There were more such acts. A thief from the RAF contingent was frogmarched to the cesspit and, fully clothed, thrust in and held down with a pole. 'When it was thought he had been punished enough, he was allowed to clamber out, and was hosed down with ice-cold water until the filth and the stench were washed away.' When he got back to his hut, he found his belongings had been thrown out and he was no longer welcome.

Thoughtful men like Younger wondered about the morality of these 'pitiful, pathetic, pettifogging little thefts, not many when one considered that here were 10,000 men, all desperately hungry'. Could any individual really be blamed? 'It makes one wonder what would happen if one's own friends succumbed to sudden temptation, or if one were to succumb oneself.' But it was hard to know what was right or wrong any more, as one small incident demonstrated. A box, sent from Stalag Luft III on the last train to leave before the Russians overran the camp, had arrived addressed to Dixie Deans. In it were the fountain pens and cigarette lighters the Germans had confiscated from the POWs years before.[11] As Younger was handed his own pen he pondered on 'the superb honesty' of the Germans, and vowed to write the first draft of his prison-camp memoirs with it.

Overhead, constant streams of Allied planes headed for Hamburg, Bremen and Hanover, their trails in the sky watched eagerly from the compound. Passmore remembered the day they hit the oil storage tanks in Hanover and 'a brown curtain climbed the southern sky until it blotted out the whole of the heavens, leaving us in near-twilight for almost two days'. Back in Heydekrug in 1944, Deans had worried that celebrating the news of D-Day might result in retaliation, and it was still just as necessary to avoid provoking the Germans too much. Jumpy guards occasionally fired a round or two in the air to remind the prisoners who was in charge, but in return they were sharply reminded that things were about to change. Passmore recalled that, when a guard attempted to arrest a prisoner who was late for parade, the prisoner began to write down the guard's name and number for future reference – future revenge – and the guard took the hint and went away.

An even greater worry for Deans was the rapid deterioration of the men's health. They were all, Younger knew, far from being in the state of concentration-camp inmates, yet 'we were suffering from malnutrition; the flesh of thighs and upper arms atrophied a little more with each day, hip-bones resembled incipient wings. We dreaded an epidemic and we dreaded being made to march again, this time eastward.' There was a lethargy about the camp, a sense of unreality, as if it was all a film in slow motion. This attitude was dangerous, because it made men weak and vulnerable just when they most needed to be strong. Deans opted for action that would give everyone a shot in the arm. The cheer of Red Cross parcels was needed. There were literally tons of them, but they were stuck at the port of Lübeck 80 miles away with no transport to bring them south, only the promise of gleaming white lorries at some unspecified time.

Deans persuaded the commandant to find a van, and he and another prisoner, along with a Russian driver and a German officer, set off for Lübeck. As they lunched in a pub along the way and slept that night in a dormitory at a German services club in Lübeck, surrounded by *Wehrmacht* soldiers on leave, Deans and his fellow prisoner concealed their identities. The town had been wrecked by Allied bombing, and to be discovered as RAF men could have been disastrous for them. They found parcels and, after great difficulty (and a little bribery), arranged for two railway wagons to be filled with them and attached to the next passenger train going south to Fallingbostel. Deans and the others then threw as many parcels as they could in the back of the van and returned to camp. There they handed out 200 parcels to the sick and waited for their delivery from Lübeck. It was a long wait. Not until 30 March, Good Friday, did the two wagons arrive with 6,000 parcels – enough for half a parcel for each man.

They were too late to save one life. According to Passmore, one room had managed to acquire a pet dog.

Nellie was a dachshund and much loved. One day she vanished and the sad traces were found in a dustbin. Nellie's owners put up a bitter notice – 'The men of [hut] C2/4 would like it to be known that on Saturday evening, March 24, 1945, their dog Nellie was eaten by some persons unknown. They would like to thank all who helped to feed her during the last few weeks. No doubt those who ate her would like to add their thanks.'

By then the prisoners were in a state of high anxiety. They knew that Patton had crossed the Rhine nine days earlier and that his tanks were eating up the miles in a mad dash across south-west Germany. But the soldier who mattered most to them was Montgomery, and his 21st Army Group in the north. Caution was the Field Marshal's watchword, particularly since the Arnhem debacle. He moved only when he was absolutely certain. For days there were reports of a massive military build-up on the Rhine's west bank and of artillery pounding the eastern bank of the river to obliterate any opposition. Impatient prisoners of war had stuck up a photograph of Monty with the word 'Wanted' printed above it. What worried them was that the Germans would try to march them out before he got there. The signals they were getting were contradictory. Some camps closer to the Allied lines had apparently been liberated, but the persistent rumour was still that their release was not going to be that easy. Passmore listed the possibilities that were endlessly discussed:

The Germans would just leave us to be liberated by the advancing Allies – which was too good to be true, of course. They would shoot, shell and bomb us all – which seemed hardly credible. They would march us away from our approaching liberators, to use us as bargaining counters in some future haggling. More exciting was the possibility that British airborne troops would be dropped into the camp under heavy air cover and wipe out the guards. At this point, the rumour split. Either we would fortify the perimeter and dig in, waiting for a tank spearhead to reach us, or we would fight our way across country to meet the advancing forces. In either case, we should have adequate air cover. Our confidence in the ability of the RAF to look after its own was boundless, almost as boundless as our collective ego-centricity.

The last was a revealing observation. Passmore was one of the few who realized the truth: that the prisoners might not be at the top of everyone's list of priorities at this crucial stage in the war. He added, 'We said our prayers unworthily, assuming that the Almighty must share *our* dominating concerns.'

Meanwhile, thousands more prisoners were arriving on foot from the camps in the east.[12] Doug Fry remembered his sheer relief at just getting there. He and his column had left Gross Tychow on 6 February. It was now 28 March. 'Thank God we're off the road,' he told himself, 'and under cover.'[13] Another of the new arrivals was Roger Allen, who was

just unbelievably filthy and ragged. My shoes were falling apart. But at least we had shelter. We were marched into an old circus-type tent with hay on the ground. That's where we met these British guys. They had been captured at Dunkirk, and been in prison camps for five years. They were about as happy as you could be. They had a really good sense of humour, and we got on well with them.[14]

Later this friendship would be a life-saver. American airman Bob Otto also got a standard British welcome – a cup of tea. He was grateful: 'it was comforting to think we had come to the end of that march. We weren't worried about going back behind the wire again, not at that stage.'[15]

Another new arrival was Cec Room, who noted in his log, 'The camp is horribly overcrowded. Grub stakes very poor. We are all herded together in a huge marquee, and I have a space one foot wide to sleep in.'[16] Things got worse: 'a mass funeral takes place. The sheets on the stretchers were flat because there was nothing left of them – they had just wasted away. I'm not feeling any too happy at this dismal sight. The atmosphere here is bloody grim.'

No sooner had they arrived when one of Room's buddies died – 'he had peritonitis and he died on the straw in that marquee. The poor bloke was in agony but nobody could do anything for him. Doc Pollock just hadn't got the equipment. All I could do was give him a few words of comfort. I felt so helpless.' He was buried with six others of various nationalities, and those who followed the coffins to the grave were embarrassed and distressed as the thin matchwood lids kept springing open.[17] The death toll did not surprise Percy Carruthers, who had arrived in the same group as Cec Room. He watched the plight of the Russians in their compound:

Most of them had their feet wrapped in rags and sacking. Their food, rough boiled potatoes, was merely tipped on the ground, and they were so hungry that they just fell upon the heap and shovelled it into their mouths. They were treated worse than animals. I feed my dogs more bulk food daily than we received in a week, but more than the Russians received in a month. Death was inevitable.

The arrivals from Gross Tychow began to take stock of what they had been through, who was fit and who was not. Carruthers realized how much he owed to one of his buddies, who had kept him going for the past months, eking out the food, keeping treats like slices of chocolate and fudge from Red Cross parcels for just that moment when the spirit was at its lowest. Now there were reunions as they began meeting up with old friends, but it was also painfully obvious how much numbers were reduced from all those who had once been together at Stalag Luft IV. The camaraderie of that camp seemed a distant memory compared with the ruthless attitude they found in their new home. Joe O'Donnell hated the atmosphere of Fallingbostel. 'It lacked comradeship, fellowship, friendship and, most of all, sharing. The only means for survival was every man for himself. I saw a French officer, impeccably dressed, clean shaven, and well fed, strutting about as though he were strolling along the streets of Paris.'[18] In contrast he found himself having to forage for vegetable skins to eat.

The general anxiety in the camp was heightened by an onslaught of German propaganda as blood-red posters appeared on walls in the camp stating that the Russians were the real enemy and that 'England will find herself isolated against a Soviet Europe and a Soviet Asia from the Atlantic to the Pacific.'[19] For the prisoners, these were issues too distant to contemplate. The only map of Europe they were interested in was one that showed the miles between them and Monty. Every day they willed the front line forward. Every day they cursed the Field Marshal's caution and prayed for 'build-up' to turn into 'advance'. In this limbo, behaviour was generally odd. One of Younger's companions became obsessively clean, scrubbing and dusting all the time, just to take his mind off thinking. Others adopted an end-of-term air and went round getting their diaries signed by friends, collecting addresses, writing down anecdotes and homilies, prematurely anticipating the end. Then came the thrill of great news. The British crossed the

Rhine on 24 March, and the days that followed were pure expectation – so much so that the arrival of the Red Cross parcels on Good Friday seemed irrelevant in the excitement to be free. Younger lay on his bunk 'with elation squirming inside me as every few minutes someone tumbled down the front step with news heard from "a reliable source". We waited, minute by minute, for liberation.'

Those 'reliable sources' placed the Americans to the south and the British to the west. Sounds of explosions could be heard nearby – though these turned out to be the Germans blowing up bridges rather than Allied artillery fire. One night a Mosquito buzzed the camp and the prisoners lay low, praying the site would be recognized for what it was. In the bright moonlight, the pilot took his time to assess the situation below and, choosing his target carefully, he dropped a bomb on the German quarters before shooting up a sentry box or two. The anxiety on the ground was genuine as the bomb fell. A former Spitfire pilot from Lancashire broke the fear-filled silence. 'Ee, if blud smells like manure, I'm wounded,' he announced, and the hundreds who heard him burst into laughter. Even the Americans got the joke straight away, an unkind Englishman noted – though it had to be explained to the German guards.[20]

The expectation strained the nerves – the more so when it was not fulfilled: 'we were emotionally exhausted as well as physically weak'.[21] The days went by, the liberators had to be closer, but the guards showed no real signs of panic or confusion. Younger watched a platoon of elderly Home Guard soldiers take part in an exercise beyond the wire, crawling on their stomachs and hiding in the bushes to smoke. They did not look defeated or in despair. They were still getting orders, but it was what those orders might contain that worried the prisoners. A macabre joke went round about 'going up the chimney', and the anxious dwelled on rumours about death camps. Nevertheless, for those who contemplated escape, the instructions over the radio from London were unchanged. 'Stay put' was still the order of the day. It was not just the British and Americans who were given this instruction. A month or so earlier, Paris Radio had carried a coded message to 'François le dentiste' in Fallingbostel. Apparently the French prisoners in the camp had acquired arms and ammunition and were intending to break out. They were told 'to lay off'.[22]

Deans needed a plan. He had managed to keep up a reasonably good relationship with the camp commandant, who assured him that no harm would befall the prisoners. However, such a promise would be meaningless if the SS arrived and took control, which seemed a distinct possibility. The SS needed no lessons in mass execution. They could herd the prisoners in groups to ditches outside the camp and mow them down en masse, or surround the camp with heavily armed men and simply dispose of a hut at a time. Deans planned for the worst. A twenty-four-hour watch was kept on the main gate of the camp to warn of the arrival of the SS. If it happened, the prisoners would rush the gate. As Vic Gammon noted, 'It was a forlorn hope but some might make it.'

Then came news. The wrong news. They were to be marched out again. 'We were to leave almost at once for the Northern Redoubt, the area of Denmark and Schleswig-Holstein in which the Germans planned to hold out indefinitely,' Younger recorded. It was Friday 6 April. Others were less certain about where they were headed and why. Passmore heard the name Lübeck mentioned, but he gathered they would just be going in a vague north-westerly direction. There were promises of regular food supplies, but he feared – with good reason – that they would be reduced to living off the land, 'like a ravaging Mongol horde'. Ken Brown, a navigator on Lancasters who had been shot down over Berlin in January 1944, had no wish to go. He had no doubt that

the safest place in Germany was behind wire. I had never seen any point in escaping, in putting myself in further danger. It seemed a stupid thing to do. There were a lot of rumours around that we might be shot or used as hostages. It was alleged that Hitler said, 'Shoot all prisoners of war.' But we also heard that Goering had countermanded the order. But it was always possible. We knew what the Nazis were like.[23]

Cec Room was following orders and preparing to leave. 'Curse it!' he wrote.

The offensive on the Western Front has opened up full blast and now we are being evacuated from Montgomery's Army. Presumably we shall meet the Russians halfway back. The Army boys are staying behind but the poor old RAF have got to march away. We are all in. In some ways I am glad to get out of here. We stand a little more chance of picking up odd bits of food on the road. Another month of this and I'm pretty sure many of us would hit the long, long trail!

Percy Carruthers was glad to be moving too, though he recognized that many of his fellow marchers from Gross Tychow were not. 'They were not in a suitable physical condition to go on the roads again.'

The news upset Joe O'Donnell. He had been so starved in his few days at Fallingbostel that he had finally sold his watch, which he had held on to since he was captured, for seven loaves of black bread. He and his buddy ate one loaf straight away, and were planning to trade the rest when they were told to prepare to leave. 'A loaf of black bread was two and a half pounds, which meant I had 21 lb, and that was just too much to carry. So I kept three loaves for me and my buddy and we gave the rest to the sick. I like to think that, as a result, someone's prayers for food were answered.' If so, his own prayers were answered in return. His worst fears were *not* realized. He was among a group of newcomers ordered by the Germans to take a shower to delouse them. 'We were forcibly marched out of the camp area to a small wooden building. There we were given a command to strip naked. We insisted that 12 prisoners must enter *and exit* the showers before another 12 would go in. Permission was granted, and we got our first shower in 55 days.' It had been a wise precaution. As the prisoners were beginning to realize, a special camp known as Bergen-Belsen was just a few miles down the road from Fallingbostel.

As best he could, the ever resourceful Deans had drawn up contingency plans. The prisoners would follow German orders, because they had no choice – he had been warned that escapers would be shot. But they would march as slowly as they could. Even though the weather was mild, each man would wear his greatcoat, and they should carry spare socks, a container of water, and food. They would march in columns of about 1,000 and each group would have its own leader plus a head of security – 'in case the Jerries turned nasty', as Mogg explained. Twenty senior men (including John Bristow with the 'canary') would form a sort of headquarters unit which would march in the middle of 'this great army of the unarmed but very bloody-minded'[24] and try to keep control. That was Deans's way. He would leave as few decisions as he possibly could to the Germans. They could settle on where the column was going and where they would be billeted each night, but *he* would remain in charge of *his* men. That way he stood a chance of getting them home safely.

However, not everyone was prepared to follow his orders on this occasion. Younger's friend Dick Vernon wanted to hide. He suggested they and two other friends should creep into a compound of army prisoners, in the hope that this compound would not be evacuated. At least they might buy some time. Younger was against the idea. 'Better to stay with our own crowd; we might be singled out among a crowd of soldiers for specially unpleasant attention. What really worried me was a premonition that if we moved in any but the appointed direction we would be beset by tragedy.' Younger lost the argument with his friends and they gathered up their kitbags and headed for a barracks in a different compound. They were lucky to find room. There was a stream of RAF prisoners with the same thought, and most of them were turned back.

Eventually they found refuge with a group of Americans, not long off the difficult march from the east, and they lay hidden while their own compound led the march-out. That night they were treated to US hospitality – boiled peas, which was all there was to eat, and a sing-song accompanied by a mournful mouth organ. Cigarettes glowed in the dark as the prisoners sang and took comfort in being together.

Most of the songs were sentimental – 'kinda corny', as the Americans put it – but they sang unashamedly, nostalgically, contentedly. It was a warm, a friendly gathering, yet full of emotion. A padre could have come in and talked about God, and had the best congregation of his life, because our thoughts were imbued with a peculiar reverence. Maybe some of us were thinking about God anyway.

Outside they could hear gunfire and the whine of aircraft engines. 'Uneasily, we slept.'

They had gained only a night's respite. Having dispatched the British compound, the Germans came next morning for the Americans. 'Before we realized it the barrack was surrounded.' Younger and his friends tried to make a dash for another compound. Other prisoners were trying to slip through a gap that had appeared in the barbed wire. It was all to no avail. They were all winkled out of hiding and relieved to find it was their regular guards who were chasing them out, not the SS. 'Toby, Dick, Ron and I were the last four prisoners to move out of the camp, just as it had been all those months ago back at Heydekrug.' Out on the road again, history was repeating itself in the most awful of ways.

*

But not for George Guderley. Not if he had anything to do with it. He had had a tough time slogging his way from Gross Tychow, trudging hundreds of miles from east to west. He told himself he was not about to retrace any one of those steps. This was as far as he was going. It was a decision based, as we will see, on inside information.

For him, as for so many of the long-distance marchers, Fallingbostel had been a relief when he first arrived. Sick and starving, the pounds had fallen off him, and, at around 8 stone, he was down to two-thirds of his normal weight. He thought that 'If there was an organized prison camp the chances were that we would be fed, and that's all that mattered. Everything revolved around getting food. The whole focus of my life was food.'[25] He quickly realized that Fallingbostel was not going to provide what he desperately needed to stay alive.

I was so frigging hungry there. We received potatoes and a green stew that was made up of boiled grass and boiled sugar beets. It tasted like nothing, and all it did was fill space. There was no nutrition in it. We used to look at the trees in the distance beyond the wire and wonder if we could get to them and scrape off the bark and eat the inner bit later. We would have eaten anything.

In his dreams, he feasted. 'I had a piece of cardboard, and I wrote endless descriptions about what I wanted to eat. For me it was anything with cream on it – whipped cream or chocolate.' These were fantasies to be shared and compared.

We would talk for endless hours about what we were going to eat when – if – we got home. There was this guy who used to talk about a product called Verner's Ginger Ale, which was sold in Cleveland, Ohio, and how you heated the ginger ale to drive off the gas and put in a dollop of ice and then this would melt down into the ginger and then you would drink it with a straw. But it had to be Verner's Ginger Ale or it was nothing. In those discussions I also got to hear about pizza for the first time. Some guy said, 'You ain't lived until you've had pizza.' Food was our obsession. We talked about it constantly.

Conversations like these also took their minds away from their deepest fears. 'Yes, I was worried. We could sense the chaos around us as things went badly for the Germans. There was always the thought in my head that they might kill us, out of retribution or anger.'

Guderley had been fortunate enough to come across one of the few friendly guards back at Gross Tychow, a middle-aged man he called Pop.

He was a sergeant and he came from the Sudetenland, part of southern Germany Hitler annexed from Czechoslovakia in 1938. His two sons were conscripted – he went into the *Luftwaffe* and they went into the Army. Both were killed on the Russian front, and I think he took a shine to us because we were the same age as them: just kids really. He was thin, balding and wore glasses. He would talk to me furtively, afraid of being seen fraternizing. But he became a sort of fatherly figure. He was torn apart by the loss of his sons.

I saw him over at the gate at Fallingbostel and I signalled to him. He looked surprised, and he came over and I asked him how he was, how things were going. He said, '*Schwer*' – 'Bad.' We chatted, then all of a sudden he said, 'Do you know that tomorrow morning all the air-force prisoners of war are going to be marched out back to the east again?' In the distance we could hear the noise of artillery. He looked round to make sure no one was watching, then he added quietly, 'You're a smart young man. If you can get over into that other compound over there' –

and he pointed to one of the laagers containing what the Germans called *Untermenschen* – 'then you will be free in ten days.' He told me he couldn't help – '*Ich kanne nicht Ihren helfen* – or he would be shot. 'But you have to get into that other compound.' Then he turned and walked back to his post.

Pop knew all this because he would be on the march himself, and as far as Guderley could tell he was far from keen to go: 'He was fifty-six years old and had just finished walking 471 miles – he wasn't looking forward to some more of the same.'

The American decided to take the advice. He told his friends and urged them to help him contrive a plan to get into the other compound, which housed Slavs, Indians and British Gurkhas in appalling conditions – much worse than the British and American prisoners were in. 'They were reluctant to try to make a break, because they felt relatively safe where they were. Most of them said they wanted to stay with the group. But eventually I got enough to agree.' His plan was desperate – mad even. There were about twenty of them, and they would carry empty swill buckets hanging at the end of poles across their shoulders and pretend they were a work detail carrying out an order. They would simply walk up to the compound gate, bold as brass, and demand to be let through. It was the same tactic Guderley had used when he stole cream at a farm for his sick friend Buck while on the march. Be positive and give the impression of doing something that cannot be questioned and it was amazing what you could get away with or who you could 'bullshit', as Guderley put it. 'It was pretty daft I now realize, but since none of us would be carrying our belongings I reasoned that we would not be suspected of trying to escape.'

They assembled, marched up to the gate, and when the sentry asked where they were going Guderley said they had been told by a German sergeant – a particularly nasty one whom he knew the rank-and-file guards were scared of – to take water to the other compound. The guard didn't argue:

He just opened up the gate and we marched out. We went down between rows of barbed wire between the individual compounds, and I was at the front calling out 'Left, right, left, right' in my best drill-sergeant manner.

We followed the same routine at the gate of the compound we wished to hide in, and the sentry there let us in. When we got to the middle of the compound, on a prearranged signal we scattered and hid ourselves in huts and tents, swapping hats and jackets with the people in them to disguise ourselves. When the Germans saw what was happening they went absolutely berserk trying to find us, but in the end they gave up. The next morning we watched all of the other Allied airmen being marched out. We were sorry to see them go, but we were damn glad we were going to stay there. We had made the right decision to stay after what my German guard friend had told me.

Guderley and his companions stayed hidden for a day, and then they went back to their old – and now empty – compound. There they met up with others who had refused to be evacuated. John Anderson was too sick:

I knew I could not march again. I was barely able to walk. The Germans didn't like it. They said if we were sick we should go to the hospital. Otherwise we should march. We were paraded and a German doctor was going to examine us to decide if we were fit or not. But there was an air raid which lasted the rest of the day, and he was unable to do this.[26]

Others who had also hidden to avoid the forced exodus began to emerge too, among them Roger Allen. He and his buddy

had preferred to stay in camp and take our chances there rather than go out on the road again. We were scared that those who went in the column were in danger of being used as hostages and might be killed. So, with the help of the British soldiers we had become friendly with, we hid. We swapped our American flying jackets for some old blankets, which we put over our heads, and the Brits just stood in a circle around us until the guards had gone.

By the next day, those Germans guards who hadn't left had virtually given up. The camp was now in the hands of German Home Guard troops, and they, as Guderley noted, 'were easily intimidated, particularly after we told them that unless they cooperated they would be in bad shape when the Allied lines arrived. They knew the war was almost over, and they were not going to take any chances.' But there was still one more major scare to come. A company of SS troops arrived at the camp gates, and there was a fierce argument with the German guards.

They wanted to come in and shoot us. They carried standard Schmeiser machine-guns, and they could have killed a lot of people. They weren't yelling or shouting, but voices were raised and the discussion went on for about twenty minutes. We watched them. It was terrifying, because we realized it was our lives they were arguing about. But those old boys in the Home Guard stood their ground, and we were damned glad they did. It was a gutsy thing for them to do. In the end the SS left.

Not long after, one of the groups that had marched out of Fallingbostel returned. Though the prisoners did not realize it at the time, the German guards were scared and had decided to disobey orders. They thought they were in real danger of stumbling into the Allied front line, which was now just west of the Hanover–Hamburg autobahn, and getting caught up in the fighting. Cal Younger recalled how, one morning after two days on the road, they were told they would be staying where they were. Other columns were not so lucky. 'They straggled past us, bent low as they plodded up the hill and long after they had disappeared over the brow we could hear their voices and the scrape of their boots on the road.' The next day the Germans told Younger's group to head back to Fallingbostel. Was it good news or bad? No one knew. As they prepared to retrace their steps, one of Younger's friends noted in his diary, 'It's likely we're going to be murdered.' There were plenty of woods on the route back 'where murder could so easily be done'. The others tried to dismiss his fears as those of a pessimist, 'but there is no doubt we were worried. We thought we had become a nuisance to the Germans, that we were getting in the way of the fighting and so they wanted to get us out of the way permanently. The truth is that we didn't know what was going to happen to us and we were afraid of the unknown.' The Germans were reassuring. They told the prisoners that there were too many columns like theirs clogging up the roads, and that was the reason they were going back. When they arrived at the camp, there was more reassurance. Those they had left behind – in the sickbay, for example – were still there. Nothing had happened despite the earlier threats.

However, Fallingbostel was even worse than when they had left. They had been away just a few days, and yet in that time even more prisoners of many nationalities had been dumped there. There were no spare beds. The compounds had turned into shanty towns of shelters made out of anything available. The first night back was spent on the concrete floor of the delousing shower room. As for food, the guards just looked the other way as prisoners cut holes in the barbed wire to get out into the fields and farms nearby. Younger and his friends lived on foraged peas and potatoes.

Everywhere order was collapsing. Germany, the POW camps and the prisoners themselves were all in disarray. And the war was getting perilously close. Guderley, ill with dysentery, was squatting over a latrine trench when an RAF Hawker Typhoon buzzed the camp and fired rockets into a barracks, killing thirty-five Russians. 'I think they had left a light blazing.' Guderley watched the trail of the rockets and began to run, forgetting that his trousers were around his ankles. He fell in the mess around the latrine, and smelled so bad he was not allowed back into his tent that night. It was clearly time to do something to protect the camp. With the agreement of the guards, the prisoners climbed on to the roofs of the buildings and painted the letters POW in whitewash. The raids stopped, replaced by morale-boosting fly-pasts and victory rolls. 'Now there was an air of excitement, not tension.'

On the road outside the camp, retreating German soldiers were passing by in an almost continuous line, on the retreat. They were in lorries, on horse-drawn wagons, or just walking, bedraggled, heads bowed. Gleefully, Guderley noted that 'they didn't give a damn about us; all they wanted to do was save their own asses'. Fallingbostel's own guards were the next to join the retreat. There was a loud explosion as they blew up the ammunition dump, and then those who wanted to disappeared. A good number decided to stay and take their chances with men who at least knew them. It needed little imagination to grasp the life-threatening chaos that was waiting for them outside. Choosing to surrender to those who had

17. Wounded POWs arriving at Moosburg.

18 & 19. Built to house 14,000, Moosburg eventually held 130,000 POWs. Towards the end of the war, living conditions became increasingly cramped and difficult.

20. Prisoners in a makeshift tent at Moosburg.

21. The toilets at Moosburg.

22. General Patton arrives at Moosburg after liberation, and is cheered in by POWs.

23. Moosburg after liberation: POWs mob a tank.

24. Stalag 11B, Fallingbostel, 16 April 1945: British POWs greet their liberators at the camp gate.

25. British and American POWs released from Fallingbostel, 17 April 1945. Months of a near-starvation diet had taken their toll.

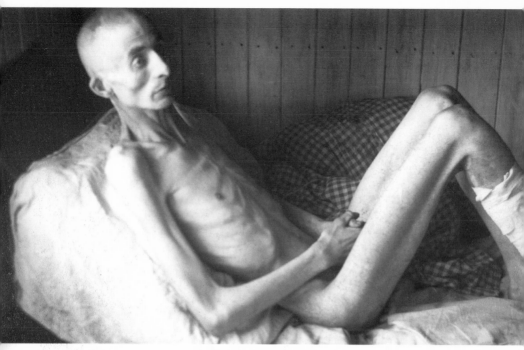

26. An American POW at Fallingbostel, 20 April 1945.

27. Fallingbostel,
20 April 1945. This
POW's feet were
gangrenous from the
forced march.

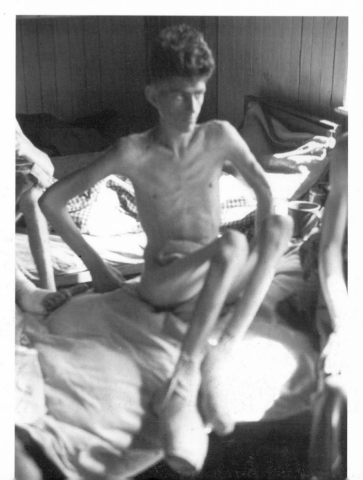

28. British prisoners at Le Havre, awaiting transport home, 5 April 1945. In the background are American transport planes.

29. Home is on the horizon: American prisoners catch their first glimpse of the Statue of Liberty.

30. George Guderley with 'Little Buck' (Wayland Buchholz), after their reunion in America, July 1944. George's mother wrote on the back of the photograph, 'George's first day out of sick bed – he looked like a skeleton when he got home – I've fattened him up from 115 to 183 lbs.'

31. (*From left to right*) Back to the site of their POW camp: George Guderley, Bob Otto and Roger Allen, at the Stalag Luft IV memorial in Poland, 2001.

been their prisoners, they laid down their arms and were then herded into a compound.

Senior Allied NCOs took charge of the camps. They followed the plan that Dixie Deans had devised months before, and though he was not there to implement it – he was on the forced march – there were enough men who had not left or who had returned to put it into action. They armed themselves with guns taken from the guards and sent out search parties to find whatever food they could in the surrounding countryside. The released Russian prisoners, however, were beyond control. They looted and raped their way through nearby towns and villages. Desperate for alcohol, they drank the area dry of beer and spirits, and then polished off a store of eau de Cologne through broken bottle necks.[27]

For those who opted for safety in the camp, sounds of heavy fighting were now coming from beyond the perimeter – 'sounds of joy', according to Guderley, but also frightening. He threw himself flat on the ground on more than one occasion. The end came on the morning of 16 April, just as John Anderson was finishing reading the last chapter of the Bible. He had come a long way. He had begun at Genesis in scripture classes back at Gross Tychow; now he was finishing Revelations. 'A tank from the British 2nd Army drove up to the gate and everyone started shouting,' he recalled. Guderley remembered a couple of Churchill tanks coming up the road,

and they drove right through the front gate, followed by a couple of Bren-gun carriers. Everyone started hollering, and the soldiers were throwing out rations and cigarettes. I stood well back, just in case. I was damned if I was going to be killed by the very British tank that was setting me free. But then the reality of the situation sank in and it was like New Year's Eve, the Fourth of July, your birthday and the wildest bacchanal you've ever been to all rolled into one.

Anderson shouted and yelled too, but his illness and his injuries meant he had to stop short of jumping up and down. Food was his priority. 'Had sauerkraut for lunch. Heated up some meat and beans. Cooked macaroni. I shall never forget this day.' Cal Younger thought the occasion unreal. He was peeling potatoes as the tank came crashing through the gate, and he just continued with what he was doing.

I was feeling pretty low at that time and at first I couldn't take part in the excitement. The potatoes boiled, and I watched the water frothing. Men went running past me – Englishmen, Frenchmen, Poles, Yugoslavs. I heard not a single voice, only the urgent pounding of feet. I stood up and watched the running men who seemed caught up in some current of magnetism. I would not be one of them. I would not. But then quite suddenly I realized that I saw only the same backs. I was running too.

Younger followed the mob.

People were in tears and yelling and screaming. Cheering prisoners surrounded the armoured cars, their arms held above their heads. Half a mile away the war went on. We could hear its sounds coming over the tank's radio. Germans were resisting in a wood nearby. A tank was sent, and then there was a message that 12 prisoners had been taken and would someone come and collect them. Another report said two cars were racing eastwards, with German senior officers in flight. They were to be headed off . . .

Roger Allen likened the sensation and the celebration that went with liberation to his team winning the Superbowl. He and Jason, his buddy since Gross Tychow, hugged each other, 'and we were jumping up and down and shouting and crying because we knew it was over and we were free'. But he was overwhelmed with sadness a little later when he went for a wander outside the barbed wire to see what he could find and

we passed this house and there was a young German mother with her little boy. He was playing with a ball and it rolled towards me. I picked it up to hand it to him, but his mother ran out and grabbed him away. If she had had a gun, I am sure she would have shot me. It made me sad that she thought I was going to hurt her son. The human race had got to such a state that she was so frightened of me. However, I must have looked pretty awful, because I had a long beard and I was filthy dirty.

Bob Otto was reflective too. He had been in the column that marched out of Fallingbostel and then came back. He yelled with all his heart when the British tanks arrived. Then he took a quiet moment for prayer, as he had done so many times since he became a prisoner. 'I thanked God that day. I was thankful that we made it, that we had had the strength to make it.' His religion had been a rock for him. So had thoughts of his wife waiting at home. He had fixed his mind on both, and he had come through the ordeal. He could barely wait to get home to see her again.

Otto would have to wait a while. For Les Allan, however, liberation meant a quick return home. He was an injured man. The march from the edge of Poland in his working clogs had crippled him. He had arrived at Fallingbostel only a matter of days before the camp was liberated. 'I was lying down on the ground when it happened. So were lots of others. We were so weak we couldn't get up and move. I was in such a dreadful state I had to have food brought to me.'[28]

It was RSM Lord who spotted Allan's plight, and dealt with it speedily.

I was leaning on a fence and he came up and asked me how long I had been a prisoner. I said, 'Five years', and he told me to go over to a point where there was a box and he said, 'Sit there.' So I went over and sat on the box, and four Americans came over with a machine. They put a nozzle up each trouser leg, up each arm, and turned the levers, and the next thing you couldn't see me for a cloud of white dust. The dust was DDT, and they were defumigating me. Then they put me in a lorry, and I was taken to a field full of marquees. Inside were long tables, and army cooks came out with dishes full to the brim with potatoes and beef. It was almost impossible to believe it. But then some doctors came in and ordered all the food to be taken away. They said too much food like that would damage us. It was heartbreaking. But they gave us a couple of spoonfuls of potato and gravy, and then we were put on planes. They had been on bombing raids over Germany, and landed on the way back to pick us up and take us to Brussels.

The ordeal really was over, and a grateful Les Allan was on his way home. He was one of the fortunate ones. For thousands of other prisoners of war out in the bleak countryside of north-west Germany, home was as far away as ever. Those who had been forced at gunpoint to join the march out of Fallingbostel were wandering through a battlefield. The first of the evacuees had left on 6 April, and various columns left at different times over the next few days. As Sergeant Alf Jenner, a veteran prisoner who was 'celebrating' exactly four years of captivity at that very time, noted, 'For the next month we were in the greatest danger since being shot down. For the whole of that time we were between the retreating Germans and the advancing Allies, often in the fighting front line itself.'[29]

For some, all that was waiting was a corner of a foreign field and the bitterest and saddest of ends.

12 Death by 'Friendly Fire'

The last place Batch Batchelder ever meant to fight his war was on the ground. As a boy, he loved the romance of the air – 'all those lovely stories of guys flying down the Nile in Empire flying boats and stopping overnight to pump fuel from 40-gallon drums. It was the one thing I longed to do. I was determined to fly.'[1] He cheered aloud the day war was declared, because his chance had come. He joined the RAF in the face of parental opposition. 'My mother and father wanted a safer occupation for me, but I wasn't frightened.' And if the Air Force had turned him down he would have joined the Navy and volunteered for submarines. Anything but the Army. 'I'd heard and read about the terrible casualties of the First World War. The one thing I was absolutely bloody sure about was that I was never going to fight on the ground.'

Yet here he was in April 1945, his feet firmly on European soil. They had not touched the rudders of a plane for nearly three years, not since his thirteenth mission over Germany, when his four-engined Halifax bomber had been hit by flak. Of the seven planes that took part in that particular attack on the industrial targets of the Ruhr valley, not one made it home. He had been through a handful of camps – Sagan, Heydekrug, Thorn, Fallingbostel. And now he was foot-slogging out of Fallingbostel and into the wild countryside of Lüneburg Heath with its mile upon mile of deep woods and rolling plains.*

Like the thousands of men around him, Batchelder had little idea of what the future held, only the fear that they were probably going to end up as hostages against a German surrender. 'There was real trepidation. We were very, very short of food, and had been for some time. Our morale was low.' This was not helped when the route of some of the columns took them past the Bergen-Belsen concentration camp, just a few miles away from Fallingbostel.

* See map 8 on page 260.

Leslie Frith remembered 'a chorus of yells from the emaciated inmates who lined the warning wire. The guards in the towers had their guns trained on them and, for a moment, the situation looked very ugly. However, we soon passed by and things calmed down.'[2] It was hardly surprising that, in that very first day, Richard Passmore felt a chill pass through him that was more than just the cold wind blowing across the open land:

We were marching towards a long, low ridge of wooded hills. Twilight was falling and there was a sudden breeze. At that moment I realized quite intensively how precarious our – my – future was. A bed in a prison camp was at least under a roof, but there were few places around here where a large party of men could sleep, not to mention many such parties. Whatever the future held, whether it was massacre, exposure, starvation – perhaps liberation – it was now hurtling towards us. This was surely the very last lap of our odyssey.[3]

He wrote his home address in the prayer book he carried with him, so that 'if the worst happened, that at least might find its way home'.
    As darkness fell, Batchelder reached the limit of his endurance.

I was at the end of my tether. I had been a prisoner for so long. I had dysentery, a severe attack this time, and I was squatting by the road. It was the most degrading time of my life. I told a German guard who tried to hustle me along that he could shoot me if that's the way he felt. I think he would have done so, but a couple of my mates grabbed hold of me and dragged me along until I came to my senses.

    Ken Brown also found the going difficult. This was no dawdle, however much Deans had encouraged them to go slowly. The Germans pushed them hard: 12 to 18 miles a day – a bruising pace, given how few rations they had to keep up their strength.

We were given a loaf of bread and a piece of sausage when we started out, and then we had to live off the land. We scrounged around for eggs and God knows what. There was a dead horse by the side of the road, and the lads I was with carved steaks off it and fried them on a fire. Then some stupid idiot punctured the horse's bowels. What a stink!

Worse than that, nothing more could be cut from it after that. Getting water was difficult. We often took it out of ditches and streams, picking out the duckweed and the slime before boiling it. And there was dysentery and disease. Every day we would see some poor bugger lying down at the side of the road. They just dropped out and couldn't move. We had to leave them, and I never knew what happened to them.

But I know some people escaped. A friend of mine ducked out of the column as we were crossing Lüneburg Heath. He ran into the gorse and the guards shot at him, but he got away. Later I found out that he made his way to the British lines and got home early.[4]

Most of the guards were reluctant to fire. When two prisoners made a run for it down an embankment, their intentions loudly announced by the crashing of the frying pan one of them had dangling from his pack, a guard stopped and lined them up in his sights. He waited a full thirty seconds while they ran into the woods before putting down his rifle and turning back to the march.[5] Cec Room had not been quite so lucky. He and his mate Jack Paul had slipped away too, got a mile down the road as the column marched in the opposite direction, but then ran into the cart for stragglers bringing up the rear. 'A German sees us and we've had it. Ah well, it was nice being free.'[6]

Hunger led to desperate meals. Room was in a group who bought a horse from a farmer. It was sick with TB,

but we didn't care. It was a bloody great cart horse, and, after the farmer shot it, four or five volunteers who knew something about butchery began to cut it up. They gave out bits and pieces. Some guys had a bit of meat and some had a bit of tail. Jack and I got a hunk of lung and the windpipe. It was like a piece of top hose from a motor car, only white. We cut it up and stewed it. It was tough and not very appetizing, but it was something to get our teeth into. Even those who had the meat found bits of hair all wrapped up in it.

They walked through a scarred landscape full of people who seemed to have nowhere to go but who filled the roads trying to get there. Villagers were hostile, though this did not stop them trading food – a few eggs or some bread – for 'luxuries' that some of the prisoners had, such as soap and cigarettes. Alf Jenner recalled the Americans being flush with cigarettes and sharing them out so that everyone had some 'currency' to trade with. 'The great trick was to be the first into a village to do your deal before the market got spoilt.'[7] Here was the chaos of a collapsing country, its people defeated in war and fearful of the future. Brown, who had been nervous about leaving the camp, found his worries eased once he was out on the road. 'We were not scared of the Germans. The main fear I had was fire. Usually we slept in a barn at night, and I remember being on the top floor, all of us lying on straw and everybody smoking. It was pretty stupid, and to this day I don't know how we got away with it.'

Others began to feel afraid of what was ahead. 'The war was nearing its end, but we didn't have any indication of what would happen to us,' according to Batchelder. The unease settled on Flight Sergeant Bob Morton. He had been happy enough as they lined up to leave Fallingbostel, concerned simply about what he could or could not take with him. Stacks of clothing had to be left behind, and a whole hut full of books. He was pleased to be leaving the camp, to be getting out beyond the wire that had been his home for the seven months since he arrived from Thorn. But once on the outside he began to feel vulnerable. The roads were crowded with columns just like theirs. Some were prisoners, mainly Russians; others were civilians in search of shelter. Some were heavily armed German soldiers with tanks and big guns heading for the front. Others had a pathetic air of fear and foreboding about them.[8] Alf Jenner noticed a detachment of boys from the German Labour Corps – 'lads in their teens', as he noted, 'poor devils!' As they passed by, he glanced up and saw Allied fighter planes – Typhoons – cruising over and 'having a look at us', their pilots clearly trying to work out who was on whose side in the complex jigsaw below. 'The next day Typhoons seemed to be around all day but gave the impression that they recognized the composition of our column.'

Down on the ground, Deans was a comforting figure for all those on the march. He tried to discourage escapers – though he did not expressly forbid anyone from trying to escape – and encouraged everyone to stick together. 'Anybody who slopes off is on his own,' he warned. 'Together, we survive.'[9] There were SS detachments out there shooting escaped prisoners of war on sight, he added. He kept in touch with news of the war via the radio which John Bristow now carried hidden in a billycan and which he would set up secretly wherever they were billeted at night.

Batchelder recalled how they marched in squads of about 500, 'and Dixie, who had managed to get hold of a bicycle, was riding from one squad to the other and arranging for barns for us to sleep in. He was amazing.' The men were in a number of different columns travelling down different roads, though all heading roughly in the same direction. In his neat RAF uniform, Deans would cycle across countryside between the columns, astonishing German troops he passed on the way. Most simply shrugged and marched on to wherever they were wearily heading, but on one occasion he was stopped and faced a gun in the hands of an irate *Wehrmacht* officer who wanted to shoot him. Coolly, in his immaculate German, Deans talked his way out of the difficulty and was allowed to ride off. He tensed his body in anticipation of a bullet in the back until he was sure he was out of sight, and only then relaxed.

To avoid similar encounters, Deans persuaded the German commandant, Oberst Ostmann, who was following the column in his staff car, to write him a letter of free passage that he could show to any Germans who stopped him in the future. In those chaotic times it would be no guarantee, but it might just help to save his life. Ostmann, who came to admire Deans as much as the prisoners did, offered the Englishman the use of his Opel, but Deans declined. That was not his idea of how a leader behaved. He would share the lot of his men, not loll in leather seats. While the German officer commandeered the best accommodation for himself each night – often in the larger farmhouses with well-stocked wine cellars, and once even in a castle – Deans slept alongside the men in barns. Cal Younger thought Deans a man who in those days had found his mission in life. 'Authority was epitomized in his voice and in his presence', and he used this to good effect on the Germans as much as on his own men. He would take on any guard who was showing signs of bullying; he fought to get the sick taken to hospitals for treatment; he constantly pressed for more food to be found. And at night he would ride from barn to barn, 'encouraging the weary and passing on any information he had gleaned that day'.

His arrival on his bicycle was usually greeted with cheers and a chorus of 'Here comes the galloping major'.[10] Alf Jenner dubbed Deans 'our heroic leader', and remembered the day (15 April) he rode up on his bicycle – an old and battered machine whose tyres were always on the point of puncturing – 'and told us that 3,000 lucky POWs who had been marched out of Fallingbostel had then been marched back to the camp and were now liberated'. It was something to cheer about, proof that the end was near. Perhaps they would be next. There was more evidence the next day, when they passed a landing strip and saw twenty or more Junkers-88 bombers burning on the ground, destroyed where they stood by a British air raid. As his column approached a German town or village, Percy Carruthers would call for a display of bravado. 'Jerry town coming up, fellows,' he would yell out.[11] 'Shoulders back, heads up, spring in your step – and remember you're British!' From behind him came a chorus of grumbles, but they followed his lead, heads held high.

*

As they trudged along, the word spread down the line that they were heading for the Elbe, and that once they had crossed it the bridge would be blown up behind them. The Germans were going to make the river their last line of defence, and the prisoners would be on the wrong side of it. Vic Gammon knew that if he and his mates John Leakey and Jock Hamilton were to escape they had to do so before that point. They seized their moment. A line of Allied planes flew low over the column, and everyone ran for cover. The three men just kept on going – into a small wood and out the other side, then throwing themselves down into a dip. No bullets thudded round them. There were no shouts. No dogs were sent in their direction. They had, however, been spotted. Gammon recalled, 'A guard was walking cautiously from the road into the wood, his rifle at the ready. We lay quite still but he saw us, and our eyes met. He stared steadily at us for 10 seconds, then, slipping his arm through the sling, he shouldered the rifle, turned and went back towards the column.' It was as if he had thought to himself, What is the point?

The three escapers set off westward, drawn by the setting sun because they had no map or compass to direct them or even tell them where they were. When it got dark they huddled in their greatcoats and slept as best they could. About midnight they were woken by someone moving around nearby, and they saw two people, one clearly a German officer in uniform. He had a woman with him, and, though it was a frosty night, they lay on the ground and made love. Just feet away from the entangled couple, the escapers dared not move until the officer and his girlfriend had finished, straightened their clothing, and walked away arm in arm. The next morning Gammon and the others set off again, keeping under cover as much as they could in the wooded countryside. At one point they ran into two men lurking, like them, in the trees. They were Russian prisoners, also on the run, and they had dug a hideaway in the forest. They invited the three Britons to join them.

The next night the three moved on, grateful to the Russians but not wanting to outstay their welcome. 'We walked through the dark countryside in silence, aware that we could be heard for long distances in the still April night.' A voice called out for them to halt as they waded through some bracken, and they ran, rushing through forest and undergrowth until they burst through some cover and found themselves beside an autobahn. On the road, a German military convoy was driving past. They stared at the officers in their open staff cars and the soldiers in their lorries, but there were barely glances for the three scruffy individuals carrying small sacks beside the road. 'As the end of the convoy disappeared, we rushed across the road and into the woods. We were grinning. A whole contingent of fighting *Wehrmacht* had passed within yards of us! "Perhaps they've got bigger worries than us," Jock chuckled.'

Their luck did not hold, and shortly afterwards they were stopped by a German soldier as they tried to slip through a village in the dead of night. They bluffed that they were French workers, but he ordered them at gunpoint to the local police station. It was early in the morning, and the village constable was incensed at being dragged from his bed. He didn't want to know anything about French workers. 'He ordered us to be taken to what he called "the French camp". We were marched to a barn and inside we were greeted by French workers who thrust bread and cheese into our hands and gave us hot drinks. We took off our boots and went to sleep.' But they were effectively prisoners again – part of a work detail labouring on a local farm.

With the French prisoners, they tilled the fields and planted seed potatoes. They kept up the pretence of being French, though the German guards knew they were not. Gammon recalled sitting on the doorstep of the farmhouse in the late-afternoon sunshine one day 'and one of the guards joined me and quietly said: "I will be glad when it is all over. At the first chance I will go back to Chicago where I had a used car business."'

It was over sooner than any of them thought. The next day they were out in the fields when they heard machine-gun fire coming from a nearby wood. The German farmers were worried. 'Will the Tommies kill my children, will they?' one of them kept asking tearfully. Gammon was taken aback when she showed him a magazine feature with an illustration showing British soldiers roasting a naked baby spiked on a bayonet. He grabbed it from her and ripped it up. 'That is disgusting Goebbels propaganda,' he told her.

Outside, a battle was shaping up around the farm. Youthful German soldiers were passing by with anti-tank weapons tied to the crossbars of their bicycles. From the direction of the front line came streams of wounded men. The three Britons were in the barn when, as Gammon recalled, 'the door crashed open and standing there was a young, grime-smeared British Army lieutenant, flanked by two privates wielding sub-machine-guns. "Any Englishmen here?" the lieutenant rapped, and we leapt to our feet. "You've got two minutes to get ready," he called out, "we are 20 miles ahead of the troops." We were ready, all right, ready and eager to go.'

As they were driven away, a British soldier offered Gammon some white bread and corned beef, butter, and a bottle of brown sauce. 'Such luxury was overwhelming and irresistible.' Then he was found a soft bed in a house in a village and managed to grab some sleep. Later he feasted on bacon and eggs. But it was a while before the three escapers could count themselves totally out of danger. There was no opportunity to return them to the front line straight away, and they had to stay with the soldiers who had released them as they advanced against the Germans.

I rode in a jeep with a tough, hard-bitten sergeant. After 20 minutes, we were halted by machine-gun fire from woods at the side of the road. Quickly men dropped off the convoy with machine-guns and flame-throwers. The skirmish was brief. German soldiers ran out from the trees, their arms held high. They were disarmed and told to walk back along the road to where the bulk of the British troops were coming. As the convoy moved again, more German soldiers were desperate to be taken prisoner.

At midday we drew into the square of a small town. German prisoners were herded into a tight group under the guns of British soldiers. Among them I saw the guard from the farm who had told me about how he wanted to go back to his home in Chicago. He was clutching a small suitcase with new boots tied to its handle but, as he was pushed with the others into a lorry, a British soldier tore it from his grasp and threw it into a ditch. I was sad that I could not help this enemy who had been so friendly to me just a few days ago. All he had wanted was peace and a return to Chicago.

By now Cec Room and Jack Paul were free too. A few days after their failed attempt to escape they had made another dash for freedom, hiding in a farmyard as the column went through.

We hid under some straw until we were discovered by two old ladies from the farm. We natter to them, though they are scared stiff and keep telling us that the Allies will kill them when they arrive. We smooth them over with some propaganda. One of them shows me a postcard from her son who is a POW in Canada. I'll bet he's more comfortable than I am.

The farmer, afraid of being caught harbouring escapers, decided to call in the authorities, and a German guard arrived to collect them. But the guard turned out to have a problem with his feet, and decided to stay on the farm with them.

We got chatting to him, and he is a disillusioned German, let down badly by the Führer. He lost his family in an air raid, and his brothers on the Eastern Front and is horribly brassed off with the war, most of all with the march. So are we. With some diplomacy we persuade him to hide us until the Allies come. He will be a prisoner in a week or so anyway, so what has he to lose?

What this meant was that he marched them very slowly in the same direction as the column but miles behind. He found them billets for the night, calming hausfraus who were still alarmed by the sight of *Terrorflieger*, and made sure there was plenty to eat – 'fried eggs (first for two years), onions and lashings of milk, all beyond our wildest dreams'.

Meanwhile German troops were overtaking them at great speed, in full retreat, and

we sensed our own troops were close. We were so bloody excited, it just wasn't true. The next morning we help the little Russian girl [a slave labourer] in the kitchen. She's about eighteen and the most beautiful girl I've ever seen. In decent clothes and with make-up I'd take her anywhere and love being seen with her. You'll soon be free, Olga. Huge breakfast – three platefuls of soup, bread, whey, cheese, jam, syrup, bacon and apples. My poor old stomach can hardly cope. That day I ate more food than in the whole of the last month. The guard has worked it out that our troops should be in the town tomorrow.

The next morning 'the great moment' really did arrive. A man came to the farm from the village saying the British had arrived, and with this the German guard surrendered. 'He whipped off his badges of rank and insignia, and they're my souvenirs. I also have his rifle, bayonet and ammunition. Do I feel good!' With their prisoner between them, the pair set off for the village and immediately heard a Cockney voice and saw the smiling faces of two English soldiers. 'We hug them in delight. We're the first liberated POWs they've met.' It was 18 April.

*

While the escapers celebrated their freedom, a tragedy was about to overtake one of the groups that had left Fallingbostel. It happened just as the men were recovering from a dip in morale. They had been on the march for a fortnight, heading roughly north-east along straight tracks through forests and fields until they had hit the flood plain of the River Elbe, criss-crossed by myriad small streams and dykes. Then they crossed the river itself. The front of the column waited until the early hours of the morning to sneak across the road bridge at the town of Lauenburg, hoping the darkness would provide cover from marauding Allied fighter planes. The danger was obvious enough: as they lay on the bank waiting,

Spitfires buzzed over and blew apart a tug and two barges. Anything that moved was a potential target, and night-time proved to be little help. The moon shone out of a cloudless sky, lighting up the bridge as if it were daytime, and they raced over it nervously, the wide Elbe flowing fast beneath them. Their luck held. As they crossed, they could see German soldiers mining the pillars of the bridge, while nearby Allied fighter planes were strafing formations of troops heading for the front. For a while the prisoners lay in a ditch as German tanks passed by with ashen-faced soldiers, many just teenagers, clinging to the sides for the last ride into battle. The tail of the column came over the river later that morning by a different route, and as they trudged through Lauenburg they heard explosions behind them as the metal-framed railway bridge they had just crossed was detonated.[12]

For some of the prisoners, crossing the Elbe was a low point. They were going backwards. Those who had come from the east only weeks earlier had rejoiced when the Elbe was behind them on their westward trek. It had stuck in the mind as a landmark, a sign pointing home. To be marched back over it in the wrong direction – the one they had come from – was painful to contemplate. Moreover, they were now on the wrong side of the river if the Germans decided to use it as a last-ditch line of defence.

To make matters worse, as they headed east into the rising sun it seemed as if the road they were on would never end. Deans thought that at this stage the Germans had run out of ideas and orders. 'They didn't seem to have any instructions and they couldn't tell us what the object of it all was. I'm sure they were helpless. We were just walking like dummies in a rough direction [towards the Baltic Sea] and nobody seemed to know where we were going.'[13] Deans, however, as always, had a plan.

The next day, a sign on the road pointed ahead to a village by the name of Gresse, and its church, high on a hill, and the rooftops of houses could be seen a little way off. The prisoners stayed the night in and around the village, and the following morning discovered that their leader had come up trumps. He had arranged for a supply of Red Cross parcels to be left for them – the first since Fallingbostel. One night he had taken advantage of the commandant's car and together they had driven 35 miles to Lübeck. The Red

Cross had agreed to send a convoy to meet up with the prisoners at Gresse. The gloom lifted. Food always had that effect. 'Euphoria,' said Batchelder. 'We had had virtually nothing to eat for days and then we got some parcels.' Morton recalled that 'we were all feeling pretty good, exploring our parcels, chattering with our mates. I was delighted as I went through mine, because it was the first time I had had an American parcel and their content was different from the British ones.'[14] Jenner was thrilled when he saw the Red Cross lorries lined up in Gresse and couldn't believe that Deans had pulled it off. 'To me he was like Jesus Christ with manna from heaven! There we were sitting in a green lane eating good food for the first time in weeks.'

Many of the columns converged on Gresse – 12,000 men in all, according to Younger. It was a tiny place – just a church, a school and a handful of houses – and so the men were encouraged to pick up their parcels – two each – and march out of the village to enjoy them in the countryside, where there was more room.

Refreshing themselves as they marched along, tearing at the boxes and stuffing themselves with goodies, the prisoners set out in a long line on the morning of 19 April, a Thursday, and headed north again, swinging along a country lane, forest on either side, and then out from the trees and into a patch of open grassland. Ken Brown was at the head of the column with his flight engineer, Gordon Reed, chatting away and munching on their Red Cross rations at the same time. The column stretched a long way behind, and those at the front were just about to pass back into the trees again when they noticed some RAF planes in the sky above. Further back in the column, Batchelder was still out in the open when he saw the Typhoons in the sky and counted nine of them, circling like hawks. 'As I watched they started to peel off, and I had the impression that they knew who we were and were just going to demonstrate their presence to us – and to the German guards, of course.' George Calvert, popping a piece of chocolate in his mouth, could see that the planes had black-and-white stripes on the underside of their wings and he thought they were probably German.[15] He took little notice as, a mile away, they made a low banking turn into line astern and disappeared behind the trees. Other prisoners, however, recognized them as British and started to wave and cheer. The Typhoons had clearly just come from attacking formations of retreating German troops, and it was marvellous to see them battering the enemy into submission.

Bob Morton was at the rear of the column and had stopped to stuff some tins of food from his Red Cross parcels into his backpack. He was standing up and getting ready to set off again when he spotted the planes,

though I didn't take much notice, because we had seen a lot of British aircraft over the previous day or two. Some people waved to them. The call came to move off, so I struggled into my backpack – a complicated web of straps, string, bundles and boxes. As I got to my feet they were diving on us, which I thought was just a bit of fun – like a mock attack, a beat-up, just as I would have done in the circumstances a few years earlier.

The planes screamed in at 30 feet above the ground, and as they roared over him Ken Brown noticed puffs of smoke from underneath the wings and, to his horror, saw clearly that their rockets had been fired, were in flight, and were heading at great speed straight for the column. He threw himself under a tree, but for those behind him it was too late to find shelter. Caught out in the open, Batchelder suddenly realized that the planes coming in low and fast 'were firing at *us*! We flung ourselves to the ground. Men were trying to bury themselves in the earth, hiding behind anything they could. We tried to get off the lane and into the fields, to use any hump that could give cover.' For some there was nowhere to hide. As the rockets hit, bodies were flung into the air like rag dolls.

Morton, still putting on his backpack, was first stunned by the horrendous noise, then terrified as

I saw sparks coming out of the machine-guns. I shouted, 'Oh my God!' and dived for the deck, scattering my belongings in all directions as I tore my harness off. After the first one had gone I got up and ran, and then I saw a second one coming and I dived to the ground again. I was trying to get as far away from the road as possible. I saw the earth being kicked up by machine-gun bullets just in front of my nose, and the next moment I felt as though my head had blown off. There was a shattering explosion and a tremendous concussion which seemed to come from inside it, and when I opened my eyes there was nothing but grey and I thought, 'Well that's that. Pity – it's been a good life.' I thought I'd died. But suddenly I found that I was running again, and as I burst out of the smoke I realized it was the smoke of a rocket that had landed just in front of me. More bullets came after me. I was in the front of the pack, and can only imagine that the pilots thought I was the leader and were deliberately picking on me. Time and again the earth kicked up just in front of me.

To Alf Jenner, who had been sitting in the sun eating from his Red Cross box, happier with food inside him than at any time on the march, what was happening was

the greatest tragedy of the whole war. They just came out of the blue and opened up on us with cannons and rockets, and, with no cover, many of my comrades were blown to pieces. As the survivors fanned out into the fields on either side of the lane, the planes came in, once, twice, three times more. I was crouched in a furrow in a ploughed field, and 50 yards away I saw one brave guy stand up and wave his blue RAF greatcoat to try and show them who we were. They just cut him down. In just a few seconds dozens were dead and as many again severely wounded. Some had been in captivity for four or five years – men we knew better than our own brothers.

Human remains lay everywhere. A torso was lodged in the branches of a tree. A head lay on the ground.

The attack went on for about ten minutes before Morton saw the last of the aircraft throttle back.

He was just cruising above us. I looked up, and I crossed my arms in the air – the sign for break off or stop firing. Then he flew off. I stood up and began to walk back to the lane. With the planes gone, there was an uncanny silence, broken only by crying and moaning. It was strange, but there wasn't a lot of loud screaming. I passed several dead and wounded bodies on the way back. Some people were wandering aimlessly, others were bending over injured friends. I saw a pair of legs with nothing attached to them – just lying in the field, complete with trousers. I remember one chap whose stomach had been ripped out. It was a scene of total carnage – by far the worst sight I'd seen through the whole war. The medical officer was doing what he could, of course, but it was a hopeless task. Nobody was talking much. We were all very silent and with our own thoughts. People were angry.

Jenner thought the end of the column had taken the worst of the battering. As usual on the marches, a horse-drawn cart had been tagging along at the end with the sick in it, and it seemed as if the Typhoons had deliberately targeted this. He shuddered at the thought. He had been sick and lame for much of the march, and until only a few days before he had either been on that cart or clinging on to the tailboard as he hauled himself along.

Now the cart was all smashed up and all around it were dead. The scene that day was like the famous pictures of Napoleon's retreat from Moscow. There were bodies lying about, and even those who hadn't been hit looked in a pretty desperate state. It was two weeks before the end of the war, after four years – almost unbelievable. So near yet so far. It was dreadful – and it was your own side that had done it. We thought that the Royal Air Force must have known that those roads were full of marching prisoners of war and other evacuees, women and children. They must have known that. I think the pilots were gung-ho. I wasn't angry at the time, but I was angry later.

Batchelder could not get out of his mind the incomprehensible stupidity of it all.

The RAF had done it. If it had been Germans I'm sure our feelings would have been different. I'm not blaming the RAF – this was just the sort of thing that happens in wartime. But that men who had been prisoners for four or sometimes nearly five years should be killed by their own side I think made it much worse. To me it was devastating.

Vic Gammon noted 'tears of deep sorrow and frustration on the faces of men hardened to death and war. These were their close friends, they had endured years of captivity and its hardships together. Now, with freedom and a reunion with their loved ones perhaps only days away, they were dead, killed by men of their service.'

Deans put the death toll at sixty in his own account of the incident.[16] 'There was a hell of a mess splattered all over the countryside. I think the last one in the flight that dive-bombed us realized that they had made a mistake, because he peeled off and went on his way. But it was too late by then. The damage had been done.' He walked among the dead and the wounded, arranged for the injured to be put in carts and taken to a hospital in a nearby town, and organized the digging of a grave and for a mass funeral to be held by the pastor from the church on the hill. The casualties included Canadians, Australians, New Zealanders, South Africans, Englishmen, Irishmen, Welshmen, Scots and an American. Many were RAF aircrew; others were soldiers taken prisoner as long ago as Dunkirk. There was grief too for the German guards who had been slaughtered, many of them older, family men who had shown kindness to the prisoners in their charge. Amid the horror and the grief, Deans knew he had to make sure this did not happen again.

The disaster could only have occurred because the column could not be distinguished from the air as being prisoners of war. Deans found that surprising, because 'we must have looked a shower of scruffs. We did try to display some indication marks to show we were prisoners of war and not troops, but it couldn't have been very successful.' Trailing the letters POW on sheets behind the column was clearly not enough. If more lives were not to be lost, he had to get a message to the Allied command.

The urgency of the situation was demonstrated within a few hours when another section of the column was hit by so-called 'friendly fire'. Prisoners had settled down for the night in a barn by the side of a river at a small hamlet called Cammin, and, as usual, had been locked in by their guards. Most of them were asleep in the hayloft when the sound of aircraft engines woke them. Doug Fry remembered looking through an opening and

I could see tracer bullets coming almost directly at my face. I thought, 'Christ!' I couldn't dig a hole, because it was a concrete floor. All I could do was turn my back to the bullets and hope. But as I turned I felt a whack across my back and blood trickling down. I'd been hit. I don't understand how more of us didn't die.[17]

Fry had been lucky. He was hit by a ricochet, but cannon shells ripping through the roof killed others as they lay. 'An American about 5 yards away from me had the top of his head blown off.' The man on one side of him slumped with a bullet through his neck, just missing his jugular vein. The man on his other side – 'his name was Reg Brown, and he'd been a kriegie for four years' – was killed outright, probably while still asleep.

The roof, which was made of thatch, caught fire, and soon the whole barn was ablaze. The prisoners battered down the doors and ran out into the cold night air, to be met initially by bullets from guards who had not grasped what was happening and thought a mass escape was in progress. The German bullets harmed no one. Once again it was British arms that had killed their own men. Four were dead and seven badly wounded, and Fry was amazed the numbers weren't higher. A mobile German army headquarters was camouflaged in trees nearby, and this may have been the real target.[18] But something had to be done to get the fly-boys in the air to be more careful. The lives of other fly-boys, on the ground, depended on it.[19]

So began a remarkable act of selfless bravery. Someone would have to cross the battlefield, through lines of German troops, then through no man's land, where the fighting was at its fiercest, and finally through the advancing ranks of British troops and tanks to find their field headquarters. The chances of being mistaken for the enemy by both sides was high. Deans could have asked for volunteers, arguing that he needed to stay at the head of his men, but he didn't.

I asked the German commandant for permission to go to Lauenburg on the River Elbe, which we knew was where the British had now reached. [It was 10 miles away, in the direction from which they had come.] He liked this idea. He even provided me with a better bike, because a tyre was going on the one I had. It was bursting out at the side like a balloon, and was going to blow out at any moment.

Oberst Ostmann had had to make a difficult decision. Just like his counterpart at Colditz, he wanted a peaceful end to his time in charge of Allied prisoners, but he was still under orders to keep them marching north and not to surrender them to the enemy. Deans played on his fears. The British had stopped at the Elbe, he told the German officer, and would not advance further because the area beyond it – the area they were in – had been designated as in the Russian zone. Did Ostmann really want to have to surrender to the Red Army? The German began to weigh his orders against thoughts of what the Russians would do to him. Then he gave Deans the go-ahead – and a written pass to get him through German lines.

Deans, whose experience of fighting was in the air, took along a British infantry officer who knew about warfare on the ground, plus a German guard by the name of Charlie Baumbach, whose presence would, he hoped, confer some sort of protection if they ran into German troops. They pedalled off back towards the sound of the guns.

I had given my parole – my word that I would not escape – but I insisted on the German accompanying me to get us out of difficulty if we ran into any problems. There was still fighting going on, still some Germans firing guns around, and I didn't want to be shot by accident. I wanted somebody there who had some authority to stop any damn fool German who was going to shoot me for the sake of it, just for fun.

It was a hazardous journey. 'All the way, there was firing around us – light arms usually, not heavy guns – and we were always running into groups of Germans,' Deans recalled. The front line always seemed to be the next village, and then the one after that. Heads down, ready to dive for cover at any second if necessary, they rode on, passed from one unit of soldiers to the next. Heavy mortar fire crashed around them, and they ran for shelter in a house. The British, they were told, were in the next village. That night, exhausted, they rested – and in the end it was the front line that found them.

When he woke the next morning, Deans was being shaken by a British soldier. It was a tricky moment. 'The British had tommy guns and a tendency to fire away at nothing in particular,' he recorded later. It was no wonder these battle-hardened front-line troops were suspicious and uncooperative to begin with. Here was a man dressed in RAF blue in the middle of a war zone, accompanied by a German soldier, and asking for any bombing of the road ahead to be halted. They thought he was a spy, or an impostor at the very least. 'Nobody would touch me,' he said.

He was passed from private to sergeant to lieutenant, and then to a major and a colonel, who promised he could see the general later that morning. Deans waited for the general. 'I had no idea about time then, and I couldn't care less. All I wanted to do was to impress on the most senior officer I could that we were out there and we shouldn't be bombed.' When the general arrived, he heard Deans out and then grabbed the field telephone. 'He knew which unit must have attacked us and he knew there was another raid just about to be carried out. He managed to stop it just in time.' Deans had prevented another slaughter.

But his war was still not over. The general offered Deans an immediate flight back to England, 'but I said no. I had come solely to contact the British and warn them about the presence of the prisoners of war, and having done that I felt I had to go back to the men I was leading.' He also felt honour-bound by the word he had given to the German commandant. 'He had allowed me to do this. I felt I ought to go back as a courtesy to him, if nothing else. It would have suited me well personally if I could have gone straight home, but I just couldn't do it.'

Deans also kept his word to the German guard, Baumbach, who had come through the lines with him. The British had disarmed him and were about to march him off to a prisoner-of-war cage, but Deans demanded his release to return with him back across to the German side. 'He is my escort, not a prisoner,' he insisted.[20] 'He volunteered to come with me, and I have given my word of honour to return.'

They went back through the front lines and into the battle zone again – though now they travelled in style in a captured Mercedes with a Red Cross flag draped across the bonnet. The party got to Gresse, where the German commandant and some of his staff were waiting. 'They were absolutely amazed to see me and tickled pink that I had been through to the British front-line troops and come back again.' As for the column, it had moved on immediately after the Typhoon attack and was still heading north towards Lübeck. Now, each night they stopped, the first priority was to lay out a big sign on the ground – 'RAF – WE ARE NOT SOLDIERS.' When Deans caught up with the column he was greeted with incredulity by his men. 'God stone the crows,' said an Australian. 'Talk about miracles. Now he's turned a bike into a flaming Mercedes-Benz!'[21]

Over the next few crucial days Deans acted as an emissary between the German and British troops. Sick prisoners were being held in a village where German forces were dug in, and it looked as if a fierce fight would break out around them. Deans persuaded the Germans to withdraw. Then, as the British front line advanced, he drove in his Mercedes to the next point of attack, a farmhouse. British tanks were hidden in the trees behind him ready to fire. A German sergeant was determined to resist, to fight to the bitter end. Encouraged by Deans, the men in his platoon were less eager to die, and the farmer and his family in whose house and barns they were dug in were eager for their home not to be blasted apart. A surrender was arranged. And so it went on. Deans went from one pocket of resistance to another, persuading the defenders to lay down their arms. Eventually he returned to the column, where Oberst Ostmann was still nominally in charge, though constantly looking over his shoulder to the east and worrying about the Russians.

What orders the Germans in charge of the columns were getting in those final days and weeks remains a mystery. One of the few commandants to give an account recalled supervising his British prisoners – mainly army privates – on various work details in the Hanover area before traipsing them round and across Lüneburg Heath, trying to escape the Americans. The number of guards was now severely depleted after many had been ordered to join the fighting on the front line, and in the end they all seem to have melted away. The commandant himself, however, tried to retain a semblance of some military order right to the end, and he described how 'the Commandant of Prisoners-of-War ordered the final dispersal of the staff' shortly before he himself 'fell into English captivity'.[22] But his report gave no explanation of what was achieved in those final weeks, or why they marched on and where they thought they were going.

It was all becoming academic. One hundred and fifty miles away, also fearful of the Russians and what they might do to him if they took him alive, Adolf Hitler put a pistol in his mouth and shot himself in his bunker in Berlin. It was 30 April 1945. When the news emerged it had an immediate consequence. His oath of loyalty to the Führer now defunct, Ostmann felt he could surrender to his one-time captive, Dixie Deans. As he took the German's Luger, Deans must have felt a sense of satisfaction. He once said that his job had simply been 'to get everything to run smoothly in the camp and to keep peace and quiet'. Now at last he had both.

*

The men who had left Fallingbostel nearly four weeks earlier were now strung out all over Lüneburg Heath, and even after Ostmann had surrendered it would be days before command was completely passed over to the Allies. Percy Carruthers was anxious that the men in his charge should not anticipate their release. He told some of them who wanted to hurry events along that their guards 'are still top dog until we get their guns; until then remember they're swinging on your balls'. They were comfortably billeted on a farm, and Carruthers's plan was to stay there. Allied planes passed over regularly, swooping low to destroy the occasional lorry on a nearby road but otherwise content with victory rolls and waggling their wings. 'We cheered them and waved encouragement.' There was more than enough food, and some prisoners were beginning to put back the weight they had lost. Men sat out in the sun, had their hair cut, sang songs for the first time in an age.

The Germans tried to move them westward, back the way they had come, to get away from the Russians, but Deans arrived in his Mercedes and told them to stay where they were. Carruthers

went round the barns and announced to the boys that we were to resist any attempt to move us. Stay put until our troops arrive within the next 24 hours. Liberation and freedom. Great cheers went up. Some leaped around like crazed natives in a war-dance. Others wept. They were extremely happy but they were also well-behaved. I was proud of them. One could have excused an outbreak of mayhem. There were deep emotions from all these young men. They had looked death in the face on many occasions but had stuck together, supporting each other when everything appeared to be against them. Behind us were the years of barbed-wire incarceration and the last three months of marching, in rain, hail and snow, sleeping in woods, fields and barns in wet and filthy clothing. The torturous, footsore 600 miles had claimed many friends and crippled many others, forcing us all beyond the point of human endurance.

The next day, 2 May, a fleet of lorries arrived along with scout cars of the 6th Airborne Division.

We went mad. Fellows were crying and laughing and hugging and congratulating each other on having survived. We got cigarettes, biscuits, choc, compo [tinned rations], matches, beautiful white bread which was so white we could hardly believe it was true, and many other impossible little treats. This was the most momentous moment of my life. I felt a great satisfaction. It was as though a whole new world was opening up before my very eyes. It was an event to dwarf the feeling I had on that day I joined the RAF. It even exceeded the satisfaction of my first solo flight.

Carruthers took charge. He called over the German officer and told him to get his men to drop their arms in a pile and fall in. '*Von hier aus, gebe ich alle Befehl*' – 'From here on, I'll give all the orders' – he added. The Germans did as they were told, and a few even saluted.

Beyond the piled arms there were knots of British airmen, now *ex*-prisoners-of-war, clad in the worn and filthy clothing they had been wearing continuously for the past three months. They were laughing and joking and looking for acquaintances and friends. This was the day they had lived for through their torture, degradation and hunger, but sometimes doubted whether they would ever live to see. It was all over at long last.

Alf Jenner was freed on the same day. After Gresse, the column he was in had kept marching, but the roads it was on became more and more congested with German civilians and soldiers fleeing from the fighting but unsure where to go. Each day was spent just trying to stay alive and out of trouble, trying to avoid concentrations of unpredictable Waffen SS troops, hoping to see a Union flag flying from a tank or a troop carrier. 'We were in a village called Harmsdorf, which was full of retreating German troops of all units, including the SS, so we expected a major attack with armour and infantry. I was cooking some oats over a camp fire when someone shouted, "There are British tanks over there."' Jenner shook his head in disbelief and carried on heating his breakfast without even bothering to look up.

But it was true. The moment of liberation had come! It was fantastic. The Army came through, and I remember being impressed by how fit the men looked. What followed was sheer delirium. My buddy and I found an abandoned car and we roared around the village in it in our excitement, until it was commandeered by the Army for a better purpose. Then we strolled down to some temporary prisoners' cage which had been set up for surrendering Germans. I recognized one who had treated me roughly on the march and mentioned it to the young soldier who was on guard. 'Here you are,' he said, handing me his Sten gun. 'Take the bugger over there and shoot him while escaping.' This guard had been rough with me when I was weak and couldn't walk fast. He had prodded me with his bayonet or hit me with the butt of his rifle. But I turned down the offer. Later on I came across another former guard who had given me a hard time. He still had his bayonet in its sheath and I snatched it from him and threatened him. His eyes turned upwards as he waited for the end, but the only thing that happened was that I had grabbed his belt too and his trousers fell down. He was completely humiliated. That was enough for me.

Richard Passmore felt sorry for one ageing guard left behind at the end.

He was in tears. He had just heard of Hitler's death and he told me he could vividly remember the last defeat in 1918 and its aftermath. He knew it would be even worse this time. Many more countries had been occupied and many more would want revenge. He took out some stamps bearing Hitler's head and gave them to me as a symbol of the ending of an era. I stuck them inside the cover of my prayer book.

Later that day Passmore saw a column of tanks with the large white star of the American forces on the side and ran to greet them.

We stood beside the road, mute, incredulous in our moment of glory. The first tank commander to pass clearly recognized our dirty and bedraggled uniforms and he bent down and re-emerged from his tank with an armful of packets and tins which he dropped down to us. We cheered and waved. Some of us wept. One tank stopped and the major in charge told us we were authorized to confiscate any vehicles we might need to make our journey back. We did not hesitate. We set up a road block for all German traffic and by nightfall we had a couple of hundred assorted vehicles, from lorries to Mercedes staff cars and a couple of BMW motor-bikes with sidecars. We also had a small armoury of machine-guns, rifles, pistols and stick-grenades. We had no intention of using them. Simply having them underlined our changed status. We had locked up our guards in a barn, and they were more than willing to accept us as the ones now issuing the orders. I slept that night in a proper bed in a house in the village. But before I turned in I looked out over the countryside. The stars were brilliant, glowing from a deep electric blue, the colour my mother used to call 'midnight madness'. All around me the night air was alive with the sound of my comrades, singing, laughing, talking in the over-loud voices of utter relief. I was approaching the end of my journey. I was no longer a prisoner. That night I slept deeply.

Liberation was not always so simple or safe. Jim Sims was in a group of 300 men from a work detail who were wandering around the edge of Lüneburg Heath. The war went around them, as if they were in a bubble. They saw its effects everywhere – 'the debris of a dying army', as Sims described it after seeing a bus full of charred German soldiers, caught in an air attack, slewed across an auto-bahn.[23] Shells were falling and black columns of smoke rising, never far away. They walked along roads where troops were dug in – 'a tough-looking crowd of truculent bullies, and we hurried past with heads down, wishing to avoid confrontation at all costs'. Their body of guards was swelled by army deserters looking for somewhere to hide from the SS. The woods were full of men who had thrown away their weapons and were sneaking from the front line to save their skins. One of them grinned at Sims from the trees and called out, 'It's a long way to Tipperary, Tommy.'

A sergeant in charge decided it was time to act. He approached the German officer and suggested that if he and his men surrendered they would get safe passage. The German quickly agreed, handing over his revolver and telling the guards to ground their rifles. The prisoners were free. They were also in the middle of a battlefield. A British tank-destroyer passed them at high speed in pursuit of a German Tiger, which was then hit by a rocket from a Typhoon overhead. Shells, mainly British, were raining down. The group took shelter in a nearby village, and Sims was keeping watch on the road when he saw a cloud of dust in the distance.

He was expecting British troops. What arrived was a German half-track manned by Hitler Youth fanatics under the command of an SS officer. Suddenly the situation had reversed. The guards were released and handed back their rifles. The British prisoners were locked up again. Things looked bad as the Hitler Youth started to dig in on the outskirts of the village for a last-ditch stand. But the sergeant seized the initiative again. He persuaded the SS officer that his position was hopeless, that British armour had already been through here and he would soon be surrounded. The German took the hint and ordered his men – his boys, given their age – to leave. Sims remembered this as the most dangerous moment of all,

because there was no knowing what they would do before they left. I fully expected them to set fire to the barn with our blokes in it. In the end they settled for threats. The SS officer ordered our guards to march us towards Berlin without delay, and threatened to return to check up if this order had been carried out. To our relief the whole gang trundled off eastwards, and everyone was let out of the barn. Once again our sergeant took over control, but he agreed that the guards should keep their weapons, in case that SS bastard kept his promise.

Sims had no illusions about what the SS and fanatics were capable of. A dozen men from his group had slipped away to make their own way to Allied lines. They had urged Sims to go with them, but he had refused. Later their bodies were found in a ditch, their hands tied behind their backs and their throats cut.

For those who were patient, liberation came the next day as a British Bren-gun carrier drove out of the trees. The men engulfed it, and there was tea and sweets and cigarettes. Pretty soon there were other unexpected delights on offer in the German village. Sims caught sight of two Polish girls who had been forced labourers and were now celebrating their freedom like everyone else.

They sauntered over, wearing tight-fitting polo-neck jumpers, black skirts and jackboots. They were after cigarettes and stood there smiling at me and my buddy, John. We gave them fags and, as they turned and walked away, John nodded towards their attractive rears and asked me: 'How would you like to have a bash at them?' I replied: 'I'd rather have a boiled egg' – and he looked at me pityingly. 'Blimey, you're in a bad way,' he said.

Many moments of liberation were amazingly low-key. Men would be sitting 'making a brew' when they looked up and saw British soldiers walking down the road towards them and heard someone say, 'Fellows, you are now free.' One group watched their twenty-five guards disappear into a barn and come out a few minutes later wearing Red Cross armbands. Joe O'Donnell was still marching, heading down a road from a farm where the column had spent the night, when he simply walked into an advance detachment of the Eighth Army.

It was a bit strange. If we had been in a camp and the Allies had come barging in, there would have been elation. But we just passed the point of liberation. We were glad, of course, but it wasn't a moment of jubilation. The British soldiers pointed us in a westerly direction to a town where we would be looked after.[24]

Few moments were as matter-of-fact as Ken Brown's. He and his mates had been bedded down in a pigsty on a farm for several days.

We had turned the pigs out, cleaned up the sty, and laid fresh straw down. About 10 a.m on Wednesday 2 May a British column drove into the farmyard and liberated us. The crew of the leading Bren-gun carrier gave me a packet of Player's Weights, a short tubby captain with a cocky attitude assured us we were free, and then they were off again in pursuit of Germans. Overnight the battlefront had passed through us and we knew nothing and heard nothing.[25]

For Batch Batchelder there were more days of captivity to go.

It was 8 May and we were still heading north towards Lübeck. We had come to the end of a normal day's march, bedded down and gone to sleep, and in the morning there were no guards. It was almost euphoria – but not quite, because we had no idea where we were or what would happen next. We were still straggling along and then a couple of scout cars of the King's Own Yorkshire Light Infantry came along. They told us to stop and they would arrange transport. Shortly after the Americans came along and gave us chewing gum, which probably wasn't very helpful for our stomachs. But then some troop-transporters arrived and picked us up, and after about 5 miles we stopped and we were given some white bread and butter and jam. I reckon that was about the finest meal I've ever had – a real banquet.

*

Hitler was dead; most of the prisoners of war were free men again; the formal German surrender to Field Marshal Montgomery on Lüneburg Heath was only hours away. By the side of an airfield, a group of casualties from the Gresse incident were lying in the grass waiting for an air ambulance to fly them out. A pilot wearing wing commander's insignia on his sleeves spotted them and came over to wish them well. 'What have you chaps been up to?' he asked.[26] 'Are you ex-POWs?' He got his answer from a soldier on a stretcher: 'Yes, we are, but a couple of weeks ago we were shot up by some bastard crowd of half a dozen Typhoons. It was at a place called Gresse.' According to accounts from the time, the face of the wing commander, a Canadian, went ashen. 'My God, I was leading that flight,' he said. There was silence as everyone tried to take in the admission, then another man on a stretcher explained that they were the lucky ones who had survived. Many had not. 'Some of them had done five years and were on the last knockings of getting towards home and this had to happen.' As the wing commander walked away, the wounded former prisoners – the victims of his overeagerness, his lack of restraint, his awful error of judgement – saw the tears roll slowly down his face.

13 A German Saviour?

Fear was the backdrop of every prisoner's life, and it did not always disappear the instant he was free. After Moosburg was liberated by Patton's Third Army, there were prisoners who could not wait to get out of the camp and into the nearest town, but Joe Lovoi stayed where he was, behind the barbed wire. 'I didn't want to do anything foolish. There might have been some *Luftwaffe* or Gestapo people out there after revenge, so I hung around in camp. Even after we were liberated there was a sense that it wasn't quite over yet.'[1] In another part of Germany, Cec Room was freed by British soldiers in the front line of the Allied advance, and while he sat drinking tea there was a battle in full swing around him, the outcome of which was uncertain for a while. 'The tanks opened up at Messerschmitts and Focke-Wulfs, and all of a sudden I was scared stiff. God, wouldn't it be awful to be captured again!'[2]

Such moments did not last long. The prisoners really were free, and, when that realization sank in, the fear that had shadowed them lifted like a cloud. It passed from over the heads of the prisoners and settled instead on their former captors. Now it was the turn of the German guards to know the stomach-turning sensation of being in the power of the enemy. Private Maurice Newey, a prisoner since the desert fighting in North Africa, watched as his former guards were rounded up and taken away in lorries. He had cause to loathe them after his forced 400-mile march, but he could not bring himself to do so:

They looked so miserable and dejected that I couldn't help but feel a little sorry for them. I knew exactly how they felt. But there was one guard who had killed one of my friends in cold blood – put his rifle against his body because he wouldn't move and just shot him through the heart. Now he was singled out to the Yanks, and they took him into the woods and shot him. Then we found out that, at the time he did what he did, his family had just been killed in the bombing at Dresden.[3]

Room was another who had thought his heart totally hardened against the Germans, but then he saw an elderly guard who had showed him some kindness.

He had lost everything – his family, the whole bloody lot. I had a hundred cigarettes and some chocolate, and I gave them to him. There was this look of gratitude on his face. Maybe I was in a mood and in the right position to be sorry for him because we were going home. But it just brought out the futility of war.

Could these pathetic figures heading off into captivity really be the same men who only hours before had held what amounted to the power of life and death? The same men who had instilled fear over many years, both as individuals and as agents of a ruthless dictatorship? Too many had indeed been the embodiment of the regime they served – little Hitlers who revelled in their power and were indifferent to the suffering they inflicted. But now, with the abject defeat of their nation, that past fear of them seemed unreal. After a happy ending, it was perhaps easier to believe that you had never really feared for your life, that you had never thought the worst would happen. And, of course, in the end the optimists proved to have been correct about the prisoners' fate. Though there were undoubtedly individual acts of murder and brutality, there was no mass massacre, no gas chambers or killing fields; the bodies of prisoners of war did not line the roads or hang from every lamp-post. So had the fears all been groundless? Had the prisoners never really been in danger after all?

At one level the answer is immaterial: the terror was real enough at the time. And there had been plenty of circumstantial evidence to justify the nightmares. George Guderley believes that the fact that his march from Gross Tychow ended at a camp just a stone's throw from Belsen was no coincidence. In his view, the extermination camp next to Fallingbostel was where he and his fellow marchers were intended to end up and that all that saved them was the rapid Allied advance and the ending of the war before this plan could be carried out. It is not a totally far-fetched theory. While many of the camp guards – *Luftwaffe* and *Wehrmacht* men – would undoubtedly have baulked at an order to murder the POWs, they may have had little alternative but to do so. Always in their mind was the spectre of the SS. And this was what had haunted Allied prisoners of war too – the revenge of the SS.

It was an SS battalion that had captured 100 men of the Royal Warwickshire Regiment manning the rearguard outside Dunkirk, herded them into a barn, and then thrown grenades inside. That had been on 28 May 1940. Four and a half years later, another SS battalion, leading the advance into the Ardennes at the start of the Battle of the Bulge, mowed down 170 American soldiers who had surrendered at Malmédy, their hands in the air, their rifles grounded. Clearly the SS had nothing to lose by more atrocities.

Jim Sims wrote of one night when he had a bad scare.

The SS swept through our huts turning us all out of bed and driving us out on to the parade ground. We were not allowed to take anything with us. We lined up outside and they fanned out around us. Two half-tracks rumbled in. One had a searchlight mounted on it which began to sweep up and down our ranks. The other had a machine-gun, cocked with the ammo belt inserted and ready to fire, its muzzle swinging backwards and forwards over our ranks. The searchlights in the watchtowers were switched on and the whole area was illuminated, and all the machine-guns in the watchtowers were manned as well. What was it all about? Was it going to be a massacre? Had Hitler given orders for all prisoners of war to be killed? Many thought so and acted accordingly. Some cried, some shouted defiance, some started to sing 'God Save the King'. Many of us just stood there mute, unable to react in any way at all. I remember feeling completely resigned. After an hour, the SS suddenly packed up everything and rumbled away. We went back to our huts. We later heard that they had been searching for a secret radio.

You were never quite sure when a prisoner of the Nazis.[4]

Sims also recorded that, when typhus swept though the neighbouring compound for Polish prisoners, threatening an epidemic, the Germans had their own unique solution. They bottled up all those with the disease in one hut and then sent for the SS, who shot everyone inside through the windows and then brought in flame-throwers to burn the hut, and its dead occupants, to the ground.

Many prisoners thought that they were marked men. Rumours abounded that Hitler had ordered their execution. At other times it was said to be Himmler or Goebbels who wanted them dead. Threats were invariably reported as hard fact, but for men behind barbed wire the only source for such information was their guards, and most of the guards had as little idea as the prisoners of what was going on in the minds of their military masters in Berlin. That did not stop them speculating, however. For instance, a prisoner on the march out of Fallingbostel overheard the guards talking. Apparently their destination was Denmark, where the prisoners were to be exterminated 'on Hitler's orders'. Fifteen years after the war, this same prisoner recorded how he was visiting Tokyo and by chance ran into a German, a former Gestapo officer, who had interrogated him when he was a prisoner of war. 'I immediately recognized him but he did not recognize me. I spoke to him, offered to shake hands, but he refused to believe I was a former POW because he said they had all been killed on Hitler's orders.'[5] Jim Sims heard another common enough story: that Hitler had ordered the murder of all prisoners of war, 'and that only the disobedience of local German commanders in the field had saved our lives'.

But it is questionable whether any such orders were ever given. Threats may have been uttered, but not orders – and orders were what mattered. For example, on more than one occasion a furious Hitler shouted out that 'The entire *Luftwaffe* staff should be hanged!'[6] But it was never taken as an instruction and acted upon. The German records show that the Führer issued a number of orders to do with Allied prisoners of war which could be confused with instructions for them all to be murdered. There was, for example, the Commando Order of October 1942. British raiding parties on the European mainland were causing the Germans so many problems that Hitler instructed that any commandos caught were 'to be slaughtered to the last man; they were not to be spared, even if they surrendered'.[7] The argument was made that, since they were operating under cover, their welfare was not protected by the Geneva Convention. In June 1944 this order was extended to include enemy parachutists caught behind the lines. They were deemed spies, and were to be treated accordingly. The following month, as German cities were pounded by British and American bombers,

Hitler turned his wrath on Allied airmen with an instruction that 'every enemy aviator who is shot down while participating in an attack on civilian targets is not entitled to treatment as a prisoner of war but will be treated as a murderer as soon as he falls into German hands'.

Interestingly, this order was made but was never actually issued and never became officially operational. Presumably someone in the German high command put forward the argument that dominated so many prisoner-of-war issues – reciprocity. If British and American pilots were held to account for deaths in Cologne and Berlin, then captured *Luftwaffe* men could expect to answer for London and Coventry. The order was downgraded and became an unofficial threat. In practice it led to the deaths of RAF and USAAF men as German police and army units were ordered not to stop civilians taking revenge on so-called *Terrorflieger* if they fell into their hands. This was an incitement to lynching, but not an instruction – and, though there were horrific examples of civilians murdering downed airmen, in practice most German military personnel did their best to protect Allied flyers from this treatment.

From the beginning of January 1945, Hitler's orders were increasingly frantic. Many were military – ordering this stronghold or that salient to be defended at all costs, and then sacking and replacing those officers who retreated. Then, in the middle of March, came the order which – as we have seen – has often been confused with an instruction that all prisoners were to be executed. The so-called Nero Order put the match to a scorched-earth policy. Everything was to be destroyed in the fight for the fatherland. Nothing was to be left for the Allies. If Germany was to be overrun, it would be destroyed first. There was no mention of prisoners of war – or at least not Allied ones. But that same month a warning was issued to German soldiers not to surrender: if they laid down their arms while unwounded, they would be regarded as traitors and their relatives would suffer the consequences.[8]

Hitler certainly instigated severe measures against Allied prisoners of war who escaped. The fifty air-force officers shot after the breakout from Stalag Luft III at Sagan in 1944 were executed on his express instructions. Earlier that year an order had gone out that recaptured escapers were to be handed over to the SS and then sent to the Mauthausen concentration camp. There they would be subjected to what was termed 'Aktion Kugel'. *Kugel* is German for bullet.[9]

But, apart from the documents mentioned, the authors have been unable to trace anything other than anecdotal evidence of orders from Hitler for the extermination of Allied prisoners. Yet the rumours persisted that he had given such instructions. When the war was over, the American Red Cross claimed that in March 1945 Hitler had ordered the execution of all American and British airmen held captive in Germany in reprisal for the Allied bombing of German cities, particularly Dresden, but that German army commanders had refused to carry out this order. A press release attributed this information to the president of the International Committee of the Red Cross, Carl Burckhardt, speaking in Switzerland. It added, 'This statement has been substantiated by American prisoners-of-war, recently liberated and returned by air from Germany, who were in a position to know the facts.'[10] The claim does not stand up to scrutiny. First, prisoners of war were the very last people in a position to know the facts. All they could report on was rumours they had heard. Second, there is no mention of Burckhardt's claim in the definitive history of the Red Cross and its activities during the Second World War,[11] and yet, if it were true, it would seem odd to omit a matter of such significance. Third, Dresden was pulverized in the middle of February – why would an angry Führer wait until the following month to order a reprisal?

The bombing of Dresden has been linked with Hitler's alleged threat on more than one occasion, and was the subject of an important discussion between United States diplomats and representatives of the Swiss Protecting Power at Berne, the Swiss capital, on 7 March 1945. The Swiss had heard rumours that 'certain German elements' wanted revenge for the attack and that reprisals on prisoners of war had been mooted.[12] The Swiss had discussed this with the Germans, 'and received assurances from the Germans that they did not contemplate such action'. A telegram from the US embassy in Switzerland to General Eisenhower at SHAEF headquarters was explicit: 'No fear is felt by Naville [the Swiss representative] personally that Allied prisoners-of-war will be massacred by the Germans or that any other rigorous action will be taken against them.' It went on to try to allay other fears:

Naville expressed little credence with respect to the rumours that it is the German intention to take British and American prisoners-of-war to a possible location as a last stand of die-hard Nazis as hostages. Should the Nazis make such a last stand, he pointed out, they did not wish to be hindered by large numbers of prisoners-of-war who might cause trouble and who would have to be guarded and fed (though they might take important/high-ranking prisoners).

What the Swiss reported – and what the US ambassador in Berne clearly accepted as the truth – was, of course, no guarantee. The German diplomats they spoke to may have been lying, or may not have known what was in Hitler's mind. But, since Gilbert Naville's judgement turned out – as we will see – to be spot-on about the implausibility of suggestions that the Nazis were planning a last redoubt, he may well also have been right that there was no threat to massacre the prisoners.

Nevertheless, the rumour surfaced again as recently as 1997, when previously classified documents on the questioning of Nazi war criminals at Nuremberg were released.[13] Now the source was the dead *Luftwaffe* chief, Hermann Goering. In 1946 he had told his American interrogators that Hitler had wanted to 'exterminate' all the prisoners and would have carried out his threat if the war had gone on any longer. All the other top Nazi officials – Goering among them, of course – had opposed the idea, as they had opposed another suggestion, made at the same time. This was that Germany should abandon the Geneva Convention because German troops were far too ready to surrender to the enemy, knowing they would be treated well in captivity. Goering was an unreliable witness. He was out of favour with Hitler at the end of the war, and would be denounced as a traitor for trying to treat with the enemy while Hitler was in his bunker in Berlin. Moreover, when he spoke to US interrogators he was fighting to save his neck,[14] and nothing served his purposes better than to portray himself as a reasonable and honourable man whereas his Führer had been out of control.

In essence, Goering's account was true – but in not telling the full story he was less than generous to his former friend, Hitler. According to Ian Kershaw's biography of Hitler, the bombing of Dresden did indeed anger the Führer, who

heard the news of the devastation stony-faced, fists clenched. Goebbels, said to have been shaking with fury, immediately demanded the execution of tens of thousands of Allied prisoners-of-war, one for each citizen killed in the air raids. Hitler was taken with the idea. Brutal German treatment of prisoners-of-war would, he was certain, prompt retaliation by the Allies. That would deter German soldiers on the western front from deserting.[15] It took the efforts of Jodl, Keitel, Dönitz, and Ribbentrop, viewing such a reaction as counter-productive, to dissuade him from such a drastic step.[16]

There the matter rested, and it was apparently never referred to again.

In summary, the suggestion of massacring prisoners came from Goebbels, and Hitler was enthusiastic because the knock-on effect would be to make his own troops fight harder. The idea was dropped when the Army (Field Marshals Jodl and Keitel), the Navy (Admiral Dönitz) and his Minister of Foreign Affairs (Ribbentrop) opposed it. It had been a momentary thought, and one that Goebbels did not even think worth noting in his extensive personal diary. He did, however, expand on the idea that the Geneva Convention should be abandoned, but without mentioning anything about massacres. Prisoners of war did surface in his diary a few weeks later. In his entry for 4 March 1945, Goebbels wrote:

The Führer is violently opposed to any steps being taken to assist Anglo-American prisoners-of-war now in the process of transfer from the East to the neighbourhood of Berlin. There are some 78,000 of them and they can no longer be properly fed; they are riddled with lice and many of them are suffering from dysentery. Under present circumstances, there is little one can do for them. Perhaps it would be possible to call in the Red Cross to help in producing a semi-human existence for them.

Not helping was what Hitler was suggesting, and that was a far cry from the sentence of death that rumour said he had passed on the prisoners – and even then the hard-line Goebbels wanted to throw them a lifeline.

In truth, Hitler gave scant thought to the Allied prisoners within his borders. He did not care about them one way or the other. His whole vision of the world was collapsing, and he would not bargain with their lives because he had no intention of bargaining at all. Others in the Nazi hierarchy, however, would do anything to try to save their own skins.

*

Generalleutnant (Lieutenant-General) Gottlob Berger had never wanted the job, and he told Hitler so to his face. At least that is what he claimed much later, when the Führer was dead and the war was over. The SS general had been put in charge of Germany's vast army of prisoners of war in the autumn of 1944, and he knew full well that a poisoned chalice had been placed in his hands. The war was almost certainly lost, and afterwards there would without doubt be recriminations. This was a time when a man with a Nazi track record like his would need to be very careful if he wanted to stay alive. Having charge of Allied POWs was a dangerous position to be in unless he found a way of using it to his advantage.

The SS had first taken over responsibility for the nation's prisoners of war through its leader, Himmler. In the aftermath of the assassination attempt on his life in June 1944, a shocked and shaken Hitler had turned to the SS Reichsführer – '*mein treuer Heinrich*' – 'my faithful Heinrich' – as the only person he could trust, and had made him head of the Reserve Army, replacing a general who had been one of the conspirators. This was a position which, among many other responsibilities, put him nominally in charge of the bureaucracy running the POW camps. Three months later this position was formalized. An order from Hitler on 25 September 1944 transferred 'the supervision of all prisoners-of-war and internees, as well as prisoner-of-war camps and establishments with guard sections' to the SS.[17]

This was a move that Himmler had long sought, arguing that only his SS and Gestapo could make the prisoner-of-war camps properly secure. Escapers had caused havoc, and had to be cracked

down on. The break-out from Stalag Luft III at Sagan was specifically cited by Hitler as a reason for transferring responsibility to
Himmler. Another – following the uprising in Warsaw in the summer of 1944, which took two months of bitter fighting to crush – was
his concern about a similar revolt among the millions of POWs in
Germany. Hitler was also convinced that the British and Americans
were planning airborne raids behind the lines to free the prisoners.[18] For all these reasons, Hitler wanted a tougher regime introduced, and turned to Himmler – his fixer on so many matters – to get it.

With Himmler nominally the man in control, the German army
and air-force officers and guards actually running the camps were
deeply worried. For years they had resisted those who would
interfere in their business, desperate to keep prisoners of war under
the military umbrella because the well-being of their own troops
in enemy hands depended on reasonable treatment on both sides.
They had endured the snap inspections by the SS and the Gestapo,
but still felt able to assert their independent authority. Now, with
Himmler at the head of the command structure, they feared a
regime of brutality and inhumanity would be forced on them. The
deputy commandant of Stalag Luft III recalled this as 'a very
unpleasant time and we always lived in fear and expectation of
some dangerous regulations and measures'.[19]

They never came. There was no increase in SS supervision. The
SS did not attempt to take over the day-to-day running of the
camps or to impose tougher regimes.[20] The prisoners and their
military guards waited for this to happen, but it never did. Himmler
did not exercise his newly acquired authority. Churchill had noticed
this discrepancy. In his discussions with Stalin and Roosevelt about
issuing an official warning to the Germans about their treatment
of prisoners of war, he noted that it was unclear whether the SS
had actually taken over from the regular army officers. 'We should
surely miss no opportunity of exploiting any duality of control,' he
added.[21] That was towards the end of March 1945, and Himmler
had been in charge for six months. In the camps themselves,
little had changed. Army and air-force guards continued to run the
prisoners' lives as they always had done, under the supervision of
the same commandants and officers as before.

One reason for Himmler's inactivity was that he was fully occupied in other areas, and his vast responsibilities increased even more after Hitler gave him command of an army in the field. In January 1945 – to the horror of the professional soldiers of the *Wehrmacht* – he was put at the head of the Vistula Army Group to mount the defence of Germany against the Russian invasion from the east. But, hard-pressed as Himmler was in pursuing the war for Hitler, he was also playing a long game. He planned to survive Hitler, make peace with the Americans and the British, and emerge at the end as his country's leader. There were dangers for himself in having charge of nationals from the very countries he knew he would want to negotiate with one day soon. Was this why he had chosen to delegate responsibility for them to his old and trusted right-hand man, Berger?

On the surface, Berger was just another SS apparatchik who had done well by doing what he was told. He was known in SS ranks as one of Himmler's 'Twelve Apostles' and was nicknamed 'der Allmaechtige Gottlob' – 'the Almighty Gottlob'.[22] It helped his career that he enthusiastically endorsed Nazi doctrines of racial supremacy and hatred of the Jews. From 1940 he ran the SS main office in Berlin and was particularly involved in liaising with the so-called 'Eastern Territories' – those where extermination camps like Auschwitz had been built. He carried out his duties with an efficiency that was seen as ruthless – and the same word was applied to his military performance in August 1944, when he was sent to deal with an uprising in Slovakia. His appointment as supremo of the prisoner-of-war camps followed immediately after, and there would have been no reason to suppose that he would not tackle it with the same brutal efficiency. But he did not. Apparently, from the very start he displayed reluctance, telling Hitler that he did not fancy being a jailer.[23] It earned him a stern rebuke and a reminder that generals should do what their Führer asked and not question it.[24]

If Berger wanted to survive, he would have to steer a course that avoided provoking the wrath of Hitler *and* the wrath of the Allies. He began by deliberately doing nothing. Instead of integrating the existing Office of Prisoner-of-War Affairs into the massive bureaucratic machine of the SS – which would have been the natural thing to do when the SS took over a new department – he kept them at arm's length from each other. They were in different buildings, two miles apart. Nor did he flood the prisoner administration with SS officers. He preferred to keep the same bureaucratic structure and the same personnel as before.

His decision not to crack down on the camps was all the more remarkable given that, by Berger's own account, Hitler gave him a dressing-down when he went to see him in the Wolf's Lair at Rastenburg on 29 September 1944. The Führer warned Berger not to be too lenient and 'to accept the more unpleasant side of my task'.[25] Berger said he was told by Hitler to destroy Red Cross supplies piling up in the camps, to stop more coming in, and to put an end to visits by Red Cross inspectors. Hitler also wanted more shootings of prisoners and more punishments. All this Berger quietly decided not to do, he later claimed. He also said that he thwarted a plan, proposed by the *Luftwaffe* and approved by the military high command, to set up special prisoner-of-war camps for British and American airmen in the centre of large cities, to act as human shields against Allied bombing raids. Realizing that this would contravene the Geneva Convention, which he was determined to maintain, Berger successfully argued that there was not enough spare barbed wire to make this possible. As a result, nothing happened.

And that was the way of it. Berger's great contribution to saving the lives of Allied prisoners of war was to stall and to procrastinate. After the war he claimed much more for himself – that he had done many positive things to protect Allied prisoners of war and defend their interests. He said that he allowed more Red Cross inspections, not fewer, and that he fought off attempts to reduce to the bare minimum the amount of food going to the camps and ensured that supplies were always at least 20 per cent above basic survival level. He claimed that he stood his ground against senior – and scary – figures such as Martin Bormann, and was even warned by Goebbels that he was putting his life in danger by defying Hitler.

There is no independent verification of any of these claims. Indeed, on food supplies, the experience of the men in the camps suggested the opposite. Rations were cut drastically towards the end of 1944 after Berger had taken charge, and Red Cross parcels were a rare luxury. Berger's claims were even more unbelievable when it came to the evacuation of the camps in the east. He said he arranged for the erection of temporary quarters along the route marches – which did not happen. He said marching prisoners were hugely helped by an idea of his to give them printed handbills appealing to locals in the areas they marched through to be compassionate – for which we have seen no evidence at all.[26] On the other hand, he said he arranged for Red Cross supplies to cross the borders into Germany, through Lübeck and Geneva – and to be fair to him, there is no reason to think he did not play a part in this.[27]

But his most important role was in keeping the SS – his own organization – off the backs of the POWs and their guards. At the same time, he made sure he was seen by the Allies as a friend of the prisoners – the British and American ones, that is. Berger showed scant concern for the Russians, the Poles and the Slavs in his charge, and there is no evidence that he did anything to alleviate their terrible conditions. It was in the West that he perceived his post-war future to be, and it was on individuals who might have influence there that he set out to make his mark.

From the ranks of the American airmen who arrived at the railhead at Spremberg after the forced march from Stalag Luft III at Sagan at the very beginning of February 1945, he had the two most senior officers picked out. Major-General Arthur Vanaman and Colonel Delmar Spivey protested as their men went off in cattle trucks to different camps all over Germany, but to no avail. They themselves were put on a train to Berlin. In the German capital, wrecked by air bombardment and awaiting the Russian onslaught, they were taken to see a young officer from Berger's staff. Vanaman seized the initiative and proposed a humanitarian mission: he should be allowed to go to Switzerland and make arrangements for food supplies stored there to be delivered to the camps in Germany. Word came back that Berger liked the idea, but he had a better one of his own. He wanted to hold a medical conference in Berlin about the problems of the prisoners of war. He wanted Allied medical staff from the camps to attend, and he needed Vanaman's authority to persuade them that this was a valid project.

It was an extraordinary suggestion, given the reality of medical aid in the camps and out on the marches. There, men were making charcoal to swallow as their only remedy for dysentery, and operations were being carried out with scalpels made from slivers of razor blades. Men like Dr Caplan could have been forgiven for asking what precisely there was to discuss. What they needed was medicines, bandages and surgical instruments. Nevertheless, the medical conference went ahead, on 28 March 1945. And it made some progress – though it was pretty late in the day to have any real effect. Allied doctors and German doctors agreed to team up to visit camps – those like Moosburg and Fallingbostel now overflowing with inmates – to see what could be done to stop epidemics. The record does not show whether they ever got there or whether anything was achieved.

Berger's presumed success with the conference led him on to his next plan for the two American officers. He wanted them to make contact with Eisenhower on his behalf. They were to leave Germany via Switzerland and take secret radio codes to the Allied commander-in-chief to enable negotiations to take place for a separate peace with the British and the Americans. Here was a familiar story: the Soviet Union was the common enemy. Make peace in the west, and let Germany turn all its attention to halting the Bolshevik tide. It was unclear whether Berger was acting on his own initiative or on behalf of others. All he declared was that he was prepared to bypass everyone – Hitler, Himmler, anyone – 'in order to save the Fatherland'.

Vanaman agreed, but in return Berger would have to do his best to make sure there were no more forced marches and to get Red Cross supplies through to those who desperately needed them. The date was 3 April 1945. It was the very day that Stalag XIIID at Nuremberg was being emptied, its prisoners heading south to Moosburg and more weeks of misery. A few days later prisoners of Fallingbostel were being pushed out on to the road again. As his part of the bargain, Berger was promising what he could not deliver. But, in fairness, the American officers found it impossible to meet their part of the deal either – through no fault of their own. It was nearly three weeks before Berger could smuggle them across the border to Switzerland, and by then there was little interest by the Allied authorities in one low-grade SS general offering to make peace.

Nevertheless, it would be wrong to call the mission a total failure. As long as Berger still had reason to think he could make a deal, he would do nothing to jeopardize the safety of the prisoners of war. On his order, death and destruction could still have been brought down on thousands of Allied prisoners waiting to be liberated. Even this late in the war, orders to kill were getting through and being acted on. Between 9 April and 20 April the last of the alleged conspirators in the 20 July bomb plot were executed on orders sent from Berlin to the concentration camps at Flossenbürg and Sachsenhausen. If Berger had wanted to issue orders to take a bloody revenge on prisoners of war, everything indicated that they would have been carried out. He did not. Moreover, his procrastination, his medical conference and then his attempt to set up a peace channel with the West via the two American generals bought valuable time for the prisoners – and, at that stage of the war, time was of the essence.

*

Berger was not the only SS officer trying to save his own life. His own commander, Himmler, was still pursuing the same course. And the time was very close when it might be right to play that trump card he still held as head of the SS – the British and American prisoners of war. Although he had put Berger in charge of them, Himmler had specifically kept for himself the international part of the job, retaining personal responsibility for the department in the Office of Prisoner of War Affairs in Berlin that liaised with the Protecting Power and the International Red Cross. He also did nothing to discourage Berger's lenient attitude to the POWs – something that Berger himself was convinced was a deliberate ploy on the part of his boss. As Berger told a war-crimes court years later, 'It was quite agreeable to Himmler if I did something special for prisoners of war because then he could tell the representatives of the Protecting Power in Switzerland that it was he, the Reich Leader SS, who had done it.'[28] At the same time, Himmler could point an accusing finger in Berger's direction should Hitler ever demand to know why the prisoners were not being more harshly treated.

Thinking he had covered his back – and his front – Himmler intensified his personal negotiations with Western contacts in the hope – incredibly – of securing some sort of amnesty for himself.

He had now set himself up with a base in the north of Germany on the Baltic coast, commandeering a castle on the Bay of Lübeck for his headquarters, and was close to a deal with the Swedes for the repatriation of Scandinavian prisoners of war. If he could pull that one off, why not a similar arrangement with the Allied authorities? A large group of men whose safe return home could be used in negotiations were conveniently gathered less than 100 miles away at the POW camp at Fallingbostel, and at the end of the first week of April 1945, as we have seen, they were told to prepare themselves to march again. On whose orders we do not know – there is no documentary evidence. But, as they headed north, many of them believed they were being taken as hostages to some last-ditch redoubt on the Baltic coast.

Events did not go the way Himmler wanted. He fell foul of both sides: the Allies refused to negotiate with him, and when Hitler found out that he had tried to make a deal he disowned him. The SS Reichsführer's power slipped out of his grasp and he committed suicide after falling into the hands of the British. However, Berger, his acolyte, survived. He proved much better than his boss at playing out that tricky endgame.

Moreover, if Berger is to be believed, he took the greatest of all risks by disobeying a direct instruction by Hitler to murder thousands of prisoners of war. And he did so, apparently, with the connivance of none other than Eva Braun, Hitler's mistress (and wife for the brief moments between their marriage in the Berlin bunker and their self-inflicted deaths).

It is an odd but fascinating tale, the sole source for which was Berger himself. He told it to an American judge who carried out an investigation into the last days of Hitler's life on behalf of the US Navy and interviewed Berger at Nuremberg in 1948. It was then repeated by a biographer of Braun,[29] who described how Hitler's mistress and Berger together saved 35,000 hostages whom Hitler had ordered to be taken to the mountains in Bavaria and held there until he could make a satisfactory deal with the Allies. If no such deal was forthcoming, they were to be executed.

Eva learned that Berger opposed the plan and that even if ordered he would not kill the prisoners. She decided that it would be best if Hitler gave the signed orders to Berger rather than to some other officer who would carry out the Führer's command. She arranged for Berger to have an appointment with Hitler, and while Hitler was discussing the matter with the general, Eva brought the typed orders pertaining to the executions into the room and handed them to the Führer. He immediately and automatically signed them and Berger left the room with the documents in his possession. Both he and Eva knew that he could stall off Hitler until the war ended without carrying out a single execution, and that is exactly what happened.

Did any of this really happen? Surprisingly, Berger did not cite this in his defence at Nuremberg; nor did he mention this supposed incident in the account of his life, where he said he only ever met Eva Braun twice, both times while waiting in the ante-room to see Hitler.[30] She had been friendly enough, warning him what sort of mood the Führer was in, but this hardly seems the basis of a secret arrangement between them to, in effect, dupe Hitler – an activity that would put both their lives in jeopardy if it had been discovered. Moreover, on the day when she allegedly made her pact with Berger to save the lives of thousands of prisoners of war, she had also turned down her last opportunity to leave the bunker in Berlin for safety, choosing to die with Hitler. It would surely be strange to decide on this ultimate act of loyalty to him and at the very same time agree secretly to betray him.

All this was said to have happened on the night of 22 April. These were some of the most significant hours in the last days of Hitler. It was on that day that the Führer had announced that he would not flee to southern Germany but would stay in Berlin and die. His generals and aides split dramatically into those who declared they would die at his side – like Goebbels, who brought his wife and six children to the bunker with the cyanide to kill them – and those who would make a run for it. Amid this high drama, in which Germany's high command was facing the destruction of everything, including the charismatic leader its members had pledged themselves to for so long, it is hard to see the fate of Allied prisoners of war being of any importance. And yet there was perhaps a grain of truth in Berger's story.

The historian Hugh Trevor-Roper, who, as a British intelligence officer with impeccable academic credentials, carried out a forensic investigation into the last days of Hitler in the months immediately after the end of the war, interviewed Berger and found him a pretty unreliable witness. He thought him good-natured and always ready with a good story, but 'his accounts of his activities in these days are all characterized by indistinct and sometimes inconsistent loquacity'.[31] Unless there was corroborating evidence, Trevor-Roper treated with suspicion any conversation the SS general said he had had with Hitler. Berger told Trevor-Roper he had arrived in Berlin from Himmler's headquarters and was heading south to Bavaria when he was summoned to see Hitler in the bunker. Berger painted a picture of a man ill and demented, purple with rage and blaming everyone else for losing the war, ranting and raving about this betrayal and that act of disloyalty. Berger claimed that he urged Hitler not to head for safety in the south and a last stand at the Alpine redoubt, but to stay in Berlin and die. This, he said he told the Führer, was his duty to the German people. Here was brave Berger apparently daring to tell Hitler to kill himself, taking the opposite line to all the other generals – Himmler included – who had been pressing Hitler to leave the shattered capital.

After hearing Berger's advice, Hitler gave him his mission. He was to track down the *Prominente*, those VIP prisoners of war who had been housed at Colditz and were now being transported into Bavaria as hostages. According to Berger, Hitler rose to his feet, 'his hand was shaking, his leg was shaking and his head was shaking; and all that he kept saying was "Shoot them all! Shoot them all!" or something like that'. Trevor-Roper added pointedly that who precisely was to be shot was unclear from Berger's 'incoherent narrative'.

Nevertheless, that this was a much more plausible account than the one involving Eva Braun, death warrants and 35,000 prisoner-of-war hostages was demonstrated by what Berger actually did next. He commandeered Himmler's private plane and flew out of Berlin, running the gauntlet of the guns of the Red Army, which was even now nearing the centre of the city. Berger headed for Bavaria. And it was there that he would next be seen – by those *Prominente* he had been sent to slaughter.[32]

As we saw in Chapter 10, the twenty-one *Prominente* – among them relations of King George VI and Winston Churchill – had been taken away from Colditz on Friday 13 April, just days before the rest of the high-risk-category prisoners of war were released by the advancing Americans. They were in two buses that headed south, making, they believed, for that fabled last redoubt in the mountains.[33] The frightened passengers still had *Wehrmacht* guards as their escort, but what lay ahead and into whose hands they were being delivered was unknown. For a fortnight they were driven from camp to camp, always afraid that at the next stop the SS would be waiting for them. It finally happened. A colonel in a long leather coat with the SS death's-head emblem on his cap took charge of them one morning, menacingly tapping his holster. Out on the road, a sign pointed to Berchtesgaden as they drove higher and higher into the mountains. But Hitler's Eagle's Nest was not their destination, and they drove on further into Austria until they reached a town called Markt Pongau. It was here that Berger appeared in an enormous Mercedes, lolling on cushions in the back seat of his car – the embodiment of all the *Prominente*'s fears.

However, Berger was all smiles. He handed out whisky and cigarettes. He told them he had been ordered to shoot them, but that he was refusing to do so. As a result, SS extremists were being sent to intercept the group and carry out the instructions, now with an extra name on the death warrant – his own. He named the feared head of the Gestapo, Ernst Kaltenbrunner, as the man leading the hunt for them. Berger told the *Prominente* he could not guarantee their safety, but he would do his best to see them across to the American lines.

The next day the prisoners set off in lorries on what they hoped was the last leg in their perilous journey. They were on alert, the threat of Kaltenbrunner around every corner, and that night it seemed he had found them. A motorcyclist ushered them off the road and down a country track to a deserted farmhouse. But there to greet them, dressed in a white uniform, was Berger, now their old friend and protector. That night they had food and drink and speeches. The jovial Berger toasted the British and Americans, shortly, he had no doubt, to join with Germany in the battle against the Russians – the 'red virus' as he called them. The next morning the *Prominente* left at dawn and were soon in American hands. Berger had saved them.

He had also saved himself. He had too much history in the SS not to face war-crimes charges after the war, and in April 1949 he was found guilty of crimes against humanity for his role in planning the 'final solution', the SS operation to exterminate the Jews. The last of the Nuremburg tribunals decided 'he was an active party in the program of persecution, enslavement and murder'.[34] His protestations that he knew nothing about this were dismissed: 'we do not believe him'. His sentence was twenty-five years, but in the event he served just a fraction of that time. At his trial he had claimed that the prisoners of war had been intended to suffer the same fate as the concentration-camp inmates in the last months of the war and that 'I prevented this plan from becoming effective . . . If today, in America, in Britain and in Russia, there are tens of thousands of mothers and wives who are welcoming home their sons and husbands healthy and safe, it is to my merit.' The court had believed him, noting in the record that 'the defendant Berger was the means of saving the lives of American, British and Allied officers and men whose safety was gravely imperilled by orders of Hitler that they be liquidated or held as hostages.[35] Berger disobeyed orders and intervened on their behalf and in so doing placed himself in a position of hazard.' On appeal two years later, a judge ruled that greater weight should have been given to this consideration, and he reduced the sentence to ten years. It was a time of clemency, for seven other convicted Nazis had their sentences cut too; but the mercy must have stretched further, because Berger was released before the end of 1951. Including the period before his trial, he had served just six years. Until his death in 1975, he spent much of the rest of his life building bridges with prisoner-of-war organizations in the United States and building up his reputation as the good German who had saved thousands of lives in those last few months of the war.

He persuaded many different people of his good deeds. His SS comrade Walter Schellenberg, who was acquitted of war crimes, told interrogators in a sworn statement at Nuremberg in January 1946 that Berger 'delayed sending many of Hitler's orders and thereby saved the lives of thousands of people who would otherwise have been evacuated from prisoner-of-war camps or executed where evacuation was impossible'.[36]

Delmar Spivey became a defender of Berger, and was responsible for a motion passed at a reunion of former prisoners of war in Dayton, Ohio, in April 1965 to honour him.[37] General Arthur Vanaman signed this motion too, though he comes over as a little more sceptical about Berger than Spivey was. In an interview with historical researchers of the USAF in 1976 he said he thought Berger had acted to save his own skin, but at the same time he thought Berger had been brave – 'his office had done things that he could have been shot for'.[38] Air-force historian Arthur Durand also gave Berger the benefit of the doubt. He considered that many of the SS man's claims were proved to be true in the years after the war, and he concluded that 'Berger was a true friend of the prisoners.'[39]

We are more sceptical. Berger claimed achievements on behalf of prisoners – better spiritual and cultural provisions, better sport and entertainment, more professional training – that reek of vainglory rather than truth. He was in charge of the prison camps for only seven months, and for the last four of those months the system was falling apart as prisoners marched across Germany, sick and starving, or eked out their lives in conditions so overcrowded that men slept on the ground. While hundreds died of dysentery, exhaustion and frostbite, he held a futile medical conference in Berlin. At his trial he had the temerity to claim that 'I prevented forced marches through my agreement with General Eisenhower', when the truth was that he had tried and failed to make contact with the Allied commander-in-chief and 'forced marches' had continued until the very end of hostilities.[40]

Having said that, we must give Berger his due. It was not what he did that was crucial in those last months of the war: it was what he did *not* do. He did not issue orders to cut down food supplies to the camps. He did not halt Red Cross supplies. He did not crack down on prisoners and make their lives even more of a misery. He did not send hard-line SS officers into the camps to replace the military guards. He did not issue orders for prisoners of war to be disposed of rather than released. He did not shoot the *Prominente* but ushered them to safety. All of which he could have done if he had seen that to be what his job – and his Führer – required.

The measure of what Berger did is what others might well have done in his place. What would have happened if someone more fanatical had been put in charge of the prisoner-of-war camps – someone more willing to follow the evil spirit behind those nebulous instructions and rumoured threats coming out of Berlin? There were plenty of candidates in the SS with the necessary mixture of cruelty, efficiency and unquestioning obedience. There were men like Adolf Eichmann, designer of death camps and gas chambers and unashamed exterminator of millions of Jews (who disappeared at the end of the war and was kidnapped from his hiding place in South America and hanged after being tried for war crimes by the Israelis in 1962); like Rudolf Hoess, the commandant of Auschwitz, brutal beyond imagination; like Ernst Kaltenbrunner, Gestapo chief, who organized the hounding and hunting down of Jews and claimed innocence on the gallows at Nuremberg because all he had ever done was his duty.

Any one of these would have run the camps in true SS style – and then how many British and American prisoners of war would ever have seen home again?

14   Heading for Home

The final leg felt like the longest of all. Suddenly, with liberation, all the prisoners' patience was gone, rushing away like the last of the sand in an hourglass. For years they had waited, because waiting was all they could do – feeding on memories, seeing off the days, the weeks, the months. They had lived for today and dammed up thoughts of tomorrow. Free men at last, the floodgates burst. Everyone wanted to be home – NOW!

Private Swift and his group had been on the road since just after Christmas. They had slogged from Poland over the mountains of Czechoslovakia into Germany, had been sent north towards Dresden, then had retraced their steps, and were now in Bavaria. They had marched 'all in all nearly halfway across Europe', as he put it, but wherever it was they were supposed to be going they never made it.[1]

We were out on the road when one day the guards told us to go home. They said, '*Nach hause*', and waved their arms in the direction of England. Then they formed up into a company and marched off. We were on our own, which was an odd feeling after five years of being guarded, starved, confined, shouted at, worked, pushed around and forced to march. It almost didn't seem right somehow.

They were in a village high above a valley with a clear view across to the snowy tops of the Alps. Home was a thousand miles away in England. 'We were like flotsam, thrown up by the tide of war and suddenly left high and dry. We just wanted to get home and be safe and sound.'

For some, particularly those who were sick or lame, getting home would be a quick process. For the majority, however, what lay ahead was dither and delay. Some took it philosophically. 'We want to rush home in a couple of hours but we'll try and be patient,' Cec Room wrote in his diary.[2] For others it was unendurable – as excruciating as anything that had gone before.

There were incidents in those days between being released and going home that many would wish they had never witnessed. Revenge was in the air. Jim Sims was appalled at how badly things had got out of hand immediately after liberation. Men had gone on the rampage – and not just the Russians, who were blamed for many outrages at this time. To his horror, British prisoners were involved too, some of them men he knew well. Sims was helpless as a gang of liberated prisoners, who had gone into the nearby town in search of German soldiers, came back dragging a terrified man with them. He was one of their former guards and had put on civilian clothes, so they accused him of being a spy. 'No, I'm not a spy,' the terrified man was shouting. 'I was one of your guards. You must remember me.'[3] Sims recalled:

The leader of the kangaroo court shouted, 'Yes we remember you all right, you bastard. String him up.' Someone got hold of a rope and made a noose which was slipped over the gibbering guard's head. The other end was slung over a beam in a barn, and they started to heave him up. It seemed incredible that British soldiers were going to lynch this German. I watched his feet dragging along the ground as willing hands took up the slack of the rope. The old guard gave a choking scream of terror as his feet left the ground. This alerted some soldiers from the British battalion that had liberated us and they came at the double to rescue him, while the mob howled with frustration.

But then Sims discovered the depth of his own anger and disgust. Newspapers arrived from England with the news and photographs of Belsen. 'These were the first pictures ever seen of this dreadful place and its obscene death-pits. It was like having a glimpse into hell. A terrible panic seized me. I wanted to get out of Germany as soon as possible.'

Even the mildest of individuals seemed to want to grab souvenirs – an activity that was often indistinguishable from looting. Leslie Frith remembered the German armoury at a *Luftwaffe* barracks being forced open and men running away with rifles, tin hats, daggers and all manner of Nazi insignia. It baffled him. 'Why on earth they wanted reminders of their stay in Germany I cannot understand. It was the very last thing I wanted.'[4] It was during this period that Sims's wallet – 'which had survived several German searches' – was stolen from his jacket when he hung it up to have a wash. 'There was nothing of any value in it, just photographs and all the names and addresses that I had collected, which were irreplaceable. I was really cut up over this.'

The near-anarchy turned to total defiance when authority tried to reassert itself, as Frith recalled:

We were told to parade in three ranks and a padre, of all people, climbed on to the roof of a truck and started shouting at us, 'Your behaviour has been disgraceful. You are back in the British Army now ... ATTEN-SHUN!' There was a disbelieving gasp from the ex-prisoners, who broke ranks and surged towards the truck, shouting, 'Fuck the British Army' and 'Let's bash the bastard.' He took one look at the angry mob advancing on him and fled.

It took an officer from the liberating battalion to calm the mob with smiles and promises. 'He told us that, if we would just be patient, he would see that we got hot food, a bath, and then every effort would be made to get us home as quickly as possible.' It was a bad lesson, but their indiscipline had paid off. 'Apparently it had originally been planned to keep us there for six weeks, but the looting and attempted lynching had changed the minds of the authorities. A fleet of trucks arrived and we set off for the west.'

American airman John Parsons found the behaviour of the Russians at Moosburg insane. He remembered his own little madnesses after being liberated – like cutting a hole in the barbed-wire fence, then stepping through it to the outside and back again into the compound and then out again and so on, just because he could, just to prove to himself that he could. But the Russians were in a league – and a world – of their own.

They found a small winery in town and they just drank its contents by the bucket and got very sick. Then someone burnt down the winery and so they drank benzene instead. They came back to the camp and they were very, very sick. Fifteen or twenty of them died right there. Their bodies were thrown outside and left to swell and rot. I was aghast that the Russians seemed to have no more feeling than that for their former comrades.[5]

Parsons was equally uneasy about the behaviour of some of the liberators. He remembered a US tank being deliberately driven over the fence around a German house and up to the window.

An American GI kicked the window out and jumped in and asked for beer. The people inside said no and he took his machine-gun out and just shot up the room. When he stopped, he demanded 'Schnapps', and, boy, I'm telling you, he got what he wanted this time. Then he rampaged through the house, looking for jewellery, which he found. The people in the house didn't want him to take it, but they did not have much choice in the matter with this maniac.

Any hint of defiance could be fatal:

I remember seeing this beautiful young German girl in a small town near the camp. She was walking down the main street in a strident Nazi goose-step. She held her head high and marched as if to the beat of a drum. Some GI just pulled out his machine-gun and shot her down in cold blood. This sickened me. I left that place immediately and went back to the camp. There was also a guard called Frederik, who had walked with me on the march from Nuremberg. He was shot by a GI. I had his address and we had promised to write to each other some day. But I saw his body lying near the camp gate.

For one dead German, however, there would be no pity or remorse. Big Stoop, the giant from Stalag Luft IV at Gross Tychow who had burst men's eardrums with one slap, had come with the prisoners all the way to Moosburg. He could not have realized how hated he was and how many men had sworn to get even with him or he would have made his escape in time. There are various accounts of his death. None is pleasant. Parsons said he saw two prisoners of war whooping with excitement as they carried the guard's head in a bushel basket. Another former prisoner recalled seeing Big Stoop's body spreadeagled across a road with a pickaxe in his head.[6] Big Stoop's reputation was such that later, when

Parsons was being debriefed by an intelligence officer, the German's name was mentioned to him, as if many men before had singled him out in their accounts of their time in captivity. He gave the officer details of Big Stoop's death, and the officer replied, 'There will be no trial for that bastard, then?' Parsons reflected and found some compassion in his heart. 'I felt sorry that he had come to the end of the war and then lost his life in such a brutal manner. I suppose he was only following orders in his fashion. In a time of peace, he would probably have had a farm, a wife and children, and lived a peaceful life.'

Others were less generous in their thoughts. Parsons met an old and close comrade, the ball-turret gunner from his plane. They had trained together and flown on missions together, and knew each other's families. The man had suffered badly on the march across Germany, and he told Parsons that when they were liberated he was asked if he had been mistreated and he pointed out a German guard who had been particularly mean and abusive. The guard – plus several others standing in a line near him – was shot where he stood. Parsons was appalled. 'I told my old friend that he should not have been that revengeful, and he said, "John, those guys were sons-of-bitches and treated us like dogs. I'm glad they are dead." We talked late into the night and promised to get together when we got home. But that was the last that I ever saw him.'

*

Now was the time for all those carefully worked-out plans by the administrators back in London and Washington to go smoothly into action. The men would be brought back under military discipline, deloused and debriefed, given their back pay, and transported home in an orderly and a fair manner. Here was the moment when the 'stand fast' order would come into its own. 'Wait' was the watchword. 'Be patient.' It was like ordering the tide not to come in.

The planners realized almost immediately that their neat schemes were about to be swamped. A communication from the British 21st Army Group at the end of March noted that, 'as a result of the increasing numbers of Allied POW likely to be uncovered', previous instructions 'will prove inadequate'.[7] Over the next month it became clear that getting more than 250,000 British and American prisoners of war home was just part of a much more massive problem. Europe was awash with homeless people, as is shown all too graphically in a memo written by the Allied authorities just ten days before the war officially came to an end.[8] Five million was a conservative estimate for the number of displaced persons in the SHAEF-controlled zones. There were more than 2 million Russians, Poles and Czechoslovaks heading *east*, and the same number again – French, Belgian, Dutch, plus German civilians – heading *west* from the Soviet side. Hundreds of thousands, maybe millions, of them could die.

The speedy return of these people to their homes is of the utmost importance not only from the standpoint of expediting the adjustment of affairs in Europe but to relieve our armies of the tremendous burden of providing food and shelter. Unless the major portion of this movement can be completed before the end of October, widespread conditions of famine and disease are almost certain to occur.

End of October! If such a note had ever fallen into the hands of ex-prisoners they would have been appalled. Were they to sit out the summer and half the autumn in squalid camps?

The answer was no. They did get priority. As soon as planes were freed from the fighting, they would bring the boys home. The RAF began Operation Exodus at the end of April, when Lancaster bombers were stood down from their daily sorties pounding Germany. However, flying out the POWs was difficult until the planes could get in, and many airfields had been wrecked by the Allied bombing or destroyed by retreating German forces. But the spirit was undoubtedly willing, and there was no shortage of enthusiastic aircrew prepared to give up rest days to get the prisoners home as soon as possible. It was just that for many of those ex-prisoners it couldn't be soon enough.

Some ex-prisoners looked around for transport of their own. Richard Passmore and his companions had been told by an American major that they could seize any vehicle they wanted, and from the ones they had stopped at a makeshift roadblock near Lübeck they selected a large Mercedes with a full tank of petrol. They were in a holiday mood as they set off west, moving along roads choked with people. They were keen to get back across the Elbe, a river they had been over twice: once on their way from their camps in Poland, and then again when they were marched out of Fallingbostel. Now it was their gateway to home.

The bridge proper had been blown by the retreating Germans, and the Royal Engineers had put up a pontoon bridge in its place. It was one lane only and we had to queue to get across. It was dark when our turn came, and a smart MP [military policeman] urged us to step on it. There was no lighting on the bridge and no side rails either. We aimed at a light on the other side and we made it, though the sight of the water only a few feet away did not inspire confidence. Early the next morning, we decided to get out of the British sector. We did not want to be washed, kitted-out, medically inspected and registered. We wanted to get to England just as we were.[9] We had heard that our people were collecting all ex-prisoners into reception camps. We thought we would be better off with the Americans, whose sector was only a few miles away. We were very much adherents of the free-enterprise system and we thought it more likely they would leave us to our own devices. To us, even a few days' delay was intolerable.

It was never going to be that easy. In the American zone, they found themselves driving against the endless traffic of US tanks, lorries and troop-carriers still going east. They were forced off the road and then stopped by two military policemen in white helmets, who suspected they might be German saboteurs trying to sneak through Allied lines. They carried no identity cards – 'don't be daft, prisoners of war don't have them' – and, in mud-encrusted army greatcoats over RAF battledress, looked suspicious. They could not satisfy their interrogators, and were about to be taken into custody for checking. Passmore and his friends were having none of that. The driver suddenly revved the engine of the Mercedes and let out the clutch.

We screamed away in a spurt of dust, and the MP with his hand on the door was sent flying. I looked through the rear window and the Americans were running for their jeep. They were quickly after us. We had the better and faster car but, after several years of captivity, our man's driving skills were rather rusty and the jeep began to close on us. Then suddenly there was a bang from behind and we looked back and the jeep was upside down on the ground, its wheels spinning in the air. We stopped and went back. They had hit a mine and both of them were dead.

The accident was a dampener, a sad outcome after the thrill of being free and heading home.

The men resumed their journey, reached the airfield at Celle between Fallingbostel and Hanover, and traded the car for a flight on a plane to Brussels. In the Belgian capital they made their way to a hotel and settled in a suite of rooms – the one, they were told by a member of staff, that Hermann Goering had always stayed in when he was in Brussels. 'This information, like the suite itself, did not move me in the slightest. A barn, a ditch, the Hotel Metropole – they were just places to lie down and sleep. Soon I was deep in my first bath for five years, watching the dirt peeling off. It took several changes of water before I was satisfied.' Then came the euphoria of clean, new clothes from an RAF depot, where they were allowed to take anything they wanted. And a shave and a haircut at a barber's shop. Afterwards 'I looked at myself in the mirror. It just wasn't me. It was a chap I had once known many years ago but whose face now showed privation, strain and shock.' Later there was a film at a cinema – *Arsenic and Old Lace*, a comedy-murder mystery with Cary Grant and Raymond Massey, the very latest release from Hollywood. The audience roared with laughter – all except Passmore. 'I understood neither the film nor why people were laughing so much. It was all foreign to me. I could not enter into the world of make-believe. Looking back, I can now see that I was like a zombie.'

Passmore's return to civilization had been too abrupt for its reality to sink in. Cal Younger had more time to adjust, though not through choice. He and his friends remained stuck at Fallingbostel. They had also 'liberated' a car – a Hanomag which had belonged to the vet in the town. Eagerly they set to work on it. 'We replaced missing engine parts, found tyres and tubes, and reconverted it from a charcoal-burning to a petrol-burning engine. But the battery was flat.'[10] They got a tow from a tank to bump-start it, though, as we raced down the cobblestone road behind the tank, there was so much noise and vibration that we could not tell whether the engine was going or not. Ours was one of hundreds of cars in the camp. Every car in every village within miles had been taken. Some men even raided villages still in German hands, and were recaptured. Others took not only cars but German uniforms, which they wanted for souvenirs, and were taken prisoner by our own forces, mistaking them for Germans.

The Allied authorities recognized the danger of ex-prisoners running wild, and ordered a curfew confining everyone to camp. Entertainments were hurriedly rushed in to help pass the time – that much the planners had promised and delivered – and Younger remembered sitting with hundreds of others watching Ralph Reader's Gang Show on a stage in one of the huts, and the gags and the vaudeville unlocked something that had been missing for far too long in the men's lives. 'I began to laugh, and as I did I realized that I had not laughed for years, and my cheeks hurt as if a thick plaster of make-up was cracking'.

Then the chance to head for home offered itself. Younger and his friends were taken aside and told where they could lay their hands on some petrol – 'enough juice to get to Paris or Brussels', according to a British corporal. They decided not to attempt the journey. They knew that the roads were clogged with men trying to beat the system home, even though they risked getting caught up in battles which were still going on in the area. 'We felt we should wait for official transport,' Younger said, and they set out instead on a local expedition to forage for food.

They were driving a few miles away from the camp when they saw two youths in German army caps and with small packs on their backs come furtively out of the forest. They were fourteen years old, and had gone into hiding with sniper rifles to be guerrilla fighters. Here, then, were Hitler's much-feared 'werewolves', sworn and ready to carry on the war at all costs. Except that they weren't. Like everyone else, they just wanted to go home, back to their families. 'They were only boys,' Younger noted, 'and doubtless they had been fanatically eager to kill the enemy. It was lucky for some British soldiers that they had wearied of this. Other boys just like them were killing British soldiers in ambushes or shooting them at point-blank range as they reached into a pocket for chocolates or chewing gum.' They handed the boys over to the army.

Later they drove down a lane looking for a farm and found six German soldiers sprawling asleep on the ground. Younger was all for turning round and getting out of there quickly, but his companions were not going to miss the chance to assert the authority of the victorious. They roused the Germans and at gunpoint – even though most of the guns were empty – escorted them back to camp as captives. Younger relished the change of role as 'we marched them along the same road which we had tramped as prisoners a few days before'.

Back at the Fallingbostel camp, a few hundred British prisoners were being shipped out each day, the general rule being that the longest-serving ones went first. Younger's turn came on 26 April.

We climbed into an army truck and, uncomfortably packed, drove out of the camp in a convoy escorted by motorcyclists. We were waved on at road junctions. All about us were wrecked homes, burnt-out shops, pale, sad-looking women, German prisoners going single file along the roadsides. That night, we stayed in a town where the Army had set up a NAAFI canteen and a makeshift cinema. We went in to watch the film but we were too restless to stay more than a few minutes. It was some months before I could sit through an entire film. We were impatient to go. This was still Germany. The next day we waited and waited, and eventually trucks came to take us to an airfield. But the one for us was late, and the driver apologized profusely and admitted he was drunk. We knew that no more planes would leave after 6 p.m. so we urged him to hurry. The man drove like fury for 17 miles, the truck whining and swaying, before he stopped and told us he was lost. He was very upset, so much so that we contained our disappointment and assured him that we did not mind spending another night in Germany. He swore he could still get us to the airfield on time, but it was long after six when we arrived – and he hunched over his wheel, and cried for us.

The airfield was a desolate place. Broken twisted aircraft and the burnt-out skeletons of aircraft littered the ground. Some had nosed into shell craters, and their tails jutted forlornly. No more aircraft were to fly to England that day. But at the end of the field a Dakota was warming up which could at least get us out of there and over the Rhine. The pilot, a nervous little man, came over to us. 'I can't take off, yet. There's broken glass all down the field. You men had better get cracking and pick it up.' We spread out, and painstakingly plodded down the field, stooping for every piece of glass or sharp metal. On my left was an Arnhem parachutist, on my right a man who had crash-landed a burning aircraft. Slowly we trod the grass back to the Dakota, and heaped our little armfuls of broken glass at the feet of the nervous pilot.

Eventually he was satisfied that the runway was clear, and they took off. Home for Younger – an Australian – was still far away, but he had reason to celebrate even so. 'I was still not home,' he noted, 'but at least I was out of Germany.'

Jim Sims, meanwhile, was travelling in a lorry and keeping his head down. As the convoy he was in bounced its way west, the ex-POWs were warned to lie on the floor for fear of sniper fire from 'werewolves' in the trees. Then they stayed overnight in a German army barracks, whose luxury, compared with the way British soldiers were housed, made him envious.

The corridors and rooms were spotless and it appeared to be centrally heated. There was even a swimming pool outside and I couldn't help thinking of places I had been stationed like Larkhill [on Salisbury Plain], which had been condemned long before World War Two, but was still in use and would be for many years after. Nothing but the best for our brave lads!

Cynicism, so typical of the post-war period ahead, had set in alarmingly quickly. But the Army had thought up a reward for them. Two unusual shoe-shine boys were produced to polish the ex-prisoners' boots. They were high-ranking German officers. The British officer who had arranged this thought it was a fine jape, and he told the men to 'kick their arses if they don't do it properly'. Sims said he and his friends 'were terribly embarrassed. I do not believe the Germans would have humiliated a British officer in this fashion and we were all glad to leave this barracks and get back in the trucks for the short trip to the airfield at Celle.'

There, as they climbed into Dakotas, many of the army men were nervous because they had never flown before. The flimsy, noisy planes, normally used for dropping paratroopers, seemed to be one risk too many for men who had come so far. Surely nothing could go wrong at this stage. But fears were stifled as they hurtled down the airstrip and up into the sky and followed a line down through Germany towards the Belgian frontier and Brussels. The pilots were proudly showing off what Bomber Command had done to the German cities below, and Sims remembered how

they even circled some towns so we could get a better look at the damage. But, as most of us had been on the receiving end [of bombings] when we were prisoners, we were not very appreciative. Some of the towns seemed to be levelled off at ground height and the people appeared to be crawling in and out of cellars. The damage to these German towns was really beyond belief, especially close to the Rhine.

We approached Brussels airport under cover of a violent thunderstorm, which was quite frightening. The Dakota landed safely and we were taken to a large hangar where ladies from the Women's Voluntary Service dished out tea and cakes to us. How nice it was to see and speak to English women again, even if they were a bit old. As I was 19 and most of them were between 35 and 45, they seemed really ancient. They also handed out soap and cigarettes and we joined the queue four times, but no one said anything. My only thought was to take a gift home to my mother, and as she was a smoker the fags seemed appropriate. All this was free of course, as none of us had any cash. One of the WVS ladies came up to me and asked if I had been at Arnhem. When I said that I had, she produced a photo of an airborne soldier and asked if I had seen him, or knew him. It was her husband. All she had received was the official War Office note that he was missing. I looked at the photo but did not know the man and handed it back to her, and I wondered how many times that sad little scene had been enacted.

Then an RAF pilot sauntered over and said, 'I want 30 men for my plane.' I was in no particular hurry, but when I turned to speak to John, who had been my constant buddy for the past eight months, he had gone. I was just in time to see him scrambling over the tailboard of this truck as it drove away towards a distant Dakota. I shouted after him, but he never even looked back. I felt stunned after all we had gone through together. I sat there feeling numb until I was shepherded over to yet another Dakota for the trip home. I found myself in this plane with 20 complete strangers from other German prison camps. I thought back over my time as a POW. It had altered me both physically and mentally for life. Although I was still only 19, I felt years older, completely different from the brash youngster who had parachuted down on the outskirts of Arnhem the previous year. I had had so many experiences and seen so much in such a short space of time that I felt I never wanted another experience of any sort ever again.

The Dakota took off and droned out over the Belgian coast towards England. Someone suddenly shouted. 'There's England!' and we all pressed our noses to the windows like street-urchins outside a sweet shop. The White Cliffs of Dover seemed as if they were suspended in space. Several of the older men wept and we patted them on the shoulder and cried, 'Never mind, old lad. We made it.'

The Dakota thundered on over a patchwork of neat fields and unspoilt countryside. Looking down, you would never have thought we had fought a terrible war. We flew inland and circled over a large castle before the plane started to descend, and we landed at an aerodrome somewhere in Hertfordshire. The doors were opened and we were helped out. As soon as my feet touched native soil, I collapsed, and had to be carried to a nearby reception area where I was put to bed. I was to spend the next eight weeks in hospital suffering from malnutrition, dysentery and various other ailments before my war was really over and I was able to go on leave.

That first sight of the White Cliffs featured in many memories. Leslie Frith's heart was close to bursting:

A glorious sight and one which at times I had thought I would never see again. It was overwhelming. A week ago we were all starving to death, just waiting for the end, and now suddenly we were crossing the English coast and we were home again. I cried with sheer joy. The Gestapo and the SS couldn't touch us now. No more rifle butts in the back, no more being herded around like cattle and being treated like the lowest form of life.

Doug Fry had a special view of the English coast on his flight home. He was loaded into a Lancaster bomber and asked the pilot if he could sit in the mid-upper gun turret, his position for all his bombing raids over Germany and in which he had very nearly been incinerated when he was shot down two years earlier. The experience had not deterred him.

I wasn't afraid of going flying again. It was going to be lovely. I was just glad there wouldn't be anybody firing at me this time. And in the event it was absolutely splendid. After all that had gone before, it was hard to take in that we really were almost home. From the turret I could see the coastline coming up – not the White Cliffs because we came a different route, over the east coast, but it was still a stupendous feeling.[11]

Percy Carruthers went one better. The pilot on his Dakota home allowed him to take the controls over the Channel, and as England loomed out of the coastal cloud bank

my eyes filled up and there was a lump in my throat so large I felt I would choke. I gripped the stick and breathed through my open mouth. Beside me, the pilot was silent. I'm sure he knew my difficulty. The engines of the old Dak sang sweetly in my ears as I checked temps, pressures, fuels, revs and so on before commencing a very shallow descent to the soil we had longed to tread for so long.[12]

In his plane, Fry peered out of the gun turret and thought about what lay ahead.

There were butterflies in my stomach as I started wondering what home was going to be like, what my life was going to be like from now on. We landed at an airfield in the Midlands, and the aircraft taxied round to a hangar. WAAFs were waiting to help us with what little kit we had. We had one on each arm as we went into this hangar with bunting all over it and a brass band playing, and tables laid out full of cakes and sandwiches. It was an absolutely astounding reception by the RAF. The feeling was indescribable. We were then taken to the base at Cosford,[13] where we had billets with a radio in each room and clean sheets. They wouldn't let us walk anywhere. They drove us round to the mess and they gave us fish and chips, but I couldn't eat it. I was too emotional. After all that time of thinking about food and looking forward to food I just couldn't manage it. Then we all bowled round to the bar. There were five of us in a group, but we were strangely subdued. There wasn't any triumphant yelling and shouting. I think we all felt that we had survived and we were lucky to have done so. Everybody had lost a lot of friends and colleagues. We were back in our homeland, but we knew there was going to be sadness for some people. So we lined up five pints at the bar – and then we couldn't drink the blinking beer either.

The emotion was finally catching up with Richard Passmore too. After a night in a luxury Brussels hotel, he deserted his companions, overwhelmed with a need to be on his own. Alone, he made his way to the airport and wangled his way on to a plane – by now there was virtually a shuttle service in operation to England. The White Cliffs of Dover left him cold. The reception with tea and cake and friendly chat at an airfield near Guildford was a blur of pleasantries. 'But then we were loaded into RAF trucks and set out for the railway station. A mob of children, eight- and nine-year-olds, ran behind, waving and cheering. They were the first children I had seen in all the long years. That was the moment when it first hit me that I was truly free.'

*

The worst journeys home and the longest delays seemed to have been reserved for those furthest away – the prisoners in southern Germany, primarily at Moosburg. Lieutenant Geoff Wright had got splendidly drunk with his American liberators and recorded in his diary that he hoped to be home 'next Sunday'.[14] Sunday was a long time coming. After three days of kicking his heels, he was raging about how much worse it was 'being a prisoner of blasted British bureaucrats than a prisoner of the Germans'. Those who had taken over the running of the camp insisted on lengthy parades every morning and banned radios because the broadcast news had not been censored and was therefore deemed unsuitable for the men to hear. Meanwhile the latrines clogged up and rubbish was piled in the compound. It angered Wright that the British contingent had been confined to camp 'while a horde of drunken swine of Russians pillage and rape the neighbourhood. If I had my way I would shoot all violent looters out of hand.' He was 'bitched, buggered and bewildered', he informed 'darling Joan', and 'I just want to get home and let you look after me.'

For Lieutenant Frank Stewart, however, there was a pleasant surprise during this period of waiting. The German headquarters at the camp was found to have all the belongings that had been taken from the prisoners when they arrived,

all neatly placed in pigeon-holes with our names and numbers attached. I got back my keyring and a heart-shaped cigarette lighter which I had bought five years ago in France before being captured. The lighter doesn't work, but it didn't when the Germans took it from me either. They are a strange race. Though they can commit the most ghastly crimes against humanity without turning a hair, they are meticulously honest when it comes to small things like this. These two trinkets have followed me round through seven camps from Bavaria to Poland and back. Amazing.[15]

The first contingent left Moosburg on 3 May, five days after liberation, but Wright was not among them and he felt let down. 'These days of waiting are very hard on the nervous system.' The ex-POWs were given no information, so all they had was rumour – 'the optimists still hope to leave tonight, the pessimists hope to be home by Christmas'. His despair deepened each day. 'No one has left today. Last night we heard that of the 3,000 who left the camp two days ago only about 550 were flown out, and the rest are still sitting on their fannies around the aerodrome. What a poxy, miserable joint this is, a stinking cesspit of mud, shit, lice and fleas.' Frank Stewart, a prisoner of Dunkirk vintage, thought he had never seen people so depressed in all his years of captivity.

We were led to expect that we'd be home any moment, but nothing has happened and no reason has been given. The weather is terrible, and we are cold, miserable and frustrated. However, things are looking up. The weather is clearing, my stomach is on the mend, and the Americans have opened up a cinema for our benefit. Someone with a fiendish sense of humour has chosen for our delectation a film called *The Thin Man Returns Home*.

Protests about conditions were cabled to Eisenhower at SHAEF headquarters, and promises of action came back – but only a handful of planes. Wright joined the thousands camping out at the airfield, waiting, counting in the planes, counting out the men in front of him in the queue, not daring to sleep in case he missed his turn. Accidents did not help. Two Dakotas collided with each other on the ground and then crashed into another three.

Stewart was also waiting at the airfield,

which was not a proper airfield at all, just an open stretch of grassy plain with no hangars and no buildings. There was no tarmac runway, only long strips of wire mesh stretched along the ground. The first plane arrived amid a great cheer, and then three more. I worked out that with 28 passengers to a plane we should be going in the 101st plane, and as we were told that 200 more were expected the prospects were looking good. Then things really started to happen. Someone sighted a plane in the distance, then another, and another, and in they came from every direction, great big moths flying low. They circled the airfield slowly and then came down along the 'runway', swinging round into line at the end. As each one landed, 28 prisoners immediately clambered in and off they went. In the first hour 40 planes came in and during the next hour another 40. That was 80 and we were nearing the magic 101 for me. I lay in the boiling sun, just looking and waiting. It was very, very exciting.

But then they stopped coming. To make matters worse, that evening we were told that the order of leaving had been changed and 1,750 Americans were to embark ahead of us. We were back to where we had started. I still needed 101 more planes to arrive. We picked up our baggage and walked into the town to look for a billet. Someone said it had just come over the BBC that the war had officially ended. [It was 8 May.] I'm afraid we laughed.

They got away the next day, and arrived in Reims to wait for a flight across the Channel. Wright was unlucky again. 'Missed England by nine planes,' he wrote wearily in his diary. It was 10 May, and he had been a free man for nearly a fortnight.

But Stewart was way ahead of him and was relaxing at a camp in Lincolnshire, asleep in a real bed. There he and those who had arrived with him were held for a day – 'endless forms to be filled up, questions to be answered, medical tests and mental checks. We were fitted out with new battledress, boots, shirts, and underclothes and, best of all, dark grey civilian suits.' Then they were let loose, 'armed with rail passes, ration books and clothing coupons, and even a little cash'. Before going home to Scotland, he and his friends headed for London and sauntered through St James's Park. They had been away a long time, and just how long now became clear.

We were all shocked by the blatancy of the couples on the benches and on the ground. We thought back to pre-war days when holding hands in public was considered rather daring. We also noticed how many women now wore trousers. We moved on to Piccadilly Circus and stood there taking in the great bustle of people. We thought they looked tired and drawn, as they had every reason to be after what they'd endured from the flying bombs and rockets. We made our way to King's Cross and sat up all night in the train, arriving at Edinburgh early in the morning of Friday 11 May. I took a taxi to my parents' house and there they were to greet me. It was also my birthday. I was 28 years old and had not been home for five and a half years.

For some, the journey back to England would be so arduous and so drawn-out that it left only bitterness. For Len Jepps, the time between liberation by the Americans at Nuremberg and arriving home was traumatic. First there was the chaos in the camp after the troops who had freed them left. No one was in charge, food stocks were dwindling, and no one knew what, if anything, was planned for them. The behaviour of the liberated Russians astounded him. Jepps remembered a group of them returning to the camp from a foraging trip with a donkey, which they then beat to death with stones and ate uncleaned and uncooked, right down to the hide. They were so starved that the shock to their digestive system killed them. Gradually order of a sort was restored, and work began to dispose of the piles of Russian corpses, the results of malnutrition and shelling. As the bodies were tipped into a communal grave, Jepps noted that there was not a stitch of clothing left on any of them, and that some had teeth marks around the thighs and upper arms as if someone had tried to eat them. He also recalled the almost complete absence of the usual stench of death, 'for there was no flesh left upon the corpses to putrefy'.[16]

After ten days of survival in these desperate circumstances, Jepps and his compatriates began their journey home. They boarded planes taking them, so they thought, to England, but, to their dismay, they got only as far as Brussels, where there were to be more disappointments and delays. After mugs of real tea, kisses from pretty girls in uniform at the airport and 'the privilege of being treated once more as real people in a real world', they hit what Jepps called 'a monumental web of frustration, the magnitude of which is still difficult to believe'. They were bussed round the city for hours, searching for accommodation. Then they were made to wait on the parade ground of an army barracks to be interrogated – a pointless exercise, as far as he could tell, 'because none of our answers was recorded and we were not even asked who we were'. After this they queued for food, though it was late into the night before some of them were fed, and were then left to sleep on a flagstoned floor. Jepps felt as though he was back in Stalag 344 at Lamsdorf.

They had been told they were to be flown home. Instead, the next day they were taken in lorries to a railway station and, after a long wait, were put on a goods train to Bruges. There they were bundled out on to the platform and, in a near-mutinous mood, were made to wait again before being taken by lorry to another camp. Starved of food and information, the prisoners were at breaking point. As Jepps told an army colonel who asked him what the problem was, 'we had been prisoners for five years, and we were not lacking in patience for we had learned that virtue in a hard school; but we needed to be treated as people instead of animals or small children'. There was an instant change in attitude. They were properly fed and properly bedded down that night. They were told they would be staying at Bruges for three days, and would then be taken to Ostend to be shipped home to Tilbury in the Thames estuary. And so it turned out, with the added pleasure of a band to play them on to the train at Bruges and then on to the waiting ship at Ostend.

But their ordeal was not over. At Tilbury there were long queues for food and no shelter from the pouring rain as they waited for trains to take them to an unknown destination. They ended up at a reception camp in Sussex, staffed, as Jepps complained, 'by a body of officers and troops who were so offhand and unhelpful that, had it been the intention of the authorities to subject us to deliberate indignities, they could not have selected a more competent staff to carry out the job'. An 'uncouth corporal' told them they had missed breakfast and that they had to be on parade in ten minutes. The growls of anger alerted him to the mistake in his manner, and he fled before he was physically thrown out.

Days of inspections and parades followed, culminating in a medical examination which Jepps thought a disgrace. 'We were returning POWs who had been incarcerated for five years, and the pipsqueak of a doctor gave each of us an average of a minute and a half. He was a disgrace to his profession, and should have been cashiered.' Finally, the men were issued with rail warrants. Their boots shining, gaiters scrubbed, and collars and buttons fastened, they could go home at last. But the experience – the delays and, more than that, the indifference – had soured their repatriation. It had been a bitter homecoming – and an unjust one, given their years of deprivation and suffering.

For some, however, there would be no homecoming at all. They would fall at the very last hurdle. RAF records report a Lancaster from 514 Squadron which took off from Juvincourt in northern France with twenty-five passengers and a crew of six. The pilot lost control, apparently because the men were not evenly distributed, and crashed. They all died. It was 9 May, the day after VE Day.

Such disasters were the exception. And, though Jepps's return had taken painfully long weeks, others, like Cec Room, made it home from northern Germany in seven days and had no complaints. While waiting, Room had his souvenirs – a pair of jackboots taken from a German flight sergeant. He was better informed – he had read his way through a three-week-old copy of the *News of the World*, a present from a British soldier. He had eaten well but sensibly on stew and rice pudding – 'a light meal but even so several of the boys are in pain; their stomachs just can't take it' – and had had his fill of cigarettes, cigars and chewing gum. He was watching newsreels and Mickey Mouse cartoons in a makeshift cinema when the call came to leave and he and his comrades piled into lorries – 'very uncomfortable, almost as bad as the cattle trucks, but we're all very cheerful'. Then came the flight that dreams were made of:

We left Germany behind, went over Belgium and France, the Channel and then the White Cliffs of Dover. Everybody rushed to the starboard side and the bloody wing dropped and there was a yell from the pilot, 'For Christ sake, keep the thing in balance.' I had a tear down my cheek, the only tear I ever shed throughout that whole time.

When they landed 'a WAAF rushes up to kiss me. That was worth all the two years. A hangar is hung with flags and a huge "Welcome home" sign fluttering from the roof. A wizard tea, £2 advance pay, a rest and off we go. All the WAAFs follow the truck on their bicycles, what a glamorous guard of honour!' They were taken to the reception centre at Cosford to be rekitted with new uniforms and interrogated by intelligence officers.

Debriefings varied enormously. Doug Fry remembered a few questions from Military Intelligence. Seated at a table in a hangar along with hundreds of others, he was asked if he wanted to name any particular German who had mistreated him. (He did not.) The main concern seemed to be to check that he was who his documents said he was. Spitfire pilot Bob Morton found that no one wanted to hear his epic story – shot down in 1941, a trail of notorious camps from Sagan to Fallingbostel, shot-up at Gresse. It would have been worth hearing, but the officer delegated to listen to him was just about to go to lunch. 'He said, "If there's anything terribly important write it down and leave a note." This really rather gave it away. They didn't want the stories. There was nobody trying to find out about what happened to us, not really. I think it was just so that we could get it off our chests if we wanted to.'[17] Morton didn't. He was home and he felt fine. 'I don't think we needed looking after,' he said.

Military Intelligence – MI9 – had in fact made elaborate plans for debriefing the ex-prisoners. It had compiled three different questionnaires: a general one for all to fill in; a specific questionnaire for the men who had been its contacts in the camps or escape leaders; a third for those wishing to report atrocities. It had then intended to send officers into all the camps immediately after liberation to hand out these questionnaires and conduct further investigations. These officers were to be specifically asked to root out alleged collaborators and hand them over to the British or

US Army. There were also deserters to be identified and caught, and Germans trying to slip into England in disguise. But MI9 had drawn up its plan in August 1944, and it proved redundant – except for the clause that said 'no interrogation shall be allowed to hold up the return to the UK of prisoners of war'. The intelligence officers did not make it to the camps in Germany in time, and the questionnaires and the interrogations had to wait until the men were either in transit camps or back on home soil.

Brigadier Norman Crockatt, who was in charge of the intelligence operation, had wanted to make completing these forms a condition of returning to England. He instructed his subordinates that no individual would be allowed on a plane home until he had filled in a form. He was gently advised that men coming home after five years in captivity were unlikely to sit like schoolboys at an examination answering questions that seemed irrelevant. 'I think we will have a lot of trouble on our hands,' he was told. Crockatt replied that he fully expected the men's reactions to be 'vociferous and occasionally violent', but 'gentlemen, those are your orders and you will carry them out'.[18]

According to MI9's historians, 'most liberated prisoners accepted, though often sullenly, the re-imposition of service discipline, and filled in the forms', though this claim of 'most' is not backed by their own figures. Around 166,000 British and Commonwealth prisoners came back from Germany, but only 54,000 forms were filled in – a hit rate of less than one in three. As Crockatt's staff had expected, many refused to cooperate at all, and others scrawled obscenities. Some could only be bothered with an unhelpful 'yes' or 'no'; others poured out their life stories and their grievances in scribbled page after angry page.

These people gave intelligence officers most trouble. Their outpourings were usually vicious accusations of collaboration with the Germans by fellow-prisoners, or self-justifications of their own activities, in the form of long rambling accounts of their unsuccessful attempts to escape. The staff could do no more than keep them supplied with paper and pencils. These essentials, notably pencils, often ran short, for the staff failed to take into account the habit acquired in prison camps of pocketing any small object that might serve some useful purpose in the future. There was much silent sympathy for those in MI9 whose task it would be to evaluate these statements.

There seems to have been little attempt to find out about missing friends – fellow prisoners of war who had died or been lost in those chaotic marches across Germany.[19] It was probably impossible anyway, given the flood of men returning. Even getting a basic list of names of those coming home proved next to impossible. 'The hope that Shaef's administrative staff would be able to supply accurate nominal rolls in the three main ex-POW transit camps, at Antwerp, Brussels and Rheims, proved unfounded,' according to MI9's historians.

Groups of liberated prisoners would arrive, frequently without warning, at all hours of the day or night, hungry, dirty, often in rags. Dealing with their immediate requirements was given priority, and on many occasions men had left on the next stage of their journey home before the interrogators saw [their names]. Then there were those who went absent without leave and then hitchhiked back to England, there rejoining the stream destined for home.

The chaos was not really surprising. Bloody-minded soldiers and airmen were always more than a match for bureaucrats with clipboards. But the failure to collect accurate data – to count them out and count them in, as would famously be said in a later conflict[20] – would have a bearing on the very end of this story, as we will see.

*

For the American prisoners, there was a staging post on the way home that became legendary – the appropriately named Camp Lucky Strike. John Parsons was there just five days after being liberated at Moosburg. Dakotas flew him and his comrades to Reims, and then they went by train to what they were told was a RAMP camp. Here was a strange new piece of jargon – it stood for Recovered Allied Military Personnel – and, as Parsons noted, the camp 'had to be better than anything we had seen since being shot down'.[21] It was.

The American authorities seemed to have a better grasp of what the men needed than their British counterparts. Information and respect. The ex-POWs were told where they were going and when. They were put in first-class rail carriages to take them to Lucky Strike, which was on the Channel coast of northern France. Here, in an area that had once been part of Hitler's supposedly impregnable Atlantic Wall, was a vast arena of pitched tents. Parsons got priority treatment. The doctors took one look at him, weighed him in at a shocking 70 lb (5 stone), and categorized him as being in the poorest of conditions. There was a thorough debriefing by an officer from Army Air Corps Intelligence, who asked especially about the 'Baltic cruise' and the 'run up the road' at Gross Tychow. 'He said there would be a War Crimes Commission investigating the bad treatment we had received. He wanted names of guards and I tried to give him as much information as possible.' Parsons told him what he knew about Big Stoop's violent ending.

Home was still 3,000 miles away, but it was now feeling closer. He could at last send a message to his wife with certainty that it would get through. Every man was allowed one cable home. 'Dearest Mai,' he wrote, 'I will see you soon. I am in good health and waiting for a boat home. All my love.' With a portion of his back pay in his pocket, he went to the camp store and found a bottle of her favourite perfume – Joy – and stowed it in his pack. Then it was the short trip by truck to the port of Le Havre.

The weather was perfect. We were quickly loaded on board. The sailors knew that we were all former prisoners of war and they handled us as if we were precious china. We had been warned at Lucky Strike that there would be so many of us that we might have to share bunks at different hours and sleep in rotation but that didn't happen to me. I had my choice of bunks in a large cabin. The dining area of the ship was immaculate with tables of stainless steel. The food was the best ever and we sat down to a dinner of steak, mashed potatoes with gravy, fresh vegetables, beautiful white bread, pies and cakes and four flavours of ice cream. The captain announced over the loudspeaker that we would be at sea about a week and would have good weather throughout. I relaxed and settled into the ship's routine.

Soon they were steaming towards the American coastline, with New York on the horizon. The captain warned them that they should not all crowd on to the port side for the best view, otherwise the ship might list, and there were marines stationed to stop this happening. But nothing could dampen the excitement. 'When we caught sight of the Statue of Liberty, it was the greatest thrill in the world for all of us. The Port Authority fire boats shot water into the sky as they came alongside, and ahead on the dock a band was playing Sousa.' There was Hawaiian music too, and girls dancing and rolling their hips. The captain's order was forgotten as everyone rushed to the rails, and the ship heaved and rolled into the timbers of the dock.

Strangely, in the excitement of reaching the shores of America, friendships that had lasted long years of hardship, and which had pulled men through when they might otherwise have collapsed, ended. Buddies parted company. Trains went in different directions. So did individual lives that had once been entwined. Roger Allen and his friend Jason Bugs had managed to stay together and were on the same boat home, though the men from Kentucky were up on the third deck and those from Oklahoma down in the hold. They had seen the Statue of Liberty together – a first for Allen, who had never been outside his home state before leaving for Europe, and certainly never to New York City. 'I said goodbye to him on the boat and we hugged and said "See you later."'[22] Back at their respective homes, their new lives had an urgency of their own. It was thirty years before they met again.

Joe Lovoi was not on the sick list for a priority voyage, and his stay at Camp Lucky Strike was longer than John Parsons's. Now that he was out of Germany and out of danger, Lovoi was excited and ready for action. The ex-prisoners were expected to rest and recover their strength, but that was the last thing he wanted as he went hunting round the tents, the mess halls, the hospital rooms and the recreation areas for old friends. Lovoi wanted to see a little more of France before he went home, though his buddy from Stalag Luft III, the guitar-playing Onafrio Brancato, disagreed. He just wanted to be home in Ohio. Lovoi decided to let him go ahead. He and another friend, Vinnie Niemann, would wait until they had seen Paris. The trouble was that the authorities, having got everyone in one place to ship them home, were not keen on strays. There were no passes-out to be had. If Lovoi and Niemann wanted to see Paris, they would have to escape.

The day came when all three were listed for the next ship leaving. Brancato left on time, but Lovoi and Niemann made sure they overslept and missed the truck to Le Havre. The next day they were out of Lucky Strike, climbing over a remote part of the perimeter fence and racing for the woods, just as they would have done if they had ever had the chance back at Sagan or Moosburg. They had not been spotted, and they headed for the main road to Paris, 100 miles away.

In smart new uniforms, fresh from the store at Lucky Strike, they soon thumbed a lift. Lovoi recalled, 'The sun was shining, the sky was blue, and the morning rain had washed the countryside clean. We were happy, joking and laughing. It was great to be alive.'[23] The lifts they got took them a long way round – via Rouen and Reims, where they marvelled at the cathedrals – and then, as afternoon turned to evening, they stood by the side of the road, their thumbs out, and contemplated the prospect of a night in the French capital.

The jeep that stopped for them was not a welcome sight. Two military policemen asked to see their passes. They had none, of course. They were taken into custody and sat in a cell in a guard-room, waiting to be returned to the camp. They were back behind bars. There was even barbed wire stretched across the window – barbed wire, it turned out, that was not securely fastened and could be pulled out with a nail file. Lovoi and Niemann made their escape, once again running for the woods. A French farmer on his way to market in Paris in a dilapidated lorry picked them up. There were baskets of apples in the back, and they feasted on them all the way into the city.

'Paris in the spring!' Lovoi recalled, and he saw the chance to be there as a reward for his twenty-nine bombing missions and the nightmare of being a prisoner of war. The farmer dropped them close to the Arc de Triomphe, and soon they were in the throngs of people on the Champs-Elysées. There were girls everywhere, and they sat at an outdoor café, ordered two beers, and took in the buzz of life around them. It did not take long to find companionship.

Two girls passing by stopped and smiled. One was a tall, slim brunette; the other a shorter, more shapely redhead. Both were extremely well dressed. The young men rose to their feet and invited them for a drink. They talked in a mixture of English, Italian and German; they walked arm in arm along the boulevards; they shared a dinner in a restaurant ... and there, eating and drinking in a Paris bistro with two beautiful French girls, Joe Lovoi chose to end his account of his war in Europe. He reached home a little later than other prisoners, sailing into Atlantic City before taking the train to Massachusetts.

John Anderson did not get to see Paris. Instead he had a number of days in Brussels, which suited him well because, as a musician, he was able to visit the Conservatory. It made for a lengthy journey home. He had been liberated on 16 April at Fallingbostel, and it was more than a month before he landed back in the USA. He missed an earlier transit home by staying too long in the shower. 'It was so refreshing I was in there at least half an hour, and when I came out the group I was with had gone.'[24] They had taken a flight on to England, and he would have to wait.

In the Belgian capital he looked at the cathedral and then gorged himself on ice cream, extravagantly ordering chocolate *and* vanilla. There was still no news of transport the next day, so he did the same again. 'Went downtown. Ate ice cream. Went to symphony concert.' He wrote to his mother:

It is Sunday morning and I'm still in Brussels. I have the opportunity to stay here as long as I want or leave by plane for either England or France any day. This seems like a wonderful chance to see things so I may delay my coming home for a while. Today I want to go to the Conservatory. Perhaps I'll go to an opera tonight.

Eventually he ended up in Camp Lucky Strike, but even then his route home was tortuous. He got on a ship at Le Havre which headed over the Channel rather than into the Atlantic. That meant he was in Southampton on VE Day, and heard Winston Churchill's voice on the radio. Anderson, always a man of conscience, was troubled. The war was over in Europe, but he wondered 'if I will see action in the South Pacific'. There was still more fighting to do, another enemy to defeat. That thought hung like a cloud over many a homecoming.

Finally the ship left England and headed west through wind and rain. On 19 May he saw his homeland in the distance and, like so many others, felt a surge of pride and emotion as he passed the Statue of Liberty. 'That's what it had all been about – liberty. We all cheered and shouted. A tear ran down my cheek.'

Soon he stood on his native soil again, as thousands of other former prisoners of war like him were doing in America, in Britain, in Australia, New Zealand and Canada, and in many other countries throughout the world. It was time to be back with those loved ones not seen for years. They would be waiting at bus stops and railway stations, at front doors and garden gates.

Wouldn't they?

15   Welcome Back

Home was the prisoner's Holy Grail. Thoughts of it often spurred him on, but they could also bring him down in despair. One of Bill Ethridge's worst days was when he wrote in his diary, 'Homesick. Our wedding anniversary. Tough all day long. Home seems pretty far away right now.'[1] But thoughts of his wife and the normal life they would one day lead were also what kept him going. Even so, there were times when prisoners had to remind themselves that there had been a previous existence – a feeling that was captured in a poem by a British prisoner by the name of Ted Beckwith, who found the right voice of nostalgia and unease when he wrote this Betjeman-like lament in 1942:

Is there really a house and a garden
Where the northbound lorries pass,
Where the summer breeze stirs the apple trees
And buttercups grow in the grass;
Where roses blow in the autumn
And the blackbird builds in the spring,
And a steady creak and a happy shriek
Was a little girl on a swing?

Was it really us in the kitchen
With a Sunday supper spread,
Making cheer with a glass of beer
With pickles and beef and bread;
You and I, and a spaniel
On the kitchen hearthrug curled,
And a sleepy head upstairs in bed –
And never a care in the world?

Did my feet once walk on a carpet?
Did I doze in my own armchair?

Was it us made merry with friends and sherry
In a house with a twisty stair?
Did we dine at a polished table
With silver bowls agleam?
Is there really a house and a garden –
Or was it all a dream?[2]

In the spring of 1945, men and women everywhere were waking up to discover the answer.

*

The last time Betty Batchelder had heard news from her husband, Batch, was in January. In the three years since he had been shot down and captured she had received just a handful of cards and letters from him as he worked his way through four different camps before ending up at Fallingbostel. She had done her bit, sending out letters and parcels regularly – even cigarettes, though he was not a smoker. He could use them for bartering and get extra food for himself, or so she thought. Later she discovered that not a single one had got through. (Sadly, the rumour was that they were stolen not by the Germans but by people handling them at the British end.) By now Betty, who was trained as a telephonist, had moved to the War Office in London to work in Signals, and that allowed her access to a little more information. Even so, as the war entered its final days, she had no idea where he was.

We knew then that the war was fizzling out and with luck our boys would be home. But those last four or five months were tense. We weren't getting any information, and of course we thought the worst. It was a really worrying time, and I am glad I was working. Just sitting at home waiting would have been dreadful. There were rumours about them being marched from their camps, but nothing about the possibility of them being tortured or killed. I'm glad about that. I think that would have sent me mad. I had an inner feeling, as if I could will them to come home. But there were conflicting messages. I would hear things from other wives, and Batch's father was also picking up pieces of information.[3]

Then newspaper war correspondents on the Allied front line in Germany reached some of the liberated camps and began filing accounts of the horrors they found. Their stories about prisoners of war were often side by side with descriptions of what had been discovered in the concentration camps. Under the headline 'Prison camp horrors will be shown to Germans', the *News of the World*'s Harry Ditton described the unearthing of Belsen's secrets and also what he had seen at nearby Fallingbostel. In the POW camp, he wrote, 'I spoke to many British prisoners of war, and their personal experiences of German barbarity and torture are bad enough in all conscience. But, inhuman and vile as the treatment of our men has been, it is not to be compared with the satanic vengeance which has been meted out to the Poles, the Yugoslavs, the Russians and the Jews.' His distinctions were carefully made, but the juxtaposition must nevertheless have been alarming to many families at home.

Released prisoners of war on the ground in Germany were also revealing details of the forced marches they had been on. On 8 April a *Sunday Times* correspondent reported an interview with three British soldiers who had been on the road from Poland for nine and a half weeks before slipping away and being rescued by the advancing Americans. They said that 7 of their group of around 170 had died and 'another 12 who fell out sick are still missing'. Five days later, a *Daily Telegraph* correspondent talked to 'some of the survivors of the British and American prisoners of war who took part in one of the worst forced marches of the war'. These were the men from Lamsdorf. 'No one knows how many died en route,' he wrote,

but I have the word of one British soldier, a lance-sergeant from the North Country, that he had seen four men die a week ago. Though they were occasionally clubbed with rifles, men died mostly from exhaustion, malnutrition and dysentery. Today, even after a few days' rest and care by an American medical unit, the majority are still too weak to talk except with long pauses.

Reports like these caused alarm at home. Betty made sure that Batch's mother, who was sick and very frail, did not see the newspapers or hear the news on the radio, because the extra worry could well have killed her. This was the toughest time of all – 'worrying, frightening, impossible', as she recalled.

When I was on my own, I just cried and cried. I hoped and prayed that Batch wasn't among those who had been forced to march. I had many sleepless nights, and, during the day, every time the phone rang I just dreaded that it was going to be bad news about him. I think my uncle in the Red Cross knew more than he was letting on about the condition of the POWs and was deliberately not telling me in order to protect me. Meanwhile, Batch's father kept telling us, 'It's no use worrying. We'll know soon enough. Keep your chin up.'

But nobody knew anything for sure, and certainly not about individuals. 'Papers would have the names and numbers of camps that had been released, but there were no lists of men and no official notification from the government at all.' The days went by with hopes rising, then dipping. Some prisoners were already home. Betty took Batch's mother to Bournemouth for a rest, and the seaside resort was full of men who had been repatriated. 'There was a rising sense of expectation, but everyone was just a little afraid to hope too much, that something might go wrong even now.'

That mixture of hope and foreboding must have affected Norman Leonard's father and stepmother when they received his last letter. They had their own problems to deal with. Their house in Hornchurch, Essex, had been blasted apart by a V2 rocket falling short of its target in London. The back of the building was reduced to rubble, and his stepmother was injured. That had happened in February 1945, so that when Leonard began writing his letter a month later he had no idea that the home he dreamed of had been shattered and the family was in temporary lodgings. He had made the long trek from Stalag 344 at Lamsdorf, been frozen, sick and strafed by Allied planes, and was now in a hospital camp at an old spa town called Bad Sulza, having been taken off the march because he was too sick to go on. It was the first time since he and his comrades had left camp in January that he had had the chance to write, and he decided to tell the truth.

'My dear mother and father,' he began, 'I am sorry that I cannot say that I am in the best of health, as I am barely recovered from dysentery which certainly made a bit of a mess of me. The last two months have been the worst I have ever experienced and I hope I ever will.'[4] A few days in hospital had helped, his strength was returning, and he was a little more optimistic than he had been, but 'unfortunately my journey is still uncompleted and I do not know what lies ahead of me. I do hope you have not worried too much although I am sure that you must know what has been happening.' He looked forward to seeing them. In the meantime they should 'start stocking the larder to fatten me up, and believe me I need it. Food will be my main interest when I get home.' The Leonard family were on standby for their son's return.

*

As the men neared home and their loved ones dared to tell themselves that the ordeal really might be over, the psychologists at the War Office were dusting off the papers and the pamphlets they had prepared years ago on returning prisoners of war and how to treat them. Back in September 1943 a meeting of army doctors in London had raised the question of rehabilitation.[5] A study had been made of ninety prisoners who had returned under a repatriation agreement with the Germans, and what had emerged was what was described as a 'Rip Van Winkle' effect. Three months after coming home, a full third of these men were diagnosed as 'sufficiently abnormal' to need treatment. The three-month interval was crucial, because, to begin with, the symptoms were masked by the excitement of getting home. The meeting agreed straight away that a rehabilitation scheme was necessary, encouraged by Major-General Sir Richard Howard-Vyse of the Red Cross, who said his organization had come under a lot of pressure from relatives of prisoners for such a scheme. The discussion then meandered off into whose responsibility this should be – particularly for men who, during the three-month interval, had 'left the Colours' and taken up civilian jobs. Would the Army then have washed its hands of them? Or should they insist that no returning prisoner of war could be demobbed for at least three months – which would seem unfair and impractical? These details were thrashed around without conclusion.

Curiously, the minutes of the meeting only once mentioned specifically what the returning prisoners might be suffering from, and that was in a comment by the man from the Ministry of Labour. 'Depression and apathy' was what they were talking about, and he wondered whether hurrying men with these ailments into jobs would not do more harm than good.

In the meantime, a lively public debate was taking place. A Captain George Collie, veteran of the First World War and a former prisoner of war himself, had published an article saying that returning prisoners of war – especially those who had been in captivity for two years or more – would need special treatment for 'minor mental abnormalities' before they were again ready for normal civilian life.[6] Collie was congratulated by those who thought such problems had been unrecognized for far too long and needed addressing urgently, and condemned by those who thought his proposals a giant fuss about nothing. One man who had been through a three-month stint in a rehabilitation centre as a repatriated prisoner thought it had been a total waste of time. He dismissed as nonsense the traumas that Collie envisaged – particularly those to do with a prisoner's ignorance of events during his absence. 'I cannot believe that to learn for the first time of the existence of the Beveridge Report [which recommended setting up the Welfare State] will produce any greater strain than to learn that utility trousers have no turn-ups.' The wife of a prisoner complained that, having been separated from her husband for years, she would then have him taken away from her for another three months. 'Please leave me my husband,' she begged. Another felt that compulsory treatment would make returning prisoners feel that they were captives again.

One wise correspondent suggested it was the relatives and friends rather than the prisoners who needed the help. 'Many people do not realize the full implications of being a prisoner of war and often speak of them as being well out of the war and living in comparative security. Anything which will remove these false ideas will ease the lot of the men who return.' The real problem for the POW coming back was going to be that real life would be 'different from the one he has been building his hopes on for years and one which may easily let him down'.

At the beginning of 1944, an article in the *British Medical Journal* by a Major P. H. Newman of the Royal Army Medical Corps looked at the precise problems that prisoners encountered in the camps.[7] Chief among these was 'the absence of female society', by which Newman meant not so much sexual starvation as lack of affection and tenderness. He was dismissive of the effect of no sexual intercourse. 'It is quite common for an Italian prisoner of war to believe that he will become mentally deranged without this physiological act, and I have heard this view expressed also by French prisoners. But never by British or German prisoners of war.' He did think, however, that there might be fears of impotence – 'quite unfounded'.

The biggest danger to the POW's mental health was the irritation that came from overcrowding in the camps and the boredom of having nothing to do. 'All this tends to make him small-minded and childish.' Newman was worried about the high expectation that prisoners would have about home – 'their exaggerated optimism and false hope'. How they handled this would depend on the reception they got from their families, and on their families' love and understanding. And loved ones should not be surprised by bouts of restlessness, irritability, irresponsibility and even dishonesty. Newman thought that most POWs would get over their experiences in six months to a year. But some might not, and there was a danger that these would sink into persistently anti-social behaviour, such as drinking heavily, or would go to the opposite extreme and become totally apathetic and indolent. Many men would need help, but the difficulty would be getting them to accept it. The task was to make that help available but to make it unobtrusive. Information, social centres and sympathetic specialists to deal with the returning POWs were his suggestions.

Finally, in February 1944, there was an authoritative report on the psychology of returning prisoners of war by the Army's expert, Lieutenant-Colonel A. T. M. Wilson.[8] This recognized that there would be particular problems for men who had been in captivity for eighteen months or more. They would have adopted what he called the Stalag Mentality, 'which was essential in the prison camp but increases the difficulties of re-adaptation on return'. He thought that the main burden prisoners would have on their return was a deep bitterness, resulting from 'the sterility, deprivations and enforced passivity of Stalag life' but also from their feeling that they had missed out on so much.

Wilson's findings had a solid basis to them. For four weeks, an exhaustive study had been made of 1,200 prisoners repatriated under an exchange agreement with the Germans. At a special camp near Aldershot they had been drilled and lectured, examined and interrogated. Most had insisted that they did not need professional psychiatric help with their problems but they did want to be understood and to be dealt with fairly by people who were sympathetic to what they had been through. They didn't need 'soft handling', but 'different handling'. There were also certain issues guaranteed to raise the blood pressure of a prisoner of war. One was his back pay; another was his entitlement to leave; a third was being given a quick decision on his health and his suitability for continued military service, if that was what he wanted. Minimizing problems over these issues would be helpful.

Most of these suggestions were taken on board by the War Office, and it did its best to offer the right sort of atmosphere and the right sort of recuperation for the men when they returned, even if the facilities were overwhelmed by the rush home at the end. But there was one howler, admitted and corrected just in time. The phrase 'mental rehabilitation' had crept into the instructions sent out for dealing with the returning prisoners of war. An early example of political correctness ruled it out. On 30 March 1945, the director of prisoners of war wrote from the War Office to all concerned:

Experience has shown that the word 'rehabilitation', although perfectly innocuous in its primary meaning, has unfortunately attracted a secondary significance in the minds of many people and is frequently taken to connote a process of mental or psychological reconditioning made necessary as the ex-prisoner of war is looked on as abnormal or even as a 'mental case'. The ex-prisoner of war who is perfectly normal and fit rather naturally feels affronted. The Adjutant-General has given instructions that the expression 'mental rehabilitation' or these words separately shall not be used in conversation or in writing. The expressions 'resettlement' or 'resettlement training' will be employed instead.[9]

Other acceptable words were 'readjustment' and 'reorientation', but 'under no circumstances should the word "mental" be used'. Similar consideration and thoughtfulness for the men coming home was urged on the government in the House of Commons by Lieutenant-Colonel Louis Gluckstein, MP for Nottingham East.[10] Gluckstein had clearly seen Wilson's report, because his speech reflected the points the army doctor had made. But the MP emphasized the point about being careful not to add to the grievances of men returning from the camps in Germany. 'In the settling of pay and allowances,' he pleaded, 'if there is any doubt, it should be exercised generously in favour of the soldier. It probably will not amount to very much in money. The Finance Branch of the War Office might consider acting generously and even improvidently. I do not think they would find themselves criticized if they did.'

This plea for leniency and understanding would not always be heeded in the days ahead. Peacetime gave the bureaucrats and the pen-pushers the upper hand again. Group Captain N. C. Hyde was a prisoner of the Germans for four years. When he returned, he filled in RAF Form 1784 requesting financial compensation for the loss of his uniform and his flying kit when he was shot down and captured. He also included on his list of items his fountain pen, which the Germans had taken. From the Air Ministry at Imperial House in central London, a civil servant – 'your most obedient servant', as he signed himself – wrote to Hyde, 'The Air Ministry is unable to pay compensation for the confiscation of your fountain pen in the absence of a receipt by the enemy.'[11] Normal service had resumed, and the realities of war were already history.

*

The bureaucrats appear to have been more considerate in the United States. The agreed plan for Americans returning from prison camps in Europe was to send them home almost immediately for sixty days' leave. Only after that two-month break would they have to present themselves for two weeks at a recreation and rehabilitation centre. Home came first.

Out of the blue, Mai Parsons received her wonderful message from Camp Lucky Strike in France saying that her husband John was on his way – followed by more days of silence as he crossed the Atlantic and landed in triumph in New York harbour. Fresh off the ship, with the cheers of welcome still ringing in their ears, the returning prisoners were taken by train to Fort Dix in New Jersey. It was there that John played a game of pool and had a few beers while waiting his turn for the telephone. He was finally called to the phone, dialled his wife's number, and heard her voice for the first time in more than a year. The feeling was 'indescribable', he said; for Mai it was 'simply wonderful, a real release of emotion'.[12]

Trains were waiting to take the servicemen westward – 'a special train with triple-A priority', according to John, 'which meant we had the right of way over all trains, scheduled or non-scheduled'. As he crossed America, he looked out of the window and marvelled at the countryside – 'the beautiful farm land in Pennsylvania and Ohio. Even the dirty and sooty rail yards were just the most wonderful sight.' At Indianapolis he had to change trains, and that meant waiting an hour – and waiting was now an impossibility. A Greyhound bus was about to leave for Lafayette. He flung himself on to it with his pack and the German rifle he had brought back as a souvenir.

Their reunion was just as Mai had imagined it would be as she had stared, for month after month in her office, at the picture of the returning soldier, resplendent in full uniform, climbing from the Greyhound bus.

I called the bus station and they said they had a bus coming in from Indianapolis late evening, and so I was right there. I was waiting. I watched the bus come down the road. It pulled up and the doors opened, and he stepped off, just like in the picture. He was the first one off, and it was so wonderful. He put his arms round me. I can't remember what we said, because we were just hugging and kissing and crying. I don't think there was much conversation. It was like a dream it was just so wonderful. It was that way for two or three days, just hard to believe that we were together again.

To John, it was

joy impossible to express as the door of the Greyhound bus opened and I was stepping off into the arms of my wife after all those long months. Unless you have been one of those who has faced death many times and stayed awake many nights thinking that never again would you see your wife and loved ones, then there is no way you can know the happiness of finally coming home.

Everything was as he remembered it. 'Mai had rented a beautiful little apartment in the same neighbourhood we had lived in before.

It was as though nothing had changed – same grocery stores, same walk to downtown. It was truly home.' But he had changed, and Mai was not the only one to think him frighteningly thin. Family and friends rallied round. John recalled:

The very next day we started visiting relatives – my father, brothers, aunts, uncles, grandparents, and so on. We were wined and dined with all my favourite foods. The butchers even saved choice cuts of meat for us. Lafayette was rather a small town, so everyone knew of my homecoming. We were approached by perfect strangers wishing us well and wondering if there was anything they could help us with. My uncle and aunt took us to Michigan for a week of fishing and boating. Mai and I had two months of this, and then I had orders to report to Miami Beach, Florida, for a two-week period of recuperation.

We left Lafayette by Pullman and felt like a king and queen travelling first class. After reporting to Miami, we were quartered at the Ocean Grande Hotel right on Miami Beach. All of our meals were provided in a mess-hall-type setting with German prisoners of war preparing the food and serving us. Also, there was a canteen-type place where we could go anytime day or night and get whatever we wanted with no charge. Many of the airmen that I had been with in the camps were also there with us. There were all sorts of activities and entertainment for us. Mai and I went deep-sea fishing and attended the dog races. On 6 August 1945, there was word on the radio that Hiroshima had been bombed with an atomic bomb. Two days later another one was dropped on Nagasaki and we heard on the radio that Japan had surrendered. Everyone was in a celebration mood. There was dancing outside around the pools until the wee hours of the morning – just knowing that the war would soon be over and everyone could come home from the far corners of the world. The news, coupled with my homecoming, was like the icing on the cake. It just overwhelmed us.

Mai remembered their time in those first few months after his return as pure joy.

We did a lot of swimming, bicycling, playing tennis, and just picked up our life as though there had been no interruption. John weighed less than 70 lb when he came back, but by the end of the summer he was up to 100 lb. He was exactly the same man that I waved off on the aircraft. He truly was the same person, and I thank God for that. Except that he did have nightmares. He used to dream about a fistfight he had had with one man in the camp. It was so real for him that one night he lashed out in his sleep and hit me and gave me a black eye. But he didn't really talk about his experiences. Every time I tried to ask him, he would say, 'Hubba hubba,' which meant, 'Forget it.' He didn't want to talk about it.[13]

Meanwhile, in Kansas City on 13 May, John Anderson's mother had received the best Mother's Day present possible – a telegram from 'her boy' that he was safe and well and on the Atlantic heading home. Perhaps she disapproved of the extra time he had had in Brussels, listening to music and eating ice cream, but now he was on his way and she was in a panic to be ready for him. He telephoned her from New Jersey, but she was out and missed the call, missed his voice. He took the train inland, long hours across the middle of America, stopping for a while at Cincinnati. 'Still going west. It won't be long,' he wrote in his diary.[14] He got to St Louis too late for his connection, and had to hang around from midnight until the morning. 'Next stop KC.'

He rang his mother from the station when he arrived, and she hurried next door and got her neighbour, Mr Barrett, to drive her down in his car. She didn't even give him time to change his shoes, and he arrived with her at the station in his slippers. 'She was crying and I was crying. She was surprised to see me looking so well. I had poured the weight back on.' The next month Anderson marched in a victory parade through the city, watched by the governors of Kansas and Missouri and General Eisenhower.

As a boy I had seen some Civil War veterans marching and veterans of World War I. Now it was my turn. I was proud, and I had reason to be. As a prisoner of war, I never thought I had failed in my mission because I had been shot down and captured. I didn't have any regrets – just that cup of water that I drank that was my friend Nelson's.[15] But apart from that, no regrets.[16]

To Roger Allen, home had always been synonymous with fried chicken. On the march and at Fallingbostel, when all the nourishment he could get was a few vegetable peelings, he had constructed imaginary meals in his head – bacon and eggs; bacon and sausage; roasts; whole steaks with mashed potatoes. But mainly it had been his mother's fried chicken that dominated his dreams. 'That was what I was thinking about when I was eating old leaves and bits of carrot. And when I got home there were lashings of it.'[17] He was overwhelmed by the welcome he received from the people of his home town of Kiowa in Oklahoma:

They wined and dined me and my family for weeks. And then I met a girl called Flo on a blind date while I was on my sixty-day leave. Three months later we were married. I was definitely not looking for matrimony, but we just hit it off – she was fun to be around. I was a boy when I left, and I came home a man. Definitely older and wiser. I knew what was important. I was just thankful to have survived. It made me value life much more. After sharing a room with so many men, I had learned to value my privacy. I didn't like standing in a crowd. It was just hard to handle after all those times being cooped up in train wagons and barns on the march. Even now I eat everything on my plate. It's so important not to waste anything.

It was a perfect homecoming for Allen. For others things did not always go to plan. Richard Burt was on that special train for ex-POWs heading west, dropping off men along the way, and he watched passenger after passenger leave at their home town. His was a long haul to Utah, and every mile his excitement grew. He left the train at Salt Lake City, took the bus to Bear River City, and then got a lift to the other side of the river to his home. He walked up to the door, pushed it open – and there was nobody there. Just the dog. 'They were all up the road at my uncle's farm but they soon came back to find me standing in the yard. I was home safe and sound at last. I was 20 years old.'[18]

As for George Guderley, thoughts of that cooling beer in Hank's Tavern with Little Buck, his friend from Chicago, had sustained him through the ordeal of Stalag Luft IV and then the march west. Guderley may have saved the desperately sick Buck with that life-saving measure of cream he stole from under the Germans' noses, but his gesture was far from being a cure, and Buck had been taken away from the column, too ill to continue. Guderley had not known if he would ever see him alive again. When he arrived at Fallingbostel, Guderley went looking for him, asking around the air-force people, but it was a hopeless task and, anyway, he was now sick himself and had to concentrate on keeping himself alive. 'I worried about him,' he recalled, 'but things were so desperate there was not much I could do.'[19]

Guderley got home to Chicago in May, and fulfilled his promise by going to see Buck's parents.

They lived not far from my home, and I went over to their house not long after I got back. I couldn't go straight away because I was in a bad way with hepatitis, dysentery and vitamin deficiency. I'd gone from about 175 lb down to about 120 lb, and just trying to walk felt like I was trying to run in waist-deep water. So when I could I walked up to their house. At that time I still didn't know if Buck was alive or dead. I hadn't seen or heard of him after getting him the cream in the barn.

Guderley had no idea what to expect. Buck had been more dead than alive when he had last seen him. Was he about to walk into a house of mourning – and face the recriminations of those who might resent his return when their own son had failed to make it? 'But he was alive. And, not only that, he was back in the United States. He was in a hospital in Chicago.' Buck had been treated well by the Germans, put on a train, and taken via Berlin and Hanover to Fallingbostel, where he arrived several weeks before Guderley.

He and I spoke on the telephone and caught up on all of the news and where we each had been. When he eventually got out of hospital he rang me and said, 'George, I'm coming round to see you', and he turned up on my doorstep, and we were both yellow! We both had hepatitis, which meant that we were in no shape to have that beer in Hank's. But it was a really great reunion. It was pretty damn good to see him again – just like finding a long-lost brother. We were both just so happy that each other had made it, and we sat talking for hours. We stood outside my house and my mother took our picture, which I still have today. We were two yellow guys, and we'd just come home from the war, and we couldn't even have a drink!

We left Bob Otto back at Fallingbostel, elated at being liberated and anxious to get home to Idaho and the childhood sweetheart he had married just before he was called up.[20] She rarely left his thoughts during his captivity, and his technique for survival on the march had been to fill his mind with dreams of their future life together. In camp at Gross Tychow he had received only the occasional letter from her, but that was not unusual. The post was a lottery. Some men got letters by the bundle, some none at all. He reckoned he was just one of the unlucky ones. At Camp Lucky Strike, nothing was going to distract him. 'Some of the fellows went to Paris, but not me. I was going home, and I was totally focused on that. I didn't want to miss the boat.'[21] He broke down when he saw the Statue of Liberty – it was the first time he had seen it – and was overwhelmed at being back on American soil. 'Crowds were waiting on the harbour, cheering and shouting. Everybody was happy. We were home again.' As he crossed the country to Idaho – three days on the train – he could see ahead of him the same sort of laughter and happiness and relief there had been on the dockside at New York. He went first to his parents' home, and they were excited to see him. Then, soon after, his wife arrived and the reception cooled.

She said she wanted to talk to me, and we went to some place alone and she said she wanted a divorce. She just said, 'I don't want to be married any more.' There wasn't much I could say, as she had pretty well made up her mind. Unknown to me, while I was away she had been enjoying life with another guy (whom I never met). Maybe she couldn't be blamed, as she had no way of knowing if I would ever come home. We talked some, to no effect as far as reconciliation. She said she would file for divorce in a different county, so the local folks wouldn't know about it. I wanted very much for our marriage to continue, as she had been the only girl I ever wanted for my wife. When she told me she wanted a divorce I was heartbroken. I had been dreaming for a year about being together and making plans for our future. Didn't happen. I don't know how others have overcome such pain, but I know much of it remained hidden in my mind for years.

He tried a traditional cure – hitting the bottle hard,

trying to drown my sorrows. I was on sixty days' leave, and I had plenty of time to pity myself. I'd gone from this incredible high of being home to an incredible low. It was like a smash in the stomach. I'd been trudging through Germany thinking I was going to get home to my family and then there was this blow to my self-esteem and to all the plans I had had in my head – the plans that had kept me going. For a few weeks I prowled around with some of my buddies who came home from the war, and I could have turned into an alcoholic.

But then he pulled himself together and found the strength that had kept him going through the camps and the marches. And there was a happy ending: a new girl in his life nine months later, who became his wife – 'my real wife, my real love', as he still calls her.

He put the first marriage behind him, along with his experiences as a prisoner of the Germans. 'I didn't talk too much about it with my parents. I don't remember them asking a lot of questions. In fact nobody said very much about what had happened. We just left it buried rather than dig up the memories.' But he was a different person when he returned:

I wasn't the same boy that had gone to war. I'd grown up about twenty years in a year. I was more mature, even if when I came back I tried to drink up all the booze that we had. I learned maturity. I learned that I could get by under almost any circumstances. I learned self-sufficiency. No matter what I faced, I could survive it. Before, I had not been a natural leader, and nor was I one in the camp or on the marches. But, when I got back, the experience had given me much more confidence in myself. I felt like I could whip the world. A few months after I got home I ran for office as county recorder. I went out and campaigned and got elected. I was respected and honoured, and it felt good.

*

Six thousand miles away, Betty Batchelder was on holiday with her mother-in-law in Bournemouth on the south coast of England. The war was over for most people, and had been for a while, but not for her. Was her husband alive? When was he coming home? It was in this state of anxiety that she looked up from what she was doing and saw her husband's father come into the lounge of their hotel. What was he doing there? It had to be bad news.

I thought, 'Oh dear God, what's he going to tell me?' Then he saw us, and he smiled, and that was enough. He just said, 'You've got to pack your bags and come home now, because he's on his way home.' I don't know how he had heard, and I never asked him. It was just such a wonderful relief. We couldn't pack our bags quickly enough to get back home.

But, back at Batch's parents' home on the outskirts of London, there was more waiting to endure. 'It was quite a little while after that before we heard on the radio that prisoners were being released and were being brought back, but we didn't know exactly when. It was like sitting on hot bricks.' Men were coming home from the camps, there were reunions everywhere, but still no Batch. Betty, seeing no point in just sitting around worrying, went back to her work at the War Office and to her lodgings in London. 'No news, no telegram, no messages,' she recalled.

In my lodgings I had the front bedroom, which had a bay window. It was a Sunday, and I was standing at the window, looking, waiting, watching. It was just after lunch, and I was just sort of star-gazing, even though it was daylight, hoping that I would see a little figure in RAF uniform. Then I saw him. He came walking along the road, this tiny little airman with a great big knapsack on his back. He was so skinny, poor little love. He looked so little, I couldn't believe it. I stumbled downstairs and rushed to the front door and opened it, and there he was. He looked wonderfully smart in his uniform, and beautifully clean, because they had been deloused, but he was so thin. He had always been quite stocky as a boy – fighting fit, never fat: slim, with nice broad shoulders. We just leaped into each other's arms and I just kept on repeating, 'Oh darling, oh darling.' It was the most wonderful moment of my life.

Batch's journey home had been laborious, as he could now tell her. He had not been liberated until the war was actually over. He and his column had been still marching towards Lübeck in complete ignorance of events such as the surrender of the German forces at Lüneburg Heath happening only miles away. They were in a world of their own until the guards disappeared on the morning of 8 May and the prisoners were spotted by British army scout cars and told they were free.

The route home was the usual one – Brussels, a flight across the Channel, and then debriefing at Cosford.

It was very superficial. I was interviewed by a psychologist for about half an hour. It just seemed a bit of a waste of time. I'd come to Cosford from London, and on the way the train had gone through New Barnet, where Betty and I had our flat, so I'd been within about half a mile of her. Then I had to go from Cosford back to London and out to Barnet again. I got the tube from Euston, and then a taxi from the underground station, but I stopped the taxi because I wanted to walk the last bit. I saw Betty at the door. We fell into each other's arms in tears. It was the end of the journey. I can't even remember what we said. Words were superfluous.[22]

But the psychologists at Cosford may not have been as irrelevant as Batch presumed, because in the days that followed his reunion with Betty he began to show signs of strain. The couple had gone to see his parents, and his mother, in her excitement, collected all the family and friends together. Betty remembered him becoming very quiet as he had to deal with a barrage of well-meaning questions. 'He didn't want to talk about camp life or anything,' she said.

I could see his face screwing up with the pain, because he wanted to forget. We had grabbed a few moments on our own, and he said, 'We must get away. I can't bear all these people coming and going.' So we packed a small case and we went into London and got on the first train available – we didn't care where it was going. It took us down to Cornwall. We were free from all the questioning and hubbub and gladness. It had all been too much. He knew he was home, he knew he was safe, and he wanted to forget what he'd been through.

Batch was not alone in these feelings. Betty continued, 'The next morning we went down to breakfast at our hotel and there was another young couple on the other side of the dining room. He was an ex-prisoner of war too, and they had done the same as us – run away from family and friends because they couldn't take the excitement of people questioning him.'

There would come a time when Batch was ready to talk, prepared to relive the horrors. His marriage endured, and, as Betty said, 'I think our love has grown stronger.' And he himself would become a leading figure in associations for former prisoners of war. For others, however, the remembering would always be a problem. The ghosts of the Stalag would haunt them for ever.

For now, though, it was a question of returning to normal life. Norman Leonard was back with his parents after a stint at Cosford. They met him at Euston station and, after the laughter and the joy that he had escaped the vengeance of the Nazis in Germany, they told him that one of Hitler's last acts of aggression had wiped out his home. They would be staying with relatives until the V2 rocket damage to their house had been repaired. Meanwhile Percy Carruthers was in the Cumbrian hills on the little farm he called home. He had been met with tears and smiles from his family, and a lot of worrying that he was so thin.

Nothing had changed in my absence. The same old black-leaded fireplace, the 10-foot settle under the window and the wall-clock on which I learned to read the time. I walked down to the familiar shops at the crossroads, and there were the same old names above the doors. But I felt a little strange. There appeared to be a frightening variety of goods on the shelves. Eggs, vegetables, cheeses, fruit, even bananas and many other lovely items I had not seen for years. I marvelled at the apparent richness of it all. I then came face to face with an old school friend. 'Hello, Perc, long time no see,' he said. 'What do you think of all this rationing? High time we were getting rid of it. And we could do with some better weather too.' I wanted to say that everything was lovely and had never been better; that what he termed 'rationing' was to me a land of milk and honey, providing four meals a day; and that as far as I was concerned the sun shone from morning till night. But obviously he would not understand. He looked so healthy. I saw him then not as a friend but as a dissatisfied, grumbling critic of all that, to me, was good. We were on entirely different planets, our senses of values were worlds apart. I learned later that he had been in a 'reserved occupation' during hostilities and had made himself a nice little fortune on the black market. I felt a certain satisfaction from what I had done.[23]

But where Carruthers's homecoming was filled with emotion, Richard Passmore's was strangely devoid of all feeling. His family were overjoyed to see him, but he remained cold inside. 'I knew how I ought to respond and I went through the motions, but I couldn't make myself *feel*.' It would be six months before the tears came, prompted by a passage in the prayer book as he sat alone in a tiny chapel. 'I remember a huge wave of grief mounting inside me and I wept for so many friends dead, for fear and suffering and frustrated hope, for uncertainty, for a happy ending which had inexplicably brought no joy. Then I dried my eyes and got on with the business of living and feeling. Life had begun again.'[24]

But leaving the old life behind and coming to terms with a new one could be troublesome, as Len Jepps discovered. His journey home had been marred by difficulties and delays and, as he was the first to admit, he had become bitter that it had been prolonged by inefficiency and error. He had expected a deliriously happy reunion:

All the years we were away, our one overriding thought had been centred round this day, and it never really occurred to us that it would be anything but an experience of pure joy. We had completely overlooked the fact that we were not the same people who had left so long before and that our experiences had changed us. Neither had we realized that our wives and families had lived the equivalent to a ten-year span during that period. My wife had been at work from the outbreak of war and had become an efficient businesswoman, had spent countless nights fire-watching, and had had to make her own life in my absence. She had made many new friends and had changed, just as I had changed. As a result, we were virtually strangers, and we had to restart our married life from scratch. I now understood why so many of my ex-comrades had had news of broken marriages while in captivity. It is difficult to lay blame on those women who were not strong enough to resist the temptation to begin a new life with somebody else. They were only human, they never knew whether the next day would be their last, and they never knew whether their husbands would ever return.

For my part, I realized I had become abnormally introspective, whereas my wife had been living a fuller life than ever before. We set about getting to know each other again. We visited all our old relatives and friends in an attempt to return to the life we had lost. Mostly I found that people were sorry for me, and I didn't need their sympathy. Small things caused infuriating embarrassment, such as being afraid of crossing the street. Then the things that had annoyed me began to amuse me, except that I would find myself convulsed with laughter at times which others thought inappropriate.[25]

Jepps was showing many of the classic symptoms of dislocation that the doctors had predicted. And, predictably too, he sought no help.

Maurice Newey sought no help and needed no help. He had been away almost as long as Jepps, having been caught by the Germans at Tobruk in North Africa in the summer of 1942, imprisoned in Italy, and then carried off to Germany when he should have been liberated by the surrender of the Italians. On his return to England, he took the train north from London and 'the grass looked so verdantly green, the trees so profuse with their blossom and the sheep so peaceful. This was the England I had always kept in my imagination. This really was peace.'[26]

He got off at York late after nightfall to discover there were no buses and no taxis. He was in a bad mood as he set off to walk home.

But then my anger just disappeared. Ahead of me the city was shimmering in bright, silver moonlight, the old buildings and walls twinkling as if they had been dusted with silver. The moat was covered in hundreds of daffodils in full bloom. I crossed the bridge over the River Ouse, running my hand along its ironwork, and then York Minster came into view, bathed in moonlight. There was absolute silence. Not a dog barked, not a single noise disturbed me as I looked up, past the towering spires, into the infinite sky and said quietly, 'Thank you, Lord, for looking after me and keeping me safe and well.' The Minster looked down at me as if to say, 'Welcome home.' A feeling of great peace spread over me.

Fifteen minutes more and he was turning into his street and marching up to his front door.

My Father was standing there. He took hold of my arm and gently pulled me in. We shook hands, and I said, 'Hello, Dad.' He opened his mouth to say something, but then my Mother came running down the stairs and flung herself into my arms. I hugged her and bent to kiss her. I noticed that she had been crying and that she had no teeth in and, God, she seemed small, all in one quick glance. She took a step back and said in a surprised voice, 'Eeh, Harold, doesn't he look well?' They told me that, after all the reports on the wireless, they had expected me to be emaciated. I laughed and told them that we had had a bit of time to fatten up since we were liberated. Suddenly we realized that we were all standing up, and my father smiled and said, 'Sit down', and motioned me to his chair. This was an honour. Nobody sat in his chair when he was in the house.

Ma was soon rustling up some sandwiches and a pot of tea. I was keen to hear about my four brothers. Bob the eldest was in the Middle East, Bill was in Austria, Norman was in Burma, and Frank was somewhere on the high seas. Peter, who was eight, was fast asleep upstairs, and I would see him tomorrow. I wondered if he would recognize me. As my Father had to go to work at 7.30 and it had just turned 3 a.m., they bade me good night, reminded me to turn out the light, and went to bed. I stayed downstairs for a while. Then I went upstairs, undressed, put my boots under the bed, and stretched out. An overwhelming desire to cry came over me and tears rushed to my eyes. I shut them tight, but one tear managed to escape and tickled my cheek as it ran down. After a while I became calmer and I felt unutterably weary. I let myself relax and I drifted into a dreamless sleep. I was home, in my own bed.

Doug Fry was almost too nervous to walk up to his own front door. He had sent a telegram to his mother from Cosford – the first communication she had had from him since January. At Cosford he had met up with an old friend, and they returned to London together.

He lived in Russell Square, and we got the tube there and he wanted me to go up to the front door with him. I said, 'Why?' And he said, 'I feel funny. I want someone with me.' I said, 'No, you're home now. You've got to go on your own.' But I had butterflies just like him as I went off in a taxi to my house. When I got there, there was bunting up and a big 'Welcome Home' banner. My mother had had a telegram saying I was coming, and she was at the top of the steps. It was early afternoon, and she'd probably been waiting there since first thing in the morning. I said to her, 'It's all over, Mum', and she cried.[27]

He had survived. Others had not, and one of his first duties was to go and see the parents of two of his friends who were not coming home. 'They'd known me since I was a little kid, and I had to stand there and say that their sons weren't coming back. It was not a nice feeling. I felt I shouldn't be there. Seeing them tempered the euphoria of my freedom and safety.'

Sad scenes like this were happening in many places. Johnny Gage's parents had no idea that he had been killed in the mistaken attack by Typhoons on the column at Gresse and they had strung up a huge banner saying, 'Welcome home, Johnny' across the front of their farmhouse. One of his comrades rang with the news of his death.[28]

For those who survived, there was the question of whether peacetime could ever live up to their dreams. Lying in his prison-camp bunk at Luckenwalde, Ron Walker had imagined a future dominated by his love of gliding. He might go back to his old job, but he really wanted something that would give him plenty of time off. 'I wonder if it is wrong to make a hobby the main reason for living,' he asked himself.[29] His dream was 'to fly during the summer and then during the winter evenings to work at a book, in a little cottage with a big fire, with my mother to keep me company and run things the way she does. Dare I expect so much happiness?' He ruled out marriage completely, because it would just get in the way of gliding, and decided instead to splash out on a sports car – either an MG or a Jaguar. 'Then later I might buy a caravan, which would be useful to take to gliding sites, and I could also use it when I was away on business and that way, by saving hotel expenses, it would pay for itself.' Back home, he got the car – a Jaguar, for which he paid £100. And at the same time he met 'the most beautiful girl in the world sitting on a bar stool in a hotel in Dorchester'. He had been home only a week. 'We were married within six months. I gave up gliding. As the Germans say, "*Man denkt, Gott lenkt*" – "Man makes plans, God decides."'

There were those for whom home would bring disappointment. Dave Radke returned to Australia with health problems that stopped him doing the things he loved. Before leaving England – and thinking he had recovered from his ordeal of marching across Germany – he went for a cricket trial and was too weak to stand up to fast bowling. The first delivery knocked the bat out of his hand. 'Against slower bowlers I performed even worse, because my legs and feet were so swollen I could not move them quickly enough.'[30] He was also unable to enjoy beer – his wrecked insides bloated after just one glass. 'A rather happy-go-lucky youth of just under 21 years of age on leaving Australia in 1941 returned as a changed and serious person of 25.'

Cal Younger found returning to civilian life difficult. Before he left Australia he had been a cinema buff who thought nothing of seeing three films a day. 'When I got back I just couldn't sit for more than five or ten minutes in a cinema. I felt a tremendous restlessness and I didn't know what I wanted to do. Also, having been cooped up, I couldn't stand being enclosed.'[31] He took a job in the London office of the Commonwealth Bank of Australia – his employer in Melbourne before he joined up. He met a girl, and was drawn into the comfort of family life, 'which at that time I craved. I had visions of my feet on the mantelpiece and a pipe in my mouth, and of course it was a mistake.' He hated talking about his experiences, and told lies when asked:

If people wanted to know how I became a prisoner, I spun them a story about going out on a boat on a pleasure trip and losing the oars and getting washed on to the French coast. I said I'd never flown in the war. I suppose I must have been feeling guilty, but I'm not sure what about. In Australia there was a feeling that those who had been captured by the Japanese had had the really bad time, and that we had had a soft number.

*

Les Allan was another who preferred fiction to fact for many years after coming home. He was one of the first to get back to England: when Fallingbostel was liberated, he was given priority because his feet had been permanently damaged by marching 600 miles in clogs. Relief and happiness flooded over him. The WAAFs at Tring looked after him. He had a brand-new uniform and a train warrant to take him to London. But he happened to see a double-decker bus going to Windsor, close to his home at Slough, and he hopped on. His first introduction to civilian life was the driver, who told him his rail warrant was not valid on a bus. But, when he explained who he was to the conductor, she allowed him on.

As he walked up the street where he lived, people came out to cheer him. 'It was a close community, and they had known me all my life. They came out of their front doors to welcome me home, rushing to take the kitbag off me and help me. The tears were flowing, mine included.'[32] And, fifty-five years on, they would flow again as he recalled the joy of his return. 'My mum had kept the faith that I would eventually get back, and they had got hold of a Union Jack and they hung it outside the house.' And, after the celebrations, he got on with his life and said nothing:

People wanted to know about my experiences as a prisoner of war, but I wouldn't tell them. Why? Because I had a feeling that they wouldn't believe it, so consequently I just bottled it up. It might also have been because of a sense of shame about being a prisoner of war – people might ask why I hadn't escaped. But it was also because I got the impression when I returned home that people believed we had, in effect, been in holiday camps, having a cushy time. That's why we didn't want to talk about it. Those who didn't know said we'd had a good time, that we were lucky to have been prisoners when so many other fellows had been killed.

Less than a year after coming home, he met the girl he was to marry and spend his life with. His reluctance to talk now made a secret of his past. It wasn't hard to do. In those days immediately after the war, talking about the war was taboo for most people anyway. Doris gathered he had been in the Army, but at first she didn't press him and he didn't volunteer any information. And when she did want to know more he told lies. 'I said I'd been in Africa, which was totally untrue, but I didn't go into details. I didn't want to make out I was a hero. I told her I'd been discharged medically unfit.'

There were aspects of his behaviour that Doris found odd. 'He wouldn't go anywhere. He preferred being at home. He wouldn't go abroad; he wouldn't go on holiday. He was always afraid to go anywhere. He just didn't want to go out of the country.' And then, after half a dozen years or so together, he began to tell her why. The truth came out gradually. 'We'd be talking to other people and things would be said, but I was pretty surprised when he finally told me he had been a prisoner of war. It didn't sink in at first. But, when it did, I began to understand some of the things he did and the way he acted.' He began meeting up with old army friends, and more information came out. Doris listened in awe as he described the conditions he had been held in and his formidable march across Germany. 'If I remember rightly,' Les said, 'I went up a couple of grades in her estimation. I was a hero after that, despite all the fibbing. I had nothing at all to worry about!'

The more Doris learned, the more she could understand. Now she could even make sense of the nightmares when he would shout in his sleep words she couldn't understand and make the sounds of a man in pain. The bad dreams had begun six months after he got home, Les recalled:

They were about being on the march, and on several occasions my father came into my bedroom. He wouldn't wake me – in those days it was thought to be dangerous to wake up anybody having a nightmare – but he would sit on the bed until I had calmed down and make sure I didn't damage myself. Then he would tell me about it the next morning. I dreamed about being on the march and helping to dress the frostbite wounds, because I was a stretcher-bearer and I had a small amount of medical knowledge. I used to see this poor fellow who had lost half his foot with frostbite and he was still marching, being helped by a couple of his friends. It was the stench – that has never left me, still never left me. The stench of frostbite. It is an appalling smell. Once you've smelled it you never ever forget.

More than half a century on, the scars are still on Les Allan's feet and still in his mind. He still wakes up in the middle of the night, according to Doris – though 'not so often now in the last few years'. His broken ankle still disables him, and he struggles to stand up for more than a short period of time. But he has a balanced perspective on his prisoner-of-war life and his escape from a death he often felt was certain at the end of the war. 'I wouldn't have missed those experiences and the comradeship they brought for the world,' he says, 'but if I was told I had to go through it all again I would shoot myself rather than let it happen.'

Epilogue

The bells of St Clement's tolled for Dixie Deans. The date was 6 May 1989 – forty-four years almost to the day after he had brought the men in his charge safely out of the hell of a collapsing Germany. Five hundred ex-servicemen who owed their survival to his leadership packed the RAF church[1] in the Strand in the centre of London for his memorial service. Tears and pride mingled as Cal Younger gave the address, praising 'a much-loved man of rare quality . . . a born leader whose very bearing was enough to bring a parade ground to silence but who was never authoritarian. His heroism, his wisdom and his compassion will never be forgotten.'[2]

But there was a sting in the tail. Deans, who had died a few months earlier at the age of seventy-six, was without doubt the most outstanding prison-camp leader of his generation, Younger declared, and yet after the war he had been all but ignored. There were murmurs of approval from the crowded pews as he laid out his heart-felt complaint on behalf of Deans: 'At the end of the war one would have thought that Dixie had a magnificent future in front of him. Unbelievably he was not offered a permanent commission in the RAF.' Unable to progress in the service he loved, Deans resigned from the RAF and put his talents into a civilian job as an executive officer at the London School of Economics.

His courage – the sort that had enabled him to stand jaw to jaw with German commandants and ride his bicycle though the middle of a raging battle – was put into a different battle. It turned out that he had multiple sclerosis, the fearful wasting disease of unknown origin that strikes without reason or warning. It was not diagnosed until he left the RAF, but, in retrospect, the first signs were probably there when he was still a prisoner. He fought the disease with a stubbornness that those who had been with him in Germany recognized instantly. His spare time was dedicated to an organization of veterans of the camps and to reunions, which he loved. He never complained, but others did on his behalf. 'Official recognition fell far short of justice,' Younger said, and there was not a single dissenting voice. For his services to his country, Deans received an MBE – an honour far short of the knighthood that many thought he deserved. But he was a non-commissioned officer, and therefore not quite a gentleman in the class terms that still had such an impact on British society in the post-war years. The MBE was decreed the right award for a sergeant. As his obituary in *The Times* said, it 'seemed scant recompense' for what he had done. To this day it remains a sore point with the likes of Cal Younger, who kept trying – without success – to get 'Sarge'[3] upgraded.

Some would see what had happened to Deans as a slight to all prisoners of war. Indeed, there were those who felt unappreciated even before they arrived home, and with reason. When liberated, each man had been issued with an official booklet explaining the plans to get them home and filling them in on matters such as the back pay and the leave they were entitled to. It began with a statement of welcome: 'We want you to know how glad we are that you are at last on your way home. We are sure you can now look forward to receiving every care and attention to make up in some way for all you have undergone.'[4] Here were words to make a man feel proud and worthwhile again, especially if they had come from the King or the Prime Minister, Field Marshal Montgomery or General Eisenhower. But the signatures underneath were B-list – the Second Sea Lord, the Adjutant-General to the Forces, and a personnel officer from the Air Ministry. Not even the *First* Sea Lord. No wonder some of the POWs felt they were the forgotten army, unrecognized for what they had been through and regarded as slightly dubious, dishonoured even, in people's estimation. Unless, as we have seen, they were heroes of the escape circuit. Years later Deans was on the popular television show *This is Your Life* – but as a guest, there to honour the much more celebrated 'Wings' Day, who had been one of the 'tally-ho boys' at Stalag Luft III.

Not all returning prisoners felt disparaged or hard done by. Just as each individual had his own particular life behind barbed wire and on his forced march, so each homecoming and each subsequent life was different from the next man's. Alf Jenner went back to his job as a journalist in Norwich and was treated as 'quite a hero'.[5] 'There was no sense that prisoners of war had not done a good job, that they hadn't done their bit in the war.' For him it would always be 'the big experience of my life. I think about it with great honour not with great horror.' Ernest Boyd never felt any reticence in chatting about his experiences to whoever would listen. Others might be silent, able to communicate their feelings only to other ex-POWs, but he 'was always willing to talk, because those were probably the best years of my life'.[6] Ken Brown bathed in the glory too. 'Nobody looked down on you for being a prisoner of war,' he said. 'Rather, the opposite. We were fêted.'[7]

Batch Batchelder was a happy man too – to begin with. He remembered tea and buns, and words of appreciation from the mayor and Corporation. But then came public indifference, and even recrimination. He felt rejected on two counts. The carpet-bombing of Germany and the destruction of fine cities like Cologne and Dresden was now felt by some to have been excessive. 'Bomber' Harris – Air Chief Marshal Sir Arthur Harris – who had master-minded that campaign, turned from hero to villain in post-war eyes, and the men in his service experienced the same cold shoulder by a no-longer-grateful nation. 'We were ignored,' said Batchelder, 'and then, if not quite animosity, there was a feeling that we shouldn't have done what we did.'[8] Having been a prisoner of war added to his sense of isolation. 'Someone once said we were heroes until the day the war ended, then nobody wanted to know us. People forgot the sacrifices we made.'

For Batchelder, the rejection was intensely personal. He knew no life other than the RAF; he had never wanted any other job than to fly. But when he got home he was told he was surplus to requirements. 'When the war ended I wanted to stay in the Air Force, but they told me they had all the pilots they needed.' Why had he been selected to be stood down? 'Because my knowledge was three years out of date.' His years in prisoner-of-war camps had left a gap in his experience that the RAF considered too great to be worth filling. Why retrain a twenty-five-year-old when they had nineteen-year-olds who knew more than he did? It was a blow to his pride and his hopes – just as it must have been for Dixie Deans when he was told he was no longer wanted on the active list.

Batchelder felt that his POW time was counting against him, and unfairly so. He hadn't chosen to be shot down, and yet he was, in effect, being penalized for it.

'I was pretty downhearted then. It had always been my intention to have a career in flying, and so I had to start from rock bottom with something new. I took a job as a process worker in a chemical factory, because I needed a job. I had a wife to support, and not long after a family as well.' His war experience became a taboo subject. 'I had to move on and forget about it. I had to establish myself in life.' As his children grew, he told them nothing. The past was a country he did not visit. But then in the mid-1960s, having made a success of himself in personnel management, he began to fall in with old companions. There were drinks in London pubs with Deans and Younger, which developed into reunions – to talk about the good times, according to Batchelder. 'Very rarely did anybody talk about the bad.' It was the beginning of what would become the RAF Ex-Prisoners-of-War Association.

His life flourished – a good job, five children, a comfortable retirement. The memories never haunted him, but, equally, they never left him. Who could forget the degradation and fear and hunger, dysentery so desperate he sat by a roadside and invited a German guard to shoot him, the horror as a friend lay dead at Gresse from bullets fired from a plane of his own side? He choked on that last recollection: his voice stuttered, and he looked away to disguise an embarrassment he had no reason to hide. 'You know, that was the first time in my life that I'd seen somebody that I knew actually killed. He was a little New Zealander, a chap I'd known for three years, ever since I first went to Sagan – name of Laurie Hope . . .' And he spoke the name with all the freshness and fondness as if it had been yesterday, not fifty-five years ago. Memories like that did not even cloud, let alone die.

I got on with my life, but I couldn't forget those experiences. They made me a very different person. There was one occasion in my job when I was having to deal with a twenty-five-year-old graduate who needed putting in his place. He was being difficult, and showing off about his degree. He was so pleased with himself, and wouldn't see sense. So I told him that when I was his age I had already lived two lifetimes. I should have died at least twice when I was flying, and then again on the march. That was what made me what I am, and I'm proud of it.

*

Some minds and personalities were badly affected by prison-camp life. Then the home that prisoners had dreamed about turned into a hell both for them and for their families. Wives and parents had been advised to take it gently with returning prisoners of war and not to worry if they were shy or moody. 'Remember that a prisoner of war is not a sick man,' they were told.[9] But the official advice did not extend to telling them what to do when he stole food from other people's plates and put it in his pocket for later, or hoarded matches and candles, or woke screaming in the night with bad dreams. Most got over the period of adjustment, helped by love and sympathy. Others cut short the leave they had following their homecoming and rushed back to the comfort and routine of military life. The British Army monitored its men, and thousands were referred by their medical officers to specialist psychiatrists in the first three months after their liberation.

The effects of the marches they had undergone were at first largely physical – they had been starved, and they needed fattening up. But readjusting from life as captives to being free men again proved more difficult to deal with – much harder than they expected. A summary of the psychiatrists' findings concluded:

They knew they had changed and that things would be different but they had not foreseen that they would be strangers in their own homes. Their general information was not up to date. They became embarrassed in company and found the noise of the children irritating. They often felt they were being watched and were suspicious even of their neighbours. It was not easy to make decisions and once the initial excitement had passed off life at home tended to fall rather flat. They were glad just to be left alone.[10]

A fifth of them showed symptoms that would be worrying if they were to continue for any length of time – restlessness and excitability, lethargy, and loss of confidence. Some wanted to make dramatic, life-changing gestures: selling up and starting afresh somewhere new – even emigrating or rushing into marriage with women they hardly knew. The group suffering the most turned out to be the airborne troops captured at Arnhem. They were characterized as being aggressive and difficult. The explanation appeared to be the short time they had been prisoners. It was generally acknowledged that it took between six months and a year for a man to adapt to Stalag life, and they had been released before they had got through the stage of anger and resentment. Hence they arrived home in the same frame of mind. 'They keep together and resent discipline,' the psychiatrists said.

There was another side to all this. For some men, being a prisoner had been 'a broadening experience – they have read, developed new hobbies and learned to understand and feel a deeper affection for their comrades'. But they, the psychiatrists concluded, were the minority. For the majority, the experience had been 'a period of regression, a return to a more egocentric pattern of life and a more emotionally determined type of life'. They were not neurotic, but they had reverted to a more childlike existence. And then there was the issue of guilt – though the doctors disagreed on this. One of them found signs of it in 90 per cent of the men he saw, one thought it extremely rare, and another concluded that it was confined to officers. The most revealing fact was how few men had ever thought in advance that they might be a prisoner – 'wounded, yes, even dead, but not being captured'. Yet being a prisoner might be every soldier's secret wish, his dark secret – 'capture provides an escape from a situation which every man desires to escape from'. So feelings of guilt would be buried deep but nevertheless capable of causing problems when they surfaced. To Lieutenant-Colonel R. F. Barbour, adviser in psychiatry to the Royal Army Medical Corps, it seemed that what mattered most in each case was 'the emotional maturity of the man concerned'. Put simply, the situation that they had been through was not going to make every man psychotic. Some coped and some didn't.

And some talked and some didn't. Bob Otto told his son, Randy, almost nothing about his experiences – until 2001, when the two of them went to the site of Stalag Luft IV at Gross Tychow. As Bob talked to us about his prisoner-of-war years, as we stood in that remote forest in Poland or retraced a few steps along the route of the 'death march' in a small village, his forty-year-old son heard for the very first time what his father had been through. Like Roger Allen's family on that same trip, he had had no idea of the hero he had lived with all his life.

Official recognition of the POWs' achievements was a long time in coming in the United States. George Guderley left the USAAF but returned to active duty for the Korean War. He retired with the rank of major after winning a Purple Heart and an Air Medal with Oak-leaf Cluster. Yet his eight months behind barbed wire, his battle to survive on the road from Stalag Luft IV to Falling-bostel, his courage and his endurance brought nothing. Twenty-five years after the end of the war, a suggestion was made that a medal should be struck for former prisoners of war in honour of their service under brutal and dehumanizing conditions. The Department of Defense rejected the idea. There was opposition to honouring men who had surrendered. It did not fit with the historic image of the American fighting man, the spirit of the Alamo, where the likes of Davy Crockett and Jim Bowie had fought to the last man and died rather than give in. The issue may also have been clouded by the undercurrents of the Vietnam conflict. Patriotism was a controversial word, and many Americans of that period were trying to forget their fighting men, not remember them.

In 1986, after a long campaign, the Prisoner of War Medal was finally authorized by Congress, but the accusations of cowardice did not stop. Two years later, the issue was still contested when an article appeared in the *Washington Post* under the headline 'Why should we honor soldiers who surrendered?'[11] The historian who wrote it argued that any medal would go to heroes and cowards alike, regardless of whether an individual 'fell into the arms of the enemy, whether he was badly wounded or willingly threw up his hands'. Senator Frank Murowski from Alaska wrote to the paper to set the record straight after this

insult to the integrity of men who have proven their dedication and loyalty to our nation under circumstances few of us can imagine and none of us would willingly endure. Few, if any, prisoners of war chose to be captured. Their aircraft were shot down or their positions overrun. POWs did not sit the war out. Almost universally their captors forced them to perform hard labor with little food, primitive sanitation, inadequate shelter and little or no medical care. They were subject to mistreatment or torture at the whim of their captors. Their loyalty to their nation was tested by pain, malnutrition and mind-numbing fatigue.[12]

Then, in 1995, when the United States Senate officially marked the fiftieth anniversary of the end of the Second World War and the victory in Europe, Senator John Warner rose to commend the prisoners of war – 'a group who made a large contribution to the Allied victory while also enduring more than their fair share of personal suffering and sacrifice. We owe them a great debt of gratitude and our undying respect.'[13]

*

They owed some of them money too. Despite all those pleas to the military bureaucrats to be generous to men returning from captivity, the rules were invariably regarded as sacrosanct and the dignity of men who for years had been humiliated was ignored. Each American prisoner of war was entitled to one dollar for every day he had been a captive of the enemy – to be paid as a lump sum when he got home. Except for those who had escaped. The Articles of War dictated that it was a soldier's duty to try to get away from a prisoner-of-war camp. It must have been some bean-counter who decided that, if a man had succeeded in his duty and escaped, then he shouldn't be paid for the days he was free. And so one GI, who had broken out and stayed on the run for twelve days before the Germans caught him and put him in solitary confinement for thirty days as a punishment, found that $12 had been deducted from his pay when he got home.

Issues like these would become irritants and then running sores. In Britain it was '*Lagergeld*' that annoyed the returning men – and still does more than half a century later. The Geneva Convention ordained that prisoners should be paid, and there was a reciprocal arrangement between warring governments so that each side could carry out this requirement. The Germans paid the prisoners in a special currency – funny money that had no value inside the camp or outside. Batchelder said it had no use at all – the notes weren't even large enough to be used as toilet paper. But, when the prisoners got home, they found that up to 10 per cent was deducted from their back pay in lieu of the *Lagergeld* they had received. Even more infuriating was that the 10 per cent was taxed as if they had actually had it in their pockets to spend. Consistently over the years, government after government has refused to restore the deduction. With inflation – and with the numbers of potential beneficiaries inexorably falling through the natural wastage of death – the sums in dispute are now molehills. But the insult still keenly felt is mountainous. Batchelder stopped resenting the Germans years ago, and even got over the RAF's rejection of him after the war. He has never lost his anger at the penny-pinching of the War Office and its successor, the Ministry of Defence. 'Little things like that really do stick in the craw.'

To some returning prisoners, official attitudes always seemed to be against them. Len Jepps's homecoming did not get any better. He had clashed with uncaring bureaucrats all the way back from Germany. In England, he remained convinced that the army doctors added several stones to his weight so that he could not claim compensation for the damage caused by malnutrition. He was logged in at 12 stone by the Army at a reception centre, but made only 10 stone 4 lb on a set of civilian scales two days later. The Army also had him down as two inches taller than he actually was, he claimed.[14]

For Les Allan, the fight goes on. After finally coming clean to his wife about his prisoner-of-war experience after years of concealing the truth from her and everyone else, he became a campaigner for fair play. He started the National Ex-Prisoners of War Association, with the aim of helping former POWs keep in touch with each other but also of coming to the aid of those who fell on hard times. His main point of contention is that the German nation as a whole has never been called to account for its treatment of prisoners of war and, as a result, no compensation has ever been demanded on their behalf. The official line of the British government since the end of the war has been that the German government did not disown the Geneva Convention – as, for example, the Japanese government did – and that breaches of the Convention and any mistreatment of prisoners were the result of individual Germans acting unlawfully.[15] Former POWs like Allan feel betrayed by what they see as the British government's connivance in denying Germany's collective responsibility. They smell a plot too. As they see it, in the post-war reconstruction period wary Western eyes were peering east towards Moscow and there was a political desire to strengthen, not weaken, the new West Germany as a bulwark against the expansion of Soviet-style Communism. In this climate – one in which war-crimes investigations were curtailed for the same reason – the hardships that the prisoners had suffered became a matter of embarrassment. It was easier to ignore POWs' complaints and their claims. The former prisoners became victims of the realpolitik of the Cold War.

Here, the men's own silence about their ordeal has acted against them. On getting home, few appear to have made official complaints about what happened to them. The files of the war-crimes investigators contain only a handful of testimonies concerning the forced marches, and those testimonies that there are – the American Dr Caplan's, for example – appear not to have led to prosecutions, largely because they lacked the precision of detail that was required by the Nuremberg tribunals. Either that or the German guards accused of specific acts of atrocity could not be properly identified or found.

There was one attempt to assign general blame for the marches, and that came four years after the war had ended. Among the long list of indictments against SS Generalleutnant Berger in his trial in 1949 was

that between September 1944 and May 1945, hundreds of thousands of American and Allied prisoners of war were compelled to undertake forced marches in severe weather without adequate rest, shelter, food, clothing and medical supplies; and that such forced marches, conducted under the authority of the defendant Berger, chief of Prisoner-of-War Affairs, resulted in great privation and deaths to many thousands of prisoners.[16]

The court accepted as 'unquestioned' the right of the Germans to evacuate prisoners to avoid their release by enemy troops, and emphasized that it was in fact the Germans' duty under the Geneva Convention to remove POWs from a potential combat zone – as long as it did not put their lives in even greater danger: 'the right to evacuate can only be exercised when it can be accomplished without subjecting evacuees to dangers and hardships substantially greater than would result if they remained at the place of imprisonment, even if thus they might be rescued by the approaching enemy'. The problem was that the right evidence was not forthcoming on what had actually happened. An English prisoner of war had made a written statement about terrible treatment on the northern line of march from Stalag XXA at Thorn, and 'the privations suffered and the mistreatment described were extreme'. Regrettably, however, the prosecution had not produced the soldier to give his evidence in person and to be cross-examined, and the court 'does not feel justified in finding guilt upon his unsupported affidavit'.

There was more evidence about hardships on the marches in the south over the Czechoslovak mountains and into Bavaria. Here the defence argued that the rapid advance of the Russians had simply caught the Germans out and, though they had planned to put the POWs on trains for the journey, in the event 'this became impractical'. Berger claimed that he had protested about the decision – made by Hitler, according to him – to move the prisoners, but he was 'without power or authority to countermand or avoid the order'. The court ruled that 'severe privations from cold and from lack of food and accommodation' had indeed occurred on this march, but the case once again foundered on evidence. 'There is no satisfactory evidence as to the actual losses sustained. No prisoner who was compelled to make the march was called as a witness. The state of the record is, therefore, unsatisfactory.' The court noted too that 'substantial casualties on protracted marches are not unusual even among well-fed troops, and would undoubtedly be larger [among] prisoners of war who have long been in confinement'.

As for Berger's role, the court decided he had acted with the best of intentions, given the state of emergency that had existed at the time. He 'honestly believed' the prisoners would be in greater danger if they were left where they were, and that was sufficient to justify his actions. Moreover, there was 'no evidence to contradict his testimony . . . that to the best of his ability, food, clothing and medical aid were furnished to the prisoners, inadequate though this was'. The court was not totally convinced by the General's pleas of self-justification. 'We may have suspicions as to parts of his story,' the judges declared, 'but suspicion does not take the place of evidence and certainly does not constitute proof of guilt beyond reasonable doubt. We therefore find that the charge against Berger in this respect is not proved and he must be acquitted.'

Looking back, it seems extraordinary that the case foundered for lack of eyewitness evidence, given the amount that was clearly there to be given – if the men, by 1949 trying to put the whole ordeal behind them, had spoken out and if they had even known about the trial in the first place. It may be significant that not one of the ex-POWs we spoke to ever mentioned the Berger trial. The vast majority of them probably had no idea it was taking place.

But the central issue remains: did German treatment of British and American prisoners of war amount to an atrocity? This book may give comfort to both sides in this argument. We have shown that it is highly unlikely that either the German high command or the German government ever gave orders for British and American prisoners of war to be systematically maltreated or massacred. At the same time, the details of the marches and their unremitting hardship – always known by the former prisoners of war themselves, but now revealed to a wider audience for the first time – show a deliberate and inexcusable cruelty that exposed men in captivity to extreme sickness, danger and death.

The prisoners were ill prepared and ill equipped for marches in the depths of winter. They received woefully inadequate supplies of food, medicines and shelter, so that deaths from exhaustion, malnutrition and disease were inevitable. And, though the very first marches away from the advancing Russians could possibly be justified under the Geneva Convention's requirement that prisoners should not be exposed to the dangers of being caught up in military action, subsequent marches could not. First, the Allied leaders had specifically lifted this requirement in the hope that the Germans would leave their prisoners of war to be liberated, but they did not. Second, the prisoners had their lives endangered by being forced to continue marching on open roads where they were liable to come under fire from aircraft of both sides. Third, the intention behind the marches rapidly became (if it had not been so from the very beginning) not to protect prisoners from danger but to use them as human shields or hostages at the end of the war. The plain fact is that their lives were deliberately and unnecessarily put at risk, and those who died on the marches were victims of cruel and inhuman treatment.

The story we have told is one of courage and endurance by more than a quarter of a million British and American servicemen. Their experiences did not result in a catastrophic loss of life – though they came close to doing so. The vast majority of men got home. At the very last, they escaped the fate that many of them had feared. But what of those who did not? The sad truth is that we do not know how many prisoners of war lost their lives in those final, frantic months of the Second World War. Almost every one of the hundreds of personal accounts we have seen and heard speaks of men dying – from sickness, from falling from exhaustion and being left to die in the snow, from being shot while trying to escape, or just from being shot for lagging behind. Sometimes the dead are named, and some lists of casualties do exist; more often they are not. Sometimes as many as three-quarters of those in a particular column dropped out through sickness, and those who marched on never found out what happened to them. And there was no systematic attempt to find out at the end of the war.

The homecomings – as we have seen – were a nightmare for the bureaucrats, and, in their eagerness to be back with their loved ones, few former POWs seem to have followed up what happened to their comrades. It would perhaps be twenty or thirty years later, when the mood swung towards reunions, that people might ask what happened to Harry or Hank; but by then no one knew for sure. Official figures produced by the American Department of Defense show that 93,941 US Army and Air Corps personnel were captured and interned in the European theatre of war between 1941 and 1945. Of these, 92,820 were logged as having returned, which leaves 1,121 who died while prisoners.[17] This figure does not distinguish between those who died during normal camp life in the course of the war and those who might have been victims of the marches and the horrendous conditions at the end.

Individual American veterans disagree with each other vehemently about the mortality figures. One article in a magazine for former prisoners of war thought the number of deaths could have been as high as 1,500 on the march from Gross Tychow alone,[18] while an ex-prisoner who had been on the same march pooh-poohed the whole idea and put the death toll at six.[19] 'None died in the group I was in,' he added, 'and I never heard anyone mention anyone's death.' He admitted to freezing conditions and shortage of food, but he rejected the term 'death march' and downgraded it to 'the misery walk'. Then again, a senior YMCA official closely involved with the POW camps gave the number of British and American prisoners who died between September 1944 and May 1945 as 8,348.[20]

British statisticians are unable to be of any greater help. Our request to the Ministry of Defence for details of the number of prisoners of war who died on the marches from the camps in the east produced an admission that no consolidated figures exist. No one has reconciled the numbers of soldiers, sailors and airmen who went to war with the numbers who were known to have been killed in action or captured and the numbers who returned home. The only figure we were offered was that in mid-1946 the Secretary of State had announced in the House of Commons that the number of 'unaccounted-for prisoners of war from German camps' had been reduced to forty-nine.[21] It left us none the wiser. The RAF came up with precise figures for its men killed in action, missing, wounded and held as prisoners of war, but could not elaborate on those who had been killed *while* prisoners of war. It remained a mystery, for example, in which category the fifty officers murdered after the great escape from Sagan had been placed. How many British, Commonwealth and American POWs died on the dreadful marches? We cannot tell for sure. But from our researches we will hazard a guess at somewhere between 2,500 and 3,500.[22]

These deaths were all the more terrible because they happened to men who had waited patiently for years with just one thought – that one day they would see their home again. They died with the worst behind them, and with home closer than it had ever been before in their captivity – both physically, because the marches took them west, and mentally, because they knew it was only a matter of time before the fighting was over. Nevertheless, more than 250,000 survived to tell their tale, however belatedly. It could have been so different. As we walked among the pine trees on the site of Stalag Luft IV, alongside men who had been given back their lives half a century ago and had used them well ever since, we were aware of the ghosts that haunt other Polish forests. Katyn, 1,000 miles away and now part of Russia, has become a byword for massacre. There, in 1940, thousands of Polish army officers were shot and buried in mass graves. For years the world blamed the Germans, until it eventually emerged that the officers had been victims of Stalin and the Soviet Union. They had committed no crime. They just happened to be men in uniform in the wrong place at the wrong time. Five years later, as the war in Europe came to an end, lives were every bit as cheap and just as likely to end with a bullet in the head or a bayonet in the back.

Not one of the men we interviewed regarded himself as a hero. In their words, they were simply 'doing their job and survived while many friends did not'. As one POW said, 'The tortures of war are many, and the chances for survival are few. Each day a new and different challenge for survival was met, and each day you prayed that you would meet that challenge face to face and pass the test.'[23] That particular man had every reason to know how thin the thread of life was. He had been in a group of prisoners accused of stealing bread, and every tenth man was lined up to be shot. Only the return of the loaf stopped the firing squad from carrying out its threat. In the violence and chaos of 1945, to have escaped with your life intact – as he and those thousands of other Allied prisoners of war did – can be counted a truly remarkable achievement, and now one never to be forgotten.

Appendix 1 Chronology of the End of the Second World War

1944

6 June	D-Day – Allied troops assault the beaches of Normandy.
13 June	V1 flying bombs begin to fall on London.
17 June	1.2 million Soviet soldiers attack German forces in Belorussia.
3 July	Red Army captures Minsk.
11 July	Roosevelt announces he will run for an unprecedented fourth term as President.
13 July	Red Army captures Vilna. Evacuation of Stalag Luft VI, Heydekrug, begins.
20 July	Hitler survives assassination attempt by von Stauffenberg.
31 July	Red Army 12 miles from Warsaw. US forces break out from Normandy.
1 August	Warsaw uprising begins.
7 August	German V1 bombs have now killed 5,000 people and destroyed 35,000 homes.
16 August	Stalin refuses to help Warsaw uprising.
25 August	Paris is liberated.
8 September	First V2 rocket lands on west London.
10 September	Himmler orders the families of all German deserters to be executed.
11 September	US First Army crosses Germany/Luxembourg border.
27 September	Beleaguered British forces surrounded at Arnhem are forced to surrender – only 2,400 men of original force of 10,000 escape. Hopes fade of an early end to the war.
5 October	All hospitals in Germany are put under military control and sixteen-year-olds are called up for military service.
8 November	Roosevelt wins fourth term as US President.
29 November	Red Army crosses the Danube and encircles Budapest.
5 December	General Patton's Third Army crosses the River Saar.

16 December	The German Army counter-attacks in the Ardennes – the Battle of the Bulge begins.
17 December	The SS massacre seventy-one American POWs captured at Malmédy.
24 December	POW work camps around Königsberg are evacuated.

1945

12 January	Red Army launches offensive in Poland and East Prussia.
17 January	Warsaw falls to the Red Army.
19 January	POWs at Stalag Luft VII, Bankau, are evacuated in blizzard conditions.
22 January	Stalag 344 at Lamsdorf is evacuated.
23 January	Marienburg evacuation begins.
27 January	Red Army liberate Auschwitz. Evacuation of POWs from Stalag Luft III at Sagan begins.
31 January	The Red Army crosses the German frontier and is 95 miles from Berlin.
4 February	Stalin, Roosevelt and Churchill meet at Yalta in the Crimea.
6 February	Stalag Luft IV at Gross Tychow is evacuated at the start of an eighty-six-day march.
9 February	British and American troops sweep through Germany's western defensive wall, the Siegfried Line.
10 February	Stalag VIIIA at Görlitz is evacuated.
13 February	Budapest falls to the Red Army after a fifty-day siege.
14 February	British and American bombers attack Dresden.
23 February	US Ninth Army crosses the Ruhr on the Dutch border.
28 February	Two million Germans flee the 'red terror' through the Baltic port of Danzig.
6 March	US troops enter Cologne.
7 March	First US troops cross the Rhine south of Cologne.
19 March	Hitler issues the 'Nero Order' for the destruction of all industry, transport and agriculture likely to fall to the Allies.

24 March	Allied troops cross the Rhine in force.
29 March	US forces capture Frankfurt am Main.
3 April	Stalag XIIID at Nuremberg is evacuated.
6 April	Stalag XIB and 357 at Fallingbostel are evacuated.
8 April	First reports of POW marches appear in British press.
9 April	Königsberg falls to the Red Army.
12 April	President Roosevelt dies.
16 April	Colditz is liberated.
	POWs left behind at Fallingbostel are liberated by the British Second Army.
17 April	Bergen-Belsen concentration camp is liberated.
19 April	A POW column is attacked by allied aircraft at Gresse.
22 April	Soviet forces liberate Stalag Luft IIIA at Luckenwalde.
27 April	US and Soviet forces link up at the River Elbe.
29 April	Stalag VIIA at Moosburg is liberated by Patton's Third Army.
30 April	Berlin falls to the Red Army after a nine-day battle. Hitler commits suicide.
2 May	British troops capture the Baltic ports of Lübeck and Wismar.
4 May	German forces in western Europe surrender on Lüneburg Heath.
8 May	VE day – the last of the POWs evacuated from Fallingbostel are liberated.
9 May	Prague is liberated.
12 May	Red Army releases British and American POWs at Luckenwalde.

Appendix 2 The Yalta Agreement on Prisoners of War, February 1945[1]

The Government of the Union of Soviet Socialist Republics on the one hand and the Governments of the United Kingdom of Great Britain and Northern Ireland, of Canada, of Australia, of New Zealand, of the Union of South Africa and of India on the other hand, wishing to make arrangements for the care and repatriation of Soviet citizens freed by forces operating under British command and for British subjects freed by forces operating under Soviet command, have agreed as follows:

Article 1

All Soviet citizens liberated by the forces operating under British command and all British subjects liberated by the forces operating under Soviet command will, without delay after their liberation, be separated from enemy prisoners of war and will be maintained separately from them in camps or points of concentration until they have been handed over to the Soviet or British authorities, as the case may be, at places agreed upon between those authorities.

British and Soviet military authorities will respectively take the necessary measures for protection of camps, and points of concentration from enemy bombing, artillery fire, etc.

Article 2

The contracting parties shall ensure that their military authorities shall without delay inform the competent authorities of the other party regarding citizens or subjects of the other contracting party found by them, and will at the same time take the necessary steps to implement the provisions of this agreement. Soviet and British repatriation representatives will have the right of immediate access into the camps and points of concentration where their citizens or subjects are located and they will have the right to appoint the internal administration and set up the internal discipline and management in accordance with the military procedure and laws of their country.

Facilities will be given for the despatch or transfer of officers of their own nationality to camps or points of concentration where liberated members of the respective forces are located and there are insufficient officers. The outside protection of and access to and from the camps or points of concentration will be established in accordance with the instructions of the military commander in whose zone they are located, and the military commander shall also appoint a commandant, who shall have the final responsibility for the overall administration and discipline of the camp or point concerned.

The removal of camps as well as the transfer from one camp to another of liberated citizens or subjects will be effected by agreement with the competent Soviet or British authorities. Removal of camps and transfer of liberated citizens or subjects may, in exceptional circumstances, also be effected without preliminary agreement, provided the competent authorities are immediately notified of such removal or transfer with a statement of the reasons. Hostile propaganda directed against the contracting parties or against any of the United Nations will not be permitted.

Article 3

The competent British and Soviet authorities will supply liberated citizens or subjects of the contracting parties with adequate food, clothing, housing and medical attention both in camps or at points of concentration and en route, and with transport until they are handed over to the Soviet or British authorities at places agreed upon between those authorities. The standards of such food, clothing, housing and medical attention shall, subject to the provisions of Article 8, be fixed on a basis for privates, non-commissioned officers and officers. The basis fixed for civilians shall as far as possible be the same as that fixed for privates.

The contracting parties will not demand compensation for these or other similar services which their authorities may supply respectively to liberated citizens or subjects of the other contracting party.

Article 4

Each of the contracting parties shall be at liberty to use in agreement with the other party such of its own means of transport as may be available for the repatriation of its citizens or subjects held by the other contracting party. Similarly each of the contracting parties shall be at liberty to use in agreement with the other party its own facilities for the delivery of supplies to its citizens or subjects held by the other contracting party.

Article 5

Soviet and British military authorities shall make such advances on behalf of their respective governments to liberated citizens and subjects of the other contracting party as the competent Soviet and British authorities shall agree upon beforehand.

Advances made in currency of any enemy territory or in currency of their occupation authorities shall not be liable to compensation.

In the case of advances made in currency of liberated non-enemy territory, the Soviet and British Governments will effect, each for advances made to their citizens or subjects, necessary settlements with the Governments of the territory concerned, who will be informed of the amount of their currency paid out for this purpose.

Article 6

Ex-prisoners of war and civilians of each of the contracting parties may, until their repatriation, be employed in the management, maintenance and administration of the camps or billets in which they are situated. They may also be employed on a voluntary basis on other work in the vicinity of their camps in furtherance of the common war effort in accordance with agreements to be reached between the competent Soviet and British authorities. The question of payment and other conditions of labour shall be determined by agreement between these authorities. It is understood that liberated members of the respective forces will be employed in accordance with military standards and procedure and under the supervision of their own officers.

Article 7

The contracting parties shall wherever necessary use all practicable means to ensure the evacuation to the rear of these liberated citizens or subjects. They also undertake to use all practicable means to transport liberated citizens or subjects to places to be agreed upon where they can be handed over to the Soviet or British authorities respectively. The handing over of these liberated citizens or subjects shall in no way be delayed or impeded by the requirements of their temporary employment.

Article 8

The contracting parties will give the fullest possible effect to the foregoing provisions of this agreement, subject only to the limitations in detail and from time to time of operational, supply and transport conditions in the several theatres.

Article 9

This Agreement shall come into force on signature.

Done at the Crimea in duplicate and in the English and Russian languages, both being equally authentic, this 11th day of February, 1945.

Appendix 3 The Senior American Officer's Complaint about Conditions at Stalag XIIID, Nuremberg

Stalag Luft III[1]

Nürnberg-Langwasser

Germany

Subject: Complaints respecting the conditions of captivity.

To: The Kommandant, Stalag Luft III

I. Under the provisions of the International Convention relating to the treatment of Prisoners of War (POW) published at Geneva, Switzerland 27 July 1929 of which the USA and the German Reich are signatory powers. The Senior American Officer (SAO) of Stalag Luft III, Nürnberg, Germany presents in writing those basic requirements violated by the detaining power at this camp citing its authority as contained in the Convention and by subject. Violations are as follows:

A.   POW Camps (Part III Section II Article 9)

1. Proximity of Military Targets: Stalag Luft III is within approx. three (3) kilometers of a major railroad choke point and marshaling yard. During the last two weeks the local area has been bombed by heavy aerial main efforts with apparent attention to the railroad targets. The dispersion of bombs, both day and night, has been close to this camp. There are no slit trenches or shelters which the POWs are permitted to use during raids. Prisoners are kept in the overcrowded huts at the point of guns. The location of this camp and local air raid precaution policy is unjust and untenable and a protest of the strongest nature is hereby registered for present and future consideration.

B.   Food and Clothing (Part III Section II Chapter II Articles 11 & 12)

1. Inadequate Diet: The present German ration to the POWs according to medical opinion is less than that required for basic metabolism and will inevitably lead to loss of weight and starvation. Under the present

unhygienic and unhealthful conditions resistance of the men will become so lowered as to render them highly susceptible to any disease.

2. German Issues: Dehydrated vegetables are consistently wormy. No ersatz jam or honey is issued. As closely as can be figured not more than twelve hundred and eighteen (1218) calories per man per day are available, which is insufficient to sustain existence for a protracted period. It is impossible even with an inflated imagination, to consider the present German issue as 'depot troop ration'.

3. Communal Issues: Permission is requested to distribute food from kitchens during an air raid in order that such preparations as are possible may be served warm.

4. Clothing Replacements and Repair Facilities: There is no stock of clothing nor is there replacements or repair facilities provided as required of the detaining power. The majority of the men arrived from the Sagan area with only the clothing in which they stand. New Purges from the Italian Theater are destitute. Clothing and shoes now being worn are rapidly wearing out. Booty overcoats and trousers are suggested.

C. Installation of Camps (Part III Section II Article 10)

1. Overcrowding of Barracks: At the present time there is only 19 sq. ft of floor space and 119 cu. ft of air space per man. In this minuscule area our men must eat, sleep and live. This is a serious condition of overcrowding which may lead to epidemics such as cerebral-spinal meningitis, pneumonia, influenza, etc. aggravated by no heat, malnutrition and filth. The present conditions are apparently condoned by the responsible authorities.

2. Lack of Heat: No coal is provided for the barracks and there is a shortage in the communal kitchens. Present ration is being used in seven kitchens. Two kitchens have been closed and still only 180 kg per day per kitchen is available. This condition enhances the unhealthfulness of the barracks, dirtiness of food, utensils and containers and means cold or lukewarm foods are supplied to the men. A minimum of 400 kg per day per kitchen is required.

3. Shortage of Bedding: Many men do not have the depot troop issue of blankets. Many have no beds of any kind and must sleep on the cold damp floors. At present there are 1,246 men sleeping on the floor in camps 5, 6, and 7. Stuffing and pallets are vermin-ridden with no

replacements and no opportunity to clean those in use. It is felt that no 'depot troops' of the detaining power are subject to this treatment.

4. Poor Lighting: Lighting of the barracks and aborts [toilets] is below standard for depot troops and no convenience of accessibility is afforded between the hours of 2300 & 0600.

D.   Hygiene in Camps (Part III Section II Chapter II Article 13)

1. Inadequate Bathing and Washing Facilities: It has been planned, but not executed in fact, to give showers to POWs once each two (2) weeks. The shower officer reports that the Abwehr Dept has interfered unnecessarily and better facilities are necessary in order to utilize the few facilities available. No laundry facilities and the lack of hot water, soap and space necessary for washing and drying clothes, dishes and food containers lead to infection and dysentery. Wash houses have not more than two (2) water faucets and due to overcrowding this means that 400 to 500 men must depend on two (2) faucets.

2. Vermin: Rats, mice, lice, bedbugs and fleas are prevalent throughout the camps. Anti-vermin powders and disinfectant are too sporadic to be effective. The present disinfectant is too weak to destroy the vermin eggs and it is doubtful even that it liquidates living organisms indicative of the filthy conditions. A blow torch is necessary for elimination of eggs.

3. No Cleaning Material: There are no cleaning materials available for cleaning the barracks, kitchens and aborts, clothing and the POWs. Soap is not available. Brushes, mops, and brooms are non-existent. Disinfectant and anti-vermin powders are not issued. Fifty (50) rolls for 5,000 men for over one month has been the issue of toilet paper.

E.   Entertainment and Recreation (Part III Section II Chapter IV Article 17)

1. Entertainment: Books are practically non-existent and congestion of billeting in camp necessitates utilization of space originally and normally used as a theater and chapel, for barracks. Intellectual and spiritual welfare is suffering under almost insurmountable obstacles.

2. Recreation: General space for calisthenics or organized athletics is not available. The total lack of facilities adds to the mental and physical discontentment of all concerned.

II. Canteen Supplies: (Part III Section II Chapter II Article 12)

1. Canteen inoperative: No provisions are available for purchase of articles such as razor and blades, soap, toothbrushes, combs, matches, barber tools and mirrors. These items are badly needed.

Authorities of the detaining power having announced their helplessness in alleviating these present deplorable circumstances due to transportation and material shortages, the Senior American Officer suggests the following course of action subject to the approval of the German Reich, the United States and the Protective Power (Switzerland):

A. Parole March & Internment

1. Prisoners of War of this camp will undertake (under parole not to escape) a march of 20 kilometers per day to the Swiss border where they will be interned for the duration of the war with Germany.

2. Food would be provided according to the German march rations or one Red Cross parcel per man per 75 kilometers.

B. Parole March to New Location

1. POWs of this camp will undertake a march of 20 kilometers per day to any location out of the military target area more accessible to the Red Cross supplies of food, clothing and medical equipment. Given the proper tools and materials they will do what construction work is necessary.

2. Food will be supplied in accordance with A. 2 (above).

3. It is requested that a representative of the Protective Power be permitted to visit this camp and confirm the veracity of these statements.

(signed) Darr H. Alkire
Col. United States Army Force
Senior American Officer

Appendix 4   The Numbers Game

It should not be a difficult problem, should it? Surely there must be a reasonably accurate answer to the simple question of how many British and American prisoners of war fell into German hands during the Second World War. But the issue bedevilled us from the very start of our researches for this book – and still does. Even an approximate, rounded-out figure seems impossible to come by. The tally of POWs seems to shift from one moment in time to the next (which is understandable) and from source to source (which is infuriating).

Of course the situation was constantly changing. Prisoners were being taken all the time – some in large numbers after set-piece battles such as Arnhem or the Ardennes offensive, others in handfuls as when a crew baled out of a bomber. And processing was slow – even at the most settled of times, when communication between the two sides was reasonably efficient, it could be many months before a name was officially notified to the authorities at home via the Germans and the International Red Cross. But as the war headed for its climax there was often not enough time (or the organization) for this to happen. Presumably, however, someone in Whitehall or at SHAEF would have been counting and categorizing the casualties – dead, wounded, missing in action – and then reconciling the figures as new information came in. Or would they? It may not have been as easy as that.

In July 1944, US Military Intelligence gave the number of American prisoners of war in Europe as 28,867 – of whom 16,593 were air-force men and 12,274 were soldiers.[1] But two months earlier the German high command's figure for the number of American POWs it held was 21,324.[2] There is a gap, but the two figures seem reasonably reconcilable given that the US figure had been boosted by 4,500 – the estimated increase in prisoners taken since D-Day. So the real comparison was between 24,367 (the US figure) and 21,324 (the German figure) – a difference of around 3,000. Except that . . . the Germans collected their figures differently. The figure of 21,324 was from only the German army-run camps. It did *not* include American POWs held in camps run by the *Luftwaffe* – presumably, most of the US airmen. So, if the German total of 21,324 predominantly comprised US soldiers (12,274 according to US figures), it could suggest an overestimate of some 9,000 men.

To complicate matters even further, in August 1944 the War Office in London gave the number of American POWs in Germany as 22,000[3] – nearly 7,000 fewer than the USA's own figures of the previous month. Apparently not even London and Washington had figures they agreed on. That same War Office memorandum also gave a figure for the number of British and Commonwealth prisoners in Germany at that time – 160,000. Then, in November 1944, a draft of the SHAEF Operation Eclipse plan for repatriation put the combined number of US and British/Commonwealth prisoners at 196,253.[4]

Such contradictory claims and calculations illustrate the problems we encountered. It becomes yet more difficult when assessing the numbers of POWs as the end of the war approached. It is here that the discrepancies really begin to matter – or at least seem to matter.

One document has special significance. On 24 March 1945, Colonel E. F. Straub, deputy director of the prisoner-of-war section at SHAEF headquarters, put his signature to a set of figures which were then widely circulated to his colleagues. It was the very day that the final assault over the Rhine and into Germany was beginning, and the paper was intended to give the very latest information on the prisoner-of-war camps the advancing troops could expect to come across, their location and their approximate numbers of inmates. It gave what appear to be very precise figures for the number of POWs of eleven different nationalities – adding up to a total of 2,173,714 – broken down according to the seventeen German military areas (*Wehrkreise*) where they were thought to be. The number of British prisoners of war in Germany was now given as 199,592, and the number of Americans as 76,854.[5] These figures were to appear in many other documents, and were the basis on which SHAEF conducted its repatriation plans.

The apparent precision of these figures is beguiling, but it should be remembered that such a degree of accuracy was extremely improbable in the circumstances. In March 1945 – as we have shown in this book – the POW-camp system in Germany was in chaos. The terrible marches from the east were still going on, German bureaucracy – so efficient for most of the war – had broken down. No one could be sure where anyone was at this particular point. Exhausted and sick prisoners arriving in new camps – Moosburg or Fallingbostel, for example – were not football supporters clicking through a turnstile. They came in hundreds and thousands, and were rarely logged or counted. There was no cross-check of how many had arrived against how many had left their previous camp. If there had been, then we would know for sure how many had become casualties along the way. But at this stage in the war, with Germany in collapse, hardly anyone was counting and reconciling figures. How could they in the circumstances? Moreover, liaison with the German authorities through the neutral agencies of the Protecting Power and the International Red Cross – which had worked efficiently for most of the war – was now virtually non-existent. Straub's document itself states clearly that its figures are only an estimate. The crucial table is headed 'Total of PW by wehrkreis – *estimating results of recent moves on Eastern front*' (our italics). And yet any estimate can only have been made with inadequate information. Inevitably there must have been guesswork, error and, above all, double-accounting.

At the time, this did not matter very much. The document was intended to provide an assessment of the size of a problem for those who had to deal with it. It was sent to all those departments who would be involved in the return of those prisoners – all the way down the line to, for example, the financial branch whose job was to hand out foreign currency. If figures were on the high side, then that was better than understating the task ahead. But, in hindsight, it seems to matter very much. That figure of 199,592 assumes a huge significance against another statistic, which is that the official figure for the number of British POWs logged as having returned home at the end of the war was 168,746.[6]

How does one explain this discrepancy of 30,846? Some people are convinced that the explanation is that tens of thousands of British POWs who were liberated by the Russians, or fell into Russian hands in other ways, were not allowed home but were sent to a terrible fate in Stalin's forced-labour camps. We could equally claim that those 30,000 were the numbers who must have died on the marches from the east. We do not do so – for the simple reason that all the figures are inherently flawed. Serious doubts about the March 1945 figure have been stated. But there must also be question marks over the official figures given for returnees. We have seen how chaotic the homecomings were. Men waiting in their thousands at improvised airstrips and at ports did not file in an orderly manner on to waiting boats and planes as officials with clipboards ticked them off – much though the administrators at MI9 would have wished them to. Some jumped on any departing boat or plane when they could. At the other end, those welcoming them back were overwhelmed by the sheer weight of numbers. Some POWs remember being interrogated. Others say they were not even asked their name. Many returned in a truculent frame of mind, unwilling to cooperate with any form of authority and simply set off home as soon as their feet were on British soil. It was all too easy for men to slip through the net of bureaucracy. And, once again, at the time the counting of heads did not seem important. Getting the men home as quickly as possible was the priority – not reconciling numbers, adding up and cross-checking.

One thing is sure: not all the British and Commonwealth prisoners of war held by the Germans got home. Some died in captivity in their camps – through illness, Allied bombing and enemy violence. (According to historian W. Wynne Mason, bombing alone accounted for around 1,000 notified deaths.)[7] Then, as we have seen, an unknown number but probably running into several thousands died on those marches from the east and in the chaos of the final months and weeks. Some men simply chose not to go home and began new lives in Poland, Germany or France. And some (though in what numbers we do not know) undoubtedly fell into Soviet hands and, for various reasons, were detained behind the rapidly descending iron curtain and died there.

As for American prisoners of war, Washington seems to have been much more energetic than the British in trying to reconcile its casualty numbers. Even before the war had ended, search teams were sent out to battlefields in Europe to track down what had happened to those listed 'missing in action' and to locate bodies, graves or records of treatment in hospital. Records from the Germans proved hopelessly out of date, giving the total number of American POWs in German hands as 72,913.[8] But this figure almost certainly did not include any or all of the 20,000-plus American soldiers captured during the Battle of the Bulge, which would have pushed the total number of US POWs in Germany much higher. A Military Intelligence report after the war (November 1945) gave the number of US prisoners of war in Germany as having been 92,965.[9]

So where do we end up after this mire of statistics? Is there any solid ground to stand on? At the beginning of our story – in the summer of 1944 – the combined number of British, Commonwealth and US prisoners of war in Germany was approximately 180,000. By the last months of the war this had risen to between 250,000 and nearly 300,000 – a wide margin which represents roughly the lowest and highest estimates. Common sense suggests that the truth – unobtainable as it is – is probably somewhere in the middle. The 199,592 so readily quoted for British POWs seems on the high side, and the figure of 180,000 quoted by the Secretary of State for War in the House of Commons in May 1945 may be more realistic.[10] The American figures – apparently more diligently arrived at – can more reasonably be relied on, at just over 90,000. A combined total of 275,000 would therefore not be unreasonable – but cannot be taken as anything other than a best guess.

Notes

Note

After a reference number in the text, all subsequent quotations come from the same source until either the next reference number appears or a quotation is attributed in the text to someone who has been cited in an earlier reference in the same chapter, in which case that earlier reference applies again.

Abbreviations

CAB   Cabinet
CHAR   Churchill Archives
FO   Foreign Office
IWM   Imperial War Museum (the Department of Documents unless stated otherwise)
JSM   Joint Staff Mission
PREM   Premier
PRO   Public Record Office (London)
USAFA   United States Air Force Academy
WO   War Office

Preface

1. Roger Allen, interviews with the authors, September 2001.
2. We were in Pomerania, near the coastline of the Baltic Sea, in an area that had been German for centuries but was handed to Poland in the post-war redistribution of territory and movement of borders. The German population was ejected by force, place names were changed, and every sign of the Germans was eradicated. Polish settlers moved in to take their place.
3. Norman Leonard, a POW who was 'almost a skeleton by the time I got home', had come across concentration-camp victims on the march and wrote, 'At the time we felt we had a certain affinity with them in our

condition and circumstances but we learned later that there was really no comparison when the horrors of the concentration camps, of which we knew nothing at the time, were full revealed' (diary and interviews with JN, 2001–2).

4. M. R. D. Foot and J. M. Langley, *MI9: The British Secret Service that Fostered Escape and Evasion 1939–1945, and its American Counterpart* (London: Bodley Head, 1979).

5. Ralph Mattera, quoted in Joseph P. O'Donnell, *The Shoe Leather Express* (privately published, n.d.).

6. Ron Walker, diaries.

1: The Russians are Coming

1. Victor F. Gammon, *Not All Glory! True Accounts of RAF Airmen Taken Prisoner in Europe, 1939–1945* (London: Arms & Armour, 1996).

2. Richard Passmore, IWM 83/1/1.

3. Cal Younger, *No Flight from the Cage* (London: Frederick Muller, 1956), and interviews with JN, 2001–2.

4. Camps of officers were led by the Senior British Officer or the Senior American Officer, a position accorded by right to the highest-ranking man there. Camps of NCOs elected their leader, who was known as the Man of Confidence. Camps of private soldiers also elected a Man of Confidence, though sometimes a non-commissioned officer might be drafted in from another camp to take the position.

5. W. Wynne Mason, *Prisoners of War* (Official History of New Zealand in the Second World War, 1939–45) (Wellington: Oxford University Press, 1954).

6. Dixie Deans interview, IWM Sound Archive 6142–1982.

7. There are differing accounts of this. Some say that Deans himself made the announcement after a conversation with the German officer, but we think this less likely. Deans was not the sort of man to have done the Germans' dirty work for them. He would have made sure that terrible news like this came initially from their mouths, not his.

8. Cec Room, diary and interviews with JN, 2001–2.

9. Nicolaus von Below, *At Hitler's Side: The Memoirs of Hitler's Luftwaffe Adjutant, 1937–1945*, trans. Geoffrey Brooks (London: Greenhill Books, 2001).

10. Affadavit for Nuremberg trials taken from *Nazi Conspiracy and Aggression*, Vol. VI (Washington DC: US Government Printing Office, 1946).

11. Hugh Trevor-Roper (ed.), *Hitler's War Directives* (London: Sidgwick & Jackson, 1964).

12. Gammon, *Not All Glory!*
13. RAF POWs referred to Thorn as Stalag 357; the British army prisoners already held there knew it as Stalag XXA.
14. Younger, *No Flight from the Cage*, and interviews with JN, 2001–2.
15. Gammon, *Not All Glory!*
16. Robert John Parsons, *The Best Seat in the House* (Indiana: privately published, 1998).
17. Percy Wilson Carruthers, *Of Ploughs, Planes and Palliasses* (Arundel: Woodfield Publishing, 1992).
18. Gammon, *Not All Glory!*
19. James Earl Taylor, *A Baltic Cruise* (http://www.members.fortunecity.com/ aries78 – accessed August 2001).
20. Gammon, *Not All Glory!*
21. Ed Hays, *The Heydekrug Run* (http://www.members.fortunecity.com/aries78 – accessed August 2001).
22. PRO WO 208/3342.
23. Carruthers, *Of Ploughs, Planes and Palliasses.*
24. The German military authorities had notified the International Red Cross of the camp's existence in May 1944. On 1 June 1944 it was logged as having 671 POWs, all American. Three months later – i.e. after the transfer from Heydekrug – the figures were given as 5,643 Americans and 865 British. (Data recorded by Commission for the Investigation of Hitler Crimes in Poland, Regional Commission in Koszalin. And see complaint by Jan Mikszo, POW number 39219, in Joseph P. O'Donnell, *The Shoe Leather Express* (privately published, n.d.).)

2: Abandoned to their Fate

1. Prepared by Military Intelligence Service, War Department, 15 July 1944.
2. USAF Oral History Interview, USAFA archive K239.0512–1130, recorded 20/21 June 1979.
3. PRO WO 32/11124.
4. Winston Churchill, *My Early Life: A Roving Commission* (London: Thornton Butterworth, 1930).
5. David Rolf, '"Blind Bureaucracy": The British Government and POWs in German Captivity 1939–1945', in Bob Moore and Kent Fedorowich (eds.), *Prisoners of War and their Captors in World War II* (Oxford: Berg, 1996).
6. W. Wynne Mason, *Prisoners of War* (Official History of New Zealand in the Second World War, 1939–45) (Wellington: Oxford University Press, 1954).

7. Quoted in David Rolf, *Prisoners of the Reich: Germany's Captives 1939–1945* (London: Leo Cooper, 1988).

8. A harsh conclusion? Perhaps – but one accepted by Mason, whose definitive work for the official New Zealand history of the war is the acknowledged authority on prisoners of war. He ventures his opinion in a footnote: 'The evidence makes it clear that the orders were meant to serve the needs of the administrative arrangements for evacuating prisoners, which, in the event of an undisturbed armistice situation, would have been all the easier if no prisoners at all had left their camps.'

9. Marienburg had 25,000 prisoners of war, of whom 9,173 were British and Commonwealth. Of these, just 856 were held in the main camp. There were 476 work detachments. War Office figures, 1 December 1944. PRO WO 32/11124.

10. Maj.-Gen. F. E. W. Simpson. PRO WO 193/346.

11. Quoted in Rolf, *Prisoners of the Reich*.

12. PRO WO 32/11124.

13. 'Instructions to commandants of British Army reception camps', 23 June 1944. PRO WO 193/347.

14. PRO WO 32/11125.

15. The expert was M. R. D. Foot: article on him by Anthony Beevor, *Daily Telegraph*, 6 December 2001.

16. Statistic from Peter Calvocoressi, Guy Wint and John Pritchard, *Penguin History of the Second World War* (London: Viking, 1989). By the middle of 1944, 3.5 million Soviet POWs had died through murder or neglect.

17. The exact numbers of Allied prisoners of war held by the Germans is almost impossible to establish: of the multitude of documents the authors read, most gave different figures. See Appendix 4 for more information on POW numbers.

18. 'Repatriation of British Commonwealth prisoners of war from German Territory occupied by the Russian Forces'. PRO WO 193/347.

19. Lt-Gen. W. B. Smith to Maj.-Gen. J. R. Dean, chief of US Military Mission, Moscow, 16 August 1944. PRO 219/1456.

20. From DPW to British Military Mission, Moscow, 24 August 1944. PRO WO 193/347.

21. From Military Mission, Moscow, to SHAEF, for Gen. Smith, 4 November 1944. PRO WO 193/347.

22. Memo to Chiefs of Staff, 7 October 1944. PRO WO 193/347.

23. Patricia Wadley, *Even One is Too Many: An Examination of the Soviet Refusal to Repatriate Liberated American World War II Prisoners of War* (http://www.aiipowmia.com/research/wadley.html – accessed June 2002).

24. Earl of Selburne, Minister of Economic Warfare, letter to PM, 25 July 1944. PRO PREM 3/364/8.

25. WSC to Foreign Secretary, 26 July 1944. PRO PREM 3/364/8.

26. Memo to Chiefs of Staff, 7 October 1944. PRO WO 193/347.

27. Telegram from Foreign Secretary to FO, 12 October 1944. PRO PREM 3/364/8.

28. PRO PREM 3/364/8.

29. 11 November 1944. PRO WO 193/347.

30. Minutes of DPW meeting, 1 December 1944 (our italics). PRO WO 193/347.

31. Wadley, *Even One is Too Many*.

32. In *Even One is Too Many*, Patricia Wadley goes step by step through the diplomatic notes and conversations and deduces that Roosevelt overruled three members of his Cabinet to change US policy on this important issue. The authors find her argument and her evidence totally persuasive and acknowledge their debt to her scholarship.

33. This decision would lead to much controversy – arguments that would go on long after the war was over about those tens of thousands of soldiers who would be forced back to the Soviet Union against their will and slaughtered. A particular row raged over the Cossack army in Austria, which was delivered up to Stalin in brutal fashion. Forty years on, British politicians and army officers involved faced accusations from historians that their involvment in this was tantamount to a crime against humanity.

34. From JSM, Washington. PRO WO 32/11124.

35. Memo by Lt-Col. R. E. A. Elwes, 11 September 1944. PRO 32/11124.

36. War Office memo by Lt M. L. Gilbert. PRO WO 32/1111.

37. Memo from Lt David James. PRO WO 32/11124.

38. 'The committing of acts of violence towards British prisoners of war', October 1944. PRO WO 32/11124.

39. 'The evacuation of Allied prisoners of war from Germany', 31 August 1944. PRO WO 193/347.

40. Minutes of Directorate of Prisoners of War meeting, 14 September. PRO WO 193/347.

41. As deputy director of Military Intelligence (Prisoners of War) – known by the designation DDMI(P/W) – Crockatt was head of MI9, the department responsible for escape and evasion of military personnel in enemy territory. Its principal activity during the war was helping airmen downed behind enemy lines and escapers from prisoner-of-war camps evade capture and get home. Its US equivalent at the Pentagon was known as MIS-X and was headed by Lt-Col. Ed Johnston, who in civilian life was the extremely

wealthy heir to the Lucky Strike cigarette fortune. The Pentagon worked very closely with MI9. 'On every point there was close, constant and cordial cooperation,' according to M. R. D. Foot and J. M. Langley, *MI9: The British Secret Service that Fostered Escape and Evasion 1939–1945, and its American Counterpart* (London: Bodley Head, 1979).

42. Distinguished Service Order, one of the highest military awards.

43. 'Possible behaviour of enemy towards Allied P/W on German collapse. Notes for conference with SHAEF', 30 September 1944. PRO WO 32/11124.

44. PRO WO 32/11124.

45. From Brig. R. H. S. Venables, SHAEF PWX Branch, 24 October 1944. PRO WO 32/11124.

46. 'Crockatt' was misspelled, and his initial was given as M instead of N – small points but ones that suggest that the writer, Brig. Venables of SHAEF's prisoner-of-war department, or his staff, was not giving the matter the fullest attention or respect.

47. 'Protection of Allied prisoners of war against acts of violence committed by SS and other German forces', 24 November 1944. PRO WO 32/11124.

48. DPW to Sub-Committee A of the Imperial War Committee, December 1944. PRO WO 163/588.

49. Phrase used in JSM memo to US Military Mission in Moscow, 24 November 1944. PRO WO 32/11124.

50. Joint Chiefs to SHAEF, 14 December 1944. PRO WO 32/11124.

3: Out into the Cold

1. 'There was no booze in the camp ... the Germans had forbidden it and confiscated all the stills' – John Hartnell-Beavis, *Final Flight* (Braunton: Merlin Books, 1985).

2. Arthur Durand, *Stalag Luft III: The Secret Story* (Wellingborough: PSL, 1988).

3. From the diary of Sqn Ldr C. N. S. Campbell, Canadian Squadron, RAF Fighter Command, IWM 86/35/1.

4. Ron Walker, diaries and interview with JN, December 2001.

5. James Vaughter, a hut leader in the south compound, said, 'We knew that many of us would die in such a mass uprising but we also knew the guards couldn't kill us all and that a good many would get away and break into the open to live off the land' (Joseph P. O'Donnell, *The Shoe Leather Express* (privately published, n.d.)).

6. Bob Neary, *Stalag Luft III* (North Wales, Pa: privately published, 1946). We thank Bob's widow for permission to quote from this.

7. Joseph W. Lovoi, *Listen ... My Children* (New York: Vintage Press, 2000), and interviews with JN, November–December 2001.

8. From Eric Hookings's diary and interviews with JN, December 2001.

9. Maj. Munro Fraser, quoted in David Rolf, *Prisoners of the Reich: Germany's Captives 1939–1945* (London: Leo Cooper, 1988).

10. Sgt Neil, quoted in Rolf, *Prisoners of the Reich*.

11. See Chapter 11.

12. From an anonymous diary held by the RAF Ex-Prisoner of War Association.

13. Lt-Col. Joseph L. Cittadini, *20th Mission* (privately published, n.d.).

14. Bill Ethridge, *Time Out* (Oregon: privately published, 1997).

15. Victor F. Gammon, *Not All Glory! True Accounts of RAF Airmen Taken Prisoner in Europe, 1939–1945* (London: Arms & Armour, 1996).

16. Diary of Walter Steck (confirmed by James Vaughter) in O'Donnell, *Shoe Leather Express*.

17. Maj.-Gen. Delmar T. Spivey, *POW Odyssey* (Massachusetts: privately published, 1984).

18. Anonymous diary – see note 12.

19. Both Moose Moulton and Walter Steck give this figure in their diaries in O'Donnell, *Shoe Leather Express*.

20. James Vaughter in O'Donnell, *Shoe Leather Express*.

21. Peter Hewitt in Gammon, *Not All Glory!*

22. There are various accounts of this incident, all slightly different in detail, depending on where the writer was in the column. This is a compilation from those accounts. It remains unclear whether anyone was hurt. Cittadini says a few were but not seriously. Walter Steck says two were badly injured.

23. Quoted in *The Longest Mission* (The Association of Former Prisoners of Stalag Luft III, 1995).

24. Anonymous diary – see note 12.

25. Geoffrey Willatt's diary, IWM 88/47/1.

26. Ethridge, *Time Out*.

27. It should be recorded, for the sake of accuracy, that some were apparently untroubled by the march. An anonymous diarist (see note 12) admitted he 'thoroughly enjoyed' the experience – 'the comparative freedom ... the novelty ... the guards were lenient'. He even thought he spoke for 'most of us'. 'It is truly remarkable how well the average man came through the ordeal.' He felt sorry for 'the few unfortunate ones who fell sick on the way'. It has to be said that this is the one and only benign interpretation of events that the authors have come across. The overwhelming weight of evidence does not support it.

4: Fears of a Massacre

1. PRO WO 32/9906.
2. PRO WO 193/343, 26 January 1945.
3. Stalag VIIIB at Teschen and Stalag 344 at Lamsdorf.
4. PRO WO 32/9906. The broadcast was monitored by the BBC.
5. Ron Walker, diaries and interview with JN, December 2001.
6. PRO WO 193/343.
7. This committee – separate from the Directorate of Prisoners of War – was concerned with POWs from Commonwealth countries.
8. PRO WO 219/1460. This seemingly simple suggestion provoked a forest of memos and myriad meetings. There were countless practical and military objections to designating an area in which prisoners of war could be safely collected. What if the Germans used such an area to hide troops and weapons? The Russians – whose agreement was essential if such a plan was to be put into action – were particularly exercised about this. They were convinced the Germans would cheat. The US Military Mission in Moscow reported, 'The Soviets believe the Germans would locate our prisoners at strategic points, which, being free from Soviet attack, would serve to cover German withdrawals. In extreme cases, they might inform the Soviet command of POW concentrations which in fact did not exist in order to free strategic areas from Soviet attack. The Soviets are convinced that unless some benefits accrue to the Germans they would not live up to the agreement' (PRO WO 193/345). Molotov dismissed the idea as 'not expedient'. He thought it might produce 'most unwished for results, especially dangerous for prisoners of war'. In the end the proposal became academic, as events overtook it. But the idea that there could ever be a 'safe area' or 'an area of immunity' had already been systematically pulled apart. In conditions of total war, it was just out of the question.
9. PRO WO 193/343.
10. Urgent memo from the International Red Cross to the Foreign Office, 17 February 1945, quoting Dr Marti, head of the delegation in Germany, who had just returned to Switzerland.
11. PRO WO 193/343.
12. JSM memo, PRO WO 32/11124.
13. PRO WO 193/343.
14. Joseph P. O'Donnell, *The Shoe Leather Express* (privately published, n.d.).
15. Doug Fry, diaries and papers and interview with JN, November 2001.
16. Norman Leonard, diary and interviews with JN, 2001–2.
17. O'Donnell, *Shoe Leather Express*.

18. *Prisoner of War* (Horace Marshal & Sons, on behalf of the British Red Cross, 1 January 1942).

19. Betty Batchelder, interviews with the authors, 2001–2.

20. Hansard, 17 November 1944.

21. Mai Parsons, interviews with JN, 2001–2.

22. Except German Military Intelligence, which had warned that the Soviets would attack with five times as many men as the Germans on this front, seven times as many big guns, and seventeen times as many planes. Hitler chose to ignore this assessment.

23. Few German documents about the handling of prisoners of war appear to have survived the war. Our enquiry to the German Military Archive at Freiburg drew a blank. The human record is equally unhelpful. Prison-camp commandants tended not to write their memoirs – perhaps there was little glory to be gleaned from being a jailer, certainly none worth recording for posterity. And most of the guards, whose stories would be interesting, were middle-aged men at the time. (For example, Theodor Lorentzen – see note 25 below – was born in 1894 and was fifty when he was commandant of Stalag XXB.)

24. Statement by von Hovel to Capt. G. Hay, 8 February 1946. PRO WO 208/4656.

25. Deposition on oath given by Theodor Lorentzen to Capt. F. Lock of No. 3 Team Field Investigation Section, War Crimes Group, at Wolfenbüttel on 1 May 1947. PRO WO 309/667.

26. Gen. Heinz Guderian – Chief of General Staff of the German Army – in his book *Panzer Leader* (London: Michael Joseph, 1952).

27. According to SS general Walter Schellenberg in evidence at Nuremberg, the first trainload of Jews under this deal crossed out of Germany in early February 1945. Himmler was paid 5 million Swiss francs.

5: The Retreat from Stalag Luft IV

1. Cec Room recorded events day by day and kept the scraps of paper in his greatcoat. On his return home it took two months to sort out the piles of paper he had collected and then write them up as his diary.

2. Report by Albert Kadler, sent by International Red Cross, Geneva, to American Legation, Berne, December 1944. The date of the visit was 10 October 1944.

3. Percy Wilson Carruthers, *Of Ploughs, Planes and Palliasses* (Arundel: Woodfield Publishing, 1992).

4. Doug Fry, interview with JN, November 2001.

5. Robert John Parsons, *The Best Seat in the House* (Indiana: privately published, 1998).

6. Testimony of Dr Leslie Caplan in the matter of the mistreatment of American prisoners of war, in Joseph P. O'Donnell, *The Shoe Leather Express* (privately published, n.d.).

7. George Guderley, interview with the authors, September 2001.

8. D. A. Harpin. PRO WO 309/667.

9. See Chapter 6 for more on the marchers from the work camps in Poland.

10. The first Soviet troops reached the Oder at Küstrin on 31 January, though it would be the middle of April before they crossed in strength and began the assault on Berlin just 40 miles away.

11. Greg Hatton, *Stories My Father Never Told Me* (privately published, n.d.).

12. O'Donnell, *Shoe Leather Express*, and interviews with JN, 2001–2.

13. From T. D. Cooke in O'Donnell, *Shoe Leather Express*. This sounds like a piece of propaganda on the part of the German guards to make themselves seem reasonable men who had the best interests of the prisoners at heart. Whether there was any truth in it remains a mystery. Hitler was alleged to have made many threats against Allied POWs. Few can be substantiated, though that does not mean they were not made. But the prisoners' reactions are interesting. Vulnerable as they were, they were prepared to believe them all – and who can blame them?

14. Roger Allen, interviews with the authors, September 2001.

15. John Anderson has a slightly different version of this. He said, in interviews with JN in 2001–2, 'When the lights were out at night in our room we would often talk, mainly about food, but we did talk about women once in a while. If we were not hungry – if we had just had a Red Cross parcel because it was Thanksgiving week or Christmas week – then men would begin to talk about women.'

16. His name was Ken Stanley.

17. John Anderson, diary and interviews with JN, 2001–2.

18. As it turned out, the Germans were panicking with no good reason. They were wrong about how close the Red Army was. The Russians did not reach the Baltic and seal off the northern corridor along the coast for another two and a half weeks. The damage done to the health of the POWs by the speed at which they were forced to march was totally unnecessary.

19. 'Kriegie' was the POWs' own abbreviation for the German *Kriegsgefangener*, meaning prisoner of war.

6: The Deadly Road to the West

1. George Guderley, interview with the authors, September 2001.
2. Statement by von Hovel to Capt. G. Hay, 8 February 1946. PRO WO 208/ 4656.
3. Bob Otto, interview with the authors, September 2001.
4. Cec Room, diary and interviews with JN, 2001–2.
5. Doug Fry, interview with JN, November 2001.
6. Percy Wilson Carruthers, *Of Ploughs, Planes and Palliasses* (Arundel: Woodfield Publishing, 1992).
7. Deposition taken by Lt-Col. William Hoffman, Minneapolis, 31 December 1947, and reproduced in Joseph P. O'Donnell, *The Shoe Leather Express* (privately published, n.d.). Caplan also recounted his experiences in his memoirs – 'Death March Medic', by Capt. Leslie Caplan, 25 August 1982, which is also in O'Donnell, *Shoe Leather Express*.
8. O'Donnell, *Shoe Leather Express*.
9. These details are recorded with precision in Room's diary.
10. O'Donnell, *Shoe Leather Express*, and interviews with JN, 2001–2.
11. Caplan, 'Death March Medic'.
12. O'Donnell, *Shoe Leather Express*.
13. Dr Caplan's report mentioned two sergeants who had legs amputated in a German hospital because of gangrene secondary to frostbite, but it is unclear if these are the same.
14. John Anderson, diary and interviews with JN, 2001–2.
15. Cec Room said of Pollack, 'He was a brilliant man, and so inventive and skilful given that he just hadn't got any equipment or medical supplies. All he had he carried in a small haversack. He cut a hole in the windpipe of a bloke who couldn't breathe with a strip of metal hacked from a milk tin.'
16. Clarence Brower was speaking in a 1994 video documentary, *Behind the Lines*, made by the US 8th Air Force Historical Society – this is the only account the authors heard of such an incident.
17. O'Donnell, *Shoe Leather Express*.
18. Greg Hatton, *Stories My Father Never Told Me* (privately published, n.d.).
19. O'Donnell, *Shoe Leather Express*.

7: The Rivers of Humanity

1. Pte Gordon Manners, IWM 95/17/1.
2. Memo to Sir Ernest Burdon, in charge of Red Cross finances, 2 February 1945. PRO WO 193/343.
3. Paraphrase of telegram received from American Legation, Berne, 28 February 1945. The telegram was also passed to the War Office in London, which circulated its own paraphrase on 2 March. PRO WO 193/345.
4. Room called this 'higher mathematics as taught by the Führer'. See Chapter 5.
5. Memo from the International Red Cross to the Foreign Office, 17 February 1945. PRO WO 193/343. Dr Marti, head of the delegation in Germany, reported:

   The delegation is unable to move food, bandages and medicines in reserve at Lübeck in the north and in Switzerland in the south. Two solutions thus strongly indicated:
   i) The immediate transport of relief by means of some hundreds of lorries to be placed at disposal of Red Cross with petrol and other necessary accessories.
   ii) Protection against air attacks on secondary railway route notified by Red Cross. We are using all means at our disposal but in view of the immensity of the problem we beg assistance in the execution of our task.

6. Report of meeting with International Red Cross representative, 18 February 1945. PRO WO 193/373.
7. PRO WO 193/373.
8. 24 February 1945. PRO WO 193/373.
9. Message from US Army Chief of Staff Gen. George Marshall, 18 February 1945: 'You are authorized to take immediately all such relief measures as you deem necessary, in co-operation with International Red Cross Committee and European representatives of the American Red Cross to the extent desired by you and without prior reference of your action to the War Department.' Ref. no. WX 39712. PRO WO 219/1640.
10. Minutes of DPW meeting of 21 February. PRO 193/373.
11. W. Bampton, IWM 94/49/1.
12. Rifleman Edgar Nance of the King's Royal Rifle Corps, IWM 95/15/1.
13. Pte Gordon Manners, IWM 95/17/1: 'Much talk of Red Cross food parcels which Geneva is supposed to have diverted for use of evacuated POWs.' He got half a box on 1 March, which lasted two days. Then a third of a box on 7 March.

14. Les Allan, interview with the authors, January 2002.
15. Stutthof, he said.
16. Rifleman Edgar Nance of the King's Royal Rifle Corps, IWM 95/15/1.
17. Affidavit by 6341491 Charles Houston to UN War Crimes Commission, 5 September 1945. In his complaint Houston named certain German officers who had failed properly to feed, shelter and provide medical treatment for the 1,000 prisoners on this march, which began on 20 January and ended on 26 April after a total of 1,200 km.
18. F. Coster, IWM 98/7/1.
19. Alan Clarke, interview with JN, January 2002.
20. Victor F. Gammon, *Not All Glory! True Accounts of RAF Airmen Taken Prisoner in Europe, 1939–1945* (London: Arms & Armour, 1996).
21. D. Swift, IWM 91/26/1.
22. Many weeks later, at the end of the march, Swift ran into what he took to be the remnants of that Auschwitz party. What had been thousands were down to 'numbers you could easily count on two hands'.
23. On the casualties on his march, Swift could only make a guess. 'All sorts were on the march and the killings and deaths must have been very many thousands. I have heard a figure of 30,000. Some of our lads died on the march, but I didn't see that happen in the bunch I was with. I don't know what happened to those we left behind with illness and frostbite or those who became exhausted and couldn't march.'
24. 28 February 1945. Recorded in War Office memo. PRO WO 163/582.
25. Minutes of DPW meeting of 21 February. PRO 193/373.
26. He mentioned 'negotiations to purchase lorries in Sweden to transport supplies from Lübeck to camps in Northern Germany' – when in fact this was an initiative by the British Red Cross. The government agreed to pay for the petrol. He spoke of 'similar projects in Switzerland' where '100 lorries from France have been assembled'. Again, this was nothing to do with the British government.
27. Telegram from American Legation at Berne, 7 March 1945, to Dept of State. PRO WO 193/343.
28. PRO WO 32/11680.
29. 'ENSA' stands for 'Entertainments National Service Association', which provided variety shows for the troops during the war.
30. 18 January 1945, SHAEF, from K. G. McLean BGS, Chief, Plans Section, to Brig. Bosville, DAC of S. G-1. Subject: Plans for Allied POW during Operation 'Eclipse'. PRO WO 219/1448.
31. From M. A. Stockholm, 3 March 1945. PRO WO 32/11124.
32. PRO WO 32/11680.

33. See Chapter 12.

34. Ian Kershaw, *Hitler: 1936–1945: Nemesis* (London: Allen Lane, 2000). The bombing of Dresden was also part of a wider strategy. Kershaw points out that in the last four and a half months of the war 471,000 tons of bombs were dropped on German towns such as Essen, Dortmund, Mainz, Munich and Nuremberg – twice as much as during the whole of 1943. In March alone, he adds, almost three times as many bombs were dispatched as during the whole of 1942.

35. From Combined Chiefs of Staff to SHAEF for Eisenhower, 26 February 1945. PRO WO 219/1466.

36. SHAEF, 5 March 1945. Report on Oflag 79 from SBO. PRO WO 219/2418.

37. SHAEF G-3 Div. PRO WO 219/2418.

38. PRO WO 32/11110.

39. Letter to SHAEF, 29 January 1945. PRO WO 219/2418.

40. PRO WO 32/11110.

41. A memo dated 25 February 1945 from SHAEF to DPW said, 'As Oflag IVC is in the Russian sphere, it is not considered that any action can be taken at present.' PRO WO 32/11110.

42. At their conference in Tehran in November 1943, Churchill, Roosevelt and Stalin agreed to set up a commission which would split Germany into three zones – British in the north-west, American in the south-west, Soviet in the east. These were meant to have purely administrative significance in making plans for the end of the war and the Allied occupation of the conquered Third Reich: they were not intended to be frontiers or demarcations for military action. But international politics quickly gave them a greater importance. Lines in the sand had, in effect, been drawn. The Russians were particularly happy with the arrangement, which gave them 40 per cent of Germany.

43. SHAEF PWX Branch, G-1 Div. PRO WO 219/3419. The authors found numerous SHAEF and War Office documents that give estimated numbers of POWs in German hands – the numbers given were rarely consistent. See Appendix 4 for more information on POW numbers.

44. Churchill to Roosevelt, 22 March 1945. CHAR 20/213A.

45. From SHAEF Main to Chiefs of Staff, 29 March 1945. Ref 2–83110. PRO WO 219/2124.

46. PRO WO 219/3419.

47. See Chapter 2.

48. From: Ops (c) sub-section. To: G-2 (O.I), 15 March 1945. PRO WO 219/2418.

49. PRO WO 219/2419.

50. PRO WO 219/1448.

51. From SHAEF to FAAA, 31 March. PRO WO 193/345.

52. PRO WO 219/1461.

53. PRO WO 219/2418.

54. Churchill to Stalin, 21 March 1945. CHAR 20/213A.

55. Study of the German National Redoubt, 25 March 1945. HQ 7th Army, Office of the AC of S, G-2, US Army. PRO WO 219/2124.

56. PRO WO 219/2418.

57. Carlo D'Este, *A Genius for War: A Life of General George S. Patton* (London: HarperCollins, 1995).

58. Oflag XIII was eventually liberated on 5 April. Stiller was not among the Americans there, but Waters was. Patton had him airlifted out to a hospital in Frankfurt, and the special treatment he received annoyed some other prisoners of war. Stiller eventually turned up at the prisoner-of-war camp at Moosburg, where he was liberated on 1 May, 10 lb lighter. Patton, who was there, greeted him in tears.

59. PRO WO 219/2418.

60. PRO WO 32/11124.

61. To be fair, even the British and Americans found agreement difficult. On 21 March, Churchill sent a proposed text to Washington for Roosevelt to consider. It was a stern warning to German soldiers that 'though you may delay, you cannot stop our overrunning your whole country both from the East and the West in the next few months'. If the fighting went into the summer, then no crops would be sown and the German people would then face starvation – 'you will condemn Germany to a winter famine the like of which has never been seen in Europe'. Churchill admitted he was worried that such a warning might backfire, and the Germans would react by 'starving all foreigners, including prisoners-of-war on the grounds that if they themselves are to starve next winter they must begin to save up as much food as they can now'. Roosevelt replied that he thought the moment 'inappropriate'. CHAR 20/213A.

8: Liberated by the Red Army

1. Stan Moss, 'Living under the Swastika' – unpublished MS made available via the RAF Ex-POW Association.

2. Ron Walker, diaries and interview with JN, December 2001.

3. Cecil Rhodes.

4. *World War II Day by Day* (London: Dorling Kindersley, 2001).

5. Interview with Capt. N. Maclean, 19 March 1945, by Maj. J. D. B. Mitchell. PRO FO 916.

6. Eric Hookings, interview with JN, December 2001.

7. Leonard Pearman, IWM Sound Archive 11191–1989.

8. Peter Hewitt, quoted in Victor F. Gammon, *Not All Glory! True Accounts of RAF Airmen Taken Prisoner in Europe, 1939–1945* (London: Arms & Armour, 1996).

9. Alan Clarke, interview with JN, January 2002.

10. Gammon, *Not All Glory!*

11. The name also had another significance. In the camps, a parcel from home with Freeman Hardy & Willis marked on it signified that it contained escape equipment.

12. Patricia Wadley, *Even One is Too Many: An Examination of the Soviet Refusal to Repatriate Liberated American World War II Prisoners of War* (http:// www.aiipowmia.com/research/wadley.html – accessed June 2002).

13. Told to Carol Mather and quoted in his book *Aftermath of War: Everyone Must Go Home* (London: Brassey's, 1992).

9: Hostages of Stalin

1. Three zones had been agreed in principle at the Tehran summit meeting in November 1943. Now a fourth zone was added – for the French.

2. Minutes of meeting between Churchill and Stalin, 10 February 1945. CHAR 23/15.

3. See Chapter 2.

4. For the text of the agreement, see Appendix 2.

5. Patricia Wadley, *Even One is Too Many: An Examination of the Soviet Refusal to Repatriate Liberated American World War II Prisoners of War* (http:// www.aiipowmia.com/research/wadley.html – accessed June 2002). This was not the only such incident Wadley lists. Later, on 29 June 1945, Soviet POWs at Fort Dix, New Jersey, were told they were going to be forcibly repatriated. They locked themselves in their barracks, which their US guards then stormed. Inside they found several had hanged themselves or killed each other. Those who were not dead were turned over to the Soviets. On 17 January 1946 at Dachau in Germany, 500 US troops needed tear gas to subdue 399 Soviets who were refusing to be sent home. There were numerous suicides.

6. To Vice-Chief, Imperial General Staff. PRO WO 193/348.

7. PRO WO 193/348.

8. P. J. Grigg, *Prejudice and Judgment* (London: Jonathan Cape, 1948).

9. PRO WO 32/11681.

10. Letter from British ambassador in Moscow to Foreign Office, London, 15 March 1945. PRO WO 193/248. According to our researches in the Soviet military archives, the dead were given a proper military funeral attended by a Russian general. The driver of the train was prosecuted.

11. PRO WO 193/348.

12. PRO WO 193/349.

13. 22 March 1945. All correspondence in PRO WO 193/348.

14. Churchill to Stalin, 21 March 1945. CHAR 20/213A.

15. Confidential SHAEF DPWX memo, 24 March 1945. The exact number of Russian POWs in German camps in the SHAEF zone was given as 496,684. It gave the total number of British and US prisoners of war as 276,446, of whom 123,507 were in the Soviet zone. Figures were as of 15 March 1945.

16. CHAR 20/213A.

17. Much of the following is from Wadley, *Even One is Too Many*.

18. Wilmeth, memoirs, from Wadley, *Even One is Too Many*.

19. Most of them had been in camps around Schubin in Poland, among them Oflag 64. They had been too sick to be evacuated west and had been overrun by the Red Army at the end of January 1945.

20. This incident remains curiously unreported and undocumented, given its apparent size. In *MI9: The British Secret Service that Fostered Escape and Evasion 1939–1945, and its American Counterpart* (London: Bodley Head, 1979), M. R. D. Foot and J. M. Langley write that 'the Red Army opened fire on the American prisoners, killing some 50 and wounding several hundred; they said they took them for Hungarians'. They name the camp as Stalag IIIB, not Stalag IIIC. But they give no more details and no description of what happened, and they quote no source. Beyond Wilmeth's comments, the US government archive is also unforthcoming on this incident, as are the military archives in Moscow. Nor have we come across any anecdotal evidence. But fifty dead and hundreds wounded was hardly a trivial matter. Did it really happen? Or was there a cover-up by US and Soviet officials, anxious to keep secret an incident that could have damaged relations between them at a particularly sensitive moment? We just don't know.

21. Wadley, *Even One is Too Many*.

22. Ron Walker, diaries and interview with JN, December 2001.

23. CHAR 20/213A.

24. Both Himmler and Goering tried individually to make deals with the West. Hitler, from his bunker in Berlin, stripped both of them of their ranks and ordered their execution as traitors, but, with the Reich collapsing, they were

out of his reach – Goering in the south in Bavaria, and Himmler in the north on the Baltic coast.

25. CHAR 20/213A.

26. On 12 May in a private message to Harry Truman, the new US President following Roosevelt's sudden death. Quoted in Roy Jenkins, *Churchill: A Biography* (London: Macmillan, 2001). This was many months before Churchill's first public use of the phrase, in the House of Commons on 16 August 1945, and almost a whole year before the meeting in Fulton, Missouri, in March 1946 when it is popularly thought he coined the expression.

27. 12 April 1945. PRO WO 32/11681.

28. Draft Paper for study of liaison officers only. Subject: Aid to POW, 15 April 1945. PRO WO 219/2420.

29. 'Summary of Operation Violet' by Brig. Nichols. PRO WO 219/2423.

30. Wadley, *Even One is Too Many*.

31. For some reason, the Norwegian general was in Moscow and he made his report to the US Mission there.

32. Wadley, *Even One is Too Many*.

33. For Allied POWs, these were to be Wismar, Wustmark, Ludwigslust, Magdeburg and Leipzig. A similar conference between the Russians and the Americans was held in Linz on 23 May to make similar arrangements for exchange of prisoners in Austria. See SHAEF report in PRO WO 219/3292.

34. Leonard Pearman, IWM Sound Archive 11191–1989.

35. Alan Clarke, diaries and interview with JN, January 2002.

36. A revealing conversation was recorded by an interpreter at a camp in England that held Russian prisoners who had been captured while fighting for the Germans. In September 1944 a Soviet general came to visit them and offered words of encouragement and sympathy. The soldiers were entirely sceptical about his reassurances. 'Don't worry. The Soviets never treat people in bulk. We shall find out who among you are guilty and who are not,' he said. He fingered the German uniform of one of the men and added, 'As for this, we shall burn it in a crematorium.' A soldier, resigned to his fate, replied, 'We know – and us inside them too!' PRO WO 32/11119.

37. Roosevelt had stunned Churchill by openly expressing at Yalta his eagerness to disengage from Europe. 'The United States would take all reasonable steps to preserve peace but not at the expense of keeping a large army indefinitely in Europe, 3,000 miles away from home.' He intended, he said, to limit American occupation of its zone in Europe to two years. It was noted by observers that Stalin looked delighted at this statement. But Churchill was so taken aback by the implications that he pushed – and got

– an additional zone of occupation in post-war Germany, to be supervised by the French. He did not relish being one-to-one against the Russians in the event of the US pulling out.

38. He added, 'I can find very little sympathy for people who are fighting against their own country, as the Cossacks were. Suppose we had fought for the Germans. Plenty of invitations were made. We were given the opportunity to fight with the *Luftwaffe* but not a single one of us took it up. We would have felt very unkind towards people enlisted in the British Army who had fought against us.'

39. Nicholas Bethell, 'A Brutal Exchange', *Sunday Times*, 8 January 1974.

40. Did they all make it home? There has been a controversy ever since over claims that many British and American prisoners of war never returned from the Soviet Union. The most notable are made in *The Iron Cage* (London: Fourth Estate, 1993) by Nigel Cawthorne, who alleged that up to 50,000 British and American prisoners of war disappeared into the Soviet gulags. According to Patricia Wadley (*Even One is Too Many*), reports of Americans in the gulag trickled out for years. Two US officers and forty-five GIs were reported to have been seen behind barbed wire in the Stalingrad area on 30 August 1945. Germans released from the Soviet Union after 1956 reported having seen American prisoners of war in some of the camps. Frenchmen reported being in camps in the Soviet Union with American and British prisoners of war. See Appendix 4 for more information on POW numbers.

41. Greg Hatton, *Stories My Father Never Told Me* (privately published, n.d.).

42. Gordon Hemmings, IWM 95/17/1.

43. Wadley, *Even One is Too Many*.

44. US Lt-Col. Francis Gabreski was on the ground at Barth, and thought that some deal had been made before the aircraft were cleared to land, but he never knew what that deal was, as he reported in Hatton, *Stories My Father Never Told Me*.

45. PRO WO 32/11119.

10: Waiting for Patton

1. *World War II Day by Day* (London: Dorling Kindersley, 2001).

2. 22 March 1945. CHAR 20/213A.

3. This had been the case since October 1944, when Generalleutnant Gottlob Berger was appointed (see Chapter 13).

4. Churchill was horrified by this suggestion: 'I am not at all pleased having my name on the same piece of paper with this gentleman while he is in his

present mood.' He was not disposed to wait for the General. 'Do please get it [the warning] out,' he wrote to Lord Halifax, the British ambassador in Washington, on 22 April 1945. PRO CAB 122/684.

5. Buchenwald was freed on 12 April and Belsen on 17 April.

6. Auschwitz had been liberated on 27 January, but the Russians kept the news of what they had discovered there until the war was over.

7. Surprisingly, it did not go as far as the warning Eisenhower – tired of waiting for the politicians to agree – had put out at the beginning of April in his capacity as Supreme Commander of the Allied Forces. This listed the obvious suspects – commandants of camps, chiefs of labour organizations and the like – but also went way down the list of responsibility to factory managers, foremen and supervisors. It then swept the net further and warned that 'the German population will be held responsible for the safety of prisoners-of-war, deportees and workers in so far as it will have neglected to protect them against any criminal attempts with which they are threatened. A passive attitude of German nationals in the face of threatened violence against Allied nationals will be held to be a crime and punished as such.' Solemn warning to Germany, 3 April 1945, in PRO WO 219/1469.

8. 'Hitler's Order for a Last Stand in the East', *New York Times*, 16 April 1945.

9. Bill Ethridge, *Time Out* (Oregon: privately published, 1997).

10. Lt-Col. Joseph L. Cittadini, *20th Mission* (privately published, n.d.).

11. 'An account of the evacuation of Allied POWs from Nuremberg to Moosburg' by Maj.-Gen. Walter Arnold, USAF (retd), in collaboration with Mike Spence. USAFA archive.

12. Bob Neary, *Stalag Luft III* (North Wales, Pa: privately published, 1946).

13. Robert John Parsons, *The Best Seat in the House* (Indiana: privately published, 1998).

14. Len Jepps, from National Ex-POW Association Archive.

15. Moose Moulton in Joseph P. O'Donnell, *The Shoe Leather Express* (privately published, n.d.).

16. Cittadini, *20th Mission*. See Appendix 3 for the text of the complaint.

17. James Oliver Badcock, IWM 99/47/1.

18. Most of this comes from Pat Reid, *The Latter Days at Colditz* (London: Hodder & Stoughton, 1953).

19. SHAEF to 12th Army Group TAC. Ref no: FWD-19 023, 12 April 1945. PRO WO 219/1461.

20. Named as Sergeant Bill Logan, a bombardier in the Eighth Air Force.

21. John Toland, *The Last 100 Days* (London: Arthur Barker, 1965).

22. This is a figure given by the author in Joseph W. Lovoi, *Listen . . . My Children* (New York: Vintage Press, 2000).

23. Maurice Newey, IWM 90/4/1.

24. USAF Oral History Interview, USAFA archive K239.0512–1130, recorded 20/21 June 1979.

25. Frank Stewart, IWM 88/20/1.

26. Lt G. B. Wright, 'The Last Days of the War', IWM 98/4/1.

27. Another account – by Capt. Kenneth Searle (IWM 92/31/1) – put the casualties at 10 dead and 42 wounded.

28. The offer was made on 11 April. PRO WO 193/349.

29. It would be nearly a week before the agreement was fully implemented. On 26 April a complaint was made that 'British, French and American officers, all allied aviators, many younger British and American non-coms and other ranks' were being moved to a possible last redoubt. The blame was placed on the SS and the Gestapo. But two days later there was confirmation from the German government that 'all transfers of POW have ceased. POW are collected as far as possible in large Stalags'. PRO WO 219/1463.

30. Later he surmised that this had been a battle between the guards and the SS, who had tried to take the camp to murder all the prisoners, on Hitler's instructions. 'The German army saved our lives.'

31. It should be said that other reports – e.g. by Bill Ethridge – say that Patton was not the first through the gates, but arrived about twenty-five minutes later. There is also dispute on how many pistols he was wearing. Joe Cittadini saw only one 'hanging jauntily from his hip' and believed the story that the General had given the other one to the American singer Dinah Shore.

32. Victor F. Gammon, *Not All Glory! True Accounts of RAF Airmen Taken Prisoner in Europe, 1939–1945* (London: Arms & Armour, 1996).

33. Patton had been restrained by the politicians. The agreement with Stalin was that the Red Army would liberate Berlin. And in any case Patton was too late and in entirely the wrong place. The Russians took the German capital the very next day, on 30 April. Patton was closing in on Munich, 300 miles away.

34. Neary, *Stalag Luft III*.

11: The Hell of Fallingbostel

1. Cal Younger, *No Flight from the Cage* (London: Frederick Muller, 1956), and interviews with JN, 2001–2.

2. Richard Passmore, IWM 83/1/1.

3. Jim Sims, 'Scar on the Soul', unpublished account of his time in captivity, from the National Ex-Prisoner of War Association.

4. Sims says that the man's name was Leslie Gemmel and that he came from Liverpool.

5. Ron Mogg published his account of POW life, *The Sergeant Escapers* (London: Allan, 1974), under the pseudonym 'John Dominy'.

6. This was the equipment that had been obtained at Heydekrug and whose theft from the Germans had been concealed by the burning down of the camp theatre. See Chapter 1.

7. Younger, *No Flight from the Cage*.

8. Younger continued his tribute to Deans: 'He had great faith in his capacity for the work, and drove himself with complete disregard of his health. Yet there was in him neither ambition nor lack of humility. It would be wrong to regard him as some paragon. He was never that. Had he been so he could never have earned the affection that was his; he was and is too human a person not to have a normal quota of weakness, but such is his make-up that he was the man the hour brought forth.'

9. According to Victor F. Gammon, in *Not All Glory! True Accounts of RAF Airmen Taken Prisoner in Europe, 1939–1945* (London: Arms & Armour, 1996), the number was 400.

10. Dominy, *The Sergeant Escapers*.

11. Deans and the other sergeants had been in Sagan (Stalag Luft III) in 1943 and had been transferred to Heydekrug (Stalag Luft VI) when Sagan became an officers-only camp.

12. Younger talks of 1,000 Americans and 800 men from K laager at Gross Tychow.

13. Doug Fry, diary and interview with JN, November 2001.

14. Roger Allen, interviews with the authors, September 2001.

15. Bob Otto, interview with the authors, September 2001.

16. Cec Room, diary and interviews with JN, 2001–2.

17. Percy Wilson Carruthers, *Of Ploughs, Planes and Palliasses* (Arundel: Woodfield Publishing, 1992).

18. Joseph P. O'Donnell, *The Shoe Leather Express* (privately published, n.d.), and interviews with JN, 2001–2.

19. Gammon, *Not All Glory!*

20. Story told in Dominy, *The Sergeant Escapers*.

21. Younger, *No Flight from the Cage*, and interviews with JN, 2001–2.

22. Recorded in a SHAEF PWX memo, 12 February 1945. PRO WO 219/1448.

23. Ken Brown, interviews with JN, January–February 2002.

24. Dominy, *The Sergeant Escapers*.

25. George Guderley, interview with the authors, September 2001.

26. John Anderson, diary and interviews with JN, 2001–2.

27. Gammon, *Not All Glory!*

28. Les Allan, interview with the authors, January 2002.

29. Alf Jenner was shot down over Berlin on 9 April 1941. From his diary and interview with JN, February 2002.

12: Death by 'Friendly Fire'

1. Batch Batchelder, interviews with the authors, 2001–2.

2. Leslie Frith, IWM 94/25/1.

3. Richard Passmore, IWM 83/1/1.

4. Ken Brown, interviews with JN, January–February 2002.

5. Cal Younger, *No Flight from the Cage* (London: Frederick Muller, 1956).

6. Cec Room, diary and interviews with JN, 2001–2.

7. Alf Jenner, diary and interview with JN, February 2002.

8. Bob Morton, interviews with JN, 2001–2.

9. Victor F. Gammon, *Not All Glory! True Accounts of RAF Airmen Taken Prisoner in Europe, 1939–1945* (London: Arms & Armour, 1996).

10. John Dominy, *The Sergeant Escapers* (London: Allan, 1974).

11. Percy Wilson Carruthers, *Of Ploughs, Planes and Palliasses* (Arundel: Woodfield Publishing, 1992).

12. Not all the crossings were by bridge. One column that came later went over the Elbe by ferry at Bleckede. This column was the one attacked in the barn by British planes.

13. Dixie Deans interview, IWM Sound Archive 6142–1982.

14. American parcel: corned beef, spam, Klim (powered milk), Oleo margarine, salmon, raisins or prunes, liver pâté, biscuits, Kraft cheese, sugar cubes, chocolate 'd' bar, orange concentrate, Nescafé, soap, cigarettes.
    British parcel: meat and vegetable, meat roll, margarine, condensed milk, jam, biscuits, cheese, sugar, chocolate, porridge, egg powder, sardines, tea, prunes, soap.

15. Gammon, *Not All Glory!*

16. This figure seems on the high side, though Deans was in charge and might be expected to have known, given what a meticulous man he was. However, most other accounts put the death toll at between 30 and 37.

17. Doug Fry, interview with JN, November 2001.

18. Carruthers, *Of Ploughs, Planes and Palliasses.*

19. There were a number of other examples of what today are known as 'friendly

fire' incidents. Geoff Wright's moving description in his diary ('The Last Days of the War', IWM 98/4/1) of one such incident at Oflag VIIB at Eichstatt in southern Germany should not go unread:

Sat. 14th April (A terrible tragic day). Got up at 5 a.m. Shared a bowl of porridge with Hendy and Maurice. We all climbed into our kit, shook hands all round and went our separate ways, Reg, Ken, Arthur and Hendy to the parade ground [where they were assembling to march to Stalag VIIA at Moosburg], Maurice and I to the hospital [they were sick and could not march]. The brigade slowly moved out by battalions. For some time one or two aeroplanes had been circling overhead. An American pilot told me they were Mustangs but his friends thought they were Thunderbolts. One of the planes came down very low and did a roll twice with his wings, from side to side. A few minutes later about six similar planes arrived and they circled and wheeled round the camp. While I was watching the leading plane it rolled over into a dive and I saw puffs of white smoke from his wings, and a second later a burst of machine-gun fire. I thought a German fighter had arrived and we were about to see a first-class dogfight. Suddenly there was a terrible roar and plane after plane roared along the road and over the camp blasting us with heavy machine-guns. God have they gone mad! I flung myself into a corner of the lavatory and pushed my head into a heavy iron basin. The hail of bullets was incessant. Just realized the roof above me is wood, these bullets weigh about 3 oz. and are high-velocity. I may as well be out in the open as lying on the lavatory floor. Looks as if you will be a widow, Jean darling, in the last few days of the war. Just one of those heavy copper-coated lead slugs will tear off an arm or a leg like a bite from a shark. This is the most horrible form of warfare I have ever seen. Hell, they are coming back. I dive for cover again. My head and my balls must be preserved. I cannot live without the one, nor do I want to live without the other. Roar, bang, crash, blast, bang. I peep out of the window and wonder if they have strafed the boys out on the road. Suddenly Hendy runs into the room. He is white as a sheet, trembling, covered in dirt and dust. 'Terrible, terrible' is all he can say. 'They're murdering the chaps.' I lie him down on a bed and cover him with my coat. 'Ben's dead,' he says. 'Lots of others dead and dying. Reg is all covered in blood but he thinks it's off someone else. The poor bastards had not moved off and caught it full blast in the open. Christ, it's murder.' Various people began to straggle into the camp. Someone comes in and says Johnnie Cousins is down, his leg completely shattered by a bullet. Ben is dead with a bullet through the heart. Paddy Heenan? Dead. Humphrey Marriot, with a bullet through the spine, looks like dying. Lowe is dead, Tranton wounded, Doug McClellan got one in the shoulder. The planes are still hovering about but seem content with their morning's work. Hendy is now showing symptoms of shock so I put him to bed, cover him with blankets and coats to stop him shivering and make him a cup of tea. The casualties are being collected and put in hospital. At present there are 8 dead, several dying and about 50 wounded, many of whom will lose arms, legs and feet. Several Germans have been killed and wounded also but the list is remarkably low considering the hail of bullets and the lack of cover. Later I hear that Johnnie has had his leg amputated below the knee but is very cheerful. Poor Johnnie, to lose a leg in the last few days of the war. Marriot has died of wounds, bringing the death toll up to six.

The official death toll would later be recorded as 11 British officers, with 50 wounded.

Official SHAEF documents also recorded an attack by two American fighter planes on a column of 700 British POWs marching westward from Breslau on 27 February. Fifteen were killed and twenty-nine wounded. Russian prisoners were marching at the rear of the column, and it was thought their greenish uniforms might have been mistaken for the khaki worn by Hungarian troops, who were known to be in the area.

20. Quoted in Dominy, *The Sergeant Escapers.*
21. Younger, *No Flight from the Cage.*
22. Statement by von Hovel to Capt. G. Hay, 8 February 1946. PRO WO 208/4656.
23. Jim Sims, 'Scar on the Soul', unpublished account of his time in captivity, from the National Ex-Prisoner of War Association.
24. Joseph P. O'Donnell, *The Shoe Leather Express* (privately published, n.d.), and interviews with JN, 2001–2.
25. Ken Brown, interviews with JN, January–February 2002.
26. Gammon, *Not All Glory!*

13: A German Saviour?

1. Joseph W. Lovoi, *Listen . . . My Children* (New York: Vintage Press, 2000), and interviews with JN, November–December 2001.
2. Cec Room, diary and interviews with JN, 2001–2.
3. Maurice Newey, IWM 90/4/1.
4. Jim Sims, 'Scar on the Soul', unpublished account of his time in captivity, from the National Ex-Prisoner of War Association.

5. T. D. Cooker in Joseph P. O'Donnell, *The Shoe Leather Express* (privately published, n.d.).

6. Hugh Trevor-Roper, *The Last Days of Hitler*, 7th edn (London: Papermac, 1995).

7. Hugh Trevor-Roper (ed.), *Hitler's War Directives* (London: Sidgwick & Jackson, 1964).

8. Recorded by Gen. Walter Warlimont in *Inside Hitler's Headquarters, 1939–45*, trans. R. H. Barry (London: Weidenfeld & Nicolson, 1964).

9. Cited in *Nazi Conspiracy and Aggression*, Vol. VI (Washington DC: US Government Printing Office, 1946), prepared by the Office of the US Chief Counsel for Prosecution of Axis Criminality as part of the indictment for the Nuremberg war crimes trials. This order was dated March 1944 and came from the Office of the Secret State Police in Cologne.

10. American Red Cross News Service, 31 May 1945. Newspapers carried fuller reports of Burckhardt's statement, which had been made on Swiss Radio. He claimed that he had met representatives of Himmler in the closing weeks of the war and had obtained permission for the Red Cross to enter POW camps and prevent 'any last-minute executions'. This seems a little fanciful on Burckhardt's part, and it does not coincide with the story told in Caroline Moorehead, *Dunant's Dream: War, Switzerland and the History of the Red Cross* (London: HarperCollins, 1998). The version there is that Burckhardt did indeed meet Himmler's representatives, but the discussions were about concentration-camp inmates and had nothing to do with POWs. Moreover, the initiative for these meetings had come from the Germans rather than from the Red Cross side, and Burckhardt prevaricated for a week – a long time at this fast-moving stage of the war – before he agreed to them. It is a mystery how these meetings were translated into having been about Allied POWs. Perhaps Burckhardt had been mistranslated – but this seems surprising, given that at least one newspaper that reported his speech had confirmed its content with Swiss Radio. It may well have been that Burckhardt wanted to improve his image with the Americans. He had been a known German sympathizer whose neutrality during the war had not always been apparent. When the war ended he was keen to re-establish his credentials, and nothing would have achieved that more than to suggest that Hitler had wanted to massacre prisoners of war but that somehow the Red Cross – with him in the lead – had played a part in preventing this. It is worth noting, perhaps, that, according to Moorehead, Burckhardt 'returned to the archives of the International Committee from time to time after the war and removed documents correcting his image for history'. Incidentally, it seems obvious that Burckhardt's information about Hitler's

alleged threat must have come from Himmler's representative and therefore
need not be taken as necessarily accurate. It was in Himmler's interest to
damn his Führer as much as possible, in the hope of being seen as a
replacement acceptable to the Western Allies.

11. Moorehead, *Dunant's Dream.*

12. PRO WO 193/343.

13. Reuter's report, printed in *Stars and Stripes*, 25 August 1997.

14. He did save his neck. Found guilty and sentenced to hang, he committed
suicide by biting on a capsule of poison the night before his execution.

15. This was not Hitler's only bizarre idea for encouraging a fighting spirit in
troops whose morale was flagging. He welcomed – according to Goebbels
– the threat by Stalin that, after the war, all German prisoners of war would
be deported to the Soviet Union as slave labour (*The Goebbels Diaries: The
Last Days*, ed. Hugh Trevor-Roper, trans. Richard Barry (London: Pan Books,
1979)). Hitler thought fear of this happening to them would discourage
thoughts of surrender among the *Wehrmacht.*

16. Ian Kershaw, *Hitler: 1936–1945: Nemesis* (London: Allen Lane, 2000).

17. Trevor-Roper, *Hitler's War Directives.*

18. Ironically, this, of course, was something that the military authorities at
SHAEF had considered but more or less abandoned at that time.

19. Quoted in Arthur Durand, *Stalag Luft III: The Secret Story* (Wellingborough:
PSL, 1988). The authors are grateful to Colonel Durand for the insights into
German prisoner-of-war administration contained in his book.

20. There was, however, one innovation that annoyed the prisoners. All cans of
food received in food parcels were to be opened immediately and their
contents ladled into other containers. This was because the Germans
believed messages and escape tools were being smuggled in this way. In fact
the bigger blow to the prisoners was that the empty cans had many uses,
including being strung together as pipes to pump air into tunnels. This new
order was inconvenient, but it was hardly draconian. Nor was it always
enforced.

21. See Chapter 10.

22. *Trials of War Criminals before the Nuernberg Military Tribunals under Control
Council Law No. 10*, Vol. XIII (Washington DC: US Government Printing
Office, 1952).

23. The word 'Apparently' is important here. The source for Berger's thoughts
and plans is Berger himself – in his evidence in his own defence at his
Nuremberg war crimes trial, in his own writings, and in the correspondence
he had with former prisoners of war in the United States long after the war.
All these are self-serving, which means not that they are necessarily untrue

but that, in the absence of independent corroboration, they need to be approached with caution. Berger wanted to present himself in the best light, naturally. But the reader is entitled to query, for example, whether he really did tell Hitler to his face that he didn't want the job he had been given. Certainly it was a brave thing for a relatively junior lieutenant-general to do in those volatile times. As we will see, many other claims by Berger appear to be fanciful rather than factual.

24. From Durand, *Stalag Luft III*, as is most of what follows on Berger. Durand's sources were Berger's testimony at his trial and the account of USAF Maj.-Gen. Delmar T. Spivey, who was a prisoner at Stalag Luft III.

25. Berger statement to Allied intelligence officers, Nuremberg, 19 October 1945.

26. If such handbills existed, they would surely have been mentioned by someone – paper was a precious commodity on the marches, for hygiene reasons. A supply like this would have attracted comment.

27. Berger's list of claims went on and on – and not just in his evidence at Nuremberg as he fought for his life but in the years after as he attempted to rehabilitate his reputation. In the account of his life by Robert Kübler (*Chef KGW: Das Kriegsgefangenenwesen unter Gottlob Berger* (Lindhorst: Askania, 1984)), Berger claimed the following actions to his credit:

- he tried to ensure the best possible treatment of all POWs;
- he introduced tolerant warders;
- he made improvements in the spiritual and cultural provisions for POWs;
- sport and entertainment for POWs were improved;
- he encouraged further professional training for POWs;
- he protected POWs against illegally enforced hard labour;
- he intervened personally on behalf of POWs who had contravened rules;
- he saw to extraordinary measures for the improvement and general care of the POWs, using every conceivable resource available to him;
- he gave Russian prisoners parity with others and released many – including Russians, Caucasians and Ukrainians – from forced labour, enabling them to work in a civilian capacity;
- he ordered direct cooperation with the International Red Cross despite the opposition of the regime and in direct defiance of Hitler. This allowed the Red Cross back into camps and also allowed many sick prisoners to get to Switzerland in empty Red Cross transports;
- he rebuilt holiday camps;
- he facilitated a successful and effective medical conference in Berlin;
- he built a special camp for Muslim prisoners;

- he allowed artist POWs to work with German artists in their studios and to exhibit their work;
- he risked his own life by handing over many sick POWs to the Red Cross;
- he successfully supervised the return of POWs from Upper Silesia.

Berger claimed that all this was accepted as true by the Red Cross.

28. *Trials of War Criminals*, Vol. XIII.

29. Glenn B. Infield, *Eva and Adolf* (London: New English Library, 1974).

30. Kübler, *Chef KGW*. However, Berger's account to an American judge carrying out an investigation into Hitler's final days suggested more than just a casual acquaintance with Eva Braun. As chief of the SS main office, he said, 'when I needed help, I asked her and she could always be convinced if the reason was good.' Since he had held that position since 1940, he seemed to be implying a friendship of many years' standing.

31. Trevor-Roper, *The Last Days of Hitler.*

32. The following account is based on Henry Chancellor, *Colditz: The Definitive History* (London: Hodder & Stoughton, 2001).

33. The last redoubt – the *Alpenfestung* – never existed in any military sense, but it was a monument to German propaganda. The idea that all true Nazis would retreat into the mountains and fight a guerrilla war that might go on for ever was a fiction created by the intelligence arm of the SS to counter the Allies' pledge to keep on fighting until they had forced the Germans into unconditional surrender. The idea took on a life of its own, and the German Army did in fact explore the feasibility of digging in and building fortifications in the Alps. But it never got beyond initial studies. The SS general Ernst Kaltenbrunner was then given the task of examining the idea, but in *Ernst Kaltenbrunner: Ideological Soldier of the Third Reich* (Princeton: Princeton University Press, 1984) his biographer Peter Black makes it clear that Kaltenbrunner had little faith in the idea himself and abandoned it altogether when, at a meeting on 23 March 1945, Hitler told him such a hiding place would not be necessary because Germany was not going to lose the war. Kaltenbrunner, a stubbornly loyal Hitler supporter right to the end and beyond, believed him. But the idea of the last redoubt successfully fooled the Allied military planners, who took very seriously the idea that they would have to winkle Nazi diehards out of some mountain retreat at the cost of considerable loss of life. In a letter to Roosevelt on 31 March 1945, Eisenhower warned of his fears that hostilities would drag on because of the problem of getting German forces to surrender in 'outlying areas ... such as the southern mountain bastion [where] ... a form of guerrilla warfare would require a very large number of troops for its suppression' (*New York Times*, 31 March 1945). A month later, Len Jepps, liberated from his camp in

Nuremberg and waiting to be repatriated, watched in awe as a seemingly endless stream of US military traffic headed south-east. There were jeeps, tanks, truckloads of infantry, ambulances, and so on, nose to tail for mile after mile, he remembered (National Ex-POW Association Archive). This was the force given the job of digging out the last-ditch defenders. It was not needed. The last redoubt was a myth – Hitler never had any intention of ending his days leading a guerrilla gang in the Alps. His war requiem was always intended to be Wagnerian, not the overture to *William Tell*. But it became a very powerful myth, clearly believed by Allied prisoners of war and by many Germans as well.

34. *Trials of War Criminals*, Vol. XIII.

35. The tribunal, sitting more than fifty years ago, seems to have taken it for granted that such orders were given, though we have established that this was almost certainly not the case.

36. Affidavit for Nuremberg Trials taken from *Nazi Conspiracy and Aggression*, Vol. VI.

37. It read, 'Whereas General Gottlob Berger, as the German general in charge of all prisoners-of-war in the last months of the war, did call a medical conference in Berlin to find ways to better take care of the medical needs of American prisoners-of-war and was instrumental in arranging for Red Cross food parcels to be distributed to American prisoners-of-war during the critical last weeks of the war, even at the risk of his own life, and ordered that the American prisoners-of-war should be treated in accordance with the rules of the Geneva Convention and not become hostages, and personally escorted American and other Allied high-ranking officers to safety through German and Allied lines, and did try during the last days of the war to bring about an honorable early conclusion of the war, therefore be it resolved that the American former prisoners-of-war assembled in Dayton, Ohio, to commemorate the 20th anniversary of the conclusion of the war . . . recognize the humanity of General Berger and thank him for the protection and care he gave prisoners-of-war during the last critical days of World War II.'

38. USAF Oral History Interview, February 1976. Office of Air Force History, USAFA archive K239.0512-855. Vanaman – interviewed when the Cold War was still very chilly – went on to praise Berger for being right in his assessment of what lay ahead. 'When you get right down to it, we would be in a much better position today if we had done what he wanted us to do – negotiate a peace with the Western Allies and let them face the Russians, with us at the back of them.'

39. Durand, *Stalag Luft III*.

40. *Trials of War Criminals*, Vol. XIII.

14: Heading for Home

1. D. Swift, IWM 91/26/1.
2. Cec Room, diary and interviews with JN, 2001–2.
3. Jim Sims, 'Scar on the Soul', unpublished account of his time in captivity, from the National Ex-Prisoner of War Association.
4. Leslie Frith, IWM 94/25/1.
5. Robert John Parsons, *The Best Seat in the House* (Indiana: privately published, 1998).
6. Joseph P. O'Donnell, *The Shoe Leather Express* (privately published, n.d.).
7. 21 Army Group Adm. Instr. 93, 30 March 1945. PRO WO 219/1448.
8. SHAEF Movement and Transportation Branch, 29 April 1945. PRO WO 219/2425.
9. Richard Passmore, IWM 83/1/1.
10. Cal Younger, *No Flight from the Cage* (London: Frederick Muller, 1956), and interviews with JN, 2001–2.
11. Doug Fry, interview with JN, November 2001.
12. Percy Wilson Carruthers, *Of Ploughs, Planes and Palliasses* (Arundel: Woodfield Publishing, 1992).
13. Cosford, in the Midlands, was the RAF's official Personnel Receiving Centre, and most returning RAF prisoners of war went through it, regardless of the airfield at which they had landed back in England. For prisoners of war of all services, the most frequently used airfields were Dunsfold, Ford, Hixon, Knettshall, Marston, Methwold, Oakley, Oldham, Seighford, Tangmere, Tarrant Rushton, Westcott and Wing. According to Percy Carruthers, Wing alone handled nearly 53,000 returning POWs in April and May, and on one particular day a total of 132 Lancaster aircraft landed there, as he put it, 'to disgorge their scruffy, louse-ridden cargoes'.
14. Lt G. B. Wright, 'The Last Days of the War', IWM 98/4/1.
15. Frank Stewart, IWM 88/20/1.
16. Len Jepps, from National Ex-POW Association Archive.
17. Bob Morton, interviews with JN, 2001–2.
18. M. R. D. Foot and J. M. Langley, *MI9: The British Secret Service that Fostered Escape and Evasion 1939–1945, and its American Counterpart* (London: Bodley Head, 1979).
19. As always in this story there are exceptions. Eric Hookings remembered being specifically asked 'questions about any missing prisoners – were there any people from your column left behind, were they taken ill?' (interview with JN, December 2001).
20. During the 1982 Falklands conflict, BBC reporter Brian Hanrahan used this

form of words to describe British raids from an aircraft carrier, making it clear that the aircraft had all returned safely while staying within the censor's rules of not giving actual numbers.

21. Parsons, *The Best Seat in the House.*
22. Roger Allen, interviews with the authors, September 2001.
23. Joseph W. Lovoi, *Listen . . . My Children* (New York: Vintage Press, 2000).
24. John Anderson, diary and interviews with JN, 2001–2.

15: Welcome Back

1. Bill Ethridge, *Time Out* (Oregon: privately published, 1997).
2. Published in *The Quill*, ed. E.G.C. ('Ted') Beckwith (London: County Life Ltd, 1947).
3. Betty Batchelder, interviews with the authors, 2001–2.
4. Norman Leonard, diary and interviews with JN, 2001–2.
5. 'Rehabilitation of repatriated prisoners of war'. Minutes of meeting, 16 September 1943. PRO WO 32/11125.
6. Collie's article was published in *The Fortnightly* in June 1943. The comments of others that follow were quoted by him in a memorandum he submitted to the War Office on 26 July 1943. PRO WO 32/11125.
7. 'The Prisoner-of-War Mentality', *British Medical Journal*, 1 January 1944.
8. 'Report to the War Office on psychological aspects of the rehabilitation of repatriated prisoners of war', February 1944. PRO WO 32/11125.
9. Memorandum signed by Lt-Col. Headley for the director of prisoners of war, 30 March 1945. PRO WO 32/11125.
10. Hansard, 2 March 1944. Report filed at PRO WO 32/11125.
11. Letter from Air Ministry to Gp Capt. N. C. Hyde, IWM 88/14/4 and 4a.
12. Robert John Parsons, *The Best Seat in the House* (Indiana: privately published, 1998), and JN interviews with Mai Parsons, 2001–2.
13. John Parsons was discharged, went to the Indiana Business College to study, and then took a job with the local telephone company. He also joined the reserve, and when the Korean War broke out in 1950 he was recalled to active duty.
14. John Anderson, diary and interviews with JN, 2001–2.
15. See Chapter 5.
16. John Anderson taught music at the University of Georgia and married one of his students; they had six children. He retired in 1982 and moved to Florida.
17. Roger Allen, interviews with the authors, September 2001.

18. Richard Burt in Joseph P. O'Donnell, *The Shoe Leather Express* (privately published, n.d.).
19. George Guderley, interview with the authors, September 2001.
20. See Chapter 9.
21. Bob Otto, interview with the authors, September 2001.
22. Batch Batchelder, interviews with the authors, 2001–2.
23. Percy Wilson Carruthers, *Of Ploughs, Planes and Palliasses* (Arundel: Woodfield Publishing, 1992).
24. Richard Passmore, IWM 83/1/1.
25. Len Jepps, from National Ex-POW Association Archive.
26. Maurice Newey, IWM 90/4/1.
27. Doug Fry, interview with JN, November 2001.
28. Victor F. Gammon, *Not All Glory! True Accounts of RAF Airmen Taken Prisoner in Europe, 1939–1945* (London: Arms & Armour, 1996).
29. Ron Walker, diaries and interview with JN, December 2001.
30. J. E. Holliday (ed.), *The RAAF POWs of Lamsdorf* (Queensland: Lamsdorf RAAF POWs Association, Australia, 1992).
31. Cal Younger, *No Flight from the Cage* (London: Frederick Muller, 1956), and interviews with JN, 2001–2.
32. Les and Doris Allan, interviews with the authors, January 2002.

Epilogue

1. Its full name is the Royal Air Force Church of St Clement Danes.
2. Cal Younger, interviews with JN, 2001–2.
3. Deans was always known as a sergeant to his men, even though he was promoted while he was a prisoner and for much of his camp life was in fact a warrant officer, the top of the non-commissioned hierarchy. He would still have been outranked by the most junior pilot officer.
4. Pamphlet published by the Directorate of Prisoners of War, February 1945.
5. Alf Jenner, interview with JN, February 2002.
6. Ernest Boyd, IWM Sound Archive 15587–1995.
7. Ken Brown, interviews with JN, January–February 2002.
8. Batch Batchelder, interviews with the authors, 2001–2.
9. War Office Advice to Relatives, PRO WO 32/11125.
10. Interim report on returned prisoners of war by Lt-Col. R. F. Barbour, adviser in psychiatry to the Royal Army Medical Corps. His team of twenty-five psychiatrists saw 8,143 men. PRO WO 208/4419.
11. Article by Brian Farwell, *Washington Post*, 8 August 1988.

12. *Washington Post*, 18 August 1988.

13. Proceedings and Debates of 104th Congress, First Session, Vol. 141, Washington DC, 8 May 1995.

14. Len Jepps, from National Ex-POW Association Archive.

15. The British government's position was set out most recently in a letter (31 July 2001) to a former POW from Dr Lewis Moonie, Parliamentary Under-Secretary of State for Defence and Minister for Veterans' Affairs, stating that 'There is no doubt that there were cases of improper treatment by individual Germans of our servicemen held prisoner of war. However, these represented improper acts by individuals, rather than acts authorized or encouraged by the German Government. The German authorities did, in general, implement The Geneva Convention with respect to the prisoners of war.'

16. *Trials of War Criminals before the Nuernberg Military Tribunals under Control Council Law No. 10*, Vol. XIII (Washington DC: US Government Printing Office, 1952).

17. Annual report of the DVA Advisory Committee on Former Prisoners of War, in cooperation with the Department of Defense, January 1999.

18. John Frisbee and George Guderley, 'Lest We Forget', *Air Force Magazine*, September 1997.

19. Claude Watkins, 'A Realistic Look at a Long Walk', *Ex-POW Bulletin*, April 2000.

20. Chris Christiansen, *Seven Years among Prisoners of War*, trans. Egede Winther (Athens, Ohio: Ohio University Press, 1994). This figure of 8,348 appears in other sources as the number of British and American POWs who died in German hands during the entire course of the war. It was also cited (as a comparison to the numbers of POWs killed in the Far East) at the trials of Japanese war criminals in Tokyo. Its accuracy is questionable, because the corresponding figure used for total numbers of British and American POWs was 235,473 – which is almost certainly an underestimate. See Appendix 4 for more information on POW numbers.

21. Quoted in personal correspondence to the authors from the Ministry of Defence (ref. HB(A)/6/3), 22 January 2002.

22. The total number of American POWs in Germany was in the region of 93,000–94,000 and 1,121 died (see note 17). The equivalent British and Commonwealth total was close to 180,000, and if we assume a similar casualty rate then the number who died would be around 2,200. What emerges is a figure approaching 3,500 American and British prisoners of war who died in German custody. Some of these would have been before the marches,

but there can be little doubt that the marches would have had the higher casualties because so many men were exposed to so much more danger as a result of them.

23. Larry Pifer in Joseph P. O'Donnell, *The Shoe Leather Express* (privately published, n.d.).

Appendix 2

1. Zygmunt C. Szkopiak (ed.), *The Yalta Agreements: Documents Prior to, During and After the Crimea Conference 1945* (London: Polish Government in Exile, 1986).

Appendix 3

1. Although Col. Alkire refers to the camp as 'Stalag Luft III', he was writing about conditions at Nuremberg, Stalag XIIIB. It was common practice for the POWs to keep their old camp designation if a large group moved to a new location. Col. Alkire was also making the point that, although they were no longer at Sagan – the original Stalag Luft III – the POWs were still under the jurisdiction of its commandant.

Appendix 4

1. 'American POWs in Germany', Military Intelligence Service, War Department, 15 July 1944.
2. Quoted in Chris Christiansen, *Seven Years among Prisoners of War*, trans. Egede Winther (Athens, Ohio: Ohio University Press, 1994).
3. PRO WO 193/347.
4. PRO WO 219/1459.
5. 'Strengths and locations of POW camps in Germany' – from Col. E. F. Straub, SHAEF PWX Branch, G-1 Div, 24 March 1945.
6. Taken from Nigel Cawthorne, *The Iron Cage* (London: Fourth Estate, 1993).
7. W. Wynne Mason, *Prisoners of War* (Official History of New Zealand in the Second World War, 1939–45) (Wellington: Oxford University Press, 1954).
8. Report from The Defence POW-Missing Personnel Office (http://www.dtic.mil/dpmo – accessed November 2001).

9. 'American POWs in Germany', Military Intelligence Service, War Department, November 1945.
10. Hansard, 15 May 1945.

Bibliography

Books

Adair, Paul, *Hitler's Greatest Defeat: The Collapse of the Army Group Centre June 1944* (London: Arms & Armour, 1994)

Ambrose, Stephen E., *D-Day June 6, 1944: The Climactic Battle of World War II* (New York: Simon & Schuster, 1994)

Bailey, Ronald, *Prisoners of War* (Chicago: Time-Life, 1981)

Barnett, Correlli (ed.), *Hitler's Generals* (London: Weidenfeld & Nicolson, 1989)

Beevor, Antony, *Berlin: The Downfall, 1945* (London: Viking, 2002)

Below, Nicolaus von, *At Hitler's Side: The Memoirs of Hitler's Luftwaffe Adjutant, 1937–1945*, trans. Geoffrey Brooks (London: Greenhill Books, 2001)

Bethell, Nicholas, *The Last Secret: Forcible Repatriation to Russia, 1944–7* (London: André Deutsch, 1974)

Black, Peter, *Ernst Kaltenbrunner: Ideological Soldier of the Third Reich* (Princeton: Princeton University Press, 1984)

Booker, Christopher, *A Looking-Glass Tragedy: The Controversy over the Repatriations from Austria in 1945* (London: Duckworth, 1997)

Brooks, Geoffrey, *Hitler's Nuclear Weapons: The Development and Attempted Deployment of Radiological Armaments by Nazi Germany* (London: Leo Cooper, 1992)

Burgess, Alan, *The Longest Tunnel: The True Story of the Great Escape* (London: Bloomsbury, 1990)

Burleigh, Michael, *The Third Reich: A New History* (London: Macmillan, 2000)

Calvocoressi, Peter, Wint, Guy, and Pritchard, John, *Penguin History of the Second World War* (London: Viking, 1989)

Carruthers, Percy Wilson, *Of Ploughs, Planes and Palliasses* (Arundel: Woodfield Publishing, 1992)

Cawthorne, Nigel, *The Iron Cage* (London: Fourth Estate, 1993)

Chancellor, Henry, *Colditz: The Definitive History* (London: Hodder & Stoughton, 2001)

Christiansen, Chris, *Seven Years among Prisoners of War* , trans. Egede
    Winther (Athens, Ohio: Ohio University Press, 1994)

Crawley, Aidan, *Escape from Germany, 1939–45: Methods of Escape used by
    RAF Airmen during World War II* (London: Stationery Office, 2001)

D'Este, Carlo, *A Genius for War: A Life of General George S. Patton* (London:
    HarperCollins, 1995)

Dominy, John, *The Sergeant Escapers* (London: Allan, 1974)

Durand, André, *From Sarajevo to Hiroshima: The History of the ICRC* (Geneva:
    International Committee of the Red Cross, 1978)

Durand, Arthur, *Stalag Luft III: The Secret Story* (Wellingborough: PSL,
    1988)

Eisenhower, Dwight D., *Crusade in Europe* (London: Heinemann, 1948)

Foot, M. R. D., and Langley, J. M., *MI9: The British Secret Service that
    Fostered Escape and Evasion 1939–1945, and its American Counterpart*
    (London: Bodley Head, 1979)

Gammon, Victor F., *Not All Glory! True Accounts of RAF Airmen Taken
    Prisoner in Europe, 1939–1945* (London: Arms & Armour, 1996)

——, *No Time for Fear: True Accounts of RAF Airmen Taken Prisoner, 1939–1945*
    (London: Arms & Armour, 1998)

Gellately, Robert, *Backing Hitler: Consent and Coercion in Nazi Germany*
    (Oxford: Oxford University Press, 2001)

Goebbels, Joseph, *The Goebbels Diaries: The Last Days*, ed. Hugh Trevor-
    Roper, trans. Richard Barry (London: Pan Books, 1979)

Grigg, P. J., *Prejudice and Judgment* (London: Jonathan Cape, 1948)

Guderian, Heinz, *Panzer Leader* (London: Michael Joseph, 1952)

Hartnell-Beavis, John, *Final Flight* (Braunton: Merlin Books, 1985)

Hinsley, F. H., et al., *British Intelligence in the Second World War: Its Influence
    on Strategy and Operations*, Vol. 3, Pt 2 (London: HMSO, 1988)

Holmes, Richard, *Battlefields of the Second World War* (London: BBC, 2001)

Horne, Alistair, and Montgomery, David, *The Lonely Leader: Monty
    1944–1945* (London: Macmillan, 1994)

Jenkins, Roy, *Churchill: A Biography* (London: Macmillan, 2001)

Kee, Robert, *A Crowd is not Company* (London: Eyre & Spottiswoode,
    1947)

Keegan, John, *Who's Who in World War II* (London: Routledge, 1995)

Kershaw, Ian, *Hitler: 1936–1945: Nemesis* (London: Allen Lane, 2000)

Kübler, Robert, *Chef KGW: Das Kriegsgefangenenwesen unter Gottlob Berger*
    (Lindhorst: Askania, 1984)

Lovoi, Joseph W., *Listen . . . My Children* (New York: Vintage Press, 2000)

Mason, W. Wynne, *Prisoners of War* (Official History of New Zealand in the Second World War, 1939–45) (Wellington: Oxford University Press, 1954)

Mather, Carol, *Aftermath of War: Everyone Must Go Home* (London: Brassey's, 1992)

——, *When The Grass Stops Growing: A War Memoir* (London: Leo Cooper, 1997)

Meltsen, Clarence R., *The Roads to Liberation from Oflag 64* (San Francisco: Oflag 64 Press, 1990)

Montgomery, Bernard L., *The Memoirs of Field-Marshal the Viscount Montgomery of Alamein, K.G.* (London: Collins, 1958)

Moore, Bob, and Fedorowich, Kent, eds., *Prisoners of War and their Captors in World War II* (Oxford: Berg, 1996)

Moorehead, Caroline, *Dunant's Dream: War, Switzerland and the History of the Red Cross* (London: HarperCollins, 1998)

Natkeil, Richard, *Atlas Of World War II* (London: Bison Books, 1985)

Nazi Conspiracy and Aggression, Vol. VI (Washington DC: US Government Printing Office, 1946)

Neave, Airey, *Nuremberg: A Personal Record of the Trial of the Major Nazi War Criminals in 1945–6* (London: Hodder & Stoughton, 1978)

——, *They Have Their Exits* (London: Hodder & Stoughton, 1953)

Padfield, Peter, *Himmler: Reichsführer SS* (London: Macmillan, 1990)

Potts, Phil, *Just a Survivor* (Arundel: Woodfield Publishing, 1999)

Powers, Thomas, *Heisenberg's War: The Secret History of the German Bomb* (London: Jonathan Cape, 1993)

Prisoner of War (Horace Marshal & Sons, on behalf of the British Red Cross, 1 January 1942)

Reid, P. R., *The Latter Days at Colditz* (London: Hodder & Stoughton, 1953)

Rolf, David, *Prisoners of the Reich: Germany's Captives 1939–1945* (London: Leo Cooper, 1988)

Smith, Michael, *Station X: The Codebreakers of Bletchley Park* (London: Channel 4 Books, 1998)

Szkopiak, Zygmunt C. (ed.), *The Yalta Agreements: Documents Prior to, During and After the Crimea Conference 1945* (London: Polish Government in Exile, 1986)

Toland, John, *The Last 100 Days* (London: Arthur Barker, 1965)

Tolstoy, Nikolai, *Victims of Yalta* (London: Hodder & Stoughton, 1977)

Trevor-Roper, Hugh (ed.), *Hitler's War Directives* (London: Sidgwick & Jackson, 1964)

——, *The Last Days of Hitler,* 7th edn (London: Papermac, 1995)

Trials of War Criminals before the Nuernberg Military Tribunals under Control Council Law No. 10, Vol. XIII (Washington DC: US Government Printing Office, 1952)

Turner, Barry, and Rennell, Tony, *When Daddy Came Home: How Family Life Changed Forever in 1945* (London: Hutchinson, 1995)

Warlimont, Walter, *Inside Hitler's Headquarters, 1939–45,* trans. R. H. Barry (London: Weidenfeld & Nicolson, 1964)

Wilson, Patrick, *The War behind the Wire* (London: Pen & Sword, 2000)

Wistrich, Robert S., *Who's Who in Nazi Germany* (London: Routledge, 1995)

World War II Day by Day (London: Dorling Kindersley, 2001)

Younger, Calton, *No Flight from the Cage* (London: Frederick Muller, 1956)

Ziegler, Philip, *London at War 1939–1945* (London: Sinclair-Stevenson, 1995)

Self-published accounts

Ball, Harry, *A Dangerous Game* (Harrogate: privately published, 1997)

Cittadini, Lt-Col. Joseph L., USAFR (retd), *20th Mission* (privately published, n.d.), j.cittadini@worldnet.att.net

Darby, Phil, *Press on Regardless* (Suffolk: privately published, 1997)

Ethridge, Bill, *Time Out* (Oregon: privately published, 1997), ethridge@whidbey.net

Hardie, Jack, *From Timaru to Stalag VIIIB* (Alexandra, NZ: privately published, 1991)

Hatton, Greg, *Stories My Father Never Told Me* (privately published, n.d.)

Holliday, J. E. (ed.), *The RAAF POWs of Lamsdorf* (Queensland: Lamsdorf RAAF POWs Association, Australia, 1992)

The Longest Mission (The Association of Former Prisoners of Stalag Luft III, 1995)

Neary, Bob, *Stalag Luft III* (North Wales, Pa: privately published, 1946)

O'Donnell, Joseph P., *The Shoe Leather Express* (privately published, n.d.), JPODPOW1414@aol.com

Parsons, Robert John, *The Best Seat in the House* (Indiana: privately published, 1998), kriegie1562@aol.com

Silk and Barbed Wire (Perth, WA: The RAAF Ex-POW Association (Australia), 2000)

Spivey, Maj.-Gen. Delmar T., *POW Odyssey* (Massachusetts: privately published, 1984)

Reports and studies

Annual Report of the DVA Advisory Committee on Former Prisoners of War, 1999

Fedorowich, Kent (University of West of England), 'Axis Prisoners of War as Sources for British Military Intelligence', *Intelligence and National Security*, 1999

Rolf, David, '"Blind Bureaucracy": The British Government and POWs in German Captivity 1939–1945', in Bob Moore and Kent Fedorowich (eds.), *Prisoners of War and their Captors in World War II* (Oxford: Berg, 1996)

Wadley, Patricia (national historian, The American Ex-POW Organization), *Even One is Too Many: An Examination of the Soviet Refusal to Repatriate Liberated American World War II Prisoners of War* (http://www.aiipowmia.com/research/wadley.html – accessed June 2002)

Letters, diaries and accounts from

Doris Allan, Les Allan, Flo Allen, Roger Allen, John Anderson, Walter Arnold, James Badcock, Charles Balaza, Harry Ball, W. Bampton, John Banfield, Batch Batchelder, Betty Batchelder, Pauline Bevan, D. Bond, K. J. Bowden, Ernest Boyd, Fred Brown, Ken Brown, Dillon Browne, Alan Bryett, George Buchan, Ron Buchanan, Wayland Buckholz, Bert Bullock, Bill Burridge, Richard Burt, C. N. S. Campbell, Dr Leslie Caplan, Roy Child, Alan Clarke, General Albert Clarke, Len Clarke, Reg Cleaver, David Codd, Arthur Cole, Bob Coles, F. Coster, John Crawbuck, Phil Darby, Dixie Deans, H. Deterding, Charles Dick, Alex East, Hilary Elsdon, Bernard Frisby, Leslie Frith, Doug Fry, Bill Garrioch, Ken Goodchild, R. Goode, George Guderley, Beryl Hart, Ed Hayes, Gordon Hemmings, David Hills, Eric Hookings, Paddy Hope, Arthur Hough, Les Howard, Peter Hughes, Stan Hurrell, Wilf Hurst, Alec Ingle, Steve

Jackson, Alf Jenner, Len Jepps, Wilf Jessop, Tony Johnson, T. Jones, John Kennedy, J. Keith Killby, Don Kirby, D. Large, Dell Laudner, Bob Lawrence, John Lenburg, Norman Leonard, Jack Lyon, Mac McCaig, James McCloskey, Gordon Manners, Arthur Minnitt, Reg Moffat, Bob Monk, Mark Moore, John Morrison, Bob Morton, Stan Moss, Moose Moulton, Gordon Moulton-Barrett, David Mowat, Robin Murray, Tom Mutton, Maurice Newey, Les Nichols, Norman Oates, David Osment, Neil Ostrom, Bob Otto, Richard Passmore, Frank Paules, Leonard Pearman, Tony Pelly, Keith Pendray, Alan Percell, Cyril Poffley, Phil Potts, Derek Price, Ray Racy, David Radke, Allen Rawlinson, Arch Riley, Vic Robins, Cec Room, Len Rose, Gerhard Rühlow, Eddie Scott-Jones, Kenneth Searle, Jim Sims, Pete Simpson, Pete Skinner, Arthur Smith, Harry Smith, Kenroy Smith, Martin Smith, Walter Steck, George Sterler, Frank Stewart, D. Swift, D. Taylor, James Taylor, Ken Timms, Tommy Tomkins, Gary Turbak, General Walter Vanaman, James Vaughter, Ron Walker, R. S. Ward, John Watson, Geoffrey Willatt, John Wilson, Ken Wood, G. B. Wright

Index

WHERE THE POWS WERE
THE PRINCIPAL CAMPS
1944–45

NETH.

LÜBECK
ROSTOCK
Stalag Luft I
BARTH
SWINEMÜNDE
STETTI
HAMBURG

BREMEN
Stalag XIB/357
FALLINGBOSTEL

Stalag XIA
ALTENGRABOW
BERLIN

HANOVER
Oflag 79
BRUNSWICK
Elbe
Stalag IIIA
LUCKENWALDE

G E R M A N Y

DÜSSELDORF
LEIPZIG
Stalag IVB
MÜHLBERG
COLOGNE
Oflag IX
ZIEGENHAIN
BAD SALZA
Oflag IVC
COLDITZ
DRESDEN

FRANKFURT AM MAIN
Rhine
Stalag XIIIC
HAMMELBURG
PRAGUE

MANNHEIM
Stalag XIIID
NUREMBERG

FRANCE
STUTTGART
Oflag VIIB
EICHSTATT
STRASBOURG
Danube
Stalag VIIA
MOOSBURG
MUNICH